# THE GUERILLA GUIDE TO THE MUSIC BUSINESS

# THE GUERILLA GUIDE TO THE MUSIC BUSINESS

2ND EDITION

Sarah Davis and Dave Laing

continuum

NEW YORK · LONDON

2006

The Continuum International Publishing Group Inc
80 Maiden Lane, New York, NY 10038

The Continuum International Publishing Group Ltd
The Tower Building, 11 York Road, London SE1 7NX

www.continuumbooks.com

Book design and composition by Susan Mark
Coghill Composition Company
Richmond, Virginia

Printed in the United States of America

**Library of Congress Cataloging-in-Publication Data**

Davis, Sarah.
    The guerilla guide to the music business / by Sarah Davis and Dave Laing.
        p.    cm.
    Includes index.
    ISBN-13: 978-0-8264-1791-6 (pbk. : alk. paper)
    ISBN-10: 0-8264-1791-4 (pbk. : alk. paper)
    1. Music trade—Vocational guidance.    2. Popular music—Writing and publishing—
Vocational guidance.    3. Music—Vocational guidance.    I. Laing, Dave.    II. Title.
ML3790.D34    2006
780.23—dc22

                                                                                        2005038042

# CONTENTS

## SECTION 1
### GIGS 1

## SECTION 2
### RECORDING    143

## SECTION 3
### OTHER STUFF    307

## SECTION 4
### BUSINESS AFFAIRS    357

## SECTION 5
### TOOLKIT    441

# CONTRIBUTORS

## AUTHORS

**Sarah Davis** is senior lecturer, Music Business Management, at the University of Westminster. She has worked in most areas of the music business—as a gigging and recording musician in Emperor Sly; as a partner in an independent record label, Zip Dog Records; in public relations and as a journalist contributing to many music and Internet magazines, including *Music Week*, dotmusic, *Future Music* and *Melody Maker*.

**Dave Laing** is a London-based researcher, writer and teacher. Since the 1970s, he has written and edited many books about music and the music business. He is an editor of the *Continuum Encyclopedia of Popular Music of the World*.

## US CONSULTING EDITORS

**Sam Howard-Spink** has been a journalist since 1992 in the UK, Asia and the US, with much of that time spent covering the international music industry and digital technologies. A Londoner by birth, Sam has lived in New York City since 1999, where he is working on a PhD at New York University.

**Lily Moayeri** has been working as a freelance music journalist since 1992. In that time she has been music editor for the music and technology magazine *Axcess* and content managing editor for the Web site of longstanding dance music brand Groove Radio B9. She also teaches mathematics to teenagers in Los Angeles, where she is based.

# INTRODUCTION

**T**HE music business has been through some big changes since we put together the first edition of this book in 2001. The major record companies have responded to the worldwide fall in sales of CDs by merging and by drastically reducing the number of recording artists they have under contract. On the other hand, the number of independent labels keeps on increasing, Apple has led the way in Internet retailing and the live scene has never been healthier in terms of the numbers of gigs and festivals held every year. But one very fundamental thing hasn't changed in those five years. As we wrote in our earlier introduction, 'It is harder than ever to get signed to a record label, to get a publishing deal or to get established as a DJ'.

How the explosion of the Internet will challenge or change this situation is not yet clear. In the meantime, it is more important than ever for anyone entering the music business to be flexible and independently minded. To be that, it is essential to be as well informed as possible about the business and the opportunities it offers. This book is offered as a tool for you to use in that process.

It's not meant as another one of those books that claim to tell you how to have a hit record or how to be a success in the music business. It is a book for the independently minded player, DJ, songwriter and music business person, a book that we hope will help you enjoy what you do, avoid too many pitfalls and, yes, maybe even help you have a hit or two along the way.

In creating music and developing a career, almost everybody starts out 'independently', that is, without the backing of a large company. However, our definition of independent musicmaking is not to do with a special type of music or even a type of music business firm, it's about a particular attitude towards the creation and distribution of music held by professional (or professionally minded) people. The attitude involves a commitment to keeping maximum control over your own work as far as is practically compatible with getting it to the largest possible relevant audience.

Of course, this does not necessarily mean that the independent musician, DJ or songwriter will do everything himself or herself. One of our main aims is to help you decide when or whether you need the services of a manager, lawyer, accountant, agent, record label, publisher and so on. We do this in the book through interviews with experienced music business professionals from both sides of the Atlantic. In our interviews, these professionals give you advice on the pros and cons of 'going it alone' in the music business.

Flip through the book and look at that advice and you'll find many of the same ideas being mentioned, whether they're coming from a press person, a publisher, a manager or an agent. You'll pick up some absolutely vital points, such as the need to make yourself known so you can actually hand over your music in person to someone. Simply sending things in to the offices of labels or publishers rarely works—even if you have a manager to do it for you.

Another important thing you'll notice as you use the book is how many people in the industry actually act as A&R people—not just 'official' A&Rs in record companies and at music publishers. A good PR company, radio plugger, agent, DJ promotions company and so on all develop a nose for hot new acts and will often work hard, and for little money, to develop their idea; if it works, it's great for the artist, plus it's kudos—and lots more work and money—for them. If your PR or plugger is really behind you, they'll go all out to help by going back again and again to magazine editors and heads of music at radio, trying to persuade them to really listen to your music.

This is especially vital because the message from 'official' A&R is 'Don't call us, we'll call you'—and this is more true now than ever. Also, the premise of this book is that you will want to develop and retain some level of independence and take this on if you get signed to a major label. This means doing a lot of the early stages of development yourself, bringing in experts at each stage as necessary. But, as you'll find out, even the experts expect some level of prior input from you before they take you on. Publishing is a different story, as you may want to sign with a publisher to exploit your work.

Another message that comes through loud and clear concerns musical style. At any time, certain styles are favoured by the music business while others are out of fashion. It can be hard if you're in the wrong style or genre at the wrong time. Check out the sections of the book on publishing and plugging—you'll see that however good you are, you may be overlooked by record companies wanting to sign new bands or by radio because they are interested in something else, something they think is more trendy and which they feel will sell more. It may be that you will have to wait for the cycle to move round so your style of music takes off again—or you may have to be content with less attention and media coverage from the specialist radio and press only.

But when the turn of your music comes around, the lesson from the experts is that hype is the key: hype if there's a bidding war for your band, hype around your club/DJing/ tune, hype a good PR can build around you—hype on the Internet if you can manufacture it. Like any commodity, your music is sold best through hype and marketing. However good or indifferent it is as music, it will succeed or fail on how you market it.

The book is divided into five sections. The first two deal with the main areas of musical activity—live performance and recording. Section 3 explains other aspects of musical activity, including songwriting and teaching, while Section 4 gets down to the nitty-gritty of the business side of making music. Finally, a Toolkit section provides examples of key industry documents, forms and contracts, plus contact details for the various companies and organizations mentioned in the book. Because the book is intended for use on both sides of the Atlantic, you will find that in many sections we have included interviews with industry professionals from both Britain and North America, interviews that highlight the differences as well as the similarities of the business in both places. For this new edition, we have added many new interviews, particularly from the United States, and fully updated the book as a whole.

We hope you enjoy reading it as much as we have enjoyed putting it together.

SARAH DAVIS AND DAVE LAING,
London

## ACKNOWLEDGEMENTS

Lily Moayeri and Sam Howard Spink wrote the North American contributions. We are grateful to all those members of the US and British industry who gave up their time to talk to us. In Britain, we wish to thank in particular Steve Barnes, Stu Lambert and Rod Lambert for their input.

# SECTION 1

# GIGS

# introduction

THE live scene is hot and happening in both the UK and the US. Most musicians would agree that gigging is by far the most exciting part of being a musician. There's nothing to compare to the rush of standing onstage, sweaty, excited, bathed in hot coloured lights and belting out your own songs to an enthusiastic audience. Sure, putting out records is a buzz too, but it doesn't have the magic of actually seeing people physically respond to your own music.

Nearly every musician's gigging goal when they start out is to move on from slumming it in a scout hut to playing the stadium gig with the stars. But of course it's not as easy as that. Gigging is not just about getting up onstage and doing your thang. There's a lot of hard graft involved in becoming a live musician: learning how to play your songs; learning how to play with the rest of your band, otherwise known as rehearsing, which is much more work than you might think; getting to know your equipment; finding gigs; promoting your gig; and on to all the mechanics of touring.

Gigging will probably be your first taste of having to market yourself or your band. And this is very important. Each gig is a golden opportunity to promote yourself and, if you've got your act together, to sell 7 CDs of your own music and other merchandise, like the ubiquitous T-shirt.

Too many new bands (and some not so new) think they can just turn up on the night, plug in and go. This attitude is the bane of the promoter or venue owner—they know they can generally fill the place with a name act but who's going to turn up for a complete unknown, even if the music is brilliant? All promoters expect an act to work on its own promotion and they are so often disappointed.

On the other hand, it's probably never been so hard to get people interested enough to make the effort to go and check out a band they've never heard of—there's so much else to do nowadays, and, let's face it, it takes quite a few gigs and some experience before a band sounds reasonably good.

According to research commissioned by the British Musicians' Union (MU), at the grassroots level, new bands need to forge a relationship with a public that is at best curious and at worst uninterested. A concern of promoters is the lack of foresight and career management shown by some local musicians as they start to present their music to a paying public.

Interestingly, the 2003 survey of the UK music business 'Counting the Notes' said that the public spent over £300 million on concerts. The equivalent US figure for 2004 was $2.8 billion, according to *Pollstar* magazine.

This all sounds great, doesn't it? But unfortunately this income is not reflected in what musicians are paid, or rather not paid, down towards the bottom of the ladder. According to research carried out for the UK government's Live Music Forum, almost half of potential venues had put on live music in 2003, rising to over 90% of student unions. A quarter of venues with music had staged over forty gigs in that year, a figure which conjures up a picture of a thriving scene. However, logic dictates that most of the bands that play at these gigs will either not get paid or get paid a nominal amount. Yet the music industry needs these young grassroots musicians to survive. This is why you must do as much as you can to help yourself in the gigging world—it's the only way forward to ever actually earning any money and achieving success for all your hard work. Promoters and venues increasingly assert that support slots and tour supports are being hogged by labels and agents trying to break new acts. Venues that want to put on name acts go along with this because otherwise they might not get the act.

In the end, all the hard work that you and your team do is only to be best prepared for a lucky break. Don't believe anyone who says, 'If you're good, you'll get noticed'. It takes more than that. There've been acts that were heartbreakingly good, had some press and radio approval and packed out gigs, and nobody ever worked out why they didn't break through. It takes all sorts of different circumstances involving different people to come about at the right time and in the right way. You can't actually make it on your own. But you can set everything in motion so you're as prepared as you can possibly be when opportunity hits.

## FINDING THE RIGHT EQUIPMENT

In this section, you'll find advice about buying all the equipment you will need for live performance.

Although each band or act has different requirements depending on the lineup, the most usual equipment/instruments needed are guitars, bass guitar, drums, percussion, keyboards/other electronic wizardry, microphones and microphone stands. The way to buy the instruments you need is through your local music shop, local paper, rehearsal studio notice boards or dedicated music magazines like *Future Music*, which carry lots of advertisements from manufacturers and from people wishing to buy and sell secondhand equipment.

## STRATEGY

For some people, getting equipment seems to be a pleasure in itself; they're always brandishing a shiny new prize. Fair enough, but buying gear and getting use to it often takes up creative time, especially if technology is involved. we've sat and listened to people droning on about the new boxes they've bought and thought, 'But they're not playing me any new tracks'. Then there's the money. For many modern musicians, spending on self-promotion in their early phases is at least as important as spending on musical or recording equipment. Think carefully about whether the gear you've got is adequate really and what you need is more songs or some CDs made or something.

Another good reason for delaying buying equipment until it's really vital is that it lets you take advantage of sales, special offers and the rising power-to-price ratio of technology. While you wait for a good price on the item you want, you can look around for a better price elsewhere, read reviews in case there's an alternative you've overlooked, and check that no wonderful new updated version or competitive product is about to be launched (and maybe watch the price of the first model drop as shops try to clear the way for the new one). When you put your money down, you should be absolutely confident that you're doing exactly the right thing.

Most advice about buying musical equipment is specific to the type of instrument or electronic item you want to buy. Here are a few assorted pieces of general advice.

Try and find reviews of the gear. Reviewers are expected to be positive about the equipment they review, don't expect a no-holds-barred hatchet job, but they are experienced at assessing gear both in its own right and compared to other similar items. Where the review mentions comparable items, try and check these out too. Reviews can be found in magazines like *Making Music*, *Future Music* and *Total Guitar*.

Get input from someone more experienced than you. They may not understand the music you want to make, but they probably know how to think about buying gear—what's the least you can spend without buying a piece of junk, whether those extra knobs make any difference or whether the salesman is trying to blind you with science. Someone from a band, or perhaps a music teacher, could help.

Consider buying the 'standard item' until you are quite familiar with different pieces of equipment and how you want to use them. Buying a Stratocaster guitar, Precision bass, Marshall amp, a Korg Trinity keyboard, a Yamaha desk or Cubase sequencer software will guarantee that you will be able to make most of the sounds on records you refer to. When you know which direction you want to pursue from there, you can choose in a more informed way. If 'industry standards' are too expensive, buy copies, cut-down versions or spin-offs. For example, most manufacturers of keyboards offer models with many of the best sounds of the flagship machines, with much less editing potential. The same applies to effects units. There are lots of copies of famous guitars and basses.

Decide what you want to play to test the instrument. You must be happy playing *your* stuff, not the music that suits the instrument. One hazard is salespeople 'demonstrating' by playing immensely flashy licks and embarrassing you. Ignore this! They're working in a shop; you're the one planning world domination. If they're so clever, they should be able to play in your genre to show that the equipment does the job.

Budget for other bits you might need to buy to use the equipment properly. Read the Bits and Bobs section at the end of the chapter about leads, cases, electricity supply stuff and more.

Don't be afraid to haggle on price. What have you got to lose? Always get prices from several shops and try to persuade your preferred shop to match the lowest.

On the other hand, think about after-sales service or help with using the equipment at first. Do you need it? (Often you won't.) If you do, it's probably worth more to you than a few quid off from someone who hasn't got time for you.

## GUITARS AND BASSES

### New or used?

To start with, buy a new instrument. This avoids problems like a distorted neck, worn frets and worn electrics. A music shop will 'set up' a guitar or bass for you. This means they will make sure the neck is true, the frets are even and the pickups adjusted for an even response. Try and get a case included in the price. Failing that, get a strap and a decent lead.

If you buy a used guitar or bass, check every single note for true tone, check that twelfth-fret harmonics agree with twelfth-fret played notes, and make sure there are no crackles or dead spots on the controls and that the jack socket is reliable.

## How do I choose?

It's a completely personal thing. Every guitar and bass has a unique feel; every model has a slightly different balance and profile. If you're serious about buying, ask for a strap and stand up, as you would for a performance.

Don't be seduced by 'knobology'. Most classic performances have been done on instruments with two or three knobs and the knobs are never moved. Active tone controls, coil tap switches, etc. are best left to those who have developed a very strong vision of what sound they want to make and can't perfect it on a standard instrument.

Don't buy a guitar with a tremolo arm (whammy bar) unless you know you want one. They tend to impair tuning stability and can affect sustain because they come between the strings and the body.

Consider resale value. Unusual body shapes or obscure makes don't have as wide a potential market as, say, a Strat copy.

✦✦✦✦✦✦✦✦✦✦✦✦✦✦✦✦✦✦✦✦✦✦✦✦✦✦✦✦✦✦✦✦✦✦✦✦✦✦✦✦✦✦✦✦✦✦✦✦✦✦✦

## CHARLES MEASURES

Charles Measures, of Chandler Guitar in London, gives top advice on buying the perfect guitar.

### What guitar would you recommend for an inexperienced player?

The cheapest electrics, lead or bass, that I can recommend are the Squier guitars, made in China or Korea, which cost about £129 new. They have a good reputation—some professional guitarists carry one as a spare—and they have good resale value, especially in the bright, custom colours. If you buy secondhand, you might be lucky and pick up a Japanese Squier. They have far superior necks to the newer guitars.

### What advice would you give about buying?

Choose your shop carefully. Do you think they will take the guitar back for adjustment if you're not happy with it? New budget guitars that come in often need a bit of adjustment or fret filing. We like to get people off to a good start. We all remember the awful guitars that we had to start on!

## What should the shop provide?

Make sure you have a standard set of strings. The standard for rock 'n' roll is .009" to .042"; heavier strings are too much work, while lighter strings are prone to fret rattle and have poor tone. D'Addario and Ernie Ball are the best-known makes. You can use any brand on any guitar—some people have assumed you had to have Fender strings if you used a Fender guitar, but you don't.

✦✦✦✦✦✦✦✦✦✦✦✦✦✦✦✦✦✦✦✦✦✦✦✦✦✦✦✦✦✦✦✦✦✦✦✦✦✦✦✦✦✦✦✦✦✦✦

# DRUMS

If you're one of the lucky ones and have the rehearsal space to allow you to splash out on a full drum kit, Dan Barrow of Drumtech explains what to look for. If not, see below.

✦✦✦✦✦✦✦✦✦✦✦✦✦✦✦✦✦✦✦✦✦✦✦✦✦✦✦✦✦✦✦✦✦✦✦✦✦✦✦✦✦✦✦✦✦✦✦

## DAN BARROW

### What is a basic kit?

Bass drum: 20" or 22" in diameter; steel snare: 14"; toms: 10", 12" and 14"; two cymbals: 20"; crash ride and 15"–17" crash; plus a pair of 14" hi-hat cymbals. The Pearl Export kit and Yamaha Stage Custom are great examples of this classic setup.

### Are there specific kinds of drums that are suitable for certain styles?

Absolutely. Rock uses bigger and deeper sizes than jazz. A jazz kit may have an 18" bass and 12 /14" toms. Rock would be 22"–24" bass, with more toms ranging from 8' to 18". In terms of the tone of a drum, there are a range of factors that affect it, especially the thickness of the shell and the kind of skin used. Rock players would go for clear plastic, thick drumheads with fairly loose tuning. Jazzers would go for coated heads, highly tuned to give their drums that bright sound.

In terms of snare drums, there are thousands to choose from. Fourteen inch is the standard and the material it's made from is the major factor. Wood, such as birch or maple, has a warmer tone than the metallic ring of a steel or brass drum. Genres such as pop and drum 'n' bass have experimented with smaller sizes, like 12″ and even 10″ snare drums, which have great, high-pitched tones. At the end of the day, it's whatever sounds good to your ear.

## Would you advise inexperienced buyers to buy secondhand?
Yes. Small classified ads in local papers are the beginner drummer's best friend.

## What problems are there to look out for?
**Shells** Warped shells destroy the drum's natural tone. If possible, check that the drumhead sits evenly on the drum. If there are ripples in the surface, especially at high tension, it's possible there is a defect, either in the drum itself or maybe just the hoop (the metal ring that holds the skin on the drum). Hoops are easily and cheaply replaceable.

**Pedals** Look out for loose rattling. It may be a case of checking that all the screws are tightened. If that doesn't eliminate it, there may be an important screw missing, which might affect your playing.

**Stands** Make sure that when the stands are extended, the drums can be secured so they don't swing about or drop down. Check the legs too. If there is any looseness, you run the risk of a cymbal falling over and damaging it.

**Cymbals/hats** Warped cymbals, or cracks, splits and holes drastically reduce the tone of a cymbal. Make sure the hats sit evenly on top of each other, so you get a nice tight 'chick' sound.

## When should heads be replaced?
Some people go for years, literally, without changing their heads. Obviously, the tone of a drum reduces over time as the head gets worn out, but with care they should last at least six months before this happens. The worst time for a head to break is at a gig, so it's a good idea to always have a spare handy, especially for your snare drum, the most important drum of all.

## Cases?
Sometimes you can get cases as part of a secondhand small-ads offer. Failing that, a cheap set for a five-piece drum kit will cost £70 to £100.

## Any other advice?
If you can, have a go at playing the whole kit before you buy any drum part. You can never tell what one drum or cymbal sounds like on its own. When you put it into the context of the whole kit, you get a better idea of how it sounds.

For many bands that start playing at home, a full drum kit is not an option to begin with. A bedroom or spare room may not have space for much more

---

than the guitar(s), bass and keyboard. This means that home rehearsal tends to be more about songwriting, arranging and learning parts than about the full band experience. Drummers can buy electric electronic drum pads quite cheaply and they are a great solution.

✦✦✦✦✦✦✦✦✦✦✦✦✦✦✦✦✦✦✦✦✦✦✦✦✦✦✦✦✦✦✦✦✦✦✦✦✦✦✦✦✦✦✦

## Electric Electronic Drums

We're not going to go deep into this because specification, price and availability will change very quickly. However, it is particularly worth knowing about drum pads for rehearsal and if you want to drum in a dance outfit or use samples with your kit.

## Integrated Pads/Sounds

The cheapest solution comes from the 'home keyboard' ranges of Yamaha (DD series) and some other manufacturers. You can buy a unit with three to six small pads which are connected to an internal sound module and to a MIDI-out socket. Some have a separate hi-hat function which can play a regular eighth beat at a tempo set by you.

The internal sounds are good enough for bedroom rehearsal and the MIDI function could be used to trigger a sampler or synth module in a basic way. If you are buying secondhand, make sure that the pads all trigger properly—not too sensitive and not too coarse.

Next come 'pro' drum pads, most famously Roland's Octapad. These typically have eight pads and comprehensive MIDI functions. The Octapad doesn't have onboard sounds, but others such as Roland's SPD-20 (and earlier SPD-11) have very good ones with onboard effects and different dynamics settings. They can be used very successfully with a sequencer instead of a drum machine or sampler. These units are much more robust and operationally flexible than the home ones. You can get bass drum pedal and hi-hat footswitch connections, too. But the pads are still postcard-sized and you can't really thrash around the kit unless you have the sticking accuracy of William Tell.

Finally, several manufacturers have made pads in drum kit format or as a pair like rack toms. Electronic kits haven't ever really caught on, even with very high-quality samples available—the playing surface responds differently from a drumhead and there is less tonal variety. The best-known (or most notorious) brand is Simmons, with polygonal 'drums' and that 'doof' sound that introduces the theme of the British soap opera *EastEnders*. Many reputable drum kit man-ufacturers such as Pearl, Roland and Yamaha have had a go at an electronic kit. Some pads give a MIDI out; some need you to connect the trigger out leads to a box which gives MIDI out. The advantage over the other configurations is that the heads are more or less full-sized and have drum kit mountings. The pads themselves rarely have sounds built in.

Otherwise, drummers can either hit some boxes or pillows, hang out and make the tea so they're in touch with things, or not come at all and practice their paradiddles in their own bedroom!

## KEYBOARDS AND SOUND MODULES

### New or Used?

It's usually okay to buy used, as there aren't many parts that can wear. But, unless you need a particular instrument which isn't made now consider that every new keyboard released gives more bangs per buck than before—it's quite unlikely that a used keyboard will have as many facilities as a new one, or that its secondhand price will be realistic compared to what you can buy new. If you do buy used, check that each key plays at different velocities, all controls and buttons work properly and audio and MIDI ins and outs work properly.

### How Do I Choose?

You'll have to read reviews and/or take specific advice on that. There's so much gear at so many prices for so many purposes that there just isn't a sim-ple answer. Don't immediately dismiss 'home keyboards', with preset styles and backings. Often the sounds are the same as the manufacturers' pro key-boards and the backing tracks are great for practising against, or even writ-ing songs with!

Apart from the subjective matter of sounds, there are a few tips for choos-ing keyboards for stage or recording use.

### Stage

Onstage, you need to change the program (single sound) or the performance (stacked/split/controlled sounds) quickly, possibly in near-dark conditions. A well-organised live keyboard player will have chains of programs to mirror the changes in the song, or use memory cards. Keyboards should have some of these facilities:

+ A footswitch socket which raises the program number by one. This is almost universal but of limited use. If a song requires you to play piano, then strings, then piano/lead synth/strings/piano, you must either fill your user locations with repeats of the three sounds or keep manually selecting piano and stepping up with the footswitch until you need piano again.

+ Lots of user locations. You don't need many different sounds for stage use, but if you have to fill the user locations with your song changes as above, it's possible that a mere sixty-four locations, for example, will be barely enough. One hundred and twenty-eight locations should be enough for all but the saddest of keyboard geeks.

+ A program change table. You enter program numbers in the table and, instead of incrementing by one, the footswitch calls the next program in the list. Excellent! You can choose sounds from different banks, mix single sounds and performances and easily change sounds in the table when necessary.

+ Memory expansion cards. These are really handy. They store a complete setup on the instrument, so you can fill the locations with sounds and performances in set-list order if you wish. And all your sounds are backed up in case of disaster, which is a good thing.

+ Some keyboards only take ROM cards with extra sounds. These are not very useful for live work. You need RAM cards, which you can 'write' to from the keyboard.

+ Some keyboards allow you to select a new sound but don't change until you lift your fingers from the keyboard. Useful for very quick changes.

## Recording

If you want to use your keyboards for recording use as well, the accent is on flexibility and control.

+ Extra outputs allow you to route different sounds to separate mixer channels. This is useful if several sounds for your arrangement are coming from one keyboard, as you can't do much to the mix if the drums, bass, chord part and special effects are all on the same channel. Many keyboards have stereo out plus two individual outs; a few have eight outs. (Onboard effects will probably be hard to use if sounds are routed to individual outputs. Sometimes these are quite important to the nature of the sound, so you may want to keep certain sounds on the main outs to get the benefit of effects.)

+ Card slots give you more choice of sounds written by experienced programmers (ROM cards) or allow you to store sounds of your own (RAM cards).

+ Memory expansion. This is another whole set of waveforms and programs which is semipermanently installed in your machine. They often specialise in certain types of sounds (orchestral, ethnic) or styles (house, classic rock).

+ Real-time controllers. Sliders or knobs which send MIDI information when moved can be used to record your 'moves'—for example, sweeping the cutoff frequency, so you can record your exact performance to a sequencer. You can use these signals to control other devices such as a MIDI-controlled effects unit as well.

+ Think about how you are going to store your sounds for safety, or if you program a lot of sounds. Some keyboards and modules can store their sounds on your computer, over Midi, or with more modern devices via USB.

## SAMPLERS

### New or used?

Samplers are obviously used in the studio for recording, but they are also taken out live and can get quite hard use. Buying used is slightly more risky because most samplers have disc drives, which can wear, and because more editing is done on samplers than on synths, frequently used buttons like '+1/–1' and 'enter/exit' get a bashing. Display screens on old Akai samplers are known to fade out.

### How do I choose?

Some of the keyboard section above applies to samplers. However, the facilities for modifying samples are much more important to most sampler users than the same facilities on keyboards. Don't worry about which one's got the editor's choice award, what do *you* need? What will you use your sampler for? Try and compare models on the same, vital functions. It's hard to do in a shop, but the sales person should be able to show you.

If you use a computer for music, your point of view on what your sampler actually needs to be able to do might be very different. Editing and sound processing are easier and more powerful on modern computers; maybe you can do all the clever stuff there and just treat your sampler as a sample player. Some budget samplers have a computer editing package supplied with them.

If you plan to take your samples to an outside studio to finish your tracks, you should consider buying a sampler which is compatible with whatever they've got, or with the industry standard. In the UK, that's Akai-S series. It's not such a big deal to take your own sampler to the studio, but consider the advantages of compatibility. Many studios have more than one sampler, so you get lots of outputs and maybe more powerful editing. The engineer may be better and faster on sampler functions than you, may have on-screen sampler editing available and may be more exact about tuning and timing. You don't necessarily need the same model; some budget samplers will at least load samples into their professional big sisters.

Samplers fall in to three categories: 19" rack format, traditional, professional models like the Akai-S series or Emu E series; cheaper, spin-off 19" rack models which have fewer facilities and fewer outputs; and drum-machine-style samplers with front-panel pads.

## Professional-Quality Samplers

Models from Akai, Emu, Roland and Yamaha all do loads of stuff, so it's a matter of priorities. For matching beats, an intuitive time-stretch screen is great. For dark or experimental music, good filters and sound-warping options are more important. If you use lots of short samples, a large, clear 'trim/truncate' screen helps.

At this level, most users will feel the advantages of using external data storage, either on your computer's hard drive or on removable media like Zip and Jaz discs. This is a standard feature on some professional machines but not all, so check and price up the external drive and discs if necessary. Digital audio boards are available for some models.

Read the next section, on budget models, and decide whether you really need all those features.

## Budget Rack–Mount Samplers

This is a hard category to discuss, as some budget models have almost as many functions as the top range, especially with add-on boards available. Others are deliberately very restricted, to make them easy to use. The kinds of things which progressively disappear as the price shrinks are:

+ Outputs. Budget samplers often have four or six, compared to ten or more on pro models
+ Effects, sometimes available as add-on board
+ Polyphony
+ Large editing screens and rapid-editing routines
+ External data storage
+ Filters, especially high-pass and band-pass
+ Time-stretch and sample processing

Read the professional model section above to get the right frame of mind, then decide what you need and what you don't care about. There aren't nearly as many samplers as keyboard modules, so it's not too hard to choose. If you barely understood the list, go for a cheap sampler. By the time it all makes sense, new gear will be much better value.

## Drum Machine–Style Samplers

These are for ragamuffin sampling! What they're best at is: 'Load up, tune up, fire up', not too much messing about. There are two very distinct divisions. The expensive ones are black music legends like the Emu SP 12(00) and its descendents, the Akai MPC1000/2000. They put the accent on immediacy and inspiration, though they have many of the features of a rack-mount . . . somewhere. The cheap ones can be very restricted indeed; some won't even retune the samples. If you're sampling from record decks or using a computer, maybe that doesn't matter. You'll also have to think about how to store the sounds if you want to use them again and you don't have a computer.

## AMPLIFIERS AND SPEAKERS

This section concentrates on amplification for playing live. In the studio, people generally use their live amp or the studio's amp.

## New or Used?

New. Amps don't get the loving treatment that instruments get and their sound doesn't improve with age. Most guitar and keyboard amps are combos (speaker/s built in) and used speakers are a poor bet. A solid-state amp head is the only safe secondhand buy here.

## Does Size Matter?

### For Guitar

No, unless you're a heavy metal monster. In fact, small is beautiful, because in most situations thirty watts is plenty and a thirty-watt amp working at three-quarter capacity sounds better than a hundred-watt beast that's barely awake. A fifty-watt combo with one twelve-inch speaker will cover just about any need. At most small or medium gigs, a fifty will only be working at about six on the volume when the engineer complains that it's cutting through his front-of-house balance and asks you to turn down.

### For Bass

Yes. Bass sounds need lots of amp power—a two hundred-watt bass amp matches a fifty-watt guitar amp—and big speakers in big cabinets make the best sound. However, refinements like ported or reflex cabinets mean that you don't actually need a bass cab the size and weight of a WWF wrestler to get a good sound, and you should remember that at all but the smallest gigs only the band will hear the direct sound of your stack anyway.

### For Keyboard

Only if you want to deliver bassy sounds. Usually a 1" x 12" plus treble unit is fine.

## How Do I Choose?

Ideally, put a couple of likely amps side by side, set them up as similarly as possible and play the same things through each, making the most rapid comparisons you can.

## For Guitar

Do you want to play 'clean' or 'dirty'? Most amps will do both reasonably well but specialise in delivering one or the other. Clean sounds should still be warm and characterful, not squeaky-clean. Solid-state or hybrid amps are fine for this and are cheaper and more robust than valve amps. For rocky, dirty sounds, look at hybrids or valve amps. If you expect to get the character of your sound from effects, you might prefer a clean amp to reproduce your careful effects programming.

## For Bass

Like guitar, the first question is 'Clean or dirty?' but dirty bass players are a minority! If you want a driving, rocky sound all the time, either look at hybrid and valve amps or choose a solid-state amp with boost controls. For most purposes, a flexible solid-state amp is fine. You don't need many facilities, so buy on the sound and the price.

## For Keyboard

You need a clean sound and may need several input channels. The range of keyboard combos is very small. Some people use small PA (public address) gear, which is fine. Choose on size and value. You can struggle by without an amp at all, in many cases, by putting your keyboards through the PA and, at gigs, hearing yourself through the stage monitors. As keyboard players often spend a lot on their equipment, they understandably want to limit expense elsewhere. It's very reassuring to have your own foldback though; you can carry on if there's a problem with the PA side.

## For Acoustic Guitar/Instruments with Pickups or 'Bugs'

You don't really need your own amp for gigs if there's a reasonable PA with an engineer. Acoustic guitarists turn up in all sorts of places, though, so if you do need your own amplification, there are some specific combos you can buy from Fender and others. Roland's Jazz Chorus (JC) series was for a long time an 'industry standard' for acoustic instrument amplification.

## Useful features

### For Guitar

✦ Switchable boost or switchable channels for clean and dirty sounds. Make sure you can get a compatible footswitch and that the footswitch socket works.

✦ 'Cascade' volume controls. Useful for dirty sounds, they create dirt early in the chain and then a second stage lets you add . . . more dirt!

✦ Headphone socket. Very useful for private practice.

✦ Onboard effects such as reverb, chorus or tremelo. Mildly useful—until you get some outboard effects, after which the onboard ones will be switched off forever.

### For Bass

✦ Multiband equalisation. Gives more precise adjustments to tone than bass, middle and treble controls. Usually graphic (vertical sliders) but sometimes on rotary knobs.

✦ Channel switching. Make sure you can get a compatible footswitch and that the footswitch socket works.

✦ Compressor. Usually switched, this can give a denser, 'present' sound, at the expense of reducing the dynamic range of your playing a bit. Generally a good thing.

✦ Wheels! Bass cabinets tend to be large and heavy and often aren't flightcased. Industrial-equipment suppliers carry a fabulous range of sets of wheels for trolleys, handcarts and so on. Go for about four-inch-diameter metal wheels with rubber tyres; get two which swivel and two which are fixed but have brakes.

## EFFECTS UNITS

There are two main types:

Floor pedals, or 'stomp boxes', are mainly used live by guitarists. Common brands include Boss and DOD.

✦ Each box has one effect, such as distortion, chorus, flanger or delay.

✦ The units are not programmable; they run on batteries or via a mains adapter and they have rugged metal cases.

- ✦ Plus points: immediate control over effects parameters, ruggedness and battery operation.
- ✦ Minus points: lack of versatility, no storage of settings and possible battery failure, limited use in studio.

Rack format effects were originally for studio use but have found their way into many live setups. Guitarists should either look for a unit which has been designed with them in mind, or look elsewhere for distortion and overdrive—the distortion effects in multi-effectors are usually no match for dedicated units.

- ✦ Some have one effect, but most are multi-effectors. Common effects include reverb, delay, chorus, flanger, pitch shifter and equaliser. Less common are distortion, cabinet simulator, compressor, noise gate and wah wah.
- ✦ They are programmable, and effects can be combined to give a very wide range of sounds.
- ✦ Changing effects settings is much less immediate—fiddly, in fact. Instead of one knob per parameter, you have to change screens/pages and use up/down buttons to alter the settings. You can't easily turn each effect on and off, as you can with floor pedals.
- ✦ The units have to be treated more carefully when gigging, as they aren't built for the road. Ideally, they should live in a rack-sized flight case, which adds quite a bit to the price.
- ✦ Plus points: lots of effects, programmable, can be used for recording.
- ✦ Minus points: harder to use, more delicate.

There are some effects which put rack power in a large floor pedal format, including a rocker pedal which can be routed to control different things, like wah wah, volume or distortion. This seems to be an ideal solution, but they're not hugely popular, probably because they aren't as immediate as effects boxes and not as recording-friendly as rack mounts. They could be just the right compromise for someone wanting both stage and studio capability without too many purchases though.

## BITS AND BOBS

### Stands

You may not have much choice of instrument stands at your music shops. There are stands for guitars and saxes, for instruments that aren't being used, and keyboard stands, which are more important—imagine a problem with a keyboard stand at a gig which sends your main keyboard to the floor as you are playing it.

## New or Used?

Buying used is okay, check for bent tubing and damage to movable parts.

## How Do I Choose?

Stages in semipro venues can be bouncy enough to topple instruments, so stability is the most important feature of any stand. Its movable parts should lock firmly so it won't collapse under pressure. It should be hard to damage; for instance, some keyboard stands are locked by bolts with knurled knobs on the end and the exposed bolts are often bent. Stands like QuikLok, where a sprung pin locates in holes on a circular plate, are quite sturdy.

You can get keyboard stands with an 'upper deck' for another keyboard or a module. Basic 'X' stands with extension arms are only just stable enough for gigging. You need to be looking for stands with more cross-members, square-section tube—stands that look like they mean business.

## Cases

You don't need full 'flight cases' like those you see at big gigs. Semiflight cases are available from music shops or directly from the makers, which advertise in the back of musicians' monthly magazines. Protecting the instrument in transit is the purpose, so the more you pay, the thicker the cut foam inside is, as is the thickness of the case shell. The inside of the case must fit the instrument as closely as is practical.

## New or Used?

Buying used is sort of okay, but the case must 'hug' the instrument, so used is not ideal. Buy oversize and pad the inside with foam or fabric. Check that the lid and base fit snugly and easily and that the fastenings work well.

## How Do I Choose?

Choose on quality and price, primarily. You may favour a local source because cases generally are made to order, not mass-produced, so you can't try before you buy. Durability is important: black leatherette covering gets ripped and hard surfaces survive better; butterfly fastenings last much better than clasp and lever fastenings. Pay a little extra for good handles, preferably broad, thick and soft. When you haul your case round three sides of a building or tackle flights of stairs, you'll be glad you did.

## OTHER EQUIPMENT

If you are not using a professional rehearsal room, you will need some way of hearing electric instruments. You can use a guitar combo or small PA equipment for amplification—it's easiest, but the result is primitive. If your amp doesn't have enough inputs, use a two-into-one 'Y' connector, available from electrical shops.

Many people use home audio gear, though some of the complete systems which have been popular since the mid-1980s have no facility for accepting an external sound source. A suitable unit will have phono (RCA) sockets marked 'Aux' or 'Ext', or—labelled for an external device—'VCR' or 'Tape 2'.

For two instruments—two guitars, guitar and bass, or keyboard and guitar, for example—you can manage with connectors and adapters. You need to adapt from male quarter-inch jack to male phono/RCA. As male usually connects to female, you may need to do this in two stages: jack–phono and male in–male out (known as a gender-bender!). Do this for each side of a stereo pair and you can monitor two instruments, using the stereo balance control to adjust levels.

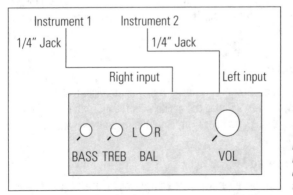

*Two instruments into home hi-fi— use the balance control to adjust the relative levels*

It is possible to monitor up to four instruments this way, using a 'Y' connector on each side of the stereo path, but it's clumsy and it becomes hard to match the levels of different instruments. And all those adapters start to cost almost as much as the more elegant solution: a line mixer. Line mixers simply combine sounds from their inputs to make a mono or stereo signal, with control over input volume. They can be bought from electrical shops and have four to eight inputs.

## SMALL PA (PUBLIC ADDRESS SYSTEM)

A conventional band using commercial rehearsal rooms doesn't need this. It's useful if:

+ You rehearse at home, too loudly for singers to sing comfortably.
+ You rehearse in a bare room, such as a school hall.
+ You want to play in venues with no PA—this usually means duos or trios in low-key pub/club/bar environments.
+ You have several acoustic instruments.
+ You have several keyboards.

The system will consist of a mixer, power amp and speakers. The mixer and power amp may be combined and may be in a mixing desk format or an amp head format. Two speakers are normal for the audience's needs. All mixing sections will offer the facility to connect at least one line of monitoring speakers for the performers as well, though these are not usually part of a basic system package.

Small mixers are now so cheap that they really represent the best option, combined with a separate power amp. The usual arguments for separate components apply: you can upgrade part of the system without changing all of it and, should something break down, you don't have to hire/borrow so much gear.

Power amps should deliver at least $2 \times 120$ watts. They don't have many functions or controls—they don't need to. All that is on the mixer. Many manufacturers take one of their mixers and put power amps inside—sometimes good-quality effects as well. Ask at your music shop.

Speakers should be able to handle one hundred and fifty watts programme and should contain at least a twelve-inch speaker plus a treble unit. If you intend to use the system for electronic keyboards or acoustic instruments with strong bass frequencies, go for at least a fifteen-inch speaker. Folding stands to bring the speakers above the soft, sound-absorbing mass that is your audience are a good idea.

The power ratings suggested are okay for vocals only, which is often how a small PA is used. A rule of thumb for small-gig PA systems, where all the instruments are coming through the PA and the music is too loud to talk over comfortably (i.e., just right), is one kilowatt of amp power per one hundred-person room capacity.

Monitor speakers are a luxury, but a nice one at times. They need their own power amp, fed by a monitor out or one of the pre-fader aux outs of the mixer.

### Miser's Tip

Use secondhand amp head format, five- or six-channel PA tops, typically by Carlsbro and HH. They have basic controls but are sturdy, functional, compact and cheap. Spend on new speakers: the difference counts much more than it does with the amp.

# rehearsal

This section assumes that most people reading it are in a 'traditional' band. Synth-led acts tend to do most of their gig preparation in the home studio. They will benefit from reading this section to help them prepare for and structure their sessions, but this is mostly about vocals, guitars, bass and drums.

## FINDING A PLACE TO REHEARSE

### WHERE TO REHEARSE?

There are three main types of rehearsal space: we'll call them domestic, community and commercial. The three very often form a 'ladder'. Artists start out rehearsing in a bedroom or garage while they are writing the set and recruiting a stable, satisfactory lineup. Eventually, they feel the need to move to somewhere less crowded, like a school, scout hut or youth club, where a full lineup can rehearse for early gigs. Proper rehearsal facilities are most useful when artists are rehearsing for a definite gig or playing regularly. In some areas, especially cities, 'alternative' rehearsal space is unobtainable; then you have to use commercial facilities early on and will need to be very together if you want to avoid wasting a lot of costly time.

## REHEARSING AT HOME

For many people, rehearsing at home is restricted by noise thresholds and a lack of space. On the other hand, it's free and doesn't involve much travel or setting-up time, so it can be productive if used properly.

### Home Rehearsal Discipline

Noise is the most common problem, especially when it annoys neighbours. Unfortunately, in many neighbourhoods, you are creating a nuisance and it's in your interest to do what you can to limit it. Try to use a room which doesn't adjoin another property. A room at the back of a house can cause less annoyance than one facing other houses. Shut all the doors and windows you can, not just those to the room you're in but doors to toilets, passageways, the lot. Try to rehearse at a time of day when adjoining rooms are less frequently occupied. The more soft things—duvets, cushions, coats—there are in the room, the better.

When you rehearse in a room for the first time, get someone who isn't playing to wander around outside listening to you playing at a volume you think is enjoyable for you but not annoying to others. It may be worth 'tweaking' the tone controls on your monitoring system to get a nice sound at the expense of volume; turn up the treble and bass a bit, or use the built-in settings that many systems have for dance or rock. Note what your main volume settings are, stick to them and get used to them. You really don't need the hassle of losing your rehearsal space at this early stage. Besides, low volumes mean you have to work on composition and technique to make exciting music, so it's good for you too.

Don't tap your feet! Because it's a physical impact as well as a sound, it can travel further and cause more annoyance than guitars and keyboards. Everyone taking off their shoes in a small, enclosed space may be unpleasant, but it helps.

Don't play loudly when you don't have to. Turning down when tuning or working things out gives other people a respite and shows you are trying not to intrude.

Another problem at home is interruptions to the rehearsal. Don't take phone calls, don't receive visitors but do have fixed rest breaks—no wandering off to the kitchen.

And generally do everything you can to get a set together, start gigging and move the band out of the bedroom!

## COMMUNITY ROOMS

Schools, scout and youth groups, arts centres, youth clubs and sports clubs may all have suitable buildings for rehearsal. If you don't know where these are, find out from your library or council leisure department; ask music shops or other bands if they know of some anywhere.

Obviously you need a room which is dry and has reasonable access for your equipment, with electric points. Heating may be a problem in winter. Don't bring your own heating without consulting the person with whom you book the room—there may be fire or electrical hazards and you may not be popular when their fuel bills come in.

You will probably have to pay something for the use of the room. Compare the cost with the rate at a commercial rehearsal room which offers a PA system, proper power provision, soundproofing, heating, security and perhaps other benefits like back-line amps, hot drinks, air-conditioning or equipment storage and hire. Generally, you can expect to encounter more petty rules and frustrations in community rooms than in commercial rehearsal rooms. They usually have poor acoustics and even poorer atmosphere. Often, though, you can play for longer than in a commercial room and, of course, it should be much cheaper.

## Equipment

You will need to bring back-line amps. In fact, you will need to bring every last little thing you might need because, unlike at home or in a commercial room, there's nothing there. Bring power extensions, fuses, toolkit, drinks and snacks. If your room doesn't have a PA, you can still rehearse everything with back-line, but you can't play loudly if the vocals aren't amplified. Singers must be careful not to damage their voices. You may know someone who has a sound system, like a DJ or a school, which you can borrow. Almost anything will do as long as it delivers fifty watts or more. The truly desperate can get a high-impedance microphone (usually cheap ones—good mics have a low signal) and borrow a back-line amp or spare channel on someone else's.

# COMMERCIAL REHEARSAL ROOMS

Hiring a proper rehearsal room is the only way to approximate the conditions of a real show. The cost can be a burden if the band isn't earning. Young bands should probably try to find another solution and put the money saved towards better gear, a recording session or saving up for a van.

Rehearsal rooms can be found through music magazines, and local music shops and studios will probably know of them. Compare costs and facilities with those of competitors—any extra travel may not cost much and be worthwhile. Firm bookings for the same slot each week are advisable—in a good suite, they're often necessary—and you should be able to negotiate a better rate for a regular booking. You will probably have to pay for a booked slot you don't use unless you give plenty of notice; ask what the terms are.

A commercial rehearsal room should have a reasonable degree of sound-proofing, so that you aren't disturbed by bands in other rooms. It should have lots of power points, spread out so that they are convenient for players in their stage positions. It should provide at least three microphones up to the standard of Shure SM58s, with stands and leads. There should be a PA system of at least $2 \times 100$ watts, with at least six working channels on the mixing desk. Most have a cassette deck, which can be useful.

An advantage of many hired rooms is that they offer back-line amps and sometimes drum kits, guitars, etc., either free or for hire. Some will store your gear for you between rehearsals. For young bands without cars, this can be very valuable. Even if you can bring everything, sometimes the carrying in and out, the wasted setup time, and the wear and tear on your gear make reasonably priced hiring seem worthwhile.

### Other useful things some rooms provide include:

+ Trolleys to make load-ins and get-outs quicker and less tiring
+ Big mirrors so you can see how crap you look and do something about it
+ 'Mood' lighting, nice for sessions over four hours or late at night
+ Natural light, which seems to help mood and alertness noticeably
+ Tea/coffee, soft drinks or water, either from a machine or from their disgusting kitchen
+ Snacks or microwaved food (from their disgusting kitchen)
+ Strings, plectrums, drumsticks, leads, gaffer tape and so on for sale
+ Musicians' noticeboard

If the room you're using doesn't offer these things, why not ask for them? The owner may not have thought of it. Most of these little extras are easy to do; some make a bit of money and it might help them keep customers.

Here are a few simple ways to get the best out of your rehearsal.

## BEFORE YOU ARRIVE

As with any music event, make sure your equipment is working properly and that you have 'spares' as necessary (e.g., strings, spare lead). Make a checklist. Perhaps it will have only a few things on it at first, but it will grow in small ways! And when you come to a gig, with five people piling into a van in the dark, an hour late, checklists—and, equally important, the habit of using them—are a godsend. Do you need refreshments? Take them or buy them on the way. Going down to the shops or over to the petrol station during the rehearsal is a massive time-waster.

Always have the phone number of your destination with you.

Plan to arrive early, then you won't be late. In a commercial studio, the previous slot may not have been booked, or the band may have packed up a few minutes early, so you can get set up before your paid-for time starts. Or they may run on late, in which case the studio owner is more likely to sympathize if you have been hanging around for a while. In a community room, you often have to find a caretaker or key-holder who will have vanished at the time you are supposed to arrive, but will be bang on time when you are supposed to leave.

## SETTING UP

This section assumes you are either in a community room and have a PA or in a commercial room.

You should set your equipment up as for a gig. Each band will have its own stage positions, but the important thing is that you are practising for a gig, so how you look onstage is important.

Small back-line amps should be angled to point diagonally across the stage, because you don't have the foldback monitors you will have at gigs. Bass speakers can point forwards because bass sounds are less directional, but the speakers should be as far back on the stage as possible—it helps you hear the bass better. Bass players should stay fairly near the drummer, as these two need to work together very closely and respond to each other's playing.

## Stage Plan

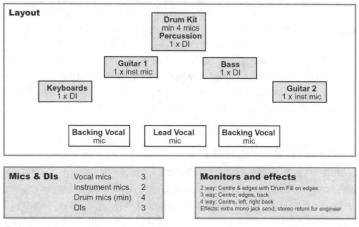

**Layout**

| Drum Kit |
| min 4 mics |
| **Percussion** |
| 1 x DI |

| Guitar 1 | | Bass |
| 1 x inst mic | | 1 x DI |

| Keyboards | | | Guitar 2 |
| 1 x DI | | | 1 x inst mic |

| Backing Vocal | Lead Vocal | Backing Vocal |
| mic | mic | mic |

| **Mics & DIs** | Vocal mics | 3 |
|---|---|---|
| | Instrument mics | 2 |
| | Drum mics (min) | 4 |
| | DIs | 3 |

**Monitors and effects**

2 way: Centre & edges with Drum Fill on edges
3 way: Centre, edges, back
4 way: Centre, left, right back
Effects: extra mono jack send, stereo return for engineer

*Typical stage layout: vox/gtr, gtr/vox, bass, drums*

Amp volumes are governed by one thing: how loud the vocals can be without starting to feed back. Your singer already has the task of singing probably about three times as much as at a gig; he or she shouldn't need to struggle to be heard as well. A damaged voice takes a lot longer to fix than a broken string. Besides, the public and the industry are more interested in the singer's contribution than in everyone else's put together, so you all need to be able to hear it clearly to make sure it's as good as possible. Whatever it takes—damping the drums, turning amps towards the wall, compromising on that amazing solo with clever feedback—you don't play louder than your singer.

Once that's sorted, you should each play a few notes to establish that you're basically all playing at about the same volume.

## PLAYING THE GIG

There are three main tasks you can tackle when rehearsing.

+ Writing material
+ Developing compositions into fully arranged works
+ Ensuring fully arranged works are gig-ready

Presumably you have written enough material to spend some of the time on the second and third tasks. Most people need some time to warm up their fingers, lips, tonsils and brains (the more often you practice, the less time), so play a couple of tunes you know to sort out tunings, volumes and technical hitches and get everyone on-stream.

It's then best to work from the top of the above list; writing demands the most creativity, so should be done when you are freshest. It's hard to return to nuts-and-bolts stuff after playing full-tilt gig material, so save that till last and work on developing arrangements in the middle of the session.

## Recording the Rehearsal

Recording parts of a rehearsal can be very valuable, but you need to treat it cautiously. Its main uses are: reminding people of new parts they wrote and might forget; catching a moment of inspiration from jamming (or making an inspired mistake); and critically evaluating the finished performance of a song you think is gig-ready.

You may be using cassette or Mini-Disc (MD). Make sure the act always has at least three blank tapes/MDs in its kit. Put the machine or the microphone where the back-line and the PA are well balanced. The first time you record with a new setup or a new mic position, play some back to make sure it's intelligible. Tape machines with auto-level controls—they don't have a record/input level control—are bad at coping with raw, uncompressed sounds. Maybe the mic or machine can be repositioned.

Label and keep everything. It may be a nuisance, but that's better than wiping something that might have the beginnings of a great idea or be a document of your struggles towards greatness.

## Writing in Rehearsal

Keep the volume reasonable so everyone can distinguish what's actually being played or sung. It can be quite boring for the rest of the band if people get into a long struggle with a particular bit; sometimes you just have to put up with it and stay alert; sometimes you can work quietly on your own part, or work in pairs—two guitarists, or drummer and bassist.

Frustrations can flare in the airless gloom of a rehearsal room, or the chilly, fluorescent-lit scout hut. Not everyone can pick up a new part at the same speed and sometimes you'll have to put up with someone stumbling through their part and promising to be ready by the next rehearsal. That's a better solution than using paid-for time struggling endlessly with something that isn't fully working anyway.

## Developing and Arranging

By now, everyone knows what they should be playing and roughly how the song goes. This is the time to iron out any weak cues, subtle discords, iffy backing vocals, loose rhythm sections and so on. You should play louder than when writing; not too loud or it will mask any problems, but loud enough to know that if a song suddenly sags, it will sag at full volume too and something needs to be done.

This is a good time to try out ideas like new riffs or solos, key changes or breakdowns, endings and so on. The band should be solid enough by now for the idea to have a fair chance. Song format ideas like doubling, halving or dropping sections are best done now too.

## Getting Gig-Ready

Rehearsing compares to gigging like cycling to the shops compares to motorbike courier riding. No matter how hard you push yourself, you can't make a rehearsal set as challenging or distracting as a gig. But it's the best chance you've got, so push as hard as you can. Don't accept second-best performances, they'll turn into third-best under the pressure of gigging. Ideally, you should by now be paying attention to stage disciplines—choreography for some, jokes between songs for others. Whatever, make it real. Try to play all the tunes you have ready, with breaks of no more than a minute between each. Time the result.

As soon as you are all happy with about thirty minutes of music, try to get some gigs. While you're waiting for those to happen, invite someone to watch the last hour of your rehearsal and to make comments.

# finding the gig

## GET READY, GET SET, GO

Okay, so you've bought your equipment, written some songs, rehearsed them, performed them in front of your mum and dad and the dog. Now you want to do the real thing. You want to play in front of the public.

The idea is thrilling but reality sets in. Where exactly are you going to play your songs? Who is going to allow complete novices to get up onstage and do their stuff?

Don't worry, there are a number of options depending on the number of people in the band and what style of music you are playing.

## GOALS

Your first goal is to go out and look for a venue and play that first, probably terrifying gig. Your second goal is to get good at it—and that means doing lots of gigs; like anything else, it's practice. Your ultimate goal is to play live gigs in front of a wildly enthusiastic crowd of your dedicated fans and, by so doing, up your profile and increase record sales.

## STRATEGY

But we've all got to start somewhere. And somewhere is finding a place to play.

## STEP 1: FIND SOMEWHERE TO PLAY

So how do you find the venue to suit your needs? First, see if you can play at a school, college or youth club, in a fairly low-key setting. If you can manage to do this, ideally more than once, you can claim at least some live experience before you approach commercial gigs and you might even gain some fans! At least you will have an audience to entertain with your antics. There will probably be someone experienced to help you—the music teacher, college events organiser or youth club arts/music worker. You aren't likely to get that help on New Band Nite at a local pub or club. Visit pubs, clubs, art centres, colleges and universities, and social clubs in your town or your local area and see who's putting on live music and what type of live music. It's no good phoning your local pub because you've seen a poster advertising 'live music' on Friday nights only to find it's a trad jazz night and you're a metal band, or six of you turn up with a full drum kit, percussionist, two guitarists, a keyboard player and a vocalist and you find the pub's got a stage the size of a coffee table. You must visit the venues, check what type of music they put on and whether they're suitable for your lineup.

## Solo Artist or Duo

If you are a solo artist or a duo, life is much simpler. Many small clubs, pubs and arts centres are keen to book people like you for a number of reasons: you won't be too noisy and you don't take up much space so the stage can be small or nonexistent. This also applies if you want to perform a PA—short for personal appearance. This means you sing over a recorded backing track, sort of karaoke really, so once again you don't need much in the way of instruments or other equipment.

## Full Band

If you're a full band of three or more members, however, you need a venue with enough space for all of you and your equipment. It also has to have a PA system large enough to do you justice, or if it doesn't have one, you will have to hire one—the venue owner or local music shop will be able to tell you where from.

## LOCAL PUBS OR CLUBS

You may be lucky to live near enough a venue that actively promotes live bands and puts on three or so a night. These promoters are used to having absolute newcomers approach them and don't expect miracles at your first gig. This is why they put new bands on in the early evening at the bottom of the bill—so you don't drive too many customers away.

Then there are venues which make a feature of putting on brand-new or freshly signed bands. In the UK, The Barfly chain has made a success of this policy—it now has club venues in cities such as Cardiff, Liverpool, Glasgow, York, Birmingham and London. The Water Rats, booked by Plum Promotions, is another. But what does a promoter at one of these venues look for in a new or up-and-coming band? We talk to one to find out. (See p. 33.)

## COLLEGES AND UNIVERSITIES

If you're at college or university you'll probably find there are opportunities either to play at a college gig or to be allowed to put on a gig yourself. Most colleges have reasonably good facilities and PA systems and, if you feel brave, you can whip up a bigger crowd by getting some promotion on the college radio network or in the college paper.

## ARTS CENTRES

Arts centres are another good bet. Good ones are usually keen on promoting local musicians and either should let you play as part of a night or support for another band, or let you put on a gig yourselves. Once again, they will have PA, lights, door staff and all the other necessary aspects of putting on a gig, so all you need to do is a bit of promotion, turn up, sound check and off you go. This is often true of social clubs. This kind of venue is particularly suitable for solo singers, duos and bands that perform popular music. They are far less likely to give you a go if you are a speed metal or skate rock band—then you're better to stick to pubs and colleges.

## STEP 2: FINDING THE GIG

## APPROACHING A VENUE

Once you find a venue that seems suitable, both musically and in its layout, approach the owner or manager and ask if you can play there. Usually they will want a CD of your music to see if they think it's right for their venue. Make sure you've got one and make doubly sure it's got your contact details on it. Also, it's important to get the name of the person you're speaking to and the venue's phone number; unless you're very lucky or strangely good for novices, it's going to be you calling them for the gig (several times probably, so don't get disheartened); they won't phone you. When you get the gig you'll probably be offered a midweek night at first or an early evening slot, which is just as well, as it gives you the latitude to learn on the job and make mistakes without too many people seeing you.

## SUPPORT A FRIEND

Another way of getting that first gig is to support a friend's band which is already gigging. Ask them if you can support them at a local gig. Most people are decent enough to let you. After all, everybody who is already gigging knows how hard it can be to make that first step.

This approach can work well, as a combination of your friends and their fans should give you a bigger audience than you might otherwise expect, which, while scary in one way, actually makes that first gig a lot more exciting. A buzzing atmosphere makes the audience a lot more forgiving of the inevitable mistakes, fluffed lines and general cock-ups that are bound to happen.

✦✦✦✦✦✦✦✦✦✦✦✦✦✦✦✦✦✦✦✦✦✦✦✦✦✦✦✦✦✦✦✦✦✦✦✦✦✦✦✦✦✦✦

## SARAH THIRTLE

Sarah Thirtle is assistant manager at Plum Promotions/Plum Music, an independent promotions company responsible for co-ordinating all live events at venues in London: the Water Rats Theatre (Kings Cross, capacity 200), the Betsey Trotwood (Farringdon, capacity 60), the Marquee Club (Leicester Square, capacity 535, plus balcony 330). Sarah explains how new artists should approach those first gigs.

### What do you do at Plum Promotions?

I am Plum Promotions' main booker for the Water Rats venue. I am also heavily involved in booking and programming the events at the Marquee Club in Leicester Square. We also book events for a small place called the Betsey Trotwood. I've been working at Plum Promotions for around four or five years. The company is owned by Allan North and he started the company about seven years ago. I started with the company just doing work experience, and through lots of hard work and determination I now book a couple of venues and am the assistant manager.

**What do you do to help support new artists?**
A lot of it is the very initial stages: once a band has got to the point where they have got a demo recorded, we might be their first port of call, the first place they send it to. So a lot of it is listening to very, very new stuff, very new bands, very new material. A lot of it is in the development stages of coming together, so our area of expertise is, out of what we receive, picking out that stuff which we think shows promise. We listen to the songs, trying to think, 'Are these bands at a stage where we can help them by working with them or are they not actually at that stage yet? And if so, can we talk to them about what else they might try and do before they are actually ready to do a gig with us?' But it's all about listening to the music and just hoping that your ear is good enough to pick something out and then forming a relationship with bands. All of us that work here have a particular band that we work with more closely with than the others; we help them with their careers, with booking in shows, or giving advice where we can.

**You have good links with the break-through panel, don't you?**
Yes, we did some break-through panels where I invited industry people down: they included A&R, management, publishing, press officers, producers or other musicians. At the panels, we listen to new demos and then the panel gives advice directly to the band. Bands find this really useful. We haven't done one of them for a while because we've been so busy. We have good strong contacts with a lot of labels, both major and indie labels, and we work closely with other independent promoters and agents and management, so we have a good working relationship across quite a few different areas of the business.

**Do you see the role of a promoter in the unsigned music industry as being very similar to that of an agent for unsigned bands; i.e., you can help them with their careers?**
I think initially yes, definitely, for those first gigs.

If they can get in with a promoter, if the promoter likes the band and it is the kind of promoter who will get behind that band in whatever way possible, then it can help with not only getting gigs at the venue that promoter works for but the promoter will pass on details to other places. It depends what kind of promoter you are. We are very much interested in doing this. I get very excited if I hear a band I like, and if it's a very new band I will get behind them and offer extra support and advice. I suppose it can help to be some kind of springboard onto other things!

As I say, it depends what kind of promoter you are. Some promoters will deal with a number of different venues because they have different club nights that they might do at a few places, so in that way I suppose it is a little more like being an agent. We tend to deal with fixed-location venues, so the bands we get coming in tend to be sourced into our main places. The promoters do venues all over London and in Manchester now as well, so that's a little bit more like, I suppose, an agent sourcing a band out at different points.

### Do you also book signed bands to play at your venues?

We do signed bands at different levels of their careers. Some bands have maybe just been signed and they are having a first or second release and they need a press show to coincide with the release for them to get prospective journalists, TV and radio down to see them, so we do quite a lot of that. We also have bands that are perhaps much further on in their career and they want to do some kind of secret show or show for their fans, so it is across all levels really. We've gone from shows with the Breeders and Alanis Morissette on different days at the Water Rats right down to the other week we had the Paddingtons, who had a little fan club gig at the Water Rats. So we put on all level of signed bands and shows for bands that are just about to get signed and they need a show for the label to come down to see them and then sign them—that's happened with loads of bands. That pretty much happened with Keane (they played and then they got signed), Boy Kill Boy and Kaiser Chiefs and bands like that. I wouldn't say that our show was the show that they got signed at, but certainly these are bands that were on the cusp of signing. Playing a venue such as ours bolsters their chances of signing the deal they wanted to sign.

### Do you do creative music programming, by putting talented unsigned bands alongside bigger acts?

Where we can. It doesn't happen as often as we would like. I know that bands like to think that we can just slot them in when we get a bigger band in, but often we get a bigger band in through another bigger promoter. For example, Live Nation will come in with a tour and they've got the whole night already booked and they'll come in and use the venue. Or an agent will come in. At the moment we've got a show coming up with Wheatus and the agent said there was already a support booked but was willing to have another support act if we wanted to. So, because we've got a good relationship with that agent, we are able to find a band to place within this particular show. Often the agent or promoter will say, 'We've already got a lineup for this. We don't need another support'. When we can, we will find a band to support a bigger act and when I do that it's usually bands we've booked a number of times and have formed a relationship with, and bands that we have got behind and know that this will be a useful gig for them. As I say, sometimes it's dictated by the agent or management or label.

## Do you pay the bands or is it normally based on ticket sales?

It's based upon ticket sales, door sales. It's a percentage split of the door after we have covered costs for staff and equipment and promotional costs and things like that, so it's a pretty standard deal. I think most venues in London do pretty similar stuff; it's a percentage split of the door.

## What do you do to promote the gigs?

We have our own Web site with full listings and previews and links to click for information about the bands and links to their Web sites. We have a pretty comprehensive database of listings and press contacts which we send all our gig listings out to, that includes the Press Association, all the main listings places like the *NME* and the *Guardian Guide,* and Web sites and fanzines get all our information as well. We print up posters for the venues and we print up listing leaflets every couple of weeks which have full listings for the venues plus pictures and previews of some particularly good bands that we think we've got coming up. We also have a large membership of people who have joined, club promotion members, normal gig-goers who can sign up for newsletters and gig listings every week. We also have an industry membership list which gets sent out, also listings and tips and previews and stuff. We are just adding new stuff to our Web site at the moment, such as chat forums for our members and for our bands so they can talk about gigs and what they like, what they don't like, any good stuff they have heard, that kind of thing, so we try and make it quite interactive. Every now and then we might place an advert in *NME* or *Time Out* or something but as that costs quite a lot of money we can't afford to do it very often.

## Do you have the sole promotion for the venues?

Pretty much. We're responsible for the programming and the organisation of the diary of events. We do work closely with promoters that come in with shows at all of the venues and all of the promoters that come in with shows. We work with people like Club Fandango and Live Nation and SJM and other promoters who have brought stuff in and little independent promoters as well that have just started out putting nights—we'll help them and give them advice for their own show. But mostly, all the events will come in through us and we'll place them in the diary and administer them, programme, everything. Most of the events are bands that we have booked but other stuff does come in.

## Do all of the venues have their own back-line?

No, we don't provide back-line. It's all PA: main PA, front-of-house, PA monitors, mixing desk, all the electronic doo dahs that go with that, but we haven't got back-line or drum kit.

## What advice would you give an unsigned band wishing to break into the industry?

It's all about the music. Don't waste time worrying about A&R people, don't waste time worrying about finding management; it is all about the music. If you create fantastic songs and you practice and practice and do fantastic gigs, you will be noticed. Good people in this industry, the people who work hard and are worth the time of day, they will notice you. It's all about the music, in my opinion.

Living in the US? See what venue promoter Mitchell Frank has to say about pulling down gigs at his two cool venues.

✦✦✦✦✦✦✦✦✦✦✦✦✦✦✦✦✦✦✦✦✦✦✦✦✦✦✦✦✦✦✦✦✦✦✦✦✦✦✦✦✦✦✦✦✦✦✦✦✦

✦✦✦✦✦✦✦✦✦✦✦✦✦✦✦✦✦✦✦✦✦✦✦✦✦✦✦✦✦✦✦✦✦✦✦✦✦✦✦✦✦✦✦✦✦✦✦✦✦

## MITCHELL FRANK

Mitchell Frank is the promoter and owner of two Los Angeles venues: Spaceland and the Echo. They have been starting points for the careers of such acts as Beck, Rilo Kiley, Moving Units and Palo Alto, among many others. The venues also play host to international talent such as the Raveonettes, M.I.A., and Embrace.

## At what point in their development should a band approach you to play?

When they have their first recordings. We start working with bands pretty early. The first time I heard Rilo Kiley was on a cassette tape and it was a demo. Or for that matter, when I first started in 1994, the bands I was dealing with barely had demos. I'm interested in a band that takes themselves seriously and has their shit together, has all the necessary parts. They've got their musicians together. They know how to promote a show.

### What do you mean by a band promoting a show?

That's the next level after a band's first show which we generally promote. We're interested in a band that at least tries to get people to go to their shows, rather than just expecting people to show up because they're a good band or something.

### How do you book headlining bands?

For shows by local bands, generally we're dealing directly with the band. For regional shows, we're generally dealing with agents. And there's always some managers we're dealing with.

### Do you give support slots to new bands? If so, how should they approach you?

Yes, but the band must make sure the headlining band knows who they are. The best way to deal with that if you're the new band is to make sure you've submitted your music to that other band or invite that other band to your show. Otherwise if I tell them, 'XYZ band wants to play with you' and they may not be that interested if they don't know who you are. And that's if it's a local show and you can actually talk to the band. If the headliners are a regional or national act, a lot of people are really good with their e-mails or their blogs. If you send the band an mp3, chances are they're probably going to listen to it and get back to you. Send it in a way where you can say, 'Here's why we fit'.

### What kind of bands do you tend to put on in either venue?

We do everything alternative, in the true sense of the word alternative, not in the genre of alternative. We started up booking indie rock before it had a name. We started booking alternative blues, alternative jazz, alternative jam bands, alternative hip-hop bands, underground hip-hop, drum 'n' bass. Basically new music styles is what we're into.

### Do you pay support bands? How does it work out?

Yes, we pretty much pay everybody. Otherwise we'll just figure it out. We have a formula of how we pay bands. We'll just figure out what each band brought in customer-wise. It's not fair to pay an opener band a lot of money if the third band or second band brought in all the people. We take our nightly expenses

---

and figure out a percentage we would pay the band. The percentage is what we feel is the standard for the industry and then we pay the bands at a pro-rata share or based on what they brought in. Say one band brought in 70% of the people and another band brought in 20% of the people and another band brought in 10% of the people, that's how we would break out the money.

## Do the bands know what they're getting paid ahead of time?
Most headliners do and then there's a bonus if they do well. Most deals are set where there's a split point. If they reach the split point then they go into bonus points. On the larger shows, support bands know exactly how much they're going to make; on smaller shows, they don't. It may be based on what you actually pull in.

## What's your method for promoting shows?
We do ground and guerilla marketing with strip flyers and postcards. We do a lot of marketing inside the club. We have a lot of posters up, a lot of flyers out. We encourage the band to come to like-minded shows to pass out flyers. We let them in for free to pass out flyers. We encourage them to come to either one of the clubs to pass out flyers or go to other clubs. We also do a lot of marketing at the local music stores. We also do advertising in the weekly magazines in Los Angeles. And we also do radio promotion. We work with all the college stations, we work with the national stations and then we also work with Internet radio. We do e-mail blasts and Internet marketing.

## What's the difference between the e-mail blasts and the Internet marketing?
E-mail blasts are when someone signs up to a list and they can specify if they want to get e-mails about reggae and underground hip-hop, so if we have one of those shows we can send them an e-mail blast about it. Then Internet marketing is where we'll go to Friendster or MySpace or Sonicbits and make sure that the band's Web site is up-to-date and any blogs that are open and available, make sure it's posted everywhere. To make sure it's in the ether. We also do a press e-mailing as well to get it out to all the listings services. There's about thirty places that list all the shows.

## Do you ever hire out the venue to a band for the whole night?
We don't really do private events or rent out the club. We pretty much focus seven nights a week times two. Sometimes at the Echo, we'll double or triple

stack events because it's a popular room. We do shows and they turn into showcases for labels. Sometimes I'll work with a manager or an agent on a new band and it'll turn into a label showcase. Typically, we don't work with a label on it. What'll happen is I'll talk to a manager and they'll be like, 'I wanted to bring out the band anyway in May or November, so if you guys will just give them $500 the label is going to fly them in and we can do a show'. On a couple of occasions we have rented out in the daytime, not for label showcases, but other kinds of showcases. We've done a couple of radio events or broadcasts to Europe but not really private events and not showcases.

### What times do the venues open and close?
Typically doors are at 8 o'clock, first band goes on at 9, 10, 11 p.m. We're done by midnight or one o'clock. We stay open while people are there and then we close down.

### How many bands do you tend to put on a night?
Three is the average, three to four depending on the night. Some headlining bands only like to play with two bands; some like to play with only one band.

### Do your support bands get a chance to sound check?
They always get to line check, sometimes they can sound check. It depends on how long the headliner takes. Sometimes the headliner takes the whole sound check time. A line check is making sure that your guitar amp is at the proper volume and that the sound engineer can hear it and it's coming through the speakers, or that your microphone is on. That's a line check. It's a five-minute sound check. It's making sure everything technically is on. It's something where you go and set levels. The engineer, by this point, has already got levels set for one band and he's trying to work your levels into that kind of thing.

### Do your bands tend to share gear?
No, everyone loves their own snare sound, everybody loves their own guitar amp, everyone loves their own keyboard. It's the nature of the beast.

✦✦✦✦✦✦✦✦✦✦✦✦✦✦✦✦✦✦✦✦✦✦✦✦✦✦✦✦✦✦✦✦✦✦✦✦✦✦✦✦✦✦✦✦

## TRIBUTE BANDS

Some people join tribute bands to make money while waiting for their own original band to make it. Others find they enjoy playing other people's songs so much they want to do it professionally, so they form a tribute band, playing no other songs than those of the band they choose to cover, and dressing to look like them too. Yet others play in a number of different tribute bands and make a living that way.

There are some tribute bands almost as famous as the real thing: Abba tribute band Bjorn Again or the Counterfeit Stones, for example. Bands like Bjorn Again tour the world and make a pretty good living out of dressing like, looking like, acting like and playing like their heroes.

There are many gigs out there for tribute bands, from pub gigs to large-scale community events. If you think this is for you, read what Patrick Haveron who founded Psycho Management has to say.

## PATRICK HAVERON

Patrick Haveron is founder and director of Psycho Management Company, which provides artists—including tribute bands—and production for all types

of events, from corporate parties, outdoor festivals, theatre shows, product launches and TV shows to university balls and weddings. Patrick once took the stage himself, playing 1970s' golden oldies. Here he explains how to enter the star-spangled world of the tribute band.

### When did you set up Psycho?

I got into it at university, around 1990. I was entertainments officer at Roehampton University and organised summer balls and other events. I was originally in a band as well. We were awful but we learned lots of 1970s' covers and played

at friends' parties and this guy saw us and booked us for the Christmas ball—our third gig in front of five hundred people. There was a big PA and we were supporting Bjorn Again on their first tour of the UK. This was when they were being very Australian and getting lots of media exposure.

My band was called the Sugar Plums—originally Sugar Plum Fairies but we dropped the fairies bit! We were totally tongue-in-cheek and we did lots of balls and so on and built up a lot of contacts. It paid my way through university! I also did it for a couple of years afterwards but I started to realise you can't quite make a living out of a seven-piece band—even though we got a good following—and we took it as far as we could, even selling out the (old) Marquee Club. The natural conclusion was that people started asking me to get them gigs and, before you know it, the agency began! It helps that I've been in a band—I know what gigging is all about, like how important it is to have a dressing room and a rider. People who get into events from sales and marketing don't have a clue.

## How easy is it to become a tribute band?

It has definitely become a business, rather than just doing it for fun, like in my day. There are hundreds of bands around, from Abba to Zappa, and some even use people who have been on the TV show *Stars in Their Eyes*. One band got in a Prince-alike from the TV show and renamed itself Prince Revolution. So now it's harder, as it's all been done before. At one point when 1970s' kitsch was at its height we had thirty-two Abba bands on our books! To get on the tribute bandwagon, lots of covers bands with one girl singer would get in another girl and become an Abba band. But since then, many Abba bands have bitten the dust and gone back to doing covers. Another example is when the Spice Girls were at their height, everyone wanted to book Spice Girls tributes. Most of the bands weren't that good and it just devalued the whole scene.

Classic bands are always in demand though, such as the Beatles and Queen—we have fourteen Queen bands on our books. We also work internationally, so if we can't get a UK Queen band for an event we will hire in a band from somewhere else in the world. I know of someone doing a festival in Holland who got in a Queen tribute band from Serbia—it shows the power of the Internet in marketing your band. At the moment, I know of twenty-five Queen tribute bands worldwide; sixty-four Beatles bands. There are eighteen Beatles bands in the UK and five Red Hot Chili Peppers, although the Peppers are not a classic tribute band, as the band is not defunct—there's certainly a nostalgia thing about dead singers like Freddie Mercury or Kurt Cobain. When bands are still going strong a tribute act has to accommodate the vagaries of that band's current career. The Red Hot Chili Peppers were very big last summer following on the success of their album so there was lots of work. The Darkness had a number of tribute bands but demand has quieted down this year. We need them to put another album out so their popularity will pick up again. Boy bands are not as popular. We have a couple of Westlife and Busted tribute bands and there's Fake That.

On the other hand there are sixteen Robbie Williams tribute acts in the UK and there's a Robbie pecking order, based on quality control! There's enough work for some to do it for a living because, as a single artist, a Robbie tribute can play pubs, clubs, all sorts of venues.

## How should you choose which band to tribute?

See how you can jump on the bandwagon, see what's new and fresh if you want to be in a tribute rock band. It's good that Coldplay is back; for example, we have three Coldplay tribute bands and their value has gone up and they are more in demand. The Foo Fighters have developed an enduring quality; Green Day are growing in popularity and we have five or six Stereophonics. If the Darkness revive in popularity there'll be two or three gigs a week for their tribute band.

We have some older musicians in AC/DC bands who regularly do two or three gigs a week and earn £400 to £700 a gig. Thin Lizzie tribute band Lime-house Lizzie also do well: these are the sort of bands that 'have PA will travel'—a bit like the Hamsters—they will get in a van and play anywhere. They all have a good reputation and can guarantee an audience. If you really just want to do nice gigs then be in an Abba band, they earn £1,000 to £1,500, regardless if they are good or not—people go for the costumes and silly accents! Abba is safe, fun and popular with parties like corporate events. So the type of band you decide to do will determine the type of gigs you will get. But if you want to leapfrog through the system and get a gig right away then you will have to do something new and fresh—something like a Franz Ferdinand. This will get you gigs at events like Freshers balls at university. They want something new—they'll have already booked their headliner act but they will want something for a different night of the week, and an indie rock tribute band is something that appeals to students. Green Day is another band good for this purpose. Or you could take something and make it a little different. There was a band that did a reggae version of White Stripes, naturally called the Red Stripes. They were fun but only trendy London gigs will take that kind of act.

## What are the most important things for a tribute band to consider?

Authentication of look and sound, give people what they expect to hear. For example, don't confuse people with reggae versions of Led Zeppelin (Dread Zeppelin!), as mostly people expect to hear the same sound as they hear on the record. This is hard, as most famous bands spend thousands on their recordings and it's not possible for a tribute band to do this. But there are ways around this. If the band plays well then you can take a mix from the desk when you are playing out live. You could do a mix of one song in the studio and present it as part of a medley of songs to show you can play other songs. Some bands buy backing tracks and record vocals and possibly a guitar, to show what they can do. This gives them a half-decent-sounding demo to send to clients, who then get the idea. What doesn't work is recording the band in a rehearsal studio. The sound is always awful and just comes across as a badly played performance.

Don't put ten songs on for an agent; two or three soundbites give the idea. In fact, we rarely send CDs out to clients now, mostly it's mp3s or we direct them to our Web site to check out music, reviews and sometimes bands have a video. If we take a band on, we'll create a page on our Web site as a promotional and selling tool. If you are creating a Web site for your band, it's worth doing an unbranded version (no contact details) for agents to send clients to as well. That way you retain control of your content whilst providing a very useful selling tool.

Costumes are important, if it's that sort of band. You can't do much if you're a soundalike for a band like the Illegal Eagles doing the Eagles or Think Floyd doing a Pink Floyd tribute band, as these bands wear jeans and T-shirts, but if you are going to do Green Day, then they wear black and red ties and a bit of makeup. You need to capture the flavour of a band. For these kinds of bands, you have to use the look as a marketing tool. In this day and age, this dressing up is the nearest thing we get to cabaret!

Then there's looking like a specific artist. U2 lookalike Achtung Baby got their Bono from *Stars in Their Eyes.* They wanted him because he looked so much the part. In contrast, Darkness tribute the Likeness got their Justin onto *Stars in Their Eyes,* which Granada TV doesn't usually allow to happen. People who go on *Stars in Their Eyes* are supposed to be builders or bricklayers and be plucked from a day job, not have experience in the industry. But if you look really good, you'll get the job. People are more interested in seeing the act than what the music has to offer.

Some acts will reconstruct an album cover and do a spoof cover, for example, Guns n' Roses's *Appetite for Destruction* —a band like Guns n' Poses will re-create the back cover but using a bottle of coke instead of Jack Daniels. I think tribute bands should retain some sense of irony!

Names are important. The bands which do best have the original band name as part of their name—they'll get twice as many gigs. If you're Coldplayer, it says exactly what you do—it's better than using a song title, although many bands do this. U2UK is better than Achtung Baby, although Achtung Baby is very successful. Think Floyd, Abba Gold, Pirate Radiohead, the list goes on.

Some people join tribute bands to make money while waiting for their own original band to make it. But playing in a tribute band may reflect on your life. The press, for example, will come down on you, as it doesn't see this way of making money as credible.

## Where can you get gigs?

There are different levels. The bottom are pubs, where you'll earn £300 to £600 a gig. The problem with pubs is they don't have a PA or lights so you have to bring your own. So it costs you more money to earn less money! Plus you have to have bigger transport, an estate car or dodgy van, to get the PA gear to the pub.

Then there's the in-between gigs, such as the Chicago Rock Club chain where you'll earn £500 to £800 a gig. These are glorified theme bars and you can find them around the UK. They'll have an in-house PA but it's geared to their own DJs so bands will need to bring a desk and monitors to add to the basic house PA.

The next step up is playing universities, which pay £800 to £1,200 a gig, possibly £1,500 if you're known. All the PA is provided for. You will be playing freshers' balls, Christmas and leavers balls.

Council events, such as summer parties in the park, pay around £1,000 to £2,000, but if you're known you might make anything up to £4,000—for example, if you're a Queen band which uses pyrotechnics and plays on an outdoor stage to five thousand people. The sorts of bands councils hire are Abba and Queen, although Gloucester did hire Green Day. Often councils have an arts remit they have to fulfil, so they need to appeal to both young and old. They'll probably use an agent to get bands in. There's a high turnover of staff and bookers at both councils and universities so they tend to use agents they know and trust.

Corporate events pay around £1,500 to £4,000 a gig and they are very hard to get. They use the same suppliers and agents because some girl in the company wants everything to run well and won't take any chances so they use the same people year after year.

Some tribute bands play theatres but I don't recommend it. Most don't make any money. Usually the theatre will give an 80:20 split, with 80% going to the band, but if the promoter makes no money from the concerts, the band won't either. There are many hidden costs in promoting a theatre show, and agreeing on a marketing budget that works for a venue is often expensive. Tribute bands don't always fit on the arts remit of a council venue. And, unless it is a very well-known tribute band—or the band puts on a special show with lights, choreography and brings their own lighting engineer and merchandiser—the public is not happy about paying £15 to see a band in a theatre when it can see the same band playing in a pub for £5. There's a lot of risk in this kind of gig and more and more promoters have been going bankrupt recently.

## When should you get an agent?
You can get one straightaway. I need a photo, biog, set list and demo. I'll use these as tools to market the band. You could get away with just a really good photo shoot if you're covering a newer band like Franz Ferdinand. People will take you on merit, even if you've not done that particular show before, especially if the players have good CVs. People don't expect you to bring a following, especially at 'closed' gigs, such as universities.

## Can you make a living from being in a tribute band?
Only just—if you're dedicated and you really love doing it. T-Rextasy looks just like Marc Bolan and he lives his life like Marc Bolan too! He not only does T-Rex songs but has got hold of unreleased Marc Bolan tracks and released them in Japan. He also has a great show. There is only one choice if you want to hire a T-Rex tribute band. No other bands can compete.

You need to be flexible. There's a Robbie Williams tribute who also plays in a Green Day tribute. Bands on the circuit get to know each other and you may play in several tribute bands. There's a bass player who does Stereophonics, the Police, and Paul Weller. Some players are in various bands, cover bands and so on. It's not an easy life but you do get to play and you do get to see all sorts of strange places—Monte Carlo one week, Dubai the next! We had a Smiths band go out to play the Fuji Rock Festival in Japan because Morrissey pulled out. There are gems in a tough lifestyle!

✦✦✦✦✦✦✦✦✦✦✦✦✦✦✦✦✦✦✦✦✦✦✦✦✦✦✦✦✦✦✦✦✦✦✦✦✦✦✦✦✦✦✦✦✦✦✦

## SUPPORT A BAND ON TOUR

Supporting a band on tour is not advisable until you have a few local gigs under your belt. Once you've achieved this and feel confident, a support slot might just give you the leg-up on to the next tier of gigging.

## THE PROS AND CONS OF BEING A SUPPORT ACT

### The Upside

+ On the upside, you don't bear the entire responsibility of bringing the crowd, which is a relief, although you will be expected to bring some fans—if you don't, as first on the bill, you may again face the empty-hall syndrome unless the fans of bands higher up the bill are willing to check you out. Some do and some don't, but you can't rely on them. If the event is well planned by the promoter, you may find that help from him or her and other bands will be forthcoming.

+ You can learn a lot by playing with other bands. Some bands will let you use their engineer if you get on well; others may help out with equipment if anything goes wrong. You might also make some lasting friends with other bands on the bill who will help out later on in the gigging process—recommending you to other bands, promoters or agents, asking you to support them on a tour or guest on a record.

### The Downside

+ You will be last to sound check and it won't be long enough—sometimes you're not even allowed to get through one song. Or you may not even get a sound check at all, just a line test to make sure all your instruments are working and coming out of the PA system. You'll inevitably feel frustrated and worried you're not going to sound good in the gig and not as good as the other bands—and sadly, this may well be the case.

+ You'll go on first and, depending on how many bands are playing—often on new-band nights it can be three or four, which can be a nightmare scenario onstage, with barely room to breathe, let alone perform—you will probably end up playing before the first people arrive.

## HOW LONG SHOULD YOU PLAY?

Do check with the promoter first about how long your set should be—he may be expecting an hour, not two hours and ten encores!

Make sure you have enough material to play—fifteen minutes isn't going to do it. If you're the only band on, you'll need either around one hour's worth of tunes or thirty minutes if you decide to do two short sets with a break in the middle.

Should you do an encore? As the headlining band, two or three songs are about right; if you're the support, one song is sufficient. But if you're the support band you probably won't be allowed an encore, although it's always worth checking. If you think you're going down a storm and decide to go for it, don't get carried away so the other bands on the bill end up going on late. You won't make many friends that way. If the headlining band has to do a short set because of your indulgence, both they and the promoter will be very unhappy with you.

## GETTING THERE ON TIME

Whether you're the only band on or one of many, it always pays to make sure you get there in plenty of time for the sound check.

Always ask what time the sound check is and try to get there before that time. Ten to one, if you're the support act you'll end up waiting around and do yours way after the time you were told. But of course, the one time you're late, someone else will have your slot or they'll have finished and the engineer will have gone off for his supper and you won't even get a line test. You'll have annoyed the promoter too by being so unprofessional. Of course, sometimes disaster happens—you break down on the way or someone is taken ill. It happens. If it happens to you, make sure you let the venue know immediately so they know what's going on and whether you can make it, but late, or not make it at all.

## PAY-TO-PLAY—DON'T!

Pay-to-play has been a burning issue with musicians for years and still rumbles on. Many pub venues in the UK try to charge bands to play, sometimes disguising the cost as 'PA Hire—£50 nonrefundable' or other such nonsense. Avoid these venues. They won't treat you well and shouldn't be encouraged. Just because you're only starting doesn't mean you have to be conned.

This isn't to say you'll get paid for playing either. You probably won't, unless you bring masses of friends and fill the place—and even then you're likely to be told the venue made no profit—but at least you've made that all-important step: your first gig.

## CRISPIN PARRY

Next, Crispin Parry goes into greater detail and offers his advice to musicians wanting to play live in Britain and overseas. Crispin is general manager of British Underground, which exists to help small labels and their bands tackle the international scene. He is also head of British Underground's parent company, Gig Right UK, which was set up to provide suitable venues for bands in the UK.

### What is Gig Right UK and why is it important to the live music scene?

Gig Right UK started in the early 1990s, sponsored by the Musicians' Union (MU) and the Arts Council. The intention was to stamp out pay-to-play. Venues in London in particular were charging bands to play by hiring the PA to them or through other ways. The Gig Right campaign to stamp out pay-to-play was a big national one that had support from BBC Radio 1. Gig Right employed someone to go round and see which were fair-play venues and link them up with other such venues. After that period, we came up with the idea of a venue directory and created a magazine called *Circuit* to support it. We contacted fair-play venues and other venues and asked if they wanted to put out the free magazines in their venues. Most were very pleased to do so. *Circuit* was also the first publication to feature some acts that became really successful, notably the Darkness and the Strokes.

### What do venues expect from bands?

One thing that bands don't understand, and this is really where they miss the point, is that venues have to live and make money. Although there are philanthropists in the industry, most venues can't do it for free. Promoters say,

'We must have something from you—the band—to cover the cost of putting on a gig'. If there are four people in a band and if they get family and friends down they can probably get at least twenty people to a gig and that amount of people will cover the promoter's costs. The more hard-bitten promoters don't seem to understand the concept of a band that doesn't understand this reality. On the other hand, bands don't realise they have to put something into things—they've got to develop themselves. They have to think philosophically about what they want to do, how they see their career in music, and plan it. They need a strategy; they need to think what they want from other people and what other people want from them.

### Should bands be prepared to play for free to start off with?

Bands shouldn't have a problem with playing for free. It's part of promoting themselves. The way to look at it is to make money some other way—if you have CDs, then sell them for £5 or £6 and you may make enough money from record sales. You don't get as much money from gigging nowadays as you did in the 1970s.

Build up a database of fans to keep them informed of what you're doing. A band should go round all their gigs handing out flyers saying, 'Fill this in and we'll put you on our mailing list and keep you informed of gigs and other things coming up'. Then you get a list of potential CD buyers. It's possible this way to get enough money to live on by gigging and selling CDs at gigs.

### What's the deal with being a support band?

If you're playing a gig in a town not local to you so you haven't got a crowd to bring, you'll probably be a support band. You should aim to impress the headlining band's crowd so that the promoter will be impressed and want to have you back. Be careful what days you play; if there's a big football match on, for example, then people won't show up. Someone in the band should be aware of things like that.

### What about industry events, are they worth playing at?

Play at things like In The City (a music industry convention that takes place each September in a different UK city; check for details and location in *Music Week*). Find out the person who's in charge of the fringe at In The City and phone up saying you're great and tell them what you've been doing and get on the bill. It's where all the A&R men are in one place and it's a good way of getting noticed.

## Is gigging still a good way of getting noticed and getting a record deal?

Yes. Someone somewhere will find out about you if you're any good and you'll get signed. Even if you're not conspicuous in the industry, someone will find you. A few years ago Gig Right did a long survey for the MU, and I saw so many bands and I can say that if you're a good unit and work well together, it should happen for you. I've seen people start with only one, two or three people in a room; I've gone to see them again and they've got a crowd. One thing I find quite disturbing is bands' obsession with record deals. Often it's the end of your career. Even if you have a Top 10 single and a Top 20 album or better, you may well end up with no career at all; the odds on being successful when you have a deal are minimal. Your career may be over. Bands should start their career and a deal should just be part of it. There are so many more people who used to have a deal than have one now.

## Do you think bands should have a manager?

Bands often think, 'If only we had a manager then things would go better. If we could get someone then we wouldn't have to do lots of work'. But managers can be even more ruthless than record companies. They want a commission for their work and, at the bottom line, a manager won't take you on if they don't think they're going to make something out of you. A band that grows from the grassroots up and learns how to manage itself will do better. The best thing is if one of the band members takes it on themselves to manage the band and learn about the industry—take the band from grassroots level onwards. This experience will help the band negotiations so much better later on. The band should be in do-it-yourself mode as long as possible—you will have so much more control.

## Nowadays, you're mainly working on British Underground projects. What is British Underground?

In 2000, after consulting with a number of small creative British labels, Gig Right UK decided to start an export company to help microlabels, which we define as small, resourceful ready-to-export record companies. And that was British Underground, which has a Web site at britishunderground.net. Basically, we organise and co-ordinate showcases and promotional CDs and vinyl for new British acts at overseas industry events. Often we also choose which bands will be featured there. So as well as organising these events, we have a curatorial role and a creative agenda, spotting the bands we think will be winners.

## Which events do you go to?

In the US, the biggest one is now South by South West, in Austin, Texas. In 2005, we co-ordinated a UK presence called SUKONTHIS when over one hundred acts went there. We had several British stages sponsored by media partners such MTV, BBC 6 Music and BBC Radio 1. There were a number of partners behind that, including UK Trade and Investment, a government agency that provides funds for export initiatives like ours. We've also taken artists to the CMJ Music Marathon. In Europe, there's MIDEM in Cannes and Sonar in Barcelona. Most recently, we organised a British Music showcase in Tokyo and took bands like the Go Team and Futureheads. In return, we're bringing Japanese bands in to play at In The City here in England.

✦✦✦✦✦✦✦✦✦✦✦✦✦✦✦✦✦✦✦✦✦✦✦✦✦✦✦✦✦✦✦✦✦✦✦✦✦✦✦✦✦✦✦✦✦✦✦✦

## DO-IT-YOURSELF

## COSTS

If you can't find anywhere in your local area that's putting on live music, or if your style just doesn't fit, you could consider hiring a venue and doing it yourself. This is going to take more than just turning up on the night and plugging in and playing; it's going to cost you money for hiring equipment, room décor and so on. You need to be fairly confident that either you have enough friends who will come to see you or you are putting on the type of music that is guaranteed to attract a crowd in your area. Otherwise you could be considerably out of pocket.

None of this comes cheap, so not only must you be sure you can attract enough people but you'll need to charge a realistic amount at the door. This of course means you'll need some system for collecting the money, giving change and for marking people so you know who's paid and who hasn't if you are going to allow people to go in and out.

## GETTING THE VENUE READY

What's involved in costs?

First of all, unless you're lucky, you're going to have to hire a PA and lights. The room will need some sort of decoration—banners, painted sheets, parachute material to give it some vibe. There's nothing more depressing than turning up for a gig in a room that looks like a village hall about to host the local flower show.

You'll need to promote the gig too—with posters (if you can get permission), flyers and general word-of-mouth advertising.

Unless one of you is a DJ, you may want to pay a friend or hire someone to play music before, after and (if there's more than one act playing) between sets, otherwise the atmosphere will fall flat.

## HOW MANY ACTS?

One way of ensuring more people turn up on the night is to share the bill with another local band in the hope they'll bring lots of their own friends and fans. If you decide to put on a gig with more than one act on the bill, think about musical style. If you play surf rock, then another similar band will please the crowd more than putting on a jazz funk outfit—unless you are lucky enough to attract an extremely eclectic audience. Think about the evening as an entertainment concept where people know roughly what to expect and what they're getting for their money.

### The Only Act—The Upside

There are pros and cons to being the only act on the bill. On the upside is the fact that you have the stage to yourself—no tripping over other people's equipment or having to let other bands share your equipment. This is especially true for drummers and bass players. Because of space restrictions, very often only one drum kit or bass cab gets used by everyone—and it may well be yours. You have plenty of time to sound check, the sound desk gets left the way you want it, you get to go on at a decent time when hopefully the venue has filled up and, best of all, within reason, you can play as long as you like and do as many encores as you like (provided the crowd's up for it, of course!).

### The Only Act—The Downside

On the downside, as the only act you will be responsible for bringing in the audience. This is also true of course if you're the only act that's been booked by a promoter. If it's a venue that hosts regular live gigs, the venue owner or promoter may have built up a crowd of regulars who are willing to check out new bands they've never heard of. But generally speaking, you should either expect, or will be expected, to bring as many friends, lovers, family as possible. If no one shows and you or the promoter's done a poor job, you will have the disillusioning experience of playing to a near-empty venue. Your consolation is that it's happened to everyone at one time or another, and if you can survive that, you can take gigging in your stride.

## GETTING TO THE GIG

### TRANSPORT

How will you get to the gig? If you're a solo player or duo you can get there by car or you may even be able to use public transport—check if the venue is near enough to suitable transport. If you're a full band you may need one or more cars to get you and your equipment there. The alternative is to hire a van. This can be expensive, and doing so may mean you end up playing at a loss.

### INSURANCE

However you get to the gig, you must be properly insured: ordinary car, van or minibus insurance isn't good enough, unfortunately. Anyone using vehicles for the entertainment industry has to have a special insurance policy, which naturally costs more than an ordinary one. On the other hand, if you don't take one out and you do have an accident, you won't be covered—and this means you and your fellow band members, should you be injured, let alone anyone else.

### SAFETY

Another aspect of driving to gigs is fitting all your gear and yourselves into the vehicles. If you are using a van or minibus, be careful of how you stack in people and gear, like bass cabs and guitar and keyboard cases. If you have an accident, or even if the driver just has to brake hard, the gear can fly about in an alarming and dangerous fashion and could easily hurt or even kill someone.

# touring

So, you've made it this far. You've done those first few tentative gigs and they've gone well. You're building up a fan base, you've got quite a repertoire of songs, you can actually play quite well now, and perhaps you've been the local support for an up-and-coming almost-name band. Stage fright is a thing of the past (or nearly!). You may even have picked up a few bits of press yourselves—mentions in the local paper, your college rag, that sort of thing. Your local promoters are keen to have you back.

## COSTING THE GIG

The time has come when the gigs start getting farther away from home and then—the great bit—your first nationwide tour is on the cards. If you book your first away-dates or tour yourselves then there are a few pointers to follow. At this stage you will probably have to pay for accommodation if you feel you need to stay somewhere after the gig. Given that you probably won't be earning much for each gig at this stage and you've got costs like van hire, insurance, petrol, maybe a sound engineer, lighting engineer or roadie to pay, you aren't going to have a lot to splash out on staying the night somewhere—especially as there may well be quite a few of you. So cost out whether it's worth driving home afterwards. Even if you're on tour it still may be better cost-wise to drive home after some of the gigs and set out again the next day rather than stay the night somewhere.

## ROUTE PLAN

When you are booking your tour dates, try to get a sensible route plan—you don't want to be doing a gig in the far north, driving south to the next gig, then over to the west, and then up north again. Try to get dates that work so you drive the shortest distance you can. Driving to gigs and home again, if that's what you've decided, is very tiring for the designated driver, and if you haven't got a dedicated driver or roadie, you are going to have to decide who will be the drivers. If anyone's over twenty-five they're the best bet because the insurance premium is lower for them. On the other hand, if it's always the same one or two people, they may feel this is a bit unfair, so you're going to have to work this out carefully if there is not to be some bad feeling in the band. Each venue should send you a detailed map which marks the location of the venue. You could also use online map services (e.g., maps.google.com/; www.multimap.com/) and print maps with different scales.

## STAYING AWAY

If you feel staying the night is the only option, as it really is too far to drive home, then look at the accommodation options. First ask the promoter or venue—if it's a pub, perhaps you can stay in the pub accommodation upstairs. Some of the nicer promoters are willing to put bands up in their homes; others will have an arrangement with a local bed and breakfast (B&B), motel or hotel to put bands up reasonably cheaply. It's always worth checking first before going through the hassle of looking for something yourselves. If the promoter isn't very helpful, B&B is usually your cheapest option. To get a list of places, contact the local tourist board, or surf the Internet—most tourist boards are now online and put accommodation lists and Web site links where available. When you find something you like, tell them you're playing in the local area and warn them that you might be late getting back to the B&B—you might find yourselves locked out otherwise.

## GETTING PAID

Whereas your local small venue will just expect you to turn up and play and pay you either an agreed sum or a percentage of the door split, things are a bit different when you go on tour. Reputable venues will send you a contract before you leave for the gig, which will say how much you will be paid and what your rider (the quantity of food and drink provided for you) will be. You will then be paid on the night, after your gig. Sometimes you will be paid in cash, sometimes by cheque. Occasionally, particularly as an unknown band, you won't get anything at all and the promoter will use the excuse that so few people turned up that he actually made a loss. This may well be true, but if you have a written contract with him, he is bound to pay you, loss or not. It should be a loss for the promoter, not you—he or she should be able to ensure enough people turn out to at least cover costs. Even with a contract, though, you will sometimes get shafted. Sarah's band, Emperor Sly, had a few occasions when they didn't get paid, including two festivals where the festival organisers ended up either bankrupt or nearly so and genuinely didn't have the money to pay the bands. Of course, this left the band hundreds of pounds out in petrol, engineer fees and other expenses.

## THE RIDER

The rider is the quantity of food and drink the promoter gives you. The farther up the scale you get, the more lavish it is, until you get to the stage where you ask for one particular kind of vodka and no other, or you refuse to play until all the blue M&Ms are removed from the candy bowl. You've heard the stories. Back at the bottom, the rider is usually a case of beer, soft drinks, some sandwiches, potato crisps and fruit. Farther up, there will be more booze and a hot meal. And on it goes. The exception is college gigs, where they tend to be more lavish with the hot food, as it comes from the student canteen.

## EQUIPMENT SAFETY

If you're staying away, you also have to consider what to do with your equipment. Leaving it in the van or minibus can be a bit risky—Emperor Sly had their bus broken into once, although nothing was taken. Some B&Bs have enough space for you to bring your gear inside—this is rare, though. Usually the best thing is to arrange with the venue to leave it there—as long as the venue is secure—and pick it up in the morning. You'll have to make sure the venue opens early enough, though, otherwise you may find yourselves late for your next gig.

## FESTIVALS

### UK

If you want to play the bigger festivals, you will usually need an agent. This is less true for Glastonbury than for the more 'corporate' festivals. Becoming eligible for these if you haven't got an agent is a process of getting your name known on your scene and networking hard with anyone who can put in a good word for you. There are smaller festivals, often for a particular music community, like It's All Tomorrow's Parties at Camber Sands, and folk festivals. Playing local outdoor events is good experience for the tougher conditions of the festival stage. Festival appearances need more confidence than most indoor gigs—you don't usually get a sound check, just a line-test; the stage is often quite big;

**FOR YOUR ENTERTAINMENT**
GREEN ROOM LINE UP FOR THE WEEKEND

**FRIDAY:**
3 SPECIAL GUESTS + FUEL RECORDS FEAT:
TIPPER, SI BEGG, FREQ NASTY, ANDREA PARKER
COLDFUSION MAFIA & HYPER WAX
PLUS: DJ FLIP (SCRATCH) + BART + FLYNN & FLORA

**SATURDAY:**
FINGER LICKIN FEAT: PLUMP DJ'S, SOUL MAN
& SERAPHIM + PLUS: SCANTY SANDWICH
MEN FROM ATLANTIS (AKA TASK & HEAR)
MISS TYSON + ALIBAT (MOODOO) + BILL RILEY +

**SUNDAY:**
DJ ROLI RHO (STO PLATOON) & DIXIE (STEEL DEVILS)
MADCUTS PLUS SPECIAL GUESTS + ORGANIC AUDIO (L)
SCRATCH FEAT: MATT SMOOTH, ROB MAC & DJ YE
PLUS: MALACHI + TIM SPENCER + RAINY HUT FUNK
AUGUST + TWINSPEED & THE WARDEN
O-JAZZY & BOWMAN

**DANCE TENT PRODUCTION**
FOREFRONT AUDIO + UTOPIUM LIGHTING
FUEL RECORDS + VISUAL BLISS [UV DECOR]

Glastonbury 2000
**PRESS**
JAZZ
B/S
J.M.    13

**RIXENSART**
**ROCK FESTIVAL 1998**
**PASS    ALL ACCESS**

BOB STATE
AKASHA
ASIAN DUB FOUNDATION
BANCO DE GAIA
BENTLEY RHYTHM ACE
BIM SHERMAN
CARDIACS
DUST JUNKYS
FREESTYLERS
HEADRILLAZ
INDIAN ROPE MAN
LEVELLERS
LIONROCK
MONKEY MAFIA
N.Y.
RED SNAPPER
SPACE MONKEYS

pendragon       nigbo tunes
mark sinclair   funksoulvision
oberon          (son of stealth)
bassista        dj food
            face        simon tobin
            juno        olly tee
            remould     (herbaliser)
            psync       return to the source

**DJ's**
ALAN BLOOMFIELD
THE AVANT        GUV'NORS
MICHAEL DOG
EVOLUTION
JOEL E
THE LIBERATORS
MR

**ART** ... and soul
you live your art in the enchanted forest,
an amalgam of dream, sensuous heaven's
canopy ... you master the galaxy
surprised by fun with shape

a team of 40 artists will animate the site
to amaze the imagination and stimulate
the senses

escort flying bicycle
funding pending theatre on
furious company still theatre
sentinel fc puppets
leotwhite anthrax t...
white dwarf theatre co
hybrid circus theatre

S.A.

**greetings**
at last, a festival with a heart,
a soul, and lucky feet

megadog and the cornish massive
are proud to present a party
with simple requests ...

enjoy yourself on a beautiful beach
in cornwall, filled with colour,
performance, art and music

...have it, love it, live it...

for three days in august leave your
everyday realities behind and bring
tents, bring friends, bring magic

**info**
tickets £80 inc. parking, shuttle bus
and on-site camping from
WAY AHEAD 0115 912 9000
TICKETZONE 01273 376447
TICKETMASTER 0990 344 4444
PICCADILLY 0161 832 1111
MIKE LLOYD MUSIC 0190 262 3939
BRISTOL OUR PRICE 0117 929 9090
BRIXTON ACADEMY 0171 771 200
Venue and all usual agents
http://www.tickets-online.co.uk
subject to booking fee
tickets ADVANCE ONLY
not available on site
children under 16 free if with parent
park+ride system - no vehicles on site
please bring minimum belongings
site open 6pm thursday to 1pm monday
no animals except guide dogs
line-up subject to change
by car: M5 + A38 + A390 + follow
        signs to car park
by train: st austell railway station
by coach: reservations call WAY AHEAD

TICKETS LIMITED TO 30,000

MEGADOG
**BEACH**
festival
14,15,16 august
cornwall
evade by funky

Mambo
**ministry**

---

**GIGS**                                                     **59**

there are more distractions, like the weather; the impact of the sound system is less outdoors; and generally you need to be on good form to pull it off.

## ABROAD

There are also festivals all over Europe and the US, and they often change name and location while being run by the same organisers. Again, while some festivals are very organised and prefer to book bands on labels or through agents, the smaller ones are usually a bit more open-minded. Apart from word of mouth, the Internet is usually the best place to check on when and where festivals are happening—often you will get the information from other bands' sites.

## TOURING ABROAD

### PASSPORTS

Touring abroad brings other problems. Remember your passports! And make sure they aren't out of date. You'd be surprised how easy it is for someone in the band to forget something so obvious.

*Emperor Sly*

Sarah's band had to leave the bass player in Belgium at the end of a tour because his passport ran out while they were away and the French border guards refused to let him into the country, even though the Belgians and Germans were fine about it. Eventually he managed to blag his way onto a ferry in Ostend and get back to the UK—although he went through rigorous questioning at the UK ferry port before they'd allow him back in the country.

And it gets more complicated: some countries, such as the US, won't let you into the country unless you have a whole six months or more left on your passport—any less and the airline won't let you on the plane. And some countries also require entry visas—make sure you check first to see if you need them.

## INSURANCE AND SAFETY

Again, making sure your vehicle is properly insured is paramount, as is the safety of the members in the vehicle. Keep that equipment under control. Emperor Sly customized its minibus, changing the seats around and boarding up the back section and making it into a gear storage compartment. It made the bus much safer in case of an accident.

## BUY A GOOD MAP

It sounds obvious, but do buy a really good map of Europe or the US or wherever you're touring. It's easy enough to get lost looking for a venue in your own country, let alone abroad in a country where you don't know the language. You should make sure your agent gets each venue to provide you with the promoter's name and a detailed (often hand-drawn) map showing the venue and its exact street location and phone numbers in case of emergency. You'd be surprised how often you get to a town and have to phone up the venue and ask where it is, only to find you're just around the corner. Some cities like Brussels or Cologne are particularly difficult because you get channelled off on to huge ring roads and it's very hard to get back to where you want to be. So make sure you really do leave plenty of time to get lost at the other end and still be in time (or nearly!) for the sound check.

## GETTING PAID

Sometimes you will be paid in cash, sometimes by cheque. You don't want to be carrying around what will add up to thousands of pounds or dollars in possibly a number of different currencies, so you need to arrange a way to bank the money as you go along. Sarah found the easiest way was to have regular meetings with the band's agent and hand over most of the money to him to bank, and then he reimbursed the band when they returned to the UK. Of course, you need to keep some cash back for expenses, pocket money for the band and so on, so someone needs to be treasurer and keep meticulous records of earnings and expenses and what's been handed to the agent.

## EQUIPMENT

If you are going to tour a country that you have to fly to, you may find that you have a problem with your equipment. It's not going to be possible to fly out with bass cabs or guitar amps, for example. Even when it comes to keyboards and guitars, if you take them with you then you have to watch the airline's weight restrictions, particularly if you're doing only one or two gigs. You might find that your gig fee doesn't even cover the cost of shipping your gear out, as excess baggage charges are so high. You could try sending the gear as cargo, but that's not cheap either. You must weigh up the pros and cons of whether it's actually worth doing the gig. If you're touring you may wish to hire equipment, which is okay for a keyboard, as all your precious sounds can be taken on disc. But it's different if you play the guitar, for example. Your own instrument will not feel or play like any other guitar, even one of exactly the same make. Guitarists have a bond with their instrument and hiring one isn't going to cut it.

❖❖❖❖❖❖❖❖❖❖❖❖❖❖❖❖❖❖❖❖❖❖❖❖❖❖❖❖❖❖❖❖❖❖❖❖❖❖❖❖❖❖❖

## BEN GRIMES

Here's Ben Grimes, from the Golden Republic, a four-piece rock group out of Kansas City, Missouri. After years of gigging relentlessly and working on their songs when they weren't on the road, the group made a multi-record

deal with Astralwerks in 2004. The Golden Republic continues to tour, drawing larger crowds than they used to, but with the same grassroots approach they've had from the beginning. Vocalist Ben Grimes gives some advice about life on the road.

### What gigging/touring tips do you have for rock bands that are just starting out?

Be prepared for the worst. Don't build expectations. That's true about the music industry in general. If you build expectations in your mind about what it's going to be like or how much money you'll make or how successful you'll be or how many people will be at your shows, you'll always be let down. Be prepared for a lot of hard work. Set your mind that you're not going to have a lot of fun doing it initially, because most of the time, unless you're some pre-packaged band that is guaranteed success from the get-go, it's going to be lots of being the opening band playing to three people.

## How do you schedule a tour if you're doing it for yourself?
We got lucky. We found friends we could leech on who would let us go out and do shows with them, small tours around the Midwest. They could draw one hundred people a night and we'd open for them. That's the way to build it, one brick at a time. It was a lot of late nights and cramped vans and not very much money. We slept in our van a lot. When we weren't in our van, we were on somebody's floor. It's not like you're in hotels partying with models.

## How you get a support slot on a tour that has a bigger band on it?
Usually, just because of the way band personalities are, you tend not to become friends with the band. As you find each other, you tend to become friends. Lots of bands get their big break because some bigger band will have heard them and heard something that appealed to them and they grabbed them and took them on tour. Every tour we've gone on, that's how it's been for us.

## How many gigs in one tour?
When you're in a van, a couple of weeks at a time is perfect. If I'm in a van for more than a month, I just about lose my mind. We did two and a half months in a van and I was nearly homicidal at the end of that tour.

## Do you recommend having a road crew and a driver?
Not initially. When we're on tour opening for a band that has a tour bus, sometimes we'll get a friend of ours to come and drive because the routing on bus

tours is always miserable. The last one we did as a support band had fifteen-hour drives between shows, through the night, every night, with no days off. We hired a friend of ours to drive through the night, sleep all day, wake up, come in, sell merchandise for us at the show, and after the show we'd jump in the van again. It was pretty punk rock.

## Where do you end up staying?

When we were first starting out, at the end of our shows in the microphone I would say, 'Hey, this is not a joke, if anybody has a place that we can stay tonight, that would be really great because we're broke'. We were getting paid $50 a show if we were really lucky and that was all going into gas. Fifty bucks and a case of beer is the classic rock 'n' roll cliché, kind of like your forty acres and a mule.

My worst night on tour was when we played the Fireside Bowl in Chicago. We couldn't find anybody to stay with because there were eight people at the show and most of them were people whose moms had dropped them off. We ended up sleeping in our van and it was maybe five degrees outside, bone-crushing cold. We ended up with every blanket, every sleeping bag, all of us wrapped up in this heap of body heat and it was so cold. We've had a lot of nights like that, although summertime was the worst, sleeping in the van in the summer down in Texas.

## How do you build your audiences at each venue?

When you first start, it's just making friends, you don't make fans. You meet everybody at the show, become good friends with them, and call them up every couple of weeks. The next time you go to town, you call those people, have them invite their friends, until you get up above a hundred people coming to see you on a regular basis. After that, it's about making fans. The more you do this, obviously the more you'll get paid and the more you build your name. It just gets better and better.

## Is it hard to get money out of promoters?

Not usually. The promoter being a business person and the rock 'n' roll band being a rock 'n' roll band, there's bound to be some kind of conflict, like some stupid thing the band does that isn't a big deal to them, but it will set the promoter off. Promoters are pretty easy to piss off and they want to run the show. But at the same time, it's the band's show too. We've always been careful to be really friendly to the people who matter.

## Do promoters expect you to pull a crowd if you're not local?

Promoters know what to expect most of the time. The only time the promoter will really give you grief is if you're a band that he had heard of and really thought would be drawing a big crowd and then didn't draw very many people.

## Have you encountered unexpected laws or restrictions from city to city or state to state?

There are lots of restrictions and little laws we found—everything from cities where no alcohol is allowed to cities where you're allowed to drink outside. For us, the most relevant stuff is noise restrictions and how late you're allowed to play. In some cities, they have local ordinances where no live band can play past 9 p.m.

## Any final words of advice?

It sounds corny but stick with it. We've almost thrown in the towel many, many times. It's really hard. It's really discouraging. You must embrace the music side of it and hold on to the passion you had to begin with. As long as you're playing music that somebody's going to care about, things will come around for you.

✦✦✦✦✦✦✦✦✦✦✦✦✦✦✦✦✦✦✦✦✦✦✦✦✦✦✦✦✦✦✦✦✦✦✦✦✦✦✦✦✦✦✦✦✦

✦✦✦✦✦✦✦✦✦✦✦✦✦✦✦✦✦✦✦✦✦✦✦✦✦✦✦✦✦✦✦✦✦✦✦✦✦✦✦✦✦✦✦✦✦

## DAVID GLEDHILL

David Gledhill is founder member, singer and rhythm guitarist in five-piece Sheffield act Gledhill. He has accrued some years of experience as an independent musician, as he was previously in cult band Slo-Mo, signed to indie label Circus. David shares his experiences and gives pointers to unsigned musicians.

## Where do you rehearse?

There's a big live scene in Sheffield and about four or five rehearsal studios. We rehearse at Yellow Arch—they know their music down there! It's somewhere A&R men drop in and it gives you a good opportunity to network. It's pretty basic but it serves its purpose. I think bands should rehearse in small rooms with a crappy PA, as it will set you up for the toilet circuit later on!

## How did you get your first gig?

We got a residency at the Grapes in Sheffield. It's a classic band venue—tiny—but we like playing there. The promoter, Mark Roberts, puts on three

bands a night, six nights a week, fifty-two weeks a year—he's always been supportive of me and my music and once I got record label interest in my music we shook hands and agreed Gledhill would play once a month—this brings people in and A&R men down. He's also editor of *Sandman*, a local music magazine which is now also published in other towns like Leeds and York. Sandman has always supported local bands like Arctic Monkeys and Harrisons. We also play at Barfly down in London and other gigs.

## When did you start touring—and who drives the van?

We did a support tour with Tears for Fears, which was good—all that catering and so on! And playing in front of three thousand people at venues like the Manchester Apollo—they may not have come to see us, but it was still brilliant! It was weird to go back to small venues after that.

Graham Smith drives the van—he's also our tour manager and is the sound engineer at the Leadmill, Sheffield's biggest venue. We do everything on a tight budget—we don't want to give our label an excuse to drop the band!

**What's the most useful thing a band can take on the road?**

Teabags, drugs and a sense of humour! We're not a Class A band—a beer and a spliff will do. We have rigid rules—no one is allowed to drink too much before playing onstage. We're quite disciplined! Probably a sense of humour is the most important thing though. After a week of being in a van with the same people, you need to see the funny side of things!

**Do you sell merchandise at gigs?**

We don't yet. It's one area we've been slack on. But we are in the process of doing it now. For a lot of unsigned bands, it's a way to keep going though—selling CDs and so on at gigs.

◆◆◆◆◆◆◆◆◆◆◆◆◆◆◆◆◆◆◆◆◆◆◆◆◆◆◆◆◆◆◆◆◆◆◆◆◆◆◆◆◆◆◆◆◆◆◆◆

# using an agent

## GETTING OFF THE BOTTOM

Bottom-of-the-league venues in Britain are not called 'toilets' for nothing. You'll have been putting up with a small stage or no stage at all, a crummy old mixing desk with a rubbish sound, possibly no sound engineer, few or no stage lights, and all in a room which probably has zilch atmosphere. That's just for starters. You've probably had to struggle to change into your stage gear because there was no dressing room and nowhere to go to chill out before having to play. You were probably given little or no rider either.

But you've done all that. So you're really getting there. You're getting the hang of touring now but you feel you've paid your dues and that it's time to move on, to get a booking agent.

## WHY USE AN AGENT?

But why should you bother with an agent?

As with everything else, there are fors and againsts. By signing with an agent, you should get better gigs, better pay, a better rider, a chance to tour your own and other countries, and support slots with bigger bands. Some venues won't even book bands unless they come through an agent—even if it's gigs in holiday camps you're after. The Leisure Service Agency books bands for all the major UK holiday camps—you can't play unless they recommend you. Agents get you off the bottom rung.

It depends on each individual band too. If a band is only doing a handful of gigs, or a handful of gigs for a record company, they don't need an agent. But if your band wants to do a national tour, or play outside your own country, it helps to have someone with experience and someone with a good relationship with the venues.

## HOW DO YOU FIND AN AGENT?

Ask promoters—if the ones you have been working with don't know, try bigger venues. Ask other bands, especially bands doing similar music to your own. Their agents will know which venues are willing or keen to put on bands like you. If you're at college or play colleges or universities, ask the college entertainment officer—they constantly deal with agents. If you're taking music or music-related courses at college or university, ask your lecturers. Look in the music industry directories, published by *Music Week* and *Pollstar*, and phone some up, checking what kind of bands they look after to see if they are suitable, or ask the Musicians' Union. If you have a manager, get them to check out agencies, as agents generally prefer to talk to management rather than the artist.

## WHAT DOES AN AGENT CHARGE?

The typical agency fee is 20% of your booking fee. Sometimes the venue will pay you direct, in which case you will pay the agent yourselves. Sometimes the agent will be paid by the promoter and pay you, less his or her commission. If the venue pays you direct, make sure you have somewhere safe to keep the money (it may well be in cash sometimes) and keep good records of who has paid you what. It's best if just one band member is in charge of taking care of tour finances—being paid by the promoter and paying expenses such as food, petrol, etc. Many bands give their members 'pocket money' out of the first night's takings to use for spending money during the tour, which is deducted from the final amount earned, minus band expenses, at the end of the tour.

# WHAT AN AGENT DOES

An agent should be able to start booking you into better-class venues than you can get yourself, or onto support tours playing at good venues. Your agent will book the date, negotiate the price (and should get a better deal than you could), issue contracts for gigs and chase them up when they haven't come back (which is often), ensure the PA system is adequate, arrange a suitable rider, make sure there's a dressing room, make sure venue costs are kept to a minimum, check ticket sales are happening and so on. If you're touring abroad, your agent will explain about the taxes liable in different countries to your or your manager and get any invoices sorted out. Your agent will explain about timings: in the UK, you tour to promote a single; whereas in Germany, for example, you gig a couple of months after your album has come out and you don't go back until the next album.

A contract with the promoter will be drawn up listing all these things, which both you and the promoter will sign, each keeping a copy. If the promoter doesn't stick to it, or cancels, he or she is obliged to pay a cancellation fee. As you get more famous, your agent will start demanding half the money up front and eventually all the money up front.

If your band is doing a headlining tour, whether in the UK, US or abroad, your agent should plan it properly so you don't have to drive too far between each gig and the promoter has booked you in each night to hotels or other suitable accommodation.

Agents deal with things that go wrong—if the band's singer gets ill and can't do a couple of gigs on the tour, the agent will sort it out with the promoters so that they don't get upset with the band. As well as chasing support tours, a good agent will inform the band of any opportunities for gigs or festivals not connected to a tour.

On a less formal note, your agent may help you and your band get on to guest lists at the after-show parties at other bands' gigs—very useful if a small band wants to meet the bigger act. Going to the right parties is a good way of making contacts and is very helpful.

# TOUR SUPPORT

A good support slot can be worth its weight in gold. Apart from the fact that supporting a famous or relatively famous band means the stage will be big, the sound and lights good and the publicity surrounding the tour will rub off

---

on you, you will probably end up with fans and reviews that you would not have gotten otherwise. If you do a particularly blinding set on the night when all the journalists are down there, you could find yourselves acing out the stars and getting well on the way to becoming stars yourselves.

This said, it's not easy getting good support slots. Either the headlining band's record label reserves the slot for another of its own bands or another record company buys into the tour for one of its own bands that needs a leg up. Then again, sometimes the headline band itself decides who it wants as support—perhaps the support act are good mates or a band the headliners toured with before and get on really well with.

## UNHAPPY WITH YOUR AGENT— WHAT CAN YOU DO?

After you've been with an agent for a while you might find yourselves grumbling about the service you're getting. You may feel that it's just not worth the fee. Common complaints are: not getting enough gigs; getting too many—but not very good ones; being asked to do gigs at ridiculously short notice—usually because someone else has dropped out, meaning the audience doesn't know anything about you and, if you are a completely different kind of band, they may actively dislike you; despite the contract, you may find the conditions at the venues are very poor (bad sound, lighting, rider, etc.); you may find it hard to get the promoter to cough up on the night; badly structured tours. (Emperor Sly once did a tour in France when the band was constantly driving right across the country for one gig, back again for another and so on. And France is a big country. Sometimes the distance between gigs was around six or seven hundred miles. These distances mean you're tired when you go onstage, you have short nights because you have to rush off early to make the next sound check and of course it's dangerous.) But if you're not happy, your agent is probably not happy either and generally speaking you can stop using the service without much trouble.

### On the Other Hand . . .

On the plus side, an agent can do more for you than just getting you gigs. Marty Diamond from the US explains exactly what is entailed touring America. From London, Concorde's Steve Hogan talks you through the UK scene.

## MARTY DIAMOND

Marty Diamond is the president of Little Big Man, a boutique booking agency based in New York City. Founded in 1994, Little Big Man represents Coldplay, Black Rebel Motorcycle Club, Avril Lavigne, Gomez, Beth Orton, the Cardigans and Doves, among many others.

**When does a band need an agent?**
A band needs an agent when a band has a reason to need an agent. That reason is predicated by a couple of things: one, they actually understand what an agent does. They have actively pursued live dates on their own so they have a sense of the process. Two, they can physically afford to go out and tour, be it supported by a record company or independently.

**Do you have to have a record deal before being taken on by an agency?**
We take a lot of things on before there are record deals, or simultaneous to record deals.

**How do you find bands you want to represent?**
There's a relationship component that factors in. We have a good sense of rhythm as to how a particular manager might work. The manager I worked with on Richard Ashcroft and the Verve also manages Gang of Four, Badly Drawn Boy, Snow Patrol and the Futureheads. We book Avril Lavigne, the Barenaked Ladies, Dido and Sarah MacLachlan through the people at Nettwerk but I don't book Sum 41 for Nettwerk. It's not a good fit. Sometimes we've heard about a band, go to see them, then start representing them. A lot of it is just downright hustle. We view this place as a boutique. We're probably one of the bigger independent agencies, but it doesn't necessarily mean that everyone's active at the same time. There might be twenty acts that are truly active.

### What are agents broadly responsible for? Does an agent liaise with the artist's manager or directly with the artist?

To procure work for the artist. I work for the artist. I've survived managers being fired and still continued to work for artists. We generally talk to managers and record labels, if that's applicable. Oftentimes we have a dialogue with the artist, keeps us all honest. But most of the time a representative, be it an assistant or a manager, will liaise with the label. For the most part, it's a relationship thing. I like having a relationship with my clients beyond the manager. It's good to have a face, but a lot of times the band should be the band and focus on their craft.

### What if an artist is unhappy with an agency agreement?

I don't have any agreements with anyone. There is no contract. There are agencies that require agency agreements, but my attitude is that I'm in a service business. If I'm in a service business and you're unhappy with the service, or I've let you down, what good is an agreement? What, I'm going to keep you here under duress? It's a protection for the artist more than a protection for the agent because to some degree it defines terms. We are a 10% agency. There have been occasions where we waive commission, and there have been occasions where we reduce commission for certain things, but the understanding is that we are a 10% agency. It's a service agreement. Do the job for me. If you do the job for me, I'm not going anywhere.

### What are some of the typical things that can go wrong at a gig?

The gig is not properly advanced so the technical needs of the band can't be met. The promoter has financial trouble. The gig has been underpromoted. The promoter said he was going to do stuff and you find out he didn't. There's always the weather issue. I've had situations where bands have been stuck on the road in a snowstorm. I have bands that were supposed to play in New York during our blackout. There's always the reality of someone getting hurt at a gig. It doesn't take a lot of time to make a phone call a couple days out from the show to say, 'Hey we're coming in. I know we haven't gotten the contract back yet, but can we get a tech rider, or can we just review what our needs are'—that way there's no surprises. To some degree a dialogue is the most important thing you can have.

### Would you advise a band to have an agent before touring abroad?

It would help. As you start to tour the world, you need visas in certain places, and there are tax issues that rear their head. It's a good idea to have an agent; then, someone is issuing a contract on your behalf.

---

**What do you think is the most instrumental element in helping bands gigging these days?**

Technology is making the live music scene incredibly healthy. Kids are finding out about bands in the most phenomenal ways—and not just swapping files of music. There's far more active participation in artists' careers. People are buying tickets through bands' Web sites. There's a much more direct connection than ever before that's important and that will continue to evolve. Before the band should get an agent, the band should get a Web site. It's almost imperative. That's the biggest tool they can have. In the pursuit of a record deal, you can reference your Web site to a record company. You can be posting dates. You can be selling CDs. You can become your own DIY business. That's almost more important than having an agent.

✦✦✦✦✦✦✦✦✦✦✦✦✦✦✦✦✦✦✦✦✦✦✦✦✦✦✦✦✦✦✦✦✦✦✦✦✦✦✦✦✦✦✦✦✦✦✦✦

✦✦✦✦✦✦✦✦✦✦✦✦✦✦✦✦✦✦✦✦✦✦✦✦✦✦✦✦✦✦✦✦✦✦✦✦✦✦✦✦✦✦✦✦✦✦✦✦

## STEVE HOGAN

**Can you tell me about yourself and your role at Concorde?**

I've been an agent for nearly ten years now. I started off life as a club DJ and then went into being an entertainments manager at Humberside University. I booked all the bands for the college ball and weekly events. And then I eventually got to work with Concorde. I got this through being just a bit cheeky one day! I was bored with working in clubs and working weekends and I asked if they were taking on anyone. It was just pure coincidence; they were just about to open another office in Bristol, and they said come down for an interview and then a month later they offered me a job. I had to start at the bottom and work my way up.

**And what acts do you have now on your books that you personally look after?**

I'm looking after dance artists such as Chicane, Andain, and Motorcycle. Concorde represents Prodigy and Apollo 440, so some of the nice big dance artists. I am also involved in a sort of R&B capacity with artists such as Jay Sean, MVP, and Alesha, who used to be in Misteeq.

**Of the acts you have at present, what sort of percentage are up-and-coming new artists?**
I try and have a steady stream. I mean, with a personal roster of about twenty different acts on it, I try and sort of nurture and encourage probably two or three new bands each year. I've just taken on a new artist called Bimbo Jones—a hot remix team. They've remixed people like Jessica Simpson, Usher, and Stonebridge. They're remix darlings in the music scene and they're called in to polish up some of the pop fraternity. They have an album deal with BMG and were signed by Mike Pickering from M People, the old Hacienda resident.

**And would you only take on artists if they have a recording or management deal?**
Generally, yes. Ninety-nine per cent of the time we do, but I have made the odd exception over the years. Just for something that I really like myself; something I feel I can do a job on. And if I can help champion something, then I'll give it a go. But 99% of the time if something comes to us, it either comes from a management company direct or we get a tip off from somebody at a label, or something will come to us. We'll get an artist coming directly and say, 'I've just signed a deal with such and such, I've just taken on new management, would you be interested in having a meeting?'

**And what are agents broadly responsible for—what are the nuts and bolts of what you do?**
The nuts and bolts of my day is really handling the sort of live side of any artist development, and obviously careers. With a new artist, the live side is an integral part of breaking the act from an early stage. So that will involve maybe doing small residencies in places, looking at some low-down festival bills, just to get the band listed—like a new-band tent such as Glastonbury, trying to get the band in there so people see them. And then we work in tandem with the labels, with the press department, with the PR people, just to try and create as much awareness about the act and to get bums on seats to go and see them. But once the act is actually broken, then it's down to us, primarily putting money into the band's pocket, especially in the pop market. With a lot of our acts, a large percentage of our roster is pop artists. They tend to have writers and producers involved in the tracks. The bands don't always get involved

in writing and producing, so they tend to see very little out of actual record sales. One way for the band to earn money is through the live side. So we cover everything from small concerts to large arena tours to UK and domestic tours and international touring. But also things like private events and corporate events, even down to such things as the Sultan of Brunei's son's birthday party or bar mitzvahs and such like.

### If an artist wanted to get a gig at a festival, is it necessary to have an agent?

It's not always necessary. If you want to be successful as an artist you need to be thinking outside the box. You don't need to do the old traditional route of just sending in a CD to the festival promoter and saying, 'Can I get a gig? Here's my band demo let me know what you think.' You have got to be talented and creative about it. Generally the agents have relationships with fes-

tival bookers because they work with them year in, year out. So an agent is more likely to get in with a new band via a festival booker than the band will themselves, calling up direct or sending in a CD or a demo.

## Would you say that the UK live music scene is healthier than it has been for a long time?

Oh most definitely; times at the moment have really changed. The music industry is going through a real transitional period. Obviously with the advances made with the Internet and file sharing and downloads, a lot of the record selling side of it has really started to suffer, although figures keep coming in from the BPI that show that we are selling more albums in the UK than we have done for a long time so that's definitely on the up. But the one thing that technological advances won't replace is that feeling of going to a gig. You know, the hairs stand up on the back of your neck when the band comes on. You hear the first few chords of the song and just the total experience of being in that gig, in that venue with a select amount of people whether it be a small-capacity gig or a 70,000-capacity arena show. You can't replace that feeling. Those memories are always there at the back of your mind whenever you hear that U2 song again, and you think back to that show you've seen at Twickenham or Cardiff, and those are the things you can't replace.

## So you are saying that the touring and live music industry wasn't really that badly hit by piracy?

Not really, I don't think so. There was a bit of a downturn. In previous times of recession when you start to feel the pinch financially as an individual, one of the first things you cut down on is your entertainment budget. So night clubs have suffered in recent times, but I think a lot of that is down to licensing laws that have changed, which allow bars to stay open later. I mean, why are you going to pay £10 entry and £4 a drink to go into your local clubs when you can go into your local bar that's open the same amount of time? You don't pay to get in and you just pay normal bar prices. So that's really hit night clubs, but I think as far as the live music side is concerned, it's probably the strongest it has been for a while.

## What are some of the typical things that go wrong at a gig? Have you got any horror stories?

I couldn't possibly name any names. . . . When you have got so many people involved in a show, there's bound to be a little bit of human error somewhere along the lines, but I couldn't possibly comment and drop any artists in it!

### What advice would you give an unsigned band wishing to break into the industry?

Like I said before, thinking outside of the box, don't go for that general sort of traditional route of going to the studio and getting money together, making a demo, sending a demo tape out to three hundred people in the hope that somebody is gonna listen to it and try and sign you up. I think these days, you need to be out there gigging; you need to be out there working. James Blunt, for example, has changed the

way that artists are getting broken. His management company set up a little residency for him every week in London at a small two hundred and fifty–capacity venue, and it was nothing more really than word of mouth that helped break him. He started off playing to around fifty people one week and then next week they bring a few more friends along, so it might be seventy people, the week after it might be ninety people and within a month or six weeks of doing the show the event has sold out and people were trying to buy advance tickets. It's all about creating some demand. I mean with James Blunt it also helped that his management company was the same management who looked after Elton John. So he managed to go on and do Elton John's tour support, which wasn't a bad thing. But for artists like James Blunt, he is a good example. There are a lot of male solo singer songwriters out there and it's very difficult to try and break yourself. You've got to be thinking of different ways of attracting attention to yourself. You've also got to think like a marketing company: how are we going to market our band? The band and the album is a product and you have to think how you are going to market it to people.

I did a marketing degree at university and that's given me a lot of useful experience and a lot of knowledge going into it. So I use something along the lines of working out and trying to identify an audience for an artist, using my old marketing experience from university. It definitely helps me in what I'm doing. There's not much else from university that helps, apart from learning how to drink and socialize and book bands!

✦✦✦✦✦✦✦✦✦✦✦✦✦✦✦✦✦✦✦✦✦✦✦✦✦✦✦✦✦✦✦✦✦✦✦✦✦✦✦✦✦✦✦✦✦✦✦✦✦

# doing the gig

## INTRODUCTION

This section takes you through the whole process from preparations to leaving for the gig to pocketing the money (if any) and waving goodbye. We'll put together a cheap little 'resources kit' which will get you through many emergencies and discomforts. You'll find out how to get the best out of the venue staff, the sound check process and the performance itself. Gigging's fun, but it's also a tiring and time-consuming way of advancing your career. You need to get the most value out of every move and avoid the frustrations and disappointments which can spoil the fun.

## THE KIT

**Mechanical:** Gaffer tape; multihead screwdriver or set; spray lubricant like WD40; self-tapping screws, about 1.5 inch; pliers with cutting ability; cut-anything scissors; nylon twine; luggage strap with ratchet (available from luggage shops); large plastic sheet for covering or wrapping; rubber bands; marker pens.

**Electrical:** Torch; two spare fuses and batteries for every fuse and battery in use; huge mains extension lead, the longer the better; insulating tape in three colours; selection of adapters covering male and female terminations of instrument jacks, mini-jack, phono and XLR; scrap lengths of signal and mains cable; 'choc block' terminal strip; multiway DC adapter; miniheadphones; small multimeter and soldering kit.

**Comfort/General:** Small first aid kit; phone card; photocopies of driving licences; parking meter change; gas lighter; Swiss Army knife (or replica); A3 sketch pad; clipboard loaded with A4 paper; box of cheap ballpoint pens; lots of old hand towels for stage; bedside lamp, for dressing rooms or merchandising tables; light bulb, 40 or 60 watts; stack of disposable cups; travel kettle, containing stashes of coffee/tea/sugar; bundle of assorted cutlery; plastic sandwich box with cereal bars, pepperami, etc.; paper towels; cling film; blanket; nylon clothesline; old pillow/cushion.

**Financial:** Securely closable plastic wallet file or similar to keep all receipts, for example, van hire, petrol, payments to crew and so on.

All this stuff will fit in a suitcase, if things are packed inside other things. There are other things you can add, of course. Sarah's band was once cruising round a market the morning after a gig and found an effects pedal–sized, four-into-one mixer with little faders for about £15. It gets used as a submixer or lead-extender in occasional tight situations. Some inventiveness is needed to see what functions the items might perform—for example, clothesline + blanket = instant dressing room; lamp = quick, safe mains tester. Many things can be used for wedging, stacking and protecting gear!

## LOADING

Often, people are late for the rendezvous owing to other commitments or laziness. The equipment checklist, discussed under the heading 'Rehearsal discipline' (p. 24), is really useful here. It makes the loading process much more purposeful. Make sure it is up-to-date and actually lists everything that goes into the vehicle(s). As well as all the equipment, the checklist should include the details of the engagement—contract, phone number, map and backup copies of the tech rider and stage diagram.

If your vehicle doesn't have a complete barrier between equipment and people, be very conscious of the possibility that things will slide into the passenger compartment, bash into the windows and generally be a danger or a nuisance.

## ARRIVING

When you arrive at the venue, park somewhere temporarily and send someone in to make contact. If a crew member has been in touch with the promoter or venue staff, he or she should go. The point of this is to let them know you are on-site and to find out where the load-in is.

Move the vehicle to the right place and ask where you should put your gear as you unload it. Get the gear in straightaway—it's more secure and the exercise is good after the journey. Find out where you can put your personal stuff.

Make sure your vehicle is appropriately parked for the evening—you don't want to get clamped!

Introduce yourself to the sound engineer and make sure they have a copy of the tech rider and stage diagram: the promoter should have organised this.

Try to meet the promoter or responsible person from the venue staff to organise dressing room, refreshment and main meal arrangements and any specific matters, such as merchandising stand placement, backstage security and so on.

## THE SOUND CHECK

If you are the main act or only act, you will be able to set up to sound check as soon as the PA and microphones are set. For a multi-artist bill, sound checks run in reverse order to the running order for the night. The last act to play, sound checks first; the preceding performers' equipment is then set up in front of the last act's and so on. So if you are supporting, you have to wait until the act which is performing immediately after you has sound checked before you can set up any equipment.

If there is time and opportunity, it's worth taking some gear out of their cases—ask where empty cases should be stowed. Use your judgement about what's possible and desirable, but here are some suggestions. Guitars and horns can be tuned and put on stands in the wings or in front of the stage. Mains leads and signal leads can be connected and coiled. Amps can be set up and quickly tested offstage.

If you're waiting around, you can usually rustle up soft drinks and maybe snacks now.

## MERCHANDISE

It's worth thinking about selling merchandise. To do this, you need a table. Establish where the table is to go: anywhere in the main hall is better than anywhere in the lobby or bar.

+ Try not to put it somewhere too busy; it's awkward and bad for security.
+ You may be constrained by fire and safety regulations—obey unquestioningly.
+ You need some light, or power for your own light.

If you are selling the stuff yourselves, set the table up, with dummy boxes/ sleeves and a clear notice saying 'Band X's music will be on sale after the show', using the A3 pad, marker pens and gaffer tape. This reduces the chance of the public taking your table, and advertises the stall.

## OTHER PEOPLE RUNNING LATE

Many sound checks run late, putting increasing pressure on the acts who are billed early. Often, these acts end up with little or no sound check. This can be due to unavoidable technical or travel difficulties, but it is often due to laziness or selfishness on the part of the other act(s). It's not easy to recommend how you should respond to this predicament to get the right result, for yourselves.

The audience is paying to see the headlining act and deserves the best performance by them which can be managed by everyone involved, with the importance of the other performances dwindling as you go down the bill. This may well be the promoter's view. The headline act has more reputation to lose than the support acts, so they will feel the same. They may have to harden their hearts if they remember what it was like to be a support, but they need to get the best result. The headliners are, to an extent, offering you access to 'their' audience, so if their show still needs attention, you may end up suffering. But this argument does not apply so strongly if it's the first support band over-running when you are second support.

But there are times when the headliners have played a couple of complete songs without changing anything and are just playing themselves in— rehearsing in your sound check time. Now you are right to apply some pressure, starting with a gentle suggestion to the sound engineer that it's time to move on.

If this doesn't work, you have to decide whose goodwill you may need in the future. You should stay on the right side of promoters. Not only do they control return engagements, but they talk to other promoters and you don't want a bad reputation. But promoters don't usually supervise sound checks very closely, so you can work on the situation without their being involved. You should be politely insistent with the sound engineer, who probably meets the promoter regularly (and will be controlling your sound check and performance). Usually this works. If not, decide whether you need the other band's goodwill, and if you don't, reason with them until they get offstage. This is rock 'n' roll; not everybody's Mr. Nice Guy all the time, and you have some rights to deliver a good show as well.

It's etiquette to wait until the previous act has left the stage before you begin setting up. Some people are flexible and friendly about this; others will scowl if you move in too soon. The second they confirm they've finished, rush the stage. Even if you have lots of time, start getting into the habit of cracking on with the sound check for those occasions when it's late. A purposefully fast but calm vibe is what you need. When you are ready with your own setup, see if you can help someone else in the band who is still setting up. Don't pack cases away now, just get them out of the main stage area, probably on the floor in front of the stage at small gigs and in the wings at larger ones. Turn off mobile phones. A well-drilled setup can easily give you time to run through a whole extra song later.

Another tricky time is when you must ask people to move their equipment to give you room. This often happens to be complicated keyboard or effects setups. Be very polite about this. Remember it's a nuisance for them—and they're not being snotty; it really is a nuisance having to put stuff together again as you are trying to get in the frame of mind to start your performance. Happily, most people have played supports, so they're cool about it. Never move anything without asking the owner or at least a member of their band, and let them move it so you're not to blame if it all falls over. If they've gone off to eat or something, either work around it or ask the sound engineer to move it for you. Under no circumstances unplug someone else's equipment without asking. Plonking your amp on top of theirs is less controversial, but still, ask if the owner is present, or check with the engineer.

Generally, set up in your standard rehearsal lineup as far in advance as possible; you should have been checking on how this looks and be comfortable with it when looking at each other for cues or doing backing vocals and so on. You may have to compensate for the width and depth of the stage, but don't feel you have to go right to the edges if the stage is big.

## YOUR SOUND CHECK

The goal is to get sounds to the mixing desk for the sound engineer to control and send to the main speakers. At a bare minimum gig, only the microphones go to the PA. The performers rely on their instruments and amps and the PA to hear what they're doing. It's a bit tough on singers, but usually a venue like this is very small and the PA is near enough to hear, with a bit of reinforcement as the sound bounces off the walls. The sound check will consist of getting the microphones to a good volume, above the drums, without feedback. Then the performers do some tunes and are asked to turn up or down until the mix is okay. Point your amps towards the opposite front corner of the stage. Then you, the audience and the other band members can all hear it.

## Tip

If there is only one engineer, ask if they will plug a spare microphone into a spare channel and communicate with you over the speakers or monitors. It saves shouting. When everything's connected, the engineer(s) will check that each signal is reaching the desk and will want each person to perform by themselves to listen for any faults, set the level and adjust EQ and effects. Performing by yourself can be embarrassing, especially for singers. Just do exactly what you expect to do in the gig as well as you can. That's the point of setting up the sound. If you sing or play too quietly because you're shy at the sound check, you won't be popular with the engineer or the crowd when you let rip later and send people diving for cover. The engineer has heard it all before—and worse—so just get on with the job. If your volume levels change because you use effects or patch changes, test the loudest sounds and the bassiest, harshest or generally most likely-to-be-trouble sounds you'll be using. The engineer may ask performers to turn up or down—usually down—to get the best result. This is okay, because you will be hearing the mic'd or DI'd sound back through the monitor mix once each signal has been heard from the PA. At the next level, all the sound sources are sent to the mixer via microphones or DI boxes. The engineer can now control all the levels that the audience hears. Each sound must be given a channel on the mixing desk. You don't have to provide the leads to go all the way to the back of the hall. The mixer is connected to a box of sockets onstage—the 'stage-box'—by a multiway cable—the 'multicore' or 'snake'—which handles signals travelling from the stage to the mixer and at least one sound—the monitor mix—going back to the stage. We'll look at the monitor mix later. The main mix is usually done first because it's more important (though you might not think so the way some bands moan about their monitor mix). You may have arranged, either in advance or on the night, to share drum kit and back-line as much as possible, so your drummer should be sorted, and possibly the guitars as well. If instruments need to be connected to the stage-box, let the sound engineers do it. There is often a team of two, one onstage and one at the desk.

## MONITORING

Each channel on the mixer has a fader to control the volume sent to the PA and knobs to control the volume sent to the monitors or foldback. Sometimes there is a whole separate mixer, the monitor desk, in the wings of the stage with someone dedicated to looking after the onstage mix. At first, you will probably only encounter this if you play at a well-equipped college or get a support slot at a biggish gig. The front-of-house engineer has to do both jobs at small gigs.

Even with only one monitor speaker, the increased control over the on-stage sound balance is usually great. However, you now rely on someone else, who is not onstage and isn't used to your sound, to be able to hear everything properly. The back-line can still be heard, but control over the mix is beginning to head in the direction of the sound engineer. As you play better gigs, you find more monitors onstage—most regular rock pubs will have four—and then a special, big cab called a drum-fill which is placed next to the drummer. (The monitors on the front of the stage are known as 'wedges', because of their shape.) Next come more monitor 'lines' or 'ways', giving different mixes to cabs or groups of cabs. After that come 'side-fills', large, square cabs that are fixed at the sides of the stage pointing across the stage front.

Note: once the volumes are set, no one must turn up their volume without asking the engineer, who should usually turn up the monitor feed and leave the front of house settings as set at the sound check. Make sure you have checked distortion settings and big synth sounds—it's worth lightly adjusting the level of the individual patch. Though each gig's monitors reinforce different frequencies, the sounds eventually settle down and there are fewer nasty surprises.

Here's what to ask the engineer to put into the monitor mix:

+ **One or two monitors, one line:** Vocals, drum machines and anything on tape/hard disc, etc. or with poor back-line.
+ **Three or more monitors, one line:** As above, plus hi-hat mic and a little bit of guitars and keyboards.
+ **Three or more monitors, two lines:** It's common for a two-way system to be organised either as wedges + drum-fill, or as centre + edges of the stage. Both setups achieve a similar thing: you keep the mix as above on the wedges or centre monitors and start feeding in some bass and drums and more of the mix generally in the drum-fill or the wedges nearer the wings. By now, you are progressing from struggling for any decent monitor mix to trying for an exciting sound onstage.
+ **More monitors and lines:** If you have side-fills, put the exciting mix through them and start trying to get other monitor mixes to meet the

performers' detailed needs, perhaps with their own sound much louder than anything else. Until you gain some experience, just rely on the sound crew's experience and let them direct you and sort out a quick mix that'll let you play, especially if time is getting tight. Don't go for detail at all at this point, even if you have time, because you don't really know how the monitor mix is working until you all perform together. You do this when each of the necessary sounds has been heard from the monitoring system and has been given a rough level.

When the engineer asks you to do a number, start with one that you know well, or at least are fairly confident of finishing. It's useful too if it also shows off lots of the things that might happen during the gig, like backing vocals, occasional flute or a searing solo. Don't ask for monitor changes; let the main mix come together this time and be ready to ask once the number is finished.

Keeping an eye on the clock, you now try to play as many songs as you can before you have to get off. It shows up more problems, if there are any, it gives the engineer a better acquaintance with what will be coming up when mixing the gig and it settles the performers. If you're told 'one more', say that you want to play about a minute each of three songs. If things are more relaxed and the main mix is settled, it's worth turning down the PA and playing with just the monitors. The PA can mislead you about the monitor sound when the room's empty—once people come in, you discover there's hardly any volume onstage. The engineer also gets to hear what you're hearing for the first time. Ask them how they would like you to signal them from the stage about which monitor level needs changing during the gig.

You may be unfortunate enough to be sound checking when the audience is let in. It's not nice (especially for the audience), but as long as your attitude makes it clear that this isn't the real deal, it doesn't really harm the atmosphere much. Just don't be thrown by it, and get finished.

Where time and running order permit, tape trailing leads to the stage. It prevents people tripping over them and makes it less likely that plugs will be yanked out of sockets. If you have excess lead length, try to run the leads clear of the main spots where you will be moving around.

## SPECIALIST KEYBOARD STUFF

Back up your data—ideally two copies, because sometimes in the heat of the moment you obliterate the data you need. Keep one somewhere else, perhaps with another band member's gear, so even if all your data gets left behind, trashed, lost or stolen you can still perform. It may seem like overkill, but it saves you from big problems—and a USB pen drive costs little more than a DVD movie (or a bottle of JD).

If you use a computer onstage, backing up is even more important, as computers are less stable than dedicated gear. Use really good quality mains supply leads, including a filtered plug or plugboard, and make everything as secure and unshakeable as you can. A CD writer is essential. Of course, there are other ways of storing large amounts of data—the specifications and prices are changing all the time.

Even nowadays, though, you should really consider whether it's necessary to tote a computer around. Could a hardware sequencer or MIDI data recorder do the job?

You shouldn't need to be editing anything and generally don't need anything other than MIDI playback. Even pocket keyboards like a Yamaha QY walkstation might do for some backing tracks. And what if your computer gets nicked?

If you use a lot of different keyboard sounds and/or need slick changes, you can usually organise MIDI patch changes to save lots of button pushing in the half-dark. The simplest method is to back up your standard set of user memories, program the sequence of changes into the memory locations and use the increment or plus button to step through them. For example:

Intro piano patch A-1
Verse 1 strings patch A-2
Chorus 1 brass patch A-3
Verse 2 strings patch A-4
Chorus 2 brass patch A-5

And so on. Cumbersome but reliable, and it lets you use a simple 'patch increment' footswitch, which most keyboards accept. This method has one nice advantage: it's easy to program slight variations, perhaps making the brass for chorus two a bit different from chorus one with a more open filter setting, almost unnoticeable but giving a little lift.

You can economize on this cumbersome method by allowing the odd change down in numbers. In the above case, the sequence would then go A-1, A-2, A-3, A-2, A-3.

There are two more complicated options. The first is to use a MIDI patch change table if your machine has one. This makes each program increment correspond to a specific destination patch instead of just the next one up.

So, for example, pressing the footswitch when you are using A-1 may give you H-8 or D-5, or whatever you have told the machine to give you, not necessarily A-2.

You can also buy MIDI foot controllers, which let you change to any patch by tapping buttons with your foot.

## WAITING

Double-check your performance time with the responsible person. If the venue is filling up slowly, you may be asked to start later. This is usually a good thing. It's better to play to a bigger, more settled crowd even if it means playing fewer songs.

It's most prudent to stay at the venue, but if you check that it's all right and you're happy about onstage and backstage security, a break might be good. Always be back at least half an hour before your appearance time and give numbers of mobile phones if you have them. Turn the phones on!

You need a main meal at some point, which may be in your contract rider. Gigging's like an exercise session. Within one hour of a performance, eat lightly or not at all and avoid spicy food or gassy drinks. You can have those later! By the time you are getting ready to leave, you're often hungry again. See if you can lay something by for a midnight snack-fest. There's a sandwich box and cling film in the kit.

People do all sorts of things while hanging about waiting to play. Car park football, Gameboy, a drink and a chat. You may want to be available for the guests you've invited or get pally with the promoter. Consider that you've put a lot of work into getting here and you want to perform well. Maybe you can take your instrument somewhere to get loosened up, or do voice exercises or some body warm-ups. Even the Rolling Stones, after all those gigs, were shown in a 1990s documentary getting in the mood before a show by playing a few easy tunes backstage. And they certainly know how to let the good times roll too, but the right time for that is after the show.

There may be an opportunity to speak to the lighting engineer. Lighting arrangements vary enormously. Some small gigs are quite clubby and have mega-lights; elsewhere, a larger place, perhaps a town hall, has hardly any. At first, if the lighting person hasn't seen the sound check, let them know where you will all be standing onstage so they can adjust lights for you if it's possible. If people are using technology onstage, ask that they are never left entirely in the dark. You can give simple cues, like 'stark lighting for the third song which is slow; mental stuff for the sixth one which begins with the taped explosion'.

Some of them are really keen and do a good show for you. Generally just let them do their job their way until you're at the point when you want to bring your own lighting engineer.

## READY TO GO ON?

The half-hour before you go on is a good time to finalize the set list. By now, you can see and smell your crowd. If it's a new place to you, look at the venue publicity to see what sort of events go on as a clue to see how people might react to your show. You know how long you're expected to play. You can do your best to choose the songs and the order to get the best result in your terms.

If you've taken anything from the stage to practice with, get it ready on-stage again. Tune instruments offstage first. Sort out set lists, drinks and towels for the stage. Keyboard players might want to sneak on and check that nothing crucial has been unplugged.

You should do all this before changing into stage clothes if you intend to, and with a decent gap before you actually go on. People wandering about picking things up and putting them down looks slack.

There will usually be music playing in the room during this time, from a DJ or at least a CD player or tape deck. (If not, see if it's possible to get something playing—anything's better than coming on in silence, as a rule.) Work out a signal for whomever's controlling it to turn it off when you are ready. Too early, and you're the object of all eyes while you fumble around getting guitars on. Very embarrassing. Too late, and you are left standing there with someone else's music playing. Both sabotage any attempt at 'creating a moment' as your show begins. Agree that they will wait for another signal before starting the music after your show—you need to be in control of this.

## PLAYING

### GOALS

This is another good moment to have a close look at the real situation. The first goal is to get a feeling going within three songs. Most people who remotely like your sort of thing will put up with a lot until the third song is under way. Anyone who leaves sooner was never going to be a fan.

The ultimate goal is to leave a good memory of your set once you have finished. Again, you can probably generate this with the last three songs. Few people will remember more if the last three are good.

Other goals include presenting the show you want, whether that's very informal or highly staged, being booked for another gig, and selling merchandise. (Extreme goals include getting out alive and seducing audience members.)

## STRATEGY

Remember that the performers are probably the only people who know exactly what's supposed to happen. Don't acknowledge problems or mistakes any more than necessary. Smile at catastrophic breakdowns as if you're having a great time—you'll be amazed what you can get away with.

Remember that the audience is there with mixed motives—talking, drinking, waiting for the main act or for the DJ session after the live bands. Try to make a strong impression without seeming desperate. Experienced performers only ask the crowd to come to the front when the very front is seeded with dancing punters already, for example. Try to work in the name of your act after every two or three tunes—just because people liked your closing songs doesn't mean they were paying attention all the time.

## BEGINNING

Assume nothing. The pin-sharp monitor mix of the sound check has mysteriously collapsed. Instruments that were fine an hour ago make no sound now. This will change, as your career progresses, especially when you can afford your own skilled engineer. Remember that the audience isn't hearing what you are hearing and the front-of-house mix is the engineer's first priority. Get through the first number by any means necessary. Whoever does the talking can now engage with the audience, thank them for coming, say who you are and where you're from or whatever suits. Now's the best time for concise instructions about the monitor mix, delivered into the vocal mic after getting the engineer's attention. Keep it brief, or you'll lose momentum. Don't apologise.

## CONTINUING

It's your show now, so set the atmosphere you want and fulfill your objectives. Here are a few tips on managing the set and coping with common problems.

## Set management

+ Get out of the habit of 'doodling' on instruments between numbers. It adds nothing.
+ Give strong cues when a number ends. Well-defined endings get well-defined reactions. You can use body language to convey this as well.
+ Running songs together (a segue) is best done sparingly.
+ Put weak or under-rehearsed material in the middle of the set, when you're settled in but not going for the climax.
+ Always announce any important song that people can buy; for example, 'This is our new single'.
+ Before you start your push to the finale, mention any other gigs you have coming up and any stuff you have for sale. Some people like to name check the other acts, the DJ, the promoter. . . . Respect costs nothing.
+ Always announce your last song; people often pay more attention.
+ When you're quite sure the final applause is over, signal the DJ.

## Common Problems

+ **Feedback** is often caused by interaction between the microphones and the front wedges. Don't cup microphones with your hands, stay away from the stage front and try to find a point onstage where the feedback doesn't happen. It's the engineer's job to find and fix the problem.

✦ **Bounce** is a feature of many stages in small venues, where the stage top is not rigid enough to support a jumping human without flexing. This can be a serious problem for keyboard players, who sometimes have to hang onto their instruments to prevent a major crash. Amps, mic stands and, especially, drinks are at risk too. Apart from (obviously) standing still, you can try to find well-supported bits of the stage, such as the point where four stage blocks meet or anywhere there is an edge or a seam.

✦ **Tough crowds** are almost inevitable at some point. Two tips here: concentrate utterly on your range of performance techniques, both instrumental/vocal and stagecraft. Play the most blindingly accurate set you've ever played; project confidently to the back row without submitting to them. Maybe they'll intuitively recognise the extra power you're bringing down. If not, you've gained valuable experience for when it really matters.

In the face of downright hostility, cut the length of the set, preferably from the middle so you don't get yanked before playing the best tunes. You have the right to play at least thirty minutes in any situation, but six numbers is enough. If the crowd is merely apathetic, play the whole set for your own delight.

## AFTER THE SHOW

You are entitled to take a quick breather. Don't be pressured into going straight back onstage to strike your gear. However, if another band is following you and, probably, things are running late, get back on within five minutes and clear down as agreed.

### Leaving the Stage

Don't pack tidily while onstage; get the stuff to a safe place offstage in any state and sort it out then. Stay mindful of security; maybe get a mate to watch the gear. Move as much stuff as you can in the available time. Recover things like mains cables first, then effects and stands, then amps and instruments. You may be able to pack completely during the next act's set—result!

If you are the last act, you can be more laid-back but there are still reasons for getting packed soon. It gives you something to do while you're still too sweaty for socializing. It lets you stop worrying about gear security. Furthermore, the PA crew are often keen to strip the stage, as it gives them less to do at the end. It's hard for the act and the crew to occupy the stage at once, so get in ahead of them or suffer a long delay. Once the PA crew starts stripping mic stands and wedges, a lively audience will often start thinking of the stage as available space—you don't need drunk people dancing around your instruments.

Don't pack gear into the vehicle unless you are really, really confident about security.

## Social Business

Now you have played, you are entitled to get any money due to you. Usually it's as well to get this done reasonably soon—sometimes it can take a while to find the promoter or responsible person. Your set is fresh in their mind, so ask if you can play for them in the future. Even if you're going, 'Nightmare! I never want to see this place again!' it's best to have the option under your control.

Thank your sound and light crew and anyone who's looked after you.

Check in with your merchandiser, if you have one. They're probably dying for a toilet break. If you went down well, they may need a hand to cover transactions and security.

If you're selling your own merchandise, set up and start chatting up nearby audience members. Some people like to add to the band's mailing list at this time. It's very useful, but let people make their own decision, then resource them quickly with clipboard and pens. A large list of people who don't really care about you once the night is over is a costly burden when it comes to mailing out. A smaller, quality list is much better. If you have a Web site, make sure you can give people something with the URL on it.

## Packing

Don't forget to use your packing list, especially as you are probably tired or in an altered state. At least two people should carefully check the stage, the dressing room and anywhere else you might have put anything.

---

# djs

## INTRODUCTION

There may have been a slowdown in the dance phenomenon during the last few years with falling record sales and the death of some so-called 'super-clubs'—as people grow tired of high door prices and overpriced drinks—this has not meant a decline in clubbing or work for DJs. As usual in the club world, as one club goes, another springs up in its place and there has been a plethora of great clubs opening and cool bars putting on excellent DJs. UK Clubs like Fabric, the Cross and God's Kitchen are doing good business, pulling in the crowds with their eclectic mix of DJ talent playing a variety of musical styles.

So a good route into musicmaking is still by becoming a DJ. If you like club or urban music, this may be the best way forward: in many ways it's easier than joining a band—you don't have to learn an instrument or learn to play with others and there's no heavy musical gear to lug around, just a record box (although that can be pretty heavy too). Unless you're part of a DJ duo or trio (or sometimes even four or more people get together to play), all the money you make on the night is yours, apart from any expenses—paying for a driver, for example. DJs are now seen as respected musical performers, not like the 'parasitic' mobile DJ of yesteryear. Many DJs release mix albums for which their name is the main selling point and they tour all over the world.

## THE RISE OF THE DJ

It's not that easy, though. Life in the smoke-filled, laser-lit world of today's DJs is ultracompetitive.

The last decade has seen a massive increase in people turning to the decks to make it in the music business, and competition for DJ slots in clubs has become commensurately tougher. So even though there are far more opportunities to play now, the rewards are much greater, hence the stiff competition. To make it as a DJ, you've got to be good and you've got to know your scene.

Most DJs also start early, some as early as eleven or twelve! This fact is recognised by BBC Radio One, which, in conjunction with UKclubculture, has for the past few years been running a national under-18 DJ competition, where young people from all over the UK have the opportunity to play their choice of dance genre at a major club in front of a large audience; the ultimate winner gets the opportunity to spend time at Radio One, learning from the experts.

## GOALS

The aim of learning to DJ is to be able to play your records to an appreciative crowd, and to do it on a regular basis. The other goal for most DJs is to make records in tandem with their DJing career in order to (a) enhance their career as a DJ and (b) make more money and be more famous. For most successful DJs, the two concepts are inextricably entwined—their own recordings are the core of their set.

## STRATEGY

By buying records, hanging around clubs and playing out, you get to find out what people are dancing (and listening) to. This gives you a good insight into the methods and techniques of making your own, we hope, successful music. Being in the right clubs and bars at the right time gives you a golden opportunity to meet and greet the right people to listen to you play, give you better and better gigs and get your music out to the masses.

## HOW TO GET STARTED

Most DJs agree on how they got into DJing, and it starts with an almost fanatical love of records, buying as many records as you can, followed by the first tentative steps into spinning tunes on the decks.

All DJs advise spending lots of time in your local dance record shop. Hang out and see what's happening. Go to clubs and hear what's being played and, just as important, how it's being played. In your favourite style of music, do you have to learn how to scratch, for example?

Once you get a feel for what turns on the crowd, start buying those records—as many as you can afford.

## EQUIPMENT

If you want to become a serious DJ, it is essential to buy turntables for your chosen format, a mixer and headphones. For the best prices and advice on what to buy, check out magazines like *DJ* and *Future Music*, which carry in-

---

depth articles on all the latest and most popular gear. They also have advertisements from manufacturers and shops dealing with DJ equipment, which will give you background on what's available and a guide to prices.

## Record Decks

Vinyl—CD—mp3—which is it to be? The world of record decks has changed dramatically over the past few years. While some DJs still swear by vinyl, others have switched to the new sophisticated CDJ decks and technology has moved on to produce an mp3/audio file format.

The first step is still to buy record decks. For vinyl lovers, the Technics brand is the most commonly used by DJs and the brand you are most likely to encounter in the clubs. If you want to spin those CDs, the Pioneer CDJ1000 is the DJ choice; it does what the vinyl deck does and has become the industry standard (see Judge Jules's description, page 132). Or you can go for a new format which combines the convenience of digital formats with the control of a turntable. Stanton's Final Scratch is a kit which allows mp3s stored on a computer to be manipulated on your turntable using special records. No need to lug around a record case to all your gigs, all you need is a laptop with all your songs stored on it.

Final Scratch lets users play mp3s or other digital music files on analogue turntables or CD players and works with both PCs and Macs. Using a special vinyl record containing a digital time-code, Final Scratch reads the movement of the record deck and plays the chosen mp3 or audio file as if it were a song sitting on the platter, exactly matching any changes in position, speed or direction. You can cut, spin, scratch and even needle drop mp3s (and other audio files such as .WAV) without losing control. Despite being in its initial stages, it has received much praise from key industry players.

A word of warning though: laptop hard drives are sensitive to magnetic impulses found in speakers. Many DJs have found that when playing near large club speakers their hard drives will crash. If you are using the Stanton Final Scratch at a club, make sure your laptop is not near any large speakers.

So cough up, get your head down and learn how to use your choice of decks. The secret is practice, practice, practice.

## Mixers

You'll also need a mixer to move smoothly, or not, depending on your mixing style, from one record deck to another. One of the best-known brands of mixer is Vestax, which has a variety of products, from entry-level mixers to scratch mixers to top-of-the-line equipment. Not only do mixers have cross faders to blend one record into another and to scratch, but you can alter the pitch, EQ, bass and so on.

## Headphones

It's often worth investing in a set of wireless headphones. Standing on or yanking the cable of your headphones when you're trying to DJ is infuriating and happens often, so the cordless option seems good, except that until recently the infra-red systems they used meant that if you turned to get a record out of your box they cut out. Now many wireless sets use radio-type UHF frequencies. They are fully enclosed, full-frequency wireless headphones which even work through walls.

## Tips

+ Gear in place, you need to get a few basics under your belt before going for the fancy stuff.
+ Stand over the decks and use one hand to cue the record; most DJs say the left is best.
+ Next, get used to counting beats and bars so you drop one record into another one to beat match seamlessly.
+ A good tip is to count four bars of eight, as most tracks are put together in sections of that length.
+ Keep an eye on melody and key. No matter how hard you try, some melodies just don't work together, or if they do, you have only once chance to drop in. Tunes in a different key rarely work together.

## GOING TO SCHOOL

DJ schools have been springing up over the past few years in response to the high demand for people wanting to get into DJ life. Most courses are still private and you can find their details in the ad section of most dedicated dance music magazines. It's worth checking your local college too. Many UK colleges now offer DJ training courses as well as general music courses. Some courses are run by local councils, such as Lewisham in South London.

One of the longest-standing private colleges is the Point (www.pointblanklondon.com), which has courses in music production and DJing. The Point has facilities in London and Sheffield and runs free workshops for budding DJs aged between sixteen and twenty-one, as well as courses you have to pay for.

Most courses teach both theory and practice. So not only do you get hands-on help with the equipment and how to mix tunes but you'll get the low-down on crowd psychology: how people react to different rhythms and styles of music, how to alter the mood of a crowd, and how to build up a set to keep those dancers moving. We wheel in the experts to tell you how.

Decks experts DJ Reid Speed from the US and the UK's DJ Kofi and CDJ turntablist Eddie Halliwell point out the intricacies of DJing different styles and explain their choice of equipment to get those block-rocking beats.

++++++++++++++++++++++++++++++++++++++++++++++++++++

## REID SPEED

Reid Speed has been DJing since 1995. Starting out in New York, then Los Angeles, she eventually got to be in demand in cities across North America on a regular basis. Reid has had two compilation albums, *Resonance* and *Life After Dark*, both released on Breakbeat Science Recordings. She was part of the Beauty and the Beats panel, alongside DJs Rap and Colette and has worked with DJ Swamp (of Beck fame) and various other producers, creating original compositions.

### What do you play out?

I most like to play drum 'n' bass, of all styles. I also like to play breakbeats and house music. But I don't like to play country music, I don't like to play trance and I'm not the biggest fan of deep house. I like to dance to it, but I don't like to play it. I'm an aggressive individual and I don't really have that soft, fluffy side in me.

### How did you get started DJing?

I used to play the violin and piano when I was younger. I also made mix tapes with my favourite songs and cut up stuff off the radio. Then I went to my first rave and I knew that's what I needed to do. It was the matter of just researching what you needed to make it happen, and making it happen.

### What did this research entail?

I went to lots of parties and watched lots of DJs to try to figure out what it was they were doing and how it worked. I was very ignorant, so I talked to

DJs, asking them what type of equipment I would need. Then, just going out and buying stuff that I needed, and working through it.

## How did you get started playing in clubs and bigger parties?

I had been in the New York scene for about two and a half years and buying records for about eight months. I was the ubiquitous girl with the glowsticks in front of the DJ booth, always watching the DJ. As a result of always being there, I think a lot of them took a liking to me and would talk to me because I was a girl, I was interested, and I was asking questions. I became friends with the people in my scene. One day someone asked me, 'You're DJing now? You want to come down and play at our little party? Bring a few records down and if you don't suck maybe we'll have some other opportunities for you'. I guess I didn't suck, so it started to take off. Bigger party promoters would see me play at the little clubs. Eventually one of them asked me to join their crew and that was a huge leap from little tiny clubs to big giant rave stages.

## How did you go from that to playing out of the city?

I got a job at my local record store [Breakbeat Science]. I made a lot of mix tapes, which I tirelessly handed out to anyone who would take one. We had a database of customers who lived out of state. I mailed out my mix tapes with the records people had ordered. I sent out thousands. I really wanted it so bad. Eventually it led to people booking me. Maybe it took a while to get a good response but within a year of starting to play out in New York I was travelling out of state.

## Was that as a result of the mix tapes?

From the mix tapes, and also from being part of this big rave crew. It gave me a lot more exposure playing at these raves, being on the same bill as other artists from out of town. Some people would want me to send out flyers with their order so they could see what was going on in New York. Then, they had a tape in there and a flyer with my name on it. People were like, 'Oh, she's somebody in the scene in New York City. We better listen'.

## How does one learn to be a DJ?

My best advice is watch other DJs and learn from their mix tapes. I bought mix tapes, went to the record store and asked for the records that were on the mix tapes. I knew the songs inside and out. When I tried to put them together the same way as those mix tapes, it was lot easier to hear what I was doing wrong because I knew how it was supposed to sound right. That's what helped me break through quickly and understand the whole beat matching thing. Until then, that was a mystery. But when you actually have two records where you know how they're mixed together on a mix tape, that's priceless.

## What about DJ schools?

I've never been to DJ school. I'm sure DJ school is good for some people who want to understand something and don't want to waste a lot of time or don't enjoy being out in clubs and watching people. I'm sure they could teach you the basics of what you need to know. But there's no way that one person is going to be able to teach you in an hour. You need to take the time to do it wrong a hundred thousand times before you're going to get it right. Learning how to DJ is about training your brain how to hear two different things at once and how to mentally calculate what's the difference between the two things, but without actually thinking about it at all. You need to retrain your brain to automatically understand and feel what's the difference. When you first do it, it seems very confusing and hard and they sound like they're the same and it doesn't make any sense. But once you can train your brain to do two or three things at once, then you're on your way.

## What equipment do you need?

You need two direct-drive turntables. Don't mess around with belt-drive turntables because they're not going to help you. Don't mess around with anything other than Technics. Headphones and a mixer that's proper. For when you're just starting, any basic Pioneer 300. My first mixer was a Gemini Scratchmaster. But as you learn the finer points of DJing, you'll definitely want to upgrade to things that include EQs and cross-fader contour and maybe effects. My personal favourite is the Pioneer 600, the Allen and Heath X-Zone series is all pretty good; the Rane scratch mixer for scratch DJs is probably the topnotch one. But when you start out, you don't really need any of that unless you know that you are committed to it in your heart. A mixer can be very expensive and at first it's not going to make any difference. You're not going to know what to do with it and you're going to be overwhelmed by too much technology. It's better to start out with something basic you can use to master the whole lining up the two records and beat matching thing before you get all crazy with it.

## How do you choose a mixer?

If you already know how to mix, go for the features you want. If what you want is to be able to scratch with it, you're going to want something that has a cross-fader contour, maybe some hamster switches and kill switches. If you're more of a house DJ and you want to do smooth blends, you might want to consider one with knobs, like a Vestax or a Urei. If you want to be an all-purpose DJ, the Pioneer is the best one because it may not have the best sound quality, but it has great EQs. It's got a couple of effects on it that are pretty fun and the cross fader is good. It doesn't have the dip in it. The Allen and Heath has a dip in the middle, and some of the Rane models have the dip in the middle too. They're not very good for cutting, only for smooth blends. In the middle of the cross fader they lower the sound by three decibels, so it's very hard to be precise on one of those when you're trying to cut it up and get freaky with it.

## What advice would you give for setting up your turntables?

Set them up in a quiet place where you have a lot of outlets. You should have your speakers somewhere near your ear level if you can. I would not recommend setting them up battle style at first unless you want to become a scratch DJ because you'll find it a lot harder to learn to manipulate the pitch control if your turntables are turned sideways. It's better if you put them at a height that's comfortable for you to stand up at because you'll have to be hunched over and it's very uncomfortable and it'll lead to 'DJ back', aka bad posture.

## Slipmats?

Slipmats are essential. It doesn't matter what kind you use. If you want to scratch, put a little piece of plastic between your thin slipmat and your platter. It makes it slippier.

## What headphones?

My personal favourite are the Sonys. There's a whole series of Sonys, the 7506. It's best if you take yourself to your local music store, bring a record and try it out for comfort. See how each one feels and which one helps you to best hear the sound.

## When you get to a club, what should you look for?

When I get there, I look to make sure that they have at least one monitor with its own booth control on the DJ mixer that I will be using. If there's an MC, I look to make sure that the MC is not plugged into the mixer that I'm going to be mixing on, so I don't have to be set up through the monitors. And I look to see if the DJ before me is redlining it because if the DJ is redlining it, the best thing to do is ask the promoter to turn it up on the amps so you can turn it down on the mixer. Your sound will then sound a lot better than the DJ before you. I check to see if there are CD players and what kind of players they are. If they're hooked up, how are they hooked up, logically or illogically? Are they front-loading or are they proper CDJs that people can DJ on and not have to wing it? Nine times out of ten, you can't move the shit around. If you can, go for it.

✦✦✦✦✦✦✦✦✦✦✦✦✦✦✦✦✦✦✦✦✦✦✦✦✦✦✦✦✦✦✦✦✦✦✦✦✦✦✦✦✦✦✦✦✦✦✦

✦✦✦✦✦✦✦✦✦✦✦✦✦✦✦✦✦✦✦✦✦✦✦✦✦✦✦✦✦✦✦✦✦✦✦✦✦✦✦✦✦✦✦✦✦✦✦

## DJ KOFI

DJ Kofi has been in the forefront of the UK DJ hip-hop scene and a top scratch DJ for more than a decade. He has been UK DMC Mixing Champion and was runner up in the World Mixing Championship of 1995. He is a popular guest on BBC Radio One's rap show and on BBC urban station IXtra. He's toured extensively around the world, including with the likes of Wu Tang Clan, and played parties for Ja Rule, Ludacris, and Ashanti. His 'deckspertise' has been used on successful records, including scratching on the Spice Girls's *Spiceworld* album! DJ Kofi also helps up-and-coming DJ talent, taking part in teaching sessions and workshops.

Here he explains why learning the DJ basics is so necessary to become a top DJ, and how the basic principles can be used, whatever style you decide to adopt—from techno to urban.

### What advice would you give for setting up your turntables?

If you're going to be a typical hip-hop DJ, there are several different ways of setting up your turntables. One of the most popular is sideways, so the arm is at the back. This is called the battle way or Cash Money's way; he was the first to do it. Now it's the standard way. It's good when you're scratching to have the arm out of the way. Other important things for setting up the turntables include the height adjustment of the arm—this depends on the size of the needles. Try and get a very solid table and make sure the height's comfortable for you. Mine's set up above my belly button so I don't have to bend over. Little things like this can really help. Slipmats should be as thin as possible, and don't get ones with textured designs, they interfere with the record.

---

One trick I have is take the platter off and polish it—with a household polish such as Mr Sheen or Pledge—to make it slippery. Another trick is to fill the hole in the record with little strips of tape so the record is quite tight on the spindle. Once you've worked out what's comfortable, and if you're doing competitions, you should set your turntables up like you do at home. It's common sense, but people often don't do it. They think the competition people know what they're doing so they leave it up to them. I've seen so many people do this and then it's a shock when they come to the decks and find it's just not right for them. It affects their playing.

### How do you choose a mixer?

I use an 05 Pro Vestax. In my opinion, it's the most versatile. If you're a house DJ and blending's your thing, there's a dial or knob that if you turn it the full way clockwise the cross fader will bring in sound at full volume, and if you turn it full on anticlockwise the sound will come in gradually, so you can do things in different ways. Also I like the way they designed the fader. If it's a normal fader you have to spray it with antistatic sprays, but with this mixer you don't need to do this. Their faders last ten times longer than normal. You've got the option of adjustment on things like bass and treble.

### What headphones should you choose?

I use ones where I can replace the leads. When you're rushing around, the leads come out and it happens so often. With my headphones you can just plug them back in; on many kinds the wire breaks, which is a bit of a disaster. I have tried radio-controlled headphones but they run on batteries and if the batteries run out you could get messed up!

### When you get to the club, what should you look out for?

When you're playing a club, check things out before you play. Check out the turntables. In some clubs the turntables are so worn out you can't adjust the height, or people have spilt beer on them. There are clubs I've played at where the actual pitch control has been mashed up. First of all, try to set the turntables up as close as possible to the way you have them at home. Check out the pitch before you start; you can turn it up to plus-eight and sometimes it'll just stay the same. Sometimes it'll go faster. Once or twice I've been in clubs where they've had the turntables serviced and they've tightened the arm so much that it's locked in a groove all the time it and sounds like the record's been scratched! There was nothing I could do and of course the crowd thinks you're doing it!

## Why do people mark records with white marks?

The object is to stop the record from slipping. Some people use Tippex and some people put sticky labels on. If you use two records that are the same and want to repeat a word or a sound on the first beat of the record, put a sticker at twelve o'clock on both sides so if it goes round you can get it to the same speed without headphones. Often the DJ will know how many times it's gone round without headphones. For example, if you want to scratch the word 'the' and you don't want to wear headphones, play the record up until that point, find the sticky label and place diagonally from the needle. Find the spot, put the tape just before the spot and put it at an angle; if you put the needle on the tape it'll slide into the groove in the exact place on the record without having to cue up. It's little things like these that help you DJ. If you're in a DMC competition, you haven't got time to wear headphones.

## People play different styles of music—any tips for different genres?

I would say regardless of what style of DJ you want to be it's good to start with the hip-hop DJing style. They do more with the record, the techniques and style that make your life a whole lot easier—and you don't *have* to scratch. People have watched me doing a normal set and said, 'However did he do that so fast?' but it's just things I have picked up from hip-hop DJing. It gives you the edge over other people, the people who just buy records and blend.

✦✦✦✦✦✦✦✦✦✦✦✦✦✦✦✦✦✦✦✦✦✦✦✦✦✦✦✦✦✦✦✦✦✦✦✦✦✦✦✦✦✦✦✦✦✦

✦✦✦✦✦✦✦✦✦✦✦✦✦✦✦✦✦✦✦✦✦✦✦✦✦✦✦✦✦✦✦✦✦✦✦✦✦✦✦✦✦✦✦✦✦✦

## EDDIE HALLIWELL

Eddie has spent nearly a decade honing his skills on the decks and he is renowned for his eclectic style and his innovative way of scratching over dance tunes. Eddie's technical ability allows him to utilise the mixer as a means to create energy and new sounds with rapid cut-ups and warped effects. And it's not just the dance floor that loves this mind-boggling trickery—Eddie DJs on BBC Radio 1 show The Residency and he is working alongside leading audio manufacture Pioneer to help develop the next generation of DJ technology!

### How did you get into DJing? And what do you play out today?

My love of music. I used to pick up instruments and mess around with them; I always wanted to find out what noises they make. I was always more into the hands-on approach than theory. Then I discovered DJing and it was amazing. I started watching DMC Mix Championship videos and saw that scratching is like another instrument in a way. I was about fifteen when I started to learn to DJ and I practiced and practiced. Then I started going clubbing and seeing how DJs worked and by the time I was eighteen I was going to all the main clubs, like Cream.

I would describe my style as energetic and uplifting. I play trance, techno, hard house and house, depending on the club, the time and so on. This allows me to vary my set. It would be boring to play just one direction: purists disagree, but I like to play whatever's good at the time.

### What advice would you give on learning to be a DJ? And how do under-18s find gigs?

If you really love it, get into it! For me, it took over my life. I came home from school and college and mucked around with it every evening and I spent all my money on records or equipment. No lads' holidays!

It's hard for under-18s and I didn't do any gigs until I was twenty. I just spent my time practising and practising. I am a perfectionist and I was always saying I had to learn more—even after five years! It was my family and friends who told me to approach people and try and get gigs. My brother got me to start talking to people at clubs—I wouldn't give a mix tape out, I just asked and I was given the chance to try out on a quiet night.

## You did a music technology course—was this helpful?

I took an HND in Music Technology at St. Helens College and I really enjoyed the course. At the time, I was thinking about being a sound engineer. I just thought of DJing as something I did at home and not as a career. The course was a very helpful: I learned about the industry from a business module and a music theory module, and my option modules were studio technology. This was very beneficial in giving me hands-on knowledge of how studios work.

## Are DJ competitions (e.g., the Radio 1 comp) another good way in?

I think they are a good way. If you think you've got something a little bit different, they give you an opportunity to step onstage and perform.

## You use scratching in your set—and some say learning how to DJ in a hip-hop style is the best, as it makes you more versatile. Would you agree? And how hard is it to learn?

Yes, it was the technical aspect of DJing that got me into hip-hop. It was very instructive, watching the DMC Mixing Championship videos and seeing that technical style. I learned to scratch and now I hear scratching in my head over tunes which I'm going to play out. But dance is a lot faster than hip-hop so you have to be as quick as you can. With hip-hop, you have more time between beats to do scratches like flares and orbits; it's a lot harder at a dance speed of 140bpm! You have to keep practising to do this—but I'm really glad I got into that side of things, as it keeps you interested, keeps you buzzing.

## What equipment do you need to start DJing?

Obviously a Pioneer CDJ1000. It's become the industry standard. I'd recommend getting a couple of CDJs and a mixer. I love the CDJ, although for scratching it's quicker and more fluid to use vinyl. But you can create some of the same sounds with CDJ—you just have to practice constantly. It's worth keeping both CDJ and vinyl decks in mind, although people are putting out less and less vinyl and this will affect the specialist record shops, and less vinyl is being sent out to DJs. It's sad to see it happen but the industry is going through a massive change. Stanton's Final Scratch is an interesting option, but at the moment it doesn't have many effects. I'm waiting for someone to come up with software that has the effects of computer software but the hands-on ability of Final Scratch—then I'd be really into it! This would bring the DJ and producer really close; it would be amazing.

### When you get to the club, what should you look out for?
First of all, make sure the gig is right for you. Take a look at it before you play there rather than going in there not knowing what it's like. You want to stand

out, to make your mark and this might not happen if the venue is not up to scratch. When you're travelling abroad, do a bit of research on the club. You can search for the club name on the Internet and find out who's played there. This is where it's good having an agent: they do the research and all the organisational things like booking flights, which means you can focus on what you're doing.

Take as much music as you can. This is another benefit of CDJ! When I used to use vinyl, I'd fill the car and my friends used to have to help carry it. You need a lot of music, as you don't know what the crowd is going to like.

### In the past, you must have ended up playing for the wrong crowd! How do you win over a difficult crowd?
It depends. Sometimes I start to muck around, scratching and so on. Sometimes I interact with them and try and connect with the crowd. If it's still not happening after that, there's not much you can do! Crowds vary around the country. In Ireland and Scotland, they're always a really good time. I've been known to leap into the crowd in Scotland!

**What do you do if your records get lost on route?**

Always take your records in your hand luggage. I take my CDs with me on plane flights—it's easy with CDs, they just fit in a wallet—and in the past, when I used vinyl, I used to split it in half and I'd take some and a friend would take some.

**Any other tips on having a safe, successful and enjoyable gig?**

Practice as much as you can!

# PLAYING OUT

Okay, you've learned how to DJ by practising hard at home and by buying an assorted collection of records that you are sure will impress the public. But how do you get to play out?

There is no one set way and everyone has a different story to tell. The most common, easiest and most successful ways are the following.

## Start Playing House Parties or Put on Your Own Parties

A large proportion of DJs started a successful career by putting on parties or illegal raves. Many budding DJs start doing this while they are at school or college. One of the world's top techno DJs, Juan Atkins, started this way: 'People used to give parties when I was in high school and I was always the one who wanted to play the music. I was always known as the guy who plays music, and when it came time to do pay parties, I was the guy'! Legendary American house DJ Marshall Jefferson also went this route. He says, 'I threw a party and got loads of money because I didn't have to pay the DJ! I think it was at Studio 21 in Chicago'.

## Start Your Own Club Night

There's a list as long as your arm of DJs who, frustrated at not having anywhere to play, started their own club night. Whether it was hassling the local bar owner or asking to play on a quiet night at a local venue, it's a great way to start. Former Underworld member Darren Emerson says, 'I started DJing at Outers in Southend when I was sixteen, around 1988. My friend Ian who I worked with thought it would be good to do a night in Southend. I was getting home at 3 a.m. and getting up for the office at 7 a.m.! I met Rick from Underworld when I was seventeen, so I was working in the studio too!'

Dub Pistols' Barry Ashworth started his own Déjà Vu night in London in the mid-1990s and it became one of the coolest clubs in town. At the time, he was also in a band called Déjà Vu and the band used to play every week and soon got a name around London and had A&R men sniffing around. Barry eventually called it a day for Déjà Vu—both the band and the club—but having built up such a solid reputation, he was able to continue to DJ under his own name. Barry was one of the pioneers of the late-1990s' British breaks scene and started another band called Dub Pistols. He got a deal with Concrete, a subsidiary of BMG, and has been both a DJ and a recording artist ever since.

First off, you need to scout around your area to find suitable venues. What makes a venue right for the purpose are things like accessibility—how near a main road it is—and if it is close to public transport. Invariably the more prominent and convenient areas will be most popular, but venues in those areas may also be very hard to get because of demand so you may need to start somewhere less prominent and start building your club night there and move later. You need to think about what night of the week to go for—weekends are obviously the most popular so a midweek night will be easiest at first and if you want a club where you play chiller vibes, a Sunday or Monday night might suit you best.

Putting on club nights and DJing is more about becoming part of a network. If your night is of a certain musical flavour you will invite along DJs and artists who are part of that scene; in turn, you will find you get invited along to other nights and events that are part and parcel of what's going on. Like everything else in music, it's about making contacts and making friends. DJs are a friendly crowd and like to help each other along.

Read on for the expert's pointers on starting and promoting a club night.

## HOW TO PROMOTE YOUR OWN CLUB NIGHT

✦✦✦✦✦✦✦✦✦✦✦✦✦✦✦✦✦✦✦✦✦✦✦✦✦✦✦✦✦✦✦✦✦✦✦✦✦✦✦✦✦✦✦✦✦✦✦

### TONI TAMBOURINE

Toni Tambourine is a DJ and Defected Records' press officer. He has several years' experience promoting his own club nights and is also involved in the larger-scale Defected nights, which take place at some of the UK's top venues and in Ibiza. Here Toni provides some small points that will stop you making big mistakes when planning your own event.

## What's the best way to start organising a party or club night?

First, work out what you want to do. Be clear on the size of your party and don't be over-ambitious. Is it an event for your friends or do you want to attract the general public? How many people is it for? I suggest that you always start small. Set a date. Allow at least four weeks to your party. You need the time to tell people properly about it.

## What about music policy?

Get the music right, as this is inevitably what sells the night. Make sure that you choose your music policy well and be clear on the style of music that you programme. *You cannot please all the people all the time.* A mish-mash of genres rarely impresses, unless that is what you want to do. A good music policy is a firm place to start your promotion. Whether it is rock, dance, urban—any type of music—you must make sure it works.

Pick your DJs carefully and don't try and please them all. You only have a set amount of time. Give them very clear times

---

that they should play. Display these times somewhere that everyone can see them. This will cut down on arguments later between DJs. The same goes for bands.

Get mates to DJ. If you choose mates to DJ and they say they'll do it for free, make sure you've got that written down. People can change their minds if they see the club doing really well that night and you're making a few hundred pounds. Making sure they can't change the deal will save arguments later.

## Will it make money?

Don't expect to make any money on the first night—or the next! If you break even, then you are doing very well. Clubs take time to grow. You will most likely lose money at first, but then if your night is working you'll make enough money, on average, to break even or make a little profit. And you'll have fun doing it!

Work out how much you have to spend. However small, the party will still inevitably cost you something. If you don't have the money now, then you may have it on the night.

Make sure that you are clear how much you will pay your DJs or bands. If they see you are doing well, they may ask for more money.

Be careful how many people you put on the guest list or how many tickets you give away. Ultimately, it's great to have a full venue and a few people on the guest list to boost numbers—especially at first—is fine, but it's no good if it costs you an arm and a leg to do it.

## What sort of venue would you recommend?

Secure a venue of the right size. The general rule is the bigger the venue, the more it costs. Choose somewhere that is accessible. Somewhere that people

know is always a good place to go, either a club or bar. It's harder to get people to go somewhere they haven't heard of before. Look locally for a venue: choose somewhere in an area you know or in an area that's 'happening' in your town. In London, at the moment, for example, I'd choose somewhere like Hoxton or Farringdon, which is cool. Go to the well-populated areas of nightlife, an area of town that has year-round destinations.

Generally any venue has its plusses and minuses wherever it is and you can make it work. Selecting a place that is known by others makes your life much easier.

When choosing your venue, find out what the gaps are—don't go for Friday and Saturday nights, as they are always booked out. Go for a Wednesday or Tuesday; there's usually a space then.

Make sure that wherever you choose to do your event, *it has a license*—that is, it's licensed to sell alcoholic drinks. If your party is in a warehouse, rehearsal room or film studio or anywhere that is not a bar or club, then find out from the owners if they have a license. If they do not, you run the risk of getting shut down if you sell alcohol.

Watch out for the deals that the venues offer. Most of the time you will pay a hire fee. This will allow you to 'rent' the bar or club for one night. This is normal. The money you pay covers the staff on the night, cleaning, etc. You will then, in turn, be able to charge on the door and that will give you your income. You will take the full 'door'.

Other deals can vary. Sometimes you can get a fixed fee to promote a party, or you could get a proportion of the bar earnings—usually between 5% and 10%.

You will usually have to pay a deposit. This is normal and shows that you are serious about the night. This is usually taken off the hire fee balance. If you cancel, then you will lose this amount.

Make sure that you find out if the cost of security is included. If you have to pay for the doormen, this could be an additional cost.

Finally, get an agreement from the venue to say what you discussed and what they said they would do, and how much it costs and when it needs to be paid (it may be hard for you to pay the hire fee upfront but on the night you may have made enough money to cover it). Venues have a habit of changing the rules without telling you and there is nothing that you can do about it. Most venues will offer you a contract. If this happens, make sure you read and understand what it says or get the venue manager to explain it.

Check what equipment they have, especially CD mixers, mixing desk, mic and lights. If you need other bits of equipment, you may have to hire it in, as the venue seldom pays for this. A DJ might want to MC, so he will need a mic, and if a club doesn't have its own lights it could be expensive if you have to bring them in. Make sure the sound system works. Have a contingency plan for when things go wrong. What if a DJ doesn't turn up? Also, always have a spare needle for the decks! Make friends with the sound engineer—it'll really help your night if he is behind you.

### How should the club night be promoted?

The best place to start is with your own address book. This is where you will get the largest number of people from. The rest will come from your mates bringing their friends and so on—get the DJs and everyone else to use their address books and help you promote the event—then a crowd will start to come. This is how Basement Jaxx made their club in Brixton successful.

Get flyers printed. Five thousand is usually enough and is sometimes the minimum quantity a printer will do. Usually, you will have to design them yourself.

Make the design look good—that goes without saying. Check the details, time, place, date. *Make sure these are all correct before you print them.* You would not believe the amount of times people have got these details wrong on their printing. It's a silly mistake. So it's worth proofreading thoroughly before sending the flyers to the printers.

Next, make sure that you put your flyers in the relevant places where people will see them. Bars, record shops, clothes shops, hairdressers' and student halls—anywhere you can. Carry a load with you so that you can give one to whomever you meet. Get your mates to help—they could be putting the flyers in shops for you. This is the art of real promotion. Tell everybody you can.

Next, don't try and do everything yourself on the night. You can't sort people out with drinks if you are DJing too. Get someone to help you out.

All the above pointers are very basic but should help you to avoid the most common pitfalls.

❖❖❖❖❖❖❖❖❖❖❖❖❖❖❖❖❖❖❖❖❖❖❖❖❖❖❖❖❖❖❖❖❖❖❖❖❖❖❖❖❖❖❖

# OTHER WAYS TO GET INTO DJING

Try DJing for a band. If you have friends in a band whose music suits a warm-up DJ, then ask if you can come along on their tours and spin your stuff while they're waiting to go on. Or they may want a DJ in their band. Either way it's a great experience and it adds to your DJ CV.

Portishead's Andy Smith started DJing as a child with a friend doing parties for little kids and it went from there. He originally met Portishead's Geoff Barrow when he was a tea boy in the studio where the band was working. The pair clicked and now Andy not only is the band's tour DJ but also meets up with Geoff on a weekly basis with lots of records and the pair listen through for inspiration for beats and samples. He calls himself a peripheral member of the band but many consider it his eclectic record collection and ear for sounds that gives Portishead's music a little something extra. On the back of his work for the band, Andy has released some highly rated mix albums.

Send in a mix tape or CD showing what you can do. This, it has to be said, is probably the least successful way of getting a gig. Most clubs are swamped with tapes from would-be hopefuls and unless they know something about you, they probably won't bother to take you on.

Mr C and Layo own the End club in London's West End. Layo says he isn't a fan of mix tapes; he prefers wannabe DJs to come to his club often, take part in the scene and get known. He feels this shows dedication to the club and its music policy. To make it as a DJ, he says you should be good but also involved in a particular scene. You have to promote yourself, but sensitively. You shouldn't hassle the promoter but you should make it clear you would love the chance to play.

If you go the tape route, you must ensure that your tape, CD or MiniDisc is at least ninety minutes long, includes a full track listing for the songs you've put on, including artist name, track title and label, and has a daytime telephone number. Obviously, when you submit a mix tape, make sure that you don't blindly copy the style of big-name DJs—develop your own with a nod to the big boys to show you know what's happening out there. Show how you can build up the set, just as you would if you were playing a club. Don't go all out on the first couple of songs or you'll have nowhere else to go.

If a promoter decides to put you on, you'll find that on your first DJ outings you must expect to be put at the bottom of the pile. You'll be playing the warm-up slot, probably from 10 p.m. until midnight, and you'll be expected to do exactly that—warm up the crowd and get them in the mood for when the big-name DJs arrive. Most DJs do this for some time until they get that all-important break. Usually, it's because said big-name DJ hasn't turned up and they need someone to fill his or her slot. Who better than you, as you're already out there spinning the tunes?

With this in mind, always take more records than you think you'll need and keep a few really top tunes back just in case!

Check out your local clubs. Some clubs, even some of the bigger ones, are willing to give new or up-and-coming DJs a chance to prove their worth. Again, it's worth making an effort to be a regular first; then you'll know what they want, and won't blow your chance. Two of London's top club promoters tell it like it is.

✦✦✦✦✦✦✦✦✦✦✦✦✦✦✦✦✦✦✦✦✦✦✦✦✦✦✦✦✦✦✦✦✦✦✦✦✦✦✦✦✦✦✦✦

## BILLY RILEY

Billy Riley is the owner of some of London's most successful and most-talked about clubs: the Cross, Pacha, Canvas and the Key. Billy may be putting on the big names but he's keen on giving new DJs and promoters a chance.

### How did you get into the club business?

I used to own a garage nearby a club called Bagley's (in London's Kings Cross) and I used to see all these kids going raving and I wanted to get involved in it all. Owning the garage before getting into clubs was a very useful thing; it gave me common sense and business sense.

I thought I'd open a wine bar at first—I didn't know anything about clubs, music, bands—but I saw this as a dream, to be involved in music and clubs. I got hold of a couple of the (railway) arches near Bagley's and built most of the venue myself; I saved a lot of money that way!

I opened the wine bar in 1993 and because I'd gotten a good deal on the premises I didn't have to worry about filling the place. I could make it work on a few people coming in the door. Then, a girl I knew who was into the club scene—she knew people like Judge Jules, Terry Francis, Junior Boys Own—asked me if Junior Boys Own could promote a night. They got seven hundred through the door, rather than the two hundred I was getting and I realised this was a good way to go and it went on from there. Then I opened another place and another and I've ended up with eight businesses: as well as the clubs, I own an events company, caterers, minicabs and a pub, the Driver, in Kings Cross.

**The right DJs/nights are important to a club's success. How do you choose which DJs/nights you want to put on?**

One of the main things behind my success is we're not that corporate, not that organised. Sometimes ignorance is bliss! For us, it's about personalities. I have a good team around me and I can tell if a promoter is going to be any good or not ten seconds after he comes in the room. I like promoters to be young and enthusiastic; either you have it or you don't. I can tell good promoters by the way they present themselves, if they have charisma—that something else that makes them stand out. If it's a good event, it's because it's a good promoter—even down to the design of the flyer or poster.

**Do you find some styles of club music more suited to your clubs than others?**

The type of music is important. We do not put on drum 'n' bass and R&B, as they don't bring in as many people or there could be trouble. We prefer to stick to mainstream dance, although the Key is quite underground and puts on more cutting-edge music. It's not one of our best earners but we like it. Everyone wants to be cool at some stage but cool doesn't make as much money. The Key attracts the cool, smaller end of the business. Cool doesn't always last either—either the music isn't as good or it pulls a dodgy crowd. I want to put on nights where kids can go out and have a good time in a safe environment. We have

**TDK CROSS CENTRAL.**

*August Bank Holiday Weekend 2005*

Kings Cross Freight Depot, York Way London N1
One month to go and things are hotting up nicely for London's only true Music, Film and Art event with a licence no-one can beat, from dusk till dawn... and not a muddy field or tent in sight.....

**SATURDAY 27TH AUGUST 2005 / 5PM - 5AM**

LIVE: GOLDFRAPP MAGIC NUMBERS THE BEES THE OTHERS THE EARLIES TOM VEK KANO LADY SOVEREIGN JAMIE LIDELL FOUR TET DUELS TEST ICICLES AMUSEMENT PARKS ON FIRE THE SHORTWAVE SET MAD PROFESSOR MU LOUIE SONGDOG PLAN B KOOKS KEITH LUDES STARS DEAF STEREO DUNGEN STROMBA + MANY MORE...

DJ's: JAMES LAVELLE X-PRESS 2 MR SCRUFF M.A.N.D.Y. KURTIS MANTRONIX OPTIMO DJS JOHN KENNEDY (XFM) MAURICE FULTON MARK RAE & RHYS ADAM Presents: A.R.P Feat. AYAK RODNEY P & SKITZ Feat. CHE MUSE NEXTMEN RICHARD X FILTHY DUKES D'JULZ EYOE DJ's DIPLO GEDDES BONES & RAMSEY BLACKBEARD DUB CARTEL Feat: DON LETTS & DAN DONOVAN SIMON & HEIDI (PHONICA RECORDS) YES PRODUCTIONS STUART BRAITHWAITE CHRIS GEDDES (BELLE & SEBASTIAN) + MANY MORE...

**SUNDAY 28TH AUGUST 2005 / 3PM - 6AM**

LIVE: GRACE JONES SOUL II SOUL FRANÇOIS K KILLA KELA MC SWAY VITALIC WHITEY DJ FORMAT Feat. ABDOMINAL & D-SISVE MOCKY LITTLE BARRIE XLOVER TEMPOSHARK GLISS + MANY MORE...

DJ's: MYLO FELIX DA HOUSECAT TIEFSCHWARZ GILLES PETERSON Feat. DYNAMITE STEVE BUG CLAUDIO COCCOLUTO GLIMMER TWINS KEB DARGE THEO PARRISH SECRETSUNDAZE RAINER TRÜBY TREVOR JACKSON ASHLEY BEEDLE NICKY SIANO JAMES HYMAN (XFM) DAN GREENPEACE (XFM) FIRST RATE & KOOBS THE LOOSE CANNONS JAMIE JONES BROOKS AARON ROSS KIKI JB NILES HESS LINDSTROM SOFT ROCKS FAT CAMP YAM WHO Feat. CHAZ JANKEL & RICO DJ COSMO RICHY PITCH, MATT SMOOTH & ROB MAC (SCRATCH) TIM RED & LUKE vB BREAKER BROTHERS GILES SMITH & JAMES PRIESTLY + MANY MORE...

Tickets:
020 7833 9944 (Office hrs) 0871 2200 260 (24 hr hotline)
WWW.GROOVETICKETS.CO.UK  WWW.SEETICKETS.COM

Fopp Outlets:
1 Earlham St, Covent Garden, London WC2H 9LL
37 Sidney St, Cambridge CB2 3HX
19 Brown St, Manchester M2 IDE
43 Park Street, Bristol BS1 5NL

Information: 020 7833 9944
CHECK WEBSITE FOR LATEST UPDATES, TRAVEL DETAILS AND SITE MAP

www.tdkcrosscentral.co.uk

DAZED METROLIFE DJ Clash GRAMMS onedotzero mr.scruff deep space secretsundaze multitoyd cypo

MADE AND PLAYED ON → TDK

THE GUERILLA GUIDE TO THE MUSIC BUSINESS

good security in the clubs and people know they can have a good time and get home safely in one of our minicabs.

## Do you help up-and-coming DJs?

I set up an organisation to promote DJs and the club industry. I said to other club owners that there weren't enough new DJs coming through and too many old DJs hanging on. I wanted to promote an environment where parents could be happy their kids were having fun in a safe environment and that a DJ should be more accountable for his fees. For example, a big-name DJ could get £3,000 and £2 for every person through the door. This would show the draw of the DJ and encourage new DJs. But the press got hold of it and people thought I was against DJs, which I'm not, so the scheme fell apart, which was a shame. We need new promoters and new talent.

## Any tips for fledgling DJs or promoters hoping to make a career out of clubworld?

Be nice to everyone if you're going to be a DJ or promoter. Nice people create a nice environment. Don't hassle a club owner, but go to the club, get known, be someone that people like to be with—then you may get a chance. If you want to be a DJ, think who you'd like to play for, who you aspire to be and make the right connections. I see every promoter who comes to me to put on a night and I know right away whether that person will be a good promoter or not. That doesn't mean every night is successful, but as an operator we're fair. We give people time for their night to work and if they lose their shirt one night we don't take the venue fee. People remember if you do good things and they tell other people. The person who lost money but didn't get charged will go on and tell people we helped out and people will think our club is a good place to put on a night, so we might end up making lots of money out of it all at the end, but you can't quantify it. But I will be tough if I have to, if someone's let me down—tough but fair.

✦✦✦✦✦✦✦✦✦✦✦✦✦✦✦✦✦✦✦✦✦✦✦✦✦✦✦✦✦✦✦✦✦✦✦✦✦✦✦✦✦✦✦✦✦✦

## STEVE BLONDE

Steve Blonde works for Fabric, one of London's best-loved and most eclectic clubs. Here he explains why Fabric is so successful and gives tips for DJs hoping to play the hallowed halls.

### How did you get into the club business, was Fabric your first club?

The real story's boring. . . . I just fell into it, unintentionally. I was friends with Keith (owner of Fabric) and he asked me if I wanted to get involved.

### Fabric is one of the most successful clubs in the UK, but how did it start?

Keith's mind was set entirely on it happening. It started many years prior to its opening as an idea, and the building took over three years to convert. The thinking was simple: we all loved going to clubs, and we wanted to make one that put right all the small things we felt other people had got wrong (hence having our own taxi firm, unisex toilets, amazing sound systems, branding-free environment, etc.). And we wanted to put music first.

### Dance music sales have slowed recently but Fabric has stayed on top. The right DJs/nights are important to a club's success. How do you choose which DJs/nights you want to put on?

The fact that Fabric is doing well has to do with us all working very hard, concentrating fully on our business (no tours, no outside events, no festivals, no merchandise), and there being an extremely large pool of talented musicians for us to showcase. And we're certainly very lucky to have attracted people who want to hear new music. We try to program original, fresh music and avoid following trends or the paths that others have set. In this industry, you need to plough your own field.

### Do you help up-and-coming DJs?

Not as often as we'd like.

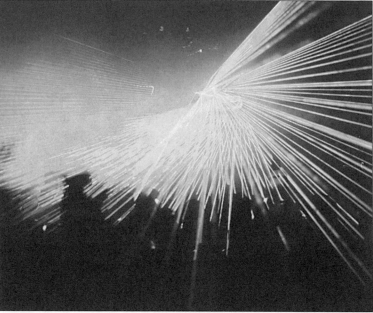

Tom Stapley

### Any tips for fledgling DJs hoping to make a career out of DJing?

Be original. Work on moulding your own sound and creating an identity for yourself. And get your sound out there—throw your own parties. . . . Do whatever it takes to get your name familiarized.

+++++++++++++++++++++++++++++++++++++++++++++++++++

## OTHER WAYS TO GET INTO DJING

+ Work in a record shop; it's one of the best ways to get known and make contacts. Working in a shop means you get to hear all the top tunes before anybody else and you can buy them first, too. It also means you get to meet DJs and promoters in your area and make those vital contacts.

Tom Stapley

Most specialist dance record shops make a point of learning what the top DJs in their area like and they keep a selection of records behind the counter for them to check out when they come to the shop. Some shops are so clued in that the DJ will just buy the tunes without even listening to them! The shop keeps them back for the DJ and he or she just picks them up.

✦ Getting to know big-name DJs in this way means that you will keep ahead of the trends and that you will make friends with the right guys. When it's appropriate, you can give them a mix CD or an mp3 to listen to, and if your mix goes down well, the DJ may well recommend you to promoters or his or her agent. The same goes if you've already made your own records. Give a white label or acetate to your chosen top DJ (someone who plays the same style of music as your record, of course) and they may well drop the record and write about it, too, if they are one of the many DJs who also review records for the music press.

The DJ may also have a radio show, or be a guest on one, and you may find your tune gets dropped on air, too. All this should see your name getting about.

Radio 1's Pete Tong found the record shop experience useful. He remembers: 'I started DJing at fifteen and was a self-employed DJ the first year after I left school. Between 1979 and 1983, I worked at *Blues & Soul* and *Black Music* magazines and joined London Records when it started. I had a lucky break in 1979 as the teenager doing the fifteen-minute dance report for Peter Powell at Radio 1'.

✦ Send in a mix CD or mp3 to one of the dance or urban magazines that have sections on new or up-and-coming DJs looking for a break. Make sure you send a passport-sized photo (with your name on the back) with your mix. The photo is because if you win, they will print your picture in the magazine alongside a description of your music preferences, DJ style and other personal information. Winners and runners-up have a good chance of securing a gig on the back of it. Also, many magazines specialising in dance have links with a specialist music radio station. This link can mean anything from having your mix CD played on a top radio show by a big-name DJ or the chance to travel to the radio station and record your mix with an engineer, taking home the finished product on CD. Generally, the station will broadcast your mix.

✦ When you get a bit farther up the ladder you should contact a DJ agency and hope to get taken onto their books. They will book you gigs around the country and abroad. There are a number of DJ agencies, some specializing in certain types of club music, such as house, techno or garage, and it's best to check with them to see who they are representing and whether they are right for you. If you're a hip-hop DJ, there's probably no point in signing up with a house DJ agent, as they won't be able to book you in with the right promoters. This is a problem suffered by many DJs. Premier US house DJs Masters at Work told Sarah one of their worst gigs ever was when they were booked in to play at a hard techno club. The clubbers hated their music and the night was a disaster.

Agents are the link between promoters, DJs and other people in the industry, including producers and record labels. As part of their gig-finding remit, they also make sure you are included on mail-outs and they manage your DJ diary and promote you. For this service, they charge around 10% to 15% of the club booking fee. Find an agent by looking in music magazines, record shops and the Internet.

Next, Charlie Harris of Serious talks you through the world of the DJ agent.

✦✦✦✦✦✦✦✦✦✦✦✦✦✦✦✦✦✦✦✦✦✦✦✦✦✦✦✦✦✦✦✦✦✦✦✦✦✦✦✦✦✦✦✦✦✦✦✦✦

## CHARLIE HARRIS

Charlie Harris is partner in Serious Artist Management and is the booking agent and manager for a top-flight roster of DJs, including Judge Jules, Norman Jay and Eddie Halliwell. Here he gives advice on making a career out of DJing and explains what would tempt him take on a new DJ.

**serious**

### What's your background in music and why has that made you a successful agent?

A misspent youth! My great friend at school was Judge Jules's younger brother Sam. When we were sixteen we used to sneak off and go to Jules's illegal warehouse parties, where Norman Jay and Soul II Soul also played. We would make ourselves useful though! Then I did business and finance at college and had a career in property letting and management for a while. But I hankered after more involvement in the music industry and spent all my leisure time going to clubs and full-on raves. I was spending more time with Jules and drove him to gigs all around the country. Serious had just started a club night with Golden at Sankey's Soap and it was a fantastic way to get into the management side of things, having developed a business sense from working in property and my college course was very helpful.

Driving Jules to all those clubs meant I met all the promoters and I'd have a beer with them in their clubs. This created a good rapport with all the major promoters of the time. So if I needed to ask a favour, it was very helpful to have had a beer with them a couple of weeks before!

### When was Serious launched?

The company was launched eleven years ago and I am a full business partner with Sam. Things are very different now then when we started. It was pretty basic in those days. It was fun and we'd get into the office knackered from the night before and take it in turns to answer the phone and go out for the bacon butties. Now it's big business, very competitive and the market is more difficult.

We had a record label, Serious Records, but that got sold to Universal. This was at the time of Sonique and I was her manager. Now we have three arms to the company: artist management and agency, club promotions and a fashion arm, primarily T-shirts and sweatshirts at the moment. I am head of artist management, which includes being the booking agency for Jules, Eddie Halliwell and our other DJs.

### Who do you have on your books?

As well as Jules, Eddie and Norman Jay, who are our more established DJs, we have some really exciting younger DJs on our books. For example, Simon Patterson, also known for his productions as Dogzilla, is our resident at Serious at The Cross and he plays at all the big clubs in the UK, including God's Kitchen, Slinky and Inside Out. Simon plays trance and techno. Then on the funky tip, there's Oliver Lang. He's brimming over with enthusiasm and he has real drive. He's a resident at Dusted at Eden on Ibiza and he has been resident at Bora Bora. He's also done a really good remix of Jamiroquai's single, Seven Days in Sunny June.

### Why should a DJ have an agency? What's in it for them?

If a DJ's career is going well, then they will have very little spare time outside of listening to and making new music.

---

A good agent will not only book their gigs for them and arrange any necessary flights, etc., but will also, if they do the job right, have a real impact in the success of the DJ's career.

As an established DJ manager and booking agent, I have an intimate knowledge of the clubbing scene worldwide. To get a DJ into the best gigs worldwide you have to know when they are! It is important to work for the best promoters of events that suit your DJing style in any one geographical area. The better promoted and attended an event is, the more it will do for the profile of the DJs who perform at it! These promoters are inundated with requests for bookings from DJs, so an agent may well have the leverage to get you in there!

An agent will contract your gigs for you, providing a level of protection from cancellations a DJ would not get on their own. They should also negotiate fees for you and chase up outstanding sums.

In addition to all this, there is the key basic service that any decent one should provide, of sorting out an itinerary for DJs for each gig they do. It is essential that you know what set time you have, who is playing before and after you, where the club is and, particularly, how to get there!

### What are you looking for in a DJ? Why would you take a DJ on?

We are looking for people with drive, with an inner belief, a self-belief. It's important that they listen to music, that they keep up-to-date with technology. A DJ needs to be media friendly. A DJ has to have something about them that sets them apart from the crowd. They can be really good and skilful at DJing, they can be not just DJs but producers, they don't have to be good looking but they have to have personality and style. They need some combination of these so if someone sees or hears them, they say, 'Wow! Who's that?'

A DJ should be organised and businesslike. There are lots of talented people out there, but if they keep missing flights or not turning up for gigs, they won't be offered any gigs in the future. An up-and-coming DJ will only get an economy flight paid for by the promoter—if the DJ doesn't make the flight, then it won't be possible to make the gig.

For me to take a DJ on, it's very important that I/we get on. If there's a problem at four o'clock in the morning and I get a phone call to sort it out, I need to feel we can work things through together as a team. It's true of the DJ as well; it's about mutual trust. You don't have to be best mates, but you do have to have mutual respect and an element of friendship.

## How should a DJ approach you? Is a CD enough?

We mostly take people on the basis of having some sort of awareness of them. It could be as simple as a mix, or they've played out.

If you send in a mix, you should always phone to ask if we've received it. Maintain that level of interest. I admit that agents like myself can be notoriously hard to get hold of. I'm so busy that people do have to wait ages to get hold of me. But you should still call and make the effort. Also, send in a CV with your mix, saying what you want, what you are, what you can do, what you can do for me and what I can do for you. It shows you've got drive and enthusiasm. You should have also done some research on my company to help you say why you have approached us out of all the other agents out there. Or if you do approach twenty-five other companies, you should have researched all of them and given a specific reason to each one as to why you chose them! The Internet is really good for this. There's lots of information out there.

If you've never done a gig, it's a bit premature to approach us. We would expect you to have played your local clubs first and be able to tell us that you've gone down well and they always want you back. Another good way in is to start your own club night. That way you get a residency and you can show how you've built up a following.

## What about magazine bedroom DJ features and Radio One's national under-18 competition. Are they useful, and would you take on a DJ by this route?

The Radio One competition is a great way of getting involved. And *Mixmag's* Bedroom Heroes is a conduit for that sort of thing. Some big companies—Bacardi did it—run DJ competitions where you send in a mix. Have good snuffle around the Internet and see what you can find.

Nowadays, with the cheapness of technology, both hardware and software, you can produce mixes and your own productions very cheaply. You won't get the level of studio-quality sound, but you can make things at home that show what you're capable of with equipment worth around £300 to £400. It's a much better way of spending your time than playing on a PlayStation all day.

## Should DJs make their own records, and when?

If you look at all the top DJs, you'll see they are all producers, too. It's a good way to start when you are under eighteen. There are loads of Internet radio stations out there you can send mixes or music to, or you can post them up on sites for people to download and listen to and get your name around that way. The amount of downloads gives you an indication of how popular your music is. Internet radio is particularly good outside the UK, in America, for example, or other countries where dance music is frowned on—even though heavy metal, where babies' heads are cut off, is considered okay!

### Any other tips?
Keep your options open. Lots of people have day jobs to supplement their income before they can earn their whole living from DJing. Other DJs, like Judge Jules, have something to fall back on—he has a law degree.

✦✦✦✦✦✦✦✦✦✦✦✦✦✦✦✦✦✦✦✦✦✦✦✦✦✦✦✦✦✦✦✦✦✦✦✦✦✦✦✦✦✦✦✦✦✦✦✦

## GETTING THERE

Another important aspect of gigging is getting there and back. In the UK, people generally go by car, as they will probably leave the club in the small hours of the morning, or in the case of big-name DJs, they may well be playing at more than one venue in the same night and need to get from one to the other. DJs tend to avoid doing the driving themselves, as they like to enjoy themselves in the club and that tends to involve a few drinks or more! Many people ask a mate or girlfriend or boyfriend to do the driving for them. The pay-off for the friend is that they get free entry to the club, and very likely some free drinks as well.

## GIGS ABROAD

If you're going to be gigging abroad, nine times out of ten you have to fly there. This often sends a shudder through a DJ, not through fear of flying but, rather, of losing records. Missing records is invariably at the top of the list of worst things DJs say can happen to them. The most likely point for records to go missing is when you're flying, in particular to another country. Airlines seem to have a unique ability to mislay record boxes. You check it in happily but it doesn't arrive at your destination. You pace the airport, begging and arguing with the airline to find out what's happened. They shrug, treat you with indifference and the records turn up days later, often back at the airport you started from. Not very helpful when you've got a gig that night.

Many DJs now refuse to be parted from their records, and if airlines kick up enough fuss about taking the tunes on board rather than putting them in the black hole of the hold, some DJs will go so far as to buy an extra seat for their precious vinyl.

In case your records do get lost, it's prudent to have a contingency plan—like taking a small number of records on board with you anyway in a soft DJ bag. You'll be able to get a set's worth in, and it's better than nothing, even if when you arrive at the club you realise that all the really best tunes for that particular crowd are naturally enough in your box. Still, you don't have to stare at the decks empty-handed or have to borrow someone else's.

## SOME DOS AND DON'TS OF PLAYING OUT

+ Never leave your record box unattended in a club; it'll walk.
+ Never leave your record box in the car outside a club, or outside your hotel or overnight accommodation if you're staying the night; it'll walk. Many big-name DJs rue the day when they went off partying after the gig, got back early next morning only to find their precious vinyl had disappeared.
+ As soon as you get in the club, check the decks and mixer—the equipment may be faulty. You may well find the stylus is broken, or even not there, for example.
+ Listen to the sound system and watch the crowd before you play, if you can. The quality of the system and the crowd response to the tunes of the DJ before you go on should influence what set you decide to play. Just because you had a certain order of records in mind, it's not worth sticking to it if it's not going to please the crowd.
+ Check with the promoter at the club on how long your set should be. You should have already been told this (or have asked in advance) but you never know; the DJ after you may be a no-show and you could luck into an extra-long set. Conversely, you may be asked to shorten it if the DJ before you takes precedence and wants a longer set. You're the up-and-coming DJ, so give way gracefully—this time!
+ If your car breaks down, your plane is delayed or, for whatever reason, you can't make the club in time, phone the promoter as soon as you know you're going to miss your slot. It can happen to anyone, but the worst thing for the club is not to know and the DJ before you putting on record after record waiting for you to show—or if you're the warm-up DJ, no one being there to put on the tunes. If you tell the club, then they can organise one of the other DJs to take your place.
+ DJs are usually given an allowance of beer, or other alcohol, soft drinks and sometimes food, depending on the promoter and the club. Check beforehand with the promoter what you should be getting and if it isn't

made available when you arrive, make sure you ask for it. That sorted, go ahead and have a brilliant night!

To round off this section, here is Judge Jules from London talking about his career in DJing.

++++++++++++++++++++++++++++++++++++++++++++++++++++++

## JUDGE JULES

Judge Jules is the UK's number one DJ and also one of the country's most successful dance producers (with myriad hits under his belt) and dance radio personalities. He's even co-written and produced a number of hit records for his wife. He's been involved in the dance scene for fifteen years since finishing his university degree and he's done the lot, from parties, to small clubs and on to the super-clubs around the world, taking in Ibiza along the way of course. He has his own Web site (www.judgejules.co.uk) which received two and a half million visitors during 2004–2005, and always has time to offer advice to budding DJs who e-mail him. His weekly BBC Radio 1 show has grown from strength to strength, broadcasting from 7 to 9 p.m. on Saturday nights to over one million listeners. He also presents his 'Global Warm Up' show in fifteen other countries. His Ibiza club night, Judgement Sundays, is one of the island's most successful, and he owns a restaurant, Kasbah, and a clothing line, Strange Love. Here he gives answers to some of the most commonly asked questions and admits he's moved on from vinyl to the CD format via the Pioneer CDJ1000!

### How did you learn to DJ?
I didn't really practice. I bought records very religiously and had a real passion about records. We'd go round mates' houses and play records and at that age—when I was around fifteen or sixteen—you always have a larger circle of friends than you do when you get older. In those days, you didn't have decks; we'd play records on one turntable in someone's bedroom. It wasn't so much DJing, it was more showing off your record collection. In my case, I had another friend who was really into music and we used to have a sort of war of the turntables, seeing who had the best records.

### How did you first get started as a DJ?
I threw parties for people in my neighbourhood. We were all underage and there were only a limited number of places we could go to.

## How did you move on from parties to DJing at clubs? Was it difficult?

For our parties, we found a particular venue willing to turn a blind eye to the fact we were fifteen or sixteen. We had a captive market—we pulled in people from all over North London. It was a dance hall above a pub and it was hard to find anything but that one venue. They didn't seem to care about our ages.

## How did you run your early club nights?

We hired the venue and charged people to go in. We also hired the decks and the sound system, which was tiny and it would be criminal to use it today. We used very cheap coloured paper to photocopy our flyers. I did the parties with Rollo from Faithless. We were the DJs and promoters.

We did our parties for three or four years but they became more grown-up, as I became more grown-up. I teamed up with Jazzie B from Soul II Soul and Norman Jay; they both came from the sound system era of the early 1980s. But Soul II Soul were in a less convenient location, so I teamed up with Norman Jay in west London and we threw illegal parties. I got my name, my Judge label, because I was the one that had to speak to the police! We threw parties at venues like the Astoria in London as well. My final stint as a promoter was in the acid era, promoting acid house parties.

## How did you rise to superstar status—what are the landmarks along the way?

There are various factors. There's the luck element of course, but mostly it's being seen to enjoy yourself. I look like I'm having fun. If I'm having fun, I don't mix as smoothly as I could, but it's more important for everyone to feel you're really having a good time. Like the records I play—you really get the feeling that I truly enjoy them, enjoy listening to them and playing them. For me it's a schoolboy enthusiasm.

The only thing that should be added is how long it takes. It takes ten to fifteen years to be a good DJ. It is an incredibly slow process; a lot of the leading DJs are in their thirties or older. I get loads of letters and e-mails from new DJs asking how they can get to play at Canvas, Ibiza or one of the big festivals. They and other events/locations like them get inundated with tapes and often don't bother to listen to them. My advice is, put on parties for your mates at a very early stage in the process; it won't work otherwise. And bear in mind, it'll take three to five years to make any money. For the first few years, I was spending more on records in a week than I was earning as a DJ. Generally

speaking, it takes a really long time. Also, think about making your own records. Many of the world's leading DJs have been recognised this way.

### Was running your own club nights helpful in becoming a successful DJ?

Yes, very helpful. They gave me an education for the market. If you do your own club nights and they're successful, you get spotted and asked by other promoters to DJ at their events. In the late 1980s, the fashion crowd was into rave music at their events—around 1988–1992, the fashion scene met up with the rave posse and were into acid house clubs. I happened to play a promoter's favourite five records in a row one night and he wanted to book me after that. A lot of it is luck, but a lot is hard work too and being in the right place at the right time.

I was lucky when I started DJing, as I began right out of university and I never had a job. It's quite hard to give up the day job and take a chance on DJing. Tony De Vit kept his job in computers for years and only gave it up and went full-time a couple of years before his death, which was very sad. In my case, I was a student so going full-time wasn't a big deal for me.

### What have you found to be the best technical setup for your style of DJing?

The biggest revolution in DJing over the past couple of years has been the huge surge in leading DJs playing CDs. If you'd asked me three years ago whether I played CDs, I would have looked at you in horror. Yet eighteen months ago I abandoned vinyl altogether in favour of the CD format, as have numerous other leading DJs. The reason is simple—the arrival of the Pioneer CDJ1000, which reinvented the wheel as far as CD mixers are concerned. Not only can you do everything that's possible with vinyl, that is, scratching, spin-backs, cueing, etc., there are numerous extra tricks and advantages. You can have a choice of cue points, you can punch in a start point like a sampler, play tracks backwards, plus perform a range of effects that are more difficult to describe. The CDJ1000 has become the industry standard in the same way that the Technics SL1200 became the essential vinyl turntable twenty-five years ago.

### You've been making your own music along the way—how and when did you get started?

I met up with Rollo again. He went to Australia and got a record deal there but the record company did nothing and he got dropped and came home again—but he came back with wads of cash. I met up with him on the street and I hadn't seen him for a couple of years. We used his cash and got a studio together. He used most of the equipment and I played keyboards. Eventually, I got my own studio. For a while it was located in the basement of my then-flat, but this destroyed relationships. Since being married, I've kept my studio in a separate location and try to maintain 9 to 5 (or 11 to 7) hours when working there.

### How has DJing helped your own music—and vice versa?

I've done hundreds of remixes and I've made loads of records. This is very valuable; it gives you a second skill alongside DJing. It's very important for getting your name around. I think it's no coincidence that the vast majority of DJs have made successful records. It supplemented their DJing. I had a very successful year in 2000, for example—three Top 10 hits and some Top 20 hits and I co-wrote the song my wife recorded and it's went Top 5. I also started a new record label—Closet Records. It's to put out the loads of tracks I get in that aren't suitable for a major label. Since that time, I've increasingly honed my production skills and even started singing on my tracks as well—although you'd hear mixed opinions about my voice!

### What tips would you give up-and-coming DJs?

Promote yourself. Promote your own parties. Make sure you make your own records. Don't bother to send tapes into the big clubs, put on your own parties, make records and make sure you get people to notice you. Be very patient and really go for it. There are lots of ways to climb that greasy pole; make sure you try as many routes as possible.

✦✦✦✦✦✦✦✦✦✦✦✦✦✦✦✦✦✦✦✦✦✦✦✦✦✦✦✦✦✦✦✦✦✦✦✦✦✦✦✦✦✦✦✦✦✦✦

# merchandising

It doesn't matter if it's *Star Wars*, *SpongeBob SquarePants*, U2, Eminem or your local band, if there are fans, there's gotta be merchandise. On top of selling records, most artists also sell lots of other products, from T-shirts to jewellery. Merchandising spin-offs were one of the big success stories of the late-twentieth century and it shows no signs of abating in the twenty-first.

## WHAT IS MERCHANDISING?

For decades, artists and/or their record labels have made extra money over and above recording and publishing royalties by selling merchandise with their band logo, faces, or signatures on it—anything you can get away with, really. Back in the 1960s, the Beatles blitzed their fans with posters, jewellery, badges, clothes, so-called Beatles wigs, pins—the list went on and on, and the Beatles' merchandisers did very well out of it, thank you. Nowadays, you can't move for boy band blow-up pillows, pens, notepads and so on. But don't throw them away as junk! Beatles memorabilia has cult status and commands high prices from collectors at auctions and fairs—perhaps thirty years down the line that dodgy Westlife blow-up pillow, once the prized possession of your kid sister, might be worth a fortune!

In addition to its records, any famous band will have a wide range of things for fans to buy. Designs and items for sale are continually changed or updated to make sure fans keep on dipping into their pockets and handing over their cash. Merchandising can include CDs, cassettes, vinyl records, videos (if you're famous enough), T-shirts, jackets, hats, posters, postcards, pens, key rings, jewellery, mugs, notepads/paper, slipmats and DJ bags—the list just goes on and on. At an early stage in the game, sticking to the ever-popular T-shirt and avoiding more expensive, gimmicky merchandise is probably your safest bet.

Most artists, or their record labels, have a good understanding of what their particular fan base is into and choose merchandise accordingly. A heavy metal fan will always want a black T-shirt with a big band logo on it and perhaps a nice gruesome design and tour dates. For someone into clubbing and the dance scene, a groovy skinny-fit T-shirt is much more the thing.

## WHAT IS THE BEST WAY TO SELL?

For new artists, your prime ways of selling your merchandise are at gigs, by mail order or through the Internet, either through your own site or using specialist e-commerce sites such as Amazon or eBay. You can also take white labels to record shops. We give lots more information on selling records in the next chapter.

## SELLING MERCHANDISE AT GIGS

There are a lot of outlets apart from the traditional record shop where you can sell your merchandise. If you're a gigging band, then your life is made simple, as touring is a great way to shift your stuff. Festivals are also one of the best outlets, whether you decide to sell yourself or go to one of the retailers that does the festival circuit, selling lots of bands' merchandise at all the festivals each season.

If you get a few gigs lined up, it's worth getting some T-shirts made up. Even if you don't sell them, you can keep them for next time, or sell through mail order (see p. 247). If it's your first tour, don't order too many and make sure they've got longevity; there's no point in putting on the tour dates and then not selling any—you won't be able to shift them after the tour's finished. If you are a band with your own record label, then having some shirts with the band logo or picture and some with the record logo is always a good idea—some fans (particularly in the dance world) get just as obsessed with independent labels as they do with musicians, and they want shirts, slipmats, bags, anything with the record company logo.

## MERCHANDISING—WHERE TO GET IT?

So you're ready to start selling T-shirts, jockey shorts and fancy pens to your unsuspecting fans. But how do you do it?

There are a number of dedicated suppliers of merchandise—check the *Music Week Directory* for a comprehensive list. To keep things easy, start with T-shirts—they may be the most basic item but they still sell the best and are the cheapest and easiest to buy. Fancy pens, cigarette lighters and the like are more expensive and more difficult to obtain at this stage. That kind of thing is usually the domain of the big artist whose record company can afford it, or as promotional items—again for the bigger stars. Make sure you phone a few different suppliers to get a good idea of prices—and don't necessarily go for the cheapest, as the quality might be poor and you want to avoid big, angry fans turning up at your next gig demanding their money back!

If you start making a name for yourself as an artist, you'll be surprised at how the merchandising can start to shift. Eventually you may find you want to hire a specialist company to handle merchandising sales for you—although they're going to take a nice bit of commission! Or, if you're in a band, you may decide that one of you will be responsible for that job, or you may delegate it to your roadie if you have one—or perhaps someone's boy- or girlfriend might be willing to take it on. However you do it, it can bring in some welcome money for the band—after all, a T-shirt that costs you around, say, £3, including printing, will be sold for more than three times that, which makes it a nice little earner. It's the same with records. If you sell your own product yourself at gigs—or through mail order—you do away with distribution and shops, which take a huge cut compared to the record label and artist. It means you can sell them cheaper, which suits your fans, and you still make a much bigger profit than if you sold them by traditional means.

Jeremy Goldsmith of Event! Merchandising, and Glen Miller from Bill Silva Management in the US, stitch in the detail on how to source and sell your act or label's merchandise.

++++++++++++++++++++++++++++++++++++++++++++++++++++

## JEREMY GOLDSMITH

Event! Merchandising has been running for over twenty-five years. It began providing tour merchandise for bands such as Led Zeppelin and Stevie Wonder, took in the likes of Gary Numan on the way, and today provides merchandise for a wide range of acts, from rock to classical, from breaking rock bands like Mohair to Pavarotti. Jeremy Goldsmith, the managing director, explains the ins and outs of band merchandise.

### What should a band bring to a supplier to get merchandise made?

Whether a band is just starting out, or whether they have a manager or a record label, they should have created a logo—an identity. They need to bring the logo artwork to the merchandiser so we can suggest which products to brand. We can also help in creating the artwork. While T-shirts used to be the most popular item, they are less so nowadays and there are many choices of products to merchandise. So you can be quirky with the products—but if you are going to do T-shirts, think carefully about how they look. T-shirts from bands have become collectable items and are back in fashion.

What items you choose depends on the type of artist or band you are. For example, heavy rock bands still go for black T-shirts, but you could go for pro-

grammes, underwear, key rings, hats and so on, right up to more exclusive merchandise. For Pavarotti, we produced enamel boxes and pashminas. Another use for merchandise is if a band wants to use a product for promotion—to get fans to buy into the brand. We have some good ideas for this!

If you are just starting out, when you bring your design to the merchandiser, he will create your merchandise on a supply basis; that is, you pay him for the merchandise and you sell it to your fans. A good merchandiser will help you to manage your order and make sure you don't overstock. He will advise you to be cautious. For example, if this is your first order, he will probably advise that you buy a hundred T-shirts rather than a thousand. This will mean the T-shirts are more expensive per item, but it's better than being left with lots of T-shirts you can't sell. Once you see how things are going, you can start to order in larger quantities if things are going well.

Once bands start to take off, they will be approached by merchandisers wanting to license their merchandise. This means the merchandiser undertakes to finance the costs of the merchandise—he takes the risk on the stock but makes a margin. He will do this by paying the band a royalty for each piece of merchandise sold—rather like a record company pays royalties on records. You need a merchandiser who understands the live and touring scene for best results. This royalty will vary on the size and success of the band, and the manager will negotiate the contract for the band.

Also, merchandising can be used for press and promotion—coming up with a high-quality original item always helps to get attention. Event! created hand-painted Russian Dolls for a greatest hits album for Bjork. This was an off-the-wall idea that won a lot of press attention.

---

## Does it cost to sell merchandise at venues?

Very small venues such as pubs will not charge you to set up a table and sell merchandise. Once you move up the gigging ladder, venues will start to charge, and it varies from venue to venue. Once you reach the theatres and big stadium venues like Wembley arena, they usually charge a 25% commission plus VAT. However, for this charge, the venue staff is responsible for displaying and selling the merchandise for you. This commission varies from country to country internationally—you will need to check. In the US, for example, it is 35% in big venues.

## Any tips on how to sell merchandise?

It's very important to make an effort to display your merchandise as well as possible. If you just have a T-shirt plonked on a table, it won't sell. You need to put up signs, have display boards—a shop dummy if possible—power for lights, anything you can come up with to make your stand look enticing. You can do it quite inexpensively. Treat your display as though it were any retail outlet—a shop—and you will tempt people to buy. Once you licence to a merchandiser, then the merchandiser will check out the display. We always go to venues to make sure our artists' merchandise is well displayed—if it's not, we make sure that things are changed so it is.

✦✦✦✦✦✦✦✦✦✦✦✦✦✦✦✦✦✦✦✦✦✦✦✦✦✦✦✦✦✦✦✦✦✦✦✦✦✦✦✦✦✦✦✦✦

✦✦✦✦✦✦✦✦✦✦✦✦✦✦✦✦✦✦✦✦✦✦✦✦✦✦✦✦✦✦✦✦✦✦✦✦✦✦✦✦✦✦✦✦✦

# GLENN MILLER

Glenn Miller started out in the worlds of music and fashion at the age of 14. Among his numerous careers have been working on the Warped Tour and Tommy Boy Records as part of, and later on, head of their street teams. He moved to Tommy Jeans PR, dressing celebrities for magazine photo shoots. Flipping back to music he has functioned as a representative for Sony Music then in special events and marketing for Giorgio Armani Corporate. Currently he is in charge of merchandising and new media at Bill Silva Management who represent Jason Mraz, Raul Midon, Dropping Daylight, and David Pack.

## What is popular in artists-related merchandise right now?

One thing we're noticing is it's all about colors. Whenever we do shirts in primary colors, they tend not to sell. Fans go for pastels and bright summer colors like baby blue, pink, purple, yellow. Every band is coming out with a different assortment of colors so people feel like they're not buying a concert shirt but that they're buying a shirt that they can wear everywhere.

People used to want to buy shirts to commemorate the event that they were going to and know that they'll probably wear it once after that day. Now it's becoming something that they put in their normal rotation of clothes. Because it doesn't say, hey I went to the show this day. Now it looks like something you would buy at Urban Outfitters or any of those specialty shops. It's making the merchandise more like clothing rather than an actual concert shirt.

Tour dates on a shirt aren't selling as much as they used to because nobody wants to wear a shirt from last year or past summer. They would rather wear a shirt that looks cool and doesn't have, necessarily, the album cover on it. Fans notice if it looks like you put a box on the shirt and inside that box is where you've put an image. One of the things we do is try to find different locations for images so that you're really buying into the person that you're there to see instead of just, 'Oh we've got to make merchandise because he's on the road.' We want to give fans back what they appreciate and they expect from the artist.

### What should a band bring a supplier to make shirts?

They have to have their idea first because their supplier can only go so far. The easiest thing is when you have the design drawn out or made up in the proper format, and you know exactly what you want your line to look like. If you go to a supplier without a direction then you're at a standstill. They can come up with ideas, but to you, that's not what you want. You have merchandise but in the artist's eyes it might suck.

Artists will say I want this kind of shirt with this design on it but then it comes down to, are people really going to buy this shirt. Suppliers will print up anything you tell them, but one of the key things is knowing your audience and knowing what your audience will buy. You don't want to come out with a line you think is going to be awesome but it doesn't connect with who you've portrayed yourself as to the fanbase and to everybody out there. You can be a bubble gum pop band and come out with these hard rock images or something that's totally artistic. With little kids coming to your show, it's a waste of your money because nobody's going to be buying your shirts.

## How many items should a band get printed?

They should have a good selection. At the most they should do four different t-shirts and an outerwear thing like a sweatshirt or a hoodie or a track jacket. Track jackets tend to be more popular now because now it's all about fashion. Quantities depend on the size of the band. If it's somebody playing 2000 capacity places for a tour that's a month and a half, we're doing 15,000 pieces total.

Smaller artists, one thing they need to watch out for because they are trying to develop their image and who they are while they're touring, while they creating their merchandise they need to be consistent with what they're trying to portray. You don't want to come up with a symbol and say this is what represents our band and then a year later, once people start recognizing you by that symbol you go, I don't like this symbol and I want to change it now. All the fanbase that you had, they're going to look for that symbol and they're not going to see it and they have to rediscover you again.

For small bands, four shirts and outerwear, especially that track jacket, even though the track jacket costs more, for a couple months run, they should easily be doing at least 144 of each style. And they have to make sure that when they come up with the guy shirts, if they want to do four guy shirts that at least two of those shirts should also become a woman's shirt. Depending what kind of band you have you don't want to make all these guy's shirts for girls that come in and can't fit into them. You kind of make sure so that you have an assortment so everybody can have a piece of you, so to speak.

## How much should you charge?

For a new band, a smaller band, developing band, I would say $12 to $15 max. A lot of times they're paying $8, $10, $15 to go see you, and when you're charging more for your merchandise than your ticket, then it's like you're buying an extra ticket to go to the show. The kids that are going to these shows obviously do not have a lot of money. When you get bigger, I look at our artist, Jason Mraz, we keep it at $20 for a t-shirt. $20 is a great price because it's easy for the people selling the merchandise, they take a 20 dollar bill and they don't have to make change. But it really goes with the ticket prices

## Any tips actually selling the merchandise?

Displaying the merchandise really well. When you go up to a merch booth and you see the front of the shirt, the back of the shirt, all the different sizes, the price, you get a feel for what that actual item is and it becomes real to you. It's accessible to the consumer. The person selling the merchandise also has to be friendly, be knowledgeable, and give good customer service. If the fan is saying, 'Oh do you have a small,' he's saying, 'Yes,' then bringing it out to the fan and letting them see the size of it.

We're learning now that fans are recognizing what kind of shirts they are. We do all our stuff on American Apparel. They're slim-fit, super-soft, every color you can think of. Fans look at the quality of the shirts. We want to give them quality but also have it affordable because we don't want to alienate our fans, we want to make sure that they're getting what they came for in this whole package.

✦✦✦✦✦✦✦✦✦✦✦✦✦✦✦✦✦✦✦✦✦✦✦✦✦✦✦✦✦✦✦✦✦✦✦✦✦✦✦✦✦✦✦✦✦

# SECTION 2

# RECORDING

# home
# recording

IN this section, you'll find out about buying the equipment you will need for home recording and how to get a good result from recording at home, not only technically but also through gaining the right perspective and strategies to do whatever you want to do. That may be quick demos to play to your fellow musicians or to get gigs, or it may be very complex, master-quality tracks ready for promotion. The process is much the same.

Because recommendations for specific models would quickly be out of date, the emphasis is on how to think about buying equipment and what, in general, are the useful features to look for.

## PERSPECTIVE

So, what is your goal here? You'll see plenty of advice around this book that emphasizes fitting the task to its purpose; it's certainly true of home record-ing. There are two common mistakes people make. The first is spending too much time on details. Even if you intend to release the recording as a CD or vinyl disc, there's a point where attention to detail damages the total project. The second is trying to make limited equipment do more than it can deliver. Tailor your recordings to show off the main ideas within the limitations of the studio. There aren't many worthwhile ideas that actually need lots of recorded tracks or racks of expensive effects to make their point.

Of course, you want to perfect your recordings, learn new techniques, meet challenges and push the boundaries. Quite right. There's no set amount of time and effort which is too much; it's a matter of taste and judgement. Just be aware that home recording will suck your life away if you let it—keep a bal-anced point of view!

## STRATEGIES

The goal is to represent your main musical ideas in a stereo recording which sounds reasonable when different people listen to it in different circumstances. You may hope some of these people will want to do something in response, by buying a record, booking you to play or approaching you with a management, recording or publishing offer.

If you want to use the recording as a demo to get gigs, the promoter will be imagining what your show will be like. Concentrate on a spirited performance, well recorded but with no clever stuff. Don't spend ages on it—by the time you have played the gigs that your first demos get you, your next recordings will probably be lots better.

A simple approach can still be best for tunes where you hope to put out a record yourself or persuade someone else to. Keep the framing of your main ideas at the front of your mind; don't get distracted by trivia. Try comparing your track, in style and technique, to a similar commercial recording. (If you can't do this, perhaps you should rework your tune!) If they have represented their key idea in an appealing way using only three or four instruments, see if you can do the same by taking a hard look at the twiddly bits to see if they really add something. If you have a good idea that's let down by the way it's been recorded, you should still be able to get enough good feedback from other people to know it's worth pushing further with, and you'll have a better notion of what to attend to.

## RECORDING EQUIPMENT

### SEATING

Often overlooked, the chair you spend many hours in is an important piece of equipment! For the price of a budget effects unit, you can buy a classy, adjustable, back-supporting chair from an office supplies outlet.

### HARDWARE-BASED SYSTEMS

A conventional recording setup needs three ingredients: a mixer, a recorder and a monitoring system. This section includes stand-alone digital hard-disc recorders which work like tape machines. For personal studios, there are good mixer-and-recorder units by Roland, Korg and others, or you can use a separate mixer linked to a dedicated recorder. The problem with the combined units is that you can't upgrade without selling the whole thing, so, if you need more inputs for Midi instruments, for example, you can't just buy a bigger mixer and keep the recorder the same. Studios producing releasable material always have separate mixer and recorder.

## THE MIXING DESK

What mixer you need depends first on how many signals you need to handle at once, whether off-tape or from MIDI gear. The smallest useful mixers have eight channels—that's really tight for a full mix of a song, though. Most desks can give extra channels for mix-downs using the monitor section; some have stereo inputs, which are fine for things which don't need treatment, like MIDI stuff. A sixteen-channel desk is the basic item nowadays and there are lots of good ones around. The mixer takes up a lot of space, so that may limit what you can have. Some mixers come in rack-mount form, which is okay if you don't change settings much.

### Features to Look for

+ EQ (tone controls) go from bass, middle and treble boot/cut (basic) to two variable-frequency, set-bandwidth boost/cut, with maybe an extra fixed treble control (midrange) to multiple sections with controls for frequency, bandwidth and gain (professional).
+ Auxiliary circuits: to route signals to effects or monitors. Three is skimpy, six is plenty.
+ Group/tape busses: you need the same number as you have recording tracks—eight for an 8-track, sixteen for a 16-track. Desks with two or three groups are for live work.
+ Channel cut and solo buttons. A nice extra on some desks is an activity light, which shows every time any signal is present.

New mixers are definitely a better bet than used ones, because of the number of moving parts—knobs, faders and switches—which can deteriorate over time as well as through use. Mixer technology hasn't changed much in the last ten years, but value for money has improved considerably.

## THE RECORDER

Recording is done on lots of formats: reel-to-reel, cassette, videotape, Mini-Disc, hard disc and solid-state memory devices.

### Do You Expect to Use Recordings You Make in a Commercial Studio, Rather Than Re-record Them?

Then it's best to record to a digital format which is saved as digital audio files.

### Do You Expect to Do Lots of Takes or Overdubs?

You need a hard-disc system. Akai, for example, makes dedicated hard disc recorders which, though they may have eight or sixteen tracks, will store a number of takes for each track. These can also mix tracks together with no quality loss and have extensive undo recovery.

For songwriting or personal studio use, budget will probably dictate whether you go for cassette (demos only), MiniDisc (nice demos) or hard disc (near-master or master).

Tape-based systems (including ADAT) have motors and read/write heads, so are best bought new, as these wear with use. Disc-based systems area a safer secondhand buy, but problems with wear are likely to be more serious and more costly.

## Miser's Tip

We're including very basic portastudios as viable units, so there isn't much scope here, what with the falling price of technology. But if you're really, really broke you could look for a unit which Amstrad made, which incorporated a four-channel mixer linked to a four-track cassette recorder; a mixdown cassette deck; a monitor amp and speakers. It was implausibly cheap new; it didn't stay on the market all that long and it wasn't well received. But it exists!

## COMPUTER-BASED SYSTEMS

The music computer nowadays can do the work of several pieces of studio gear. As this book goes to press, a fairly classic home setup is an Apple Mac running Logic software, using a soundcard interface. There are lots of PC alternatives, with Steinberg's Cubase being very popular, but the Apple/Logic approach gives best compatibility if you take your recordings to a professional studio. Programs like Cubase, Logic and ProTools—and others, higher or lower in price and specification—can record many tracks of live sound, play samples, generate synth sounds and let you mix it all, with effects, to releasable standard. Almost all of this is done within the digital audio package.

## New or Used?

Computers are getting better and cheaper all the time, so if you can afford to buy new, it's almost definitely worthwhile. If you can't, then a used computer will do. The essentials of digital recording can be done with about 200Mhz upwards.

## How Do I Choose?

Nobody knows! It's almost as hard to say which sequencer you should choose as to say which guitar you should choose. If you've used a MIDI sequencer before, go with the current version of the package you are most familiar with. If not, it might be best to go with whatever is used by the most experienced sequencer user you know. If you plan to finish your recordings in a commercial studio, there are advantages to compatibility.

Mac and PC are about equally supported now, though historically the Mac has taken precedence in music. There's more budget software, shareware and freeware for PCs and PCs usually start at lower prices than Macs. Macs are generally agreed to be easier to set up, which is quite important in this case. Computers can be fussy about soundcard sharing and device assignment generally.

You'll need to get a better soundcard for PCs straight away and the same applies to Macs once you get beyond the basics. Creative Labs serve the budget end well and is a good reference for price. The more serious market is ever-changing, so check the magazines' verdicts on the latest batch of goodies.

## Miser's Tip

The Magix range of music software is very wide—and very cheap: www.magix.com or Amazon.

## THE MONITOR SYSTEM

## Speakers

Studio monitor speakers have a different role to domestic speakers. Studio monitors should give a ruthlessly clear sound as widely across the frequency spectrum as cost and size permit. There really isn't much point in buying humongous speakers for a home studio, because the room probably isn't acoustically flat, so the result will be misleading. Apart from that, the decision will be made mostly on budget and available space.

## Miser's Tip

At the bottom end of the price scale, you don't actually have to buy 'proper' monitors. A big part of the point, at this level, is just to be able to hear back what you're playing, which you can do on any pair of speakers or even headphones. You can actually get some quite good speakers for little dosh. Old, large hi-fi speakers are often cheap because the cardigan-wearing hi-fi buffs have gotten fed up with having them in the living room. Celestion Ditton were very popular and are good value.

The challenge then is to make sure that your mixes will play reliably on different systems, because the relative levels of trebly, middly and bassy sounds on your speakers are not well set up. Follow the mix-checking procedure in the studio chapter (p. 197). You will have lots of chances at this, so you might want to progressively adjust the tone controls on your monitor amp to compensate for the weighting of your sound caused by cheaping out on your monitors! It's a trial-and-error procedure; broadly, you need to match the problem with the solution—if your mixes are frighteningly bass-heavy on Dad's stereo (having checked that *his* system is set flat), it means that you weren't hearing enough bass in the studio, so turn up the bass on your amp. Similarly, for mixes where the toppy ingredients, like hi-hats, are too quiet or dull, turn down the treble on your amp to compensate.

Moving up the scale, there are now many monitor speakers suitable for home studios, from companies such as Tannoy, Soundcraft and Alesis, as well as more exotic brands.

Buying secondhand is okay, but try to see the environment in which the speakers were used. If it's a neat personal studio with shiny gear, fine. If it's a stale bunker where pounding dance mixes till 4 a.m. are normal . . . maybe not.

## THE MONITOR AMP

Commercial studios use a dedicated power amp, which gives plenty of headroom and the cleanest signal path. For the home, a chunky hi-fi amp is fine.

You need one rated at thirty watts (RMS) per channel at least, preferably fifty. You might need to handle the following sources:

+ Mixing desk in
+ CD player in
+ Phono (turntable) in
+ Master recorder in/out
+ Cassette recorder in/out

A very valuable amp feature in a small setup is the capacity to handle two tape decks with routing between them.

## HEADPHONES

### New or Used?

Buy headphones new, as the wiring to the earpieces often fails.

### How Do I Choose?

Headphones for performers should have a closed earpiece to minimise spill into microphones. They should be robust, especially the earpiece wiring. Recordists should favour comfort—earpieces and headband—and a warm sound.

The studio standard is the Beyer DT100 set. They aren't fantastically comfortable and they don't sound great, but they're very robust and most components can be replaced individually. Sennheiser semi-open headphones are also popular. These are very good for home studios, but not ideal for monitoring recordings using a microphone because there is more chance of sound from the headphones spilling on to the mic signal than with closed-earpiece systems.

Cordless headphones are fun for people playing instruments—it's great, not having to stand awkwardly because of the headphone wire.

## EFFECTS UNITS

Effects might be divided into 'obvious', like distortion, delay and reverb, and 'subtle', like compression and gating. Of course, you can use 'obvious' effects subtly and vice versa! Some products chain effects together, sometimes sacrificing editability of parameters. These are a good buy for the 'obvious' effects, but 'subtle' effects are usually rudimentary. In the late 1990s, though, a new configuration, often called a 'vocal channel' or similar, put 'subtle' effects like compressor, parametric EQ and noise gate in a line.

## New or Used?

Since about 1997, the price of a decent, flexible effects unit has dropped considerably. This makes it hard to get good value in the used market, but otherwise buying used is fine but check for worn controls.

## How Do I Choose?

Budget units from Alesis, Digitech, DOD, Fostex, Lexicon and Zoom (and probably others) offer good quality effects cheaply. The snag with these is that they usually only provide one, or possibly two, effects at once and the effect types are often rather conventional, with the exception of Zoom.

You can buy single boxes which house more than one independent effect unit, typically two effects and sometimes four. This is different to multi-effects, where only one signal can be treated, but with chained effects, the independent effects have their own inputs and outputs and it's just like having two or four separate boxes. This saves space and electric points and, so far as one can compare, works out cheaper than buying four boxes but might feel less immediate and less varied than having separate units.

## MASTERING AND COPYING

So you've created a fantastic mix—you need to capture it in glorious stereo and, ultimately, transfer it to CD. You could master straight to cassette if you just want a copy of the mix for yourself. If you then want to make another copy, though, you have to get two cassette machines talking to each other and the sound of the copy will be worse. Any mastering machine will record to a higher standard than any cassette deck and you can make as many cassettes as you like from the master tape with no change in quality.

The mastering machine should use a no-loss or low-loss medium like DAT, CD or MiniDisc.

---

## New or Used?

New. All forms of mastering machine have delicate bits that wear. Besides, this is the point where all your hard work is captured and frozen in time. Be proud of it.

## DAT

DAT is old hat now, but still a useful format for no-loss, uncompressed, re-recordable mastering. It is the standard mastering medium in the recording industry. It uses a matchbox-sized cassette tape which can record up to one hundred and eighty minutes of music at CD quality (44.1KHz stereo). Some portable machines are available.

+ Plus points: CD quality or better; accepted by all studios and duplication houses; machines always have digital transfer ability; can be used for data storage with suitably equipped samplers
+ Minus points: machines are relatively expensive; not used outside studios; no editing or compiling possible within the machine; no direct program access

## CD-R

## STAND-ALONE

A CD recording machine is now as cheap as the cheapest DAT recorder and a twin-deck machine, which will duplicate CDs you record and costs less than most DAT decks.

Great! A no-loss system which lets you make your own CDs—problem solved. Naturally, it's not that simple. Though rewritable CDs exist, it's not as straightforward as recording over a DAT, MiniDisc or cassette. You can only delete material *before* the CD is 'finalised'—and until it's finalised, it won't play on a normal CD player. On the other hand, a CD-R machine is a superbly useful thing to have. And if you haven't yet got a CD player for the studio, you can put the budget for that towards the CD-R deck, as there's no need for both.

+ Plus points: CD quality; widely used format; cheap media
+ Minus points: fairly expensive and hard to find used

## BUILT-IN

If you are using a computer to record with, you will probably have a CD-R drive in it. If not, they are cheap and can either replace your CD-ROM drive or be added in a spare bay. Digital audio packages will allow you to 'bounce' your finished mixes to a file, which you can then burn to CD.

## MiniDisc

MiniDisc uses a disc which looks like a computer floppy disc, only smaller. The sound is compressed onto the disc, and there is fractional loss of quality, but the sound is still very good.

Discs hold up to seventy-four minutes of music and can be re-recorded easily. MiniDisc also supports track titling and in-machine recompilation. Many duplication houses are equipped for MiniDisc. If you go for a portable machine—lots are available—make sure it has digital I/O.

+ Plus points: price; size; in-machine compiling; direct program access; track titling
+ Minus points: not CD standard; not widely accepted in the industry

## Cassette Recorders

Although no good for mastering, cassette is still the format which everyone can play, anywhere. Just about any new machine will do a reasonable job. You won't use noise reduction, so budget and opportunity can largely dictate your choice. Don't buy a machine with automatic record level control. Avoid auto-reverse decks unless you're already used to them, even professional engineers find them confusing. Twin-deck machines have never been favoured, but they're certainly handy and if the convenience means more to you than extra quality, you probably won't regret buying one. (They often don't have a tape counter at all, though, which is a pain.)

## USEFUL FEATURES

+ Remote control—can be really useful, as it means you don't have to be able to reach the cassette deck at all except to put tapes in
+ Return to zero/memory locate
+ Minute/second counter

- ◆ Tape type recognition so you don't have to switch for chrome and ferric tapes
- ◆ Cue/review, for finding the end of the recording, etc.
- ◆ 'Three-head' machines let you hear the actual sound off-tape as it's being recorded. Technically best, far from vital, but it does usually mean you can listen to source sounds without having the cassette machine in record ready, using the 'source/tape' switch.

+++++++++++++++++++++++++++++++++++++++++++++++++++++++

## ALAN THOMPSON

Alan Thompson is sales manager of Turnkey, Charing Cross Road, London, one of the UK's largest and longest-running music technology specialists. Here he gives the lowdown on what gear to splash out on and when.

### We're talking about the entry–level act's needs. We discuss two typical acts: a rock band and a hip–hop act. How can you help?

Our strength is that we know music technology inside out, where your general music shop also has to know about all the instruments they sell.

### For a band which has decided it's time to record at home, what is the best setup and what do you need for it?

There are two routes you can use for recording. One is the multi-tracker, or all-in-one studio, where all you need is a microphone and you are set up to record a CD of demo quality. Or there's the PC route, which, if you have the PC already, you can get going for about £200.

The smallest multi-trackers are around £250. They give you four tracks and limited channels and mic inputs, so you have to track everything, recording a bit at a time. They all have MIDI in and out, and will work as a slave to a system, but they don't have MIDI sequencing included. Most of them can hook up to a computer or media card to store your data and your music. Small multi-trackers use up to 2Gb compact flash or 1Gb smart media card. All the machines we are discussing can be archived via USB, so that's very easy.

At the top end, machines go up to about £2,000 for twenty-four tracks of high-quality audio. There are bargains out there—an end-of-line multi-tracker will come in at about half its original price and also new products tend to have more features. Something like the Yamaha AW1600—on the market in 2005 for about £750—gives you sixteen tracks of audio at highest quality and has a CD burner in it. That's cheaper than a PC system that would do the same job.

## What should a hip-hop crew be looking for?

For recording hip-hop, it has to be the MPC [Akai MPC1000/2000]. There's no comparison. It has a very hip-hop sound because of the quantisation, the groove in the way it sequences audio and Midi—it just has this really nice swing to it that people try to emulate but they just can't. MPC stores sixteen minutes of audio and sequences audio. You need samples: get yourself sample CDs of kick drums, snares and hi-hats. Seventy pounds will get you a sample CD with thousands and thousands of single hits. The CDs that are free on the cover of magazines have loads of good sounds too. The MPC lets you work with loops, which are fundamental to hip-hop. For recording vocals, you would need to link your MPC with a small multi-tracker like the Korg D4, a new small portable recorder which is quite high quality. If you have a PC, you could use fairly basic software to record the vocals.

## Microphones?

For microphones, while an AKG drum kit set will set you back about £500 and will give you all you need, Superlux do a similar set for about £200. For vocals, a Shure SM58 is the classic vocal mic, but on a budget you can get the Shure PG58 or PG48; they go down to £30 with cable, case and clip. They sound really good. They aren't as robust as an SM58 but it's essentially the same capsule. The PG58 is also good for acoustic instruments. Behringer do a three-microphone set for £20, which we sell —if you're on a really tight budget they will get you by for a demo.

## Monitoring?

If you are going to spend some serious money, spend it on monitoring. You have two options, active or passive monitors. [Active monitors have their own amplifier built in to the speaker cabinet.] Most people have a stereo at home and you can use that with passive monitors. You can improve the speakers on the system from about £90, say Tannor Revolution X speakers which are really good quality for the money. If you need an amp, you can get a one hundred and seventy–watt Power amp for about £80. Or you can go for active monitors where you don't need the amp. You can get Alesis active monitors now for about the £200 mark. The main benefit of active over passive is that the amp and speakers are matched up properly; there's less cabling, so generally the sound quality would be a bit better. Headphones are really important. I can recommend Sennheiser HD25s, which are £70 to £100. Budget AKGs will give you decent quality for £20 to £30. The industry standard headphone is the Beyer DT100, which you would expect to pay about £80 for.

### Effects—is there a killer one-stop does it all?

Yes! Without a shadow of a doubt the M300 by TC Electronics for £140. You get reverbs, which are the same quality as their £3,000 units, though you can't adjust the parameters as much—plus, all the multi-effects you can think of. Lexicon also does good multi-effects. They cost a bit more.

### Are compressors important?

Not at first. It's probably better not to compress your demos. As your quality increases it helps. You can pick up a really good stereo compressor by Mackie called the Tapco Squeeze for £50.

### What's the hot buy for keyboard players on a budget?

If you want an all-singing, all-dancing synth which does a good job on piano I would recommend the Roland Juno D, at about £300. Up from that, the Korg Triton LE, you get the classic Triton sounds—the Triton is the industry-standard *Top of the Pops* keyboard that everyone uses—and it's got a sixteen-track sequencer as well.


## FIRST STEPS

The basics of a recording setup are a mixer to plug instruments in and connect to the recorder, the recorder to record the music and a monitoring system to play back the music and headphones. Of course, you'll need a microphone too, if you are going to sing.

So let's make sure what we play is actually going to be recorded in a good state. You may have to work with your equipment manuals and/or brain to do this, as this book can't cover all the different sorts of equipment and computer software included!

- ✦ If you have a drum machine or sequencer, it's often helpful to program it to play four beats to the bar at the same tempo continuously. If not, you or someone else will have to repeatedly make a noise to test things out.
- ✦ Connect a pair of headphones to the mixer/recorder. If a signal is getting that far, things are off to a good start!

◆ Set your recorder to 'record ready' on Track 1. A red, possibly blinking light should come on somewhere.

◆ Set the mixer channel to send to that track. It might be 'Track 1–2', 'Group 1–2', or 'to Tape'. Make sure that the EQ is 'flat'—no cut or boost on any controls.

◆ You should see the meter for the track moving when a signal is present.

### RECORDING THE VOCAL

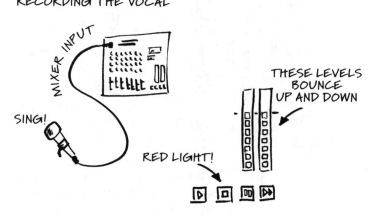

☺ Yes! Adjust the coarse input volume control (trim) and/or the volume fader on the mixer channel until the loudest signal just flickers on to 0dB on the meter.

☹ No! Check all connections and routings. If you can actually hear the signal back from the monitors, the battle is part won. Try changing the send routing to see if the signal appears on any of the tracks (set them all to the 'record ready' setting first).

That's basically it. If you can route any mixer channel to any track and adjust the level, you're in business for recording live, or semi-live, music.

## MONITORING WHEN RECORDING

The point of multi-track recording is to have each instrument on its own track—for a while, at least. So you should do your best to stop sound from other instruments getting onto the track you're recording. External sounds leak into a track when people are playing along with whomever is recording and when performers listen to playback while recording their take.

---

MONITORING USING HEADPHONES

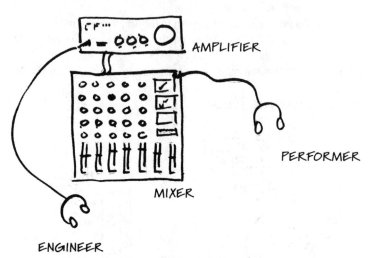

Headphones are the solution. The headphones of the musician whose performance is being recorded should be plugged into the mixer/recorder, as you
can probably set up a separate mix for them without disturbing the controls
you are using to record with, by means of the monitor section of the mixer.
They might want a distracting part turned off, or a timing track particularly
loud. The monitor amp usually has a headphone socket too, so both the main
participants, performer and engineer, can monitor on headphones if they want.
(The amp will offer the main desk mix, unless you change what's going to the
main desk outputs.)

## KILLING NOISE

Unwanted noise can subtly drain the life from home recordings. You'll have to
live with some level of noise from equipment and environment, but it's worth
getting into the habit of regulating it.

With all the mixer channels turned up to default level but no instruments
playing, cautiously turn up your monitor system to 'nearly frightening'. A system in good shape has a pleasant midrange hum, like ambient noise on a star-
ship. Rough, low noises are usually to do with earthing, of either instruments
or mains gear. Harsh hissing is often instrument amps or effects and high

wheezing is usually keyboards. Radio breakthrough can be caused by faulty cables, especially long cables. Fade channels up and down until you find the culprits and do whatever you can to sort the problem. If 'bad' noise continues with all the channels down, maybe it's in the monitoring system. That doesn't really matter so much unless it's distractingly loud.

Turn off any channels which aren't going to be at work during a take. Try to get effects pedal users to turn them on only when needed.

Noise from the environment often can't be helped, but you can watch out for nasty noises caused by fridges, heating thermostats and so on. You can buy special mains plugs or distribution boards which reduce these. Use a suppressed mains distribution board for the mixer and the monitor amp at least. If you're using a computer, that's another good place for a suppressed mains plug.

## RECORDING SONGS

In this section, we take you through the process of recording with a basic instrumental/vocal format: we'll record drums (or drum machine) on Track 1, bass on 2, backing instrument (guitar/keyboard) on 3 and vocal(s) on 4.

### DRUMS

Drummers have to record first, so that everyone can follow their timing. The same, only much more so, goes for drum machines and sequencers, unless you are recording them rather than synchronizing MIDI. These parts can't realistically be re-recorded once other tracks have been laid: you have to start again. It's worth trying to get them right, or right enough for the job.

### Vibe

Drummers should be given the best possible vibe, especially if they're inexperienced. They should have as much of the arrangement as possible to play to, unless any part puts them off. Positive body language is good: get everyone grooving along in a slightly overstated way! Don't worry too much about other sounds going to their track. Of course it's best if they don't, but drums are loud and anything that spills into the drum track will probably be covered up by other parts later.

## Timing

Drummers' timing is an awkward subject. Drumming that works with the vibe and eye contact of group playing doesn't always work when players try to follow the drummer's performance from the recording. Click-tracks are an answer, but rarely a good one. Drummers who haven't played with click-tracks before are more likely to be nervous and mess up than if left to struggle with doing a proper job by themselves. Additionally, a performance which is good enough for the players to adjust to may still sound deficient against a regular click. Only very good drummers can play to a click and preserve the spirit of their playing.

## The Recording

Studio recording of a drum kit is often the single most complex and time-consuming process of a session, involving numerous microphones, recording tracks and treatments. There are many technical books which show how to do this if you're interested. For now, we will assume that you have only two microphones at most and that the kit will be recorded as a mono track. This means that the various drums and cymbals must be balanced as well as possible before recording. Your only control is by moving the mic(s) around and trying a few short takes to check. We'll assume you're using one mic to start with. Start by placing the mic about one to two metres in front of the kit, at about the height of the hi-hats and slightly on the hi-hat side of the bass drum (see diagram on the next page). Record a short piece of representative drumming—don't bother about floor toms or splash cymbals, for example. Here's a list of what you need to capture, in order of importance:

+ Snare
+ Hi-hats (these first two are the only really important things)
+ Bass drum
+ Crash cymbal

Anything else can take its chances in the mix. You might think the bass drum is important, but it's often quite buried in the mix by other instruments playing on the same beat and it's fairly easy to bump it up later with some bass boost without affecting the other drum sounds much. The snare is the absolutely vital sound to capture properly, and if the snare is okay, the hi-hats will be okay.

## ONLY ONE MIC ON THE DRUMKIT

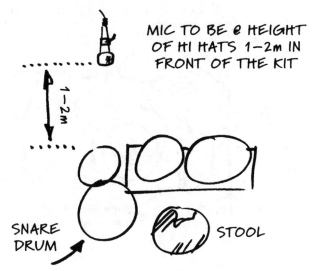

MIC TO BE @ HEIGHT
OF HI HATS 1–2m IN
FRONT OF THE KIT

1–2m

SNARE
DRUM

STOOL

Because you are listening closely to the playback, you may notice noises from the bass drum pedal, drum stool or other fittings. Squirt WD40 if you really care, but the noises probably won't show in the mix and may even give a subliminal exciting feel!

Similarly, you may have seen drums 'damped' for recording, with gaffer tape and dusters on the skins, blankets or pillows in the bass drum. Suit yourself, but it's a bit passé in the age of sampled drum sounds. Best to make a virtue of 'real drums', within reason, and keep the natural kit sound.

## More Mics

If you can use two mics and desk channels, there are two options. The first is to go for a wide left/right setup, which will give you two slightly different-sounding signals to play with but may not be very useful unless you have enough tracks to keep the drums in stereo till the mix.

The second approach is to use one mic right beside the snare, on the hi-hat side, and the other farther away from the kit, slightly on the other side. This allows you to catch those really important sounds, then balance them with the other drums and the room ambience. Unless you're recording on to a

CLOSE MICING THE KIT

OVERHEAD MIC

SNARE & HI HAT MICS AS CLOSE AS YOU CAN!

MIC THE TOMS FROM UNDERNEATH

INSIDE THE BASS DRUM IF POSSIBLE!

really bottom-end machine, like a portastudio with Dolby B, you could consider using two tracks for this and bouncing them to a single track afterwards. This gives you more chances to get a good mix. Not crucial though. (See the diagram for mic positioning.)

## Rewind, Retake

In principle, the drums define the rhythmic base for the track and drummers shouldn't have to play in time with other tracks. But it can be difficult to get a single, complete recording of drums that is good enough throughout. If other people are playing along, they may get bored, which doesn't help. One solution is to record other instruments temporarily as a guide, leaving the drummer able to concentrate on a good performance, no matter how long it takes.

Alternatively, you could try for a drop-in or two. The results won't be great, because drumming is quite continuous. You should do drop-ins only if you think the best take has been recorded and you want to fix it a little bit. To do this, you will need to record a guide part of some kind on another track. Drummers don't need much pitch information, so sometimes a running commentary—'Break coming up: one–two–three–four'—is easy to record and gets the job done.

## RECORDING MORE TRACKS

When the drum, or drum machine, track is down properly, you need to set up your equipment so that the other players can hear the drums and guide vocal to play to when they record their performances. Read the 'monitoring' sections in your manuals. It's important that the sound of the drums from the recording isn't allowed to get on to the new tracks you are recording. You won't be able to adjust the mix if it does.

Now that you've got a recording which is the length and shape of the song, make notes of the times or counter numbers when the changes in the tune happen. The roll of masking tape comes in handy here. Stick a bit in plain sight—on the meter bridge or a speaker cabinet, perhaps—and note the positions on it. Much better than a bit of paper.

It's quite standard studio practice to stick masking tape on the frame of the desk, below the faders, and mark up which instruments are on which channel. Some people go so far as to stick them to the ceiling afterwards, in case they do another mix! You may like to do this, unless you've got a fancy wipe-clean strip—or a four-channel mixer.

Again, make sure the EQ is flat and the signal is not more than 0dB at any time. (Some people believe in recording 'hot' on analogue tape. They have a (minor) point but let's play safe and make some good recordings.) It's quite common for people to play louder when they are in the throes of their performance than they did when you were testing their level before starting, so keep an eye on the meter.

STICK SOME MASKING TAPE TO THE FRAME OF THE DESK TO HELP KEEP TRACK OF YOUR TRACKS!

MASKING TAPE!

DRUMS1 DRUMS2 BASS GUITAR B/V LEAD VOX

Each time you move on to record a new track, you must check that:

✦ All the approved tracks are in 'safe' mode—including the one you've just finished—and can't be accidentally erased.
✦ The channel(s) you want to record next are routed to the right track.
✦ The destination track definitely has no valuable material recorded on it. It can then be set to 'record ready'.
✦ No other sounds are routed to the 'record ready' track.

## BASS

Bass players should be able to record their part over drums and guide vocal. Other players can still play along, provided that their sound isn't being recorded. Bass players can record in front of the main speakers; they don't need to use headphones unless noise is a problem.

Generally, bass can be recorded straight from the instrument. This lacks the gut-punch of miced-up bass but hopefully the player can rise to the challenge and give his or her take extra energy to make up for it. If the bass amp has a line-out socket, this will give a more authentic sound but it's noisier. Don't use the desk EQ or a compressor; you can add that later, and if you do it now, you can't undo it once it's recorded.

## GUITAR

Electric guitar can't usually be recorded direct; it sounds too weedy. There are three possibilities:

✦ Put a microphone in front of the guitar amp's speaker.
✦ Use a line output from the guitar amp.
✦ Use guitar effects in line before the mixer channel.

Micing the amp is standard studio policy and gives the best result because you get the 'colouration' from the amp and speaker and the sympathetic resonance between the guitar and strings and the sound from the speaker.

Put the mic smack in front of the grille, near the centre of the speaker. Keep the master volume moderate, because the benefits of playing really loudly are offset by all the extra noise when you're not playing. If you have volume restrictions, put the speaker face down on a sofa or carpet with the mic sand-

MAKE SURE THE
MIC IS NICE &
CLOSE!

wiched between. It's usually best for the guitarist to wear headphones, partly to stop monitor sounds being recorded but more because the guitar will drown out the monitors!

The other two methods are straightforward. If using effects, keep to those which improve the 'real' sound of the guitar, like overdrive/cab simulation, EQ or subtle compression. Noticeable effects like reverb and chorus can be added later. The player can record in front of the main speakers.

For all of these, especially the first, you might want to use a noise gate so there is no extraneous noise on the track when the guitar isn't playing.

For acoustic guitar, place a mic about thirty to forty centimetres from the soundhole of the guitar. Experiment with moving the mic a bit nearer for more warmth but less room ambience, or towards the neck or bridge for warmer or more cutting tones. If you have an electro-acoustic, it's much easier to get a good sound by using the output than setting up a mic.

## KEYBOARDS

Keyboards are generally recorded straight from the output socket. (Electro-mechanical instruments like Rhodes and Clavinet might be better if recorded like guitar—it's best to experiment.) The only tricky decision is whether to use

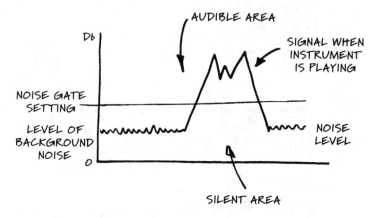

BACKGROUND NOISE? TRY USING A NOISE GATE

onboard effects. It's really down to the size and flexibility of your recording setup. If you are confident that you will be able to add effects to the track later, strip them away from the keyboard sound. Start by switching off the 'obvious', like echo and reverb. Subtler effects are sometimes so important to the pro-grammed sound that it's best to keep them.

If you don't have many channels or effects, it's probably best to use the keyboard sound 'as is', or even work more with the onboard effects to go for the finished sound you imagine, which saves stress on your rack boxes later.

If a keyboard part is played simultaneously by more than one instrument, you have the choice of trying to keep enough tracks free to record the parts separately later, or routing all the relevant desk channels to one track. Record-ing on one track is probably better, but it means that the balance between the instruments can't be changed later. So pay close attention to it before okay-ing the take and moving on.

## VOCALS

The vocal is usually the single most important part of a song. Certainly in the commercial world, a good vocal performance is almost the only thing you need apart from a good song. So it's worth taking a lot of care to get it right.

Vocalists need special consideration in home recording. They must get all the help you can give with their performance. Fuss over their monitoring, keep any fiddling with effects, EQ, etc. to a minimum and let them know when it must be done so they can relax for a minute or two. Generally, try to keep a suitable positive and progressing vibe going.

## When?

The vocalist and whoever is planning the session should think about the best time for the singer to record. Different singers work best at different times of day. A common mistake is to leave the recording of the main vocal until too late in the session. While it's true that singers usually deliver best over the fullest possible representation of the track, that doesn't apply if they start their recording too late in the day. They also need to rest their voices between takes sometimes, and leaving them till last makes this difficult.

At any time of day, there is less time to get the best from singers than from instrumentalists, because their voices are fragile. They do warm up like players, but the length of time they can stay on top form is shorter. It's a good idea to get a generally good and spirited take within the first four to six attempts and then discuss its imperfections and do some version of the 'comping' procedure. (See p. 174.)

## Where?

Somewhere quiet but in reach of the headphone and microphone arrangements. It's important to get in the habit of recording 'clean' vocals—more than it is for other parts. Voices aren't very loud compared to most acoustic sound sources, so background noise is relatively louder. Vocals are usually loud in a mix, so noises are accentuated. Because it's so important, it's more likely that trickery (see p. 173) will be used to get the best result, and trickery really needs a clean vocal.

## How?

You will see studio shots of singers standing about half a metre from a microphone, sometimes with a mesh shield in front of it. The purpose of the shield is to prevent the vocal sound from 'popping' when it is amplified. If you have a classy condenser mic like a Neumann, Oktavia or similar, this is the way to do it. You can make a pop shield with a wire coat hanger and a pair of tights. At least it makes you look as though you mean business, even if you're not sure whether it does anything!

0·5m

EXPENSIVE MIC!

CHEAP MIC!

POPPING
SCREEN

EXPENSIVE MIC 1/2M &
GAUZE POPPING
SCREEN

CHEAP MIC – GET AS
CLOSE AS YOU CAN!

If you have a stage vocal mic or worse, the singer should stand as close as possible. These mics deliver more bass or 'body' at close distance. Don't use a pop shield.

Watch out for uneven recording levels. By lightly compressing the vocal on the way in, you can make sure that a powerful performance isn't spoiled by distortion.

If you have enough spare tracks, you should try to keep vocal takes which have good performances, even if it's only on one part of the song. When you have an approved vocal recording, you can check to see whether any of the other takes have a better performance of a particular section or phrase. Some hard disc recorders have a facility to store 'takes' as well as tracks. (See 'Trickery', p. 173.)

## PLAYBACK!

So now you have recorded the basic tune. Up to now, you should have been listening to the recorded tracks through the monitor section of the desk. But you can't change the sound much, if at all, with the monitor controls. So turn those off and switch channels one through four to listen to the tracks instead

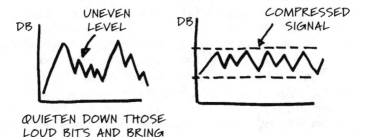

QUIETEN DOWN THOSE
LOUD BITS AND BRING
UP THE QUIET BITS!

of 'input' or 'line'. Pull the four channel faders down and make sure the EQs are flat to start with. Play the recording back and push the faders up. All being well, you can hear the four tracks and you can easily mix them and start improving their sound with some EQ. We'll do proper mixing later.

## MORE TRACKS

Set everything back the way it was for recording. You can now carry on putting down more tracks, but at some point you may fill up all the tracks you have and still want more. There are two things you can do to get them. You can 'bounce' tracks together, combining them on to a new track and leaving two or more tracks free. And you can synchronize MIDI instruments to run in time with the recording. These include samplers, which can be used to sample recorded performances and free up tracks.

## TRACK BOUNCING

If you're using a four-track recorder, you're stuck now because you've filled up all the tracks. People with more tracks can follow the example but bounce on to empty tracks. Some machines aren't happy bouncing to tracks adjacent to those which are playing in the bounce mix. You'll have to plan for this, but it's not too restricting. Many books about home recording will have sections to help you through this.

Sorry guitarist/keyboard player, we're going to treat your track as a guide and record the drums and bass over it. Get the tracks of drums and bass back on the desk channels and balance their volumes roughly. Apply any EQ you want, because the sounds won't be separate after this. It was once common practice to add a little treble to tracks with a treble component—drums in this case—to compensate for the loss of treble after the track bounce (the technical term is 'pre-emphasis'). If you only have a Dolby B–equipped recorder, do this cautiously. Otherwise, it's probably best not to do it. Now finalize the balance, switching in the vocal for reference if you like. Route the drums and bass channels to Track 3 and check that they are getting there but that nothing else is. When you're happy, record the two instruments to Track 3.

Make sure the two source tracks aren't playing, and check the result. You can reconsider and do the bounce again up until you erase the drums or bass. You now have two tracks free, so you could record the guitar or keyboard and one more part, or you could record one part and bounce it with the vocal to the empty track, freeing up two more tracks.

There are two drawbacks to all this wonderful freedom. First, you lose control of the mix to some extent because you are making decisions you can't go back on every time you do a bounce and erase the source tracks. Second, the noise from each source track is bounced across to the new track, where it is added to the track's own noise. How soon this becomes a problem depends on how good your recorder is and what you intend to do with the recording. If

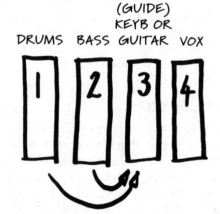

### BASIC TRACK BOUNCING

DRUMS  BASS  (GUIDE) KEYB OR GUITAR  VOX

1  2  3  4

BOUNCE DRUMS AND BASS OVER
GUIDE GUITAR OR KEYBOARDS –
FREES UP TRACKS 1 AND 2

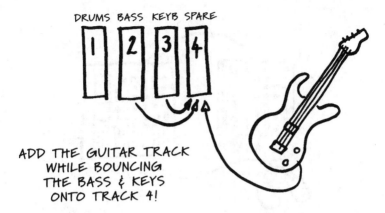

DRUMS BASS KEYB SPARE

1 2 3 4

ADD THE GUITAR TRACK
WHILE BOUNCING
THE BASS & KEYS
ONTO TRACK 4!

it's a demo for the rest of the band, or preparation for going to a larger studio, then the fidelity doesn't matter.

One way of getting more bounce per ounce is to set up a bounce as before and also set up to record another performance, which goes to the bounce track as well. In our case, we might re-record the guitar and mix it with the drums and bass. The guitarist still has the chance to get the take right, as you can just keep playing the recorded tracks and his or her performance until you're happy. Check early on that the performance track is balanced to the recorded tracks. You might not manage convincing drop-ins in this mode, but it's a good quick 'n 'dirty method for getting more tracks in less time with less noise.

## MIDI SYNC

Sequencers, including drum machines, can be sent a time-code (sometimes interpreted by a special box) which gives the song's location so that the sequencer always plays in time with the code. The humans then play in time with the MIDI. With this facility, you don't need to record MIDI instruments at all; the MIDI parts will play from the sequencer until the tune is mixed. This is great news—not only do you save tracks, but the MIDI parts and the balance between them can be revised right up until the final mix. If you have a sampler, you can save more tracks if you need to, by sampling the performances from the recordings—backing vocals which repeat for each chorus are a simple example.

You need more mixer channels than you have tracks to do this properly, as you need to mix all the track returns and the MIDI sources at the same time.

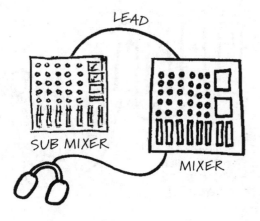

SUB MIXER

MIXER

If your own setup doesn't have this, you can use a submixer—another mixer, maybe borrowed or a cheap line mixer with few controls—and feeding the submixer's output into a channel on the main mixer.

Some (older) sync systems will only work if you play from the beginning of the track every time, but if it has 'SMPTE' in the description of what it does, any gizmo will pick up anywhere in the track.

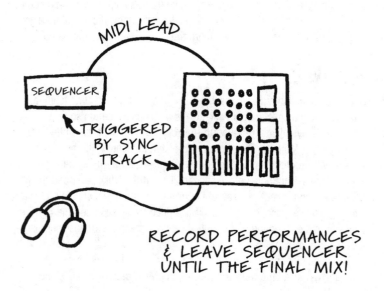

MIDI LEAD

SEQUENCER

TRIGGERED BY SYNC TRACK →

RECORD PERFORMANCES & LEAVE SEQUENCER UNTIL THE FINAL MIX!

# TRICKERY

There are some things you can do to get a good result without tirelessly going for master-quality, track-length takes all the time. Only the two or three most important components of a tune are worth this attention: the timing of the rhythm track, the lead vocal part and possibly the most noticeable instrumental part.

## Sampling

You may not need an actual sampler for this: many rack effects can take samples and may suffice, as we don't want to change the sample in any way.

Samplers can be used to capture a good performance and repeat it. You can take the best vocal chorus and use it for all the choruses, for example. Or you can take a spot-on piece of back-beat drumming and a few fills and piece together a drum track which is more solid, if less subtle, than the one from which the parts were sampled. (This doesn't always work, as the slight variations in human timing might confound it.)

If you have sync, you can then program the sequencer to play the samples in the right place. If you don't, no worries. Just play it in from the keyboard—either your timing or your drummer's should be up to it!

## Compiling Takes

This mostly applies to those with eight tracks or more. It's most frequently used on vocals, but it can be used for other parts too.

Record several takes on different tracks, ideally leaving at least one free track. Make a chart (see the table below), which has the song format on one axis and the tracks on the other. If you think you know which take has the largest amount of acceptable material, listen to that first and note the faulty or weak sections. You could use a grading system of 1 to 3, as we have done. Then try to find better performances of these sections on other takes. When you have a complete track of class 1 material across various takes, follow the track-bouncing procedure (p. 170) to compile it all to a free track, or one which didn't have parts you're using for compiling. Fade the sections rapidly in and out as needed. You may need to keep an eye on the chart, or mark it with a highlighter or felt-tipped pen, to know when the changes come.

Try to use a take for as long as possible before switching to another one, for the most natural result.

In our example, Take 2 is the best one overall. Chorus 2 is supplied by

Take 3, and after the solo, Take 4 is used. Take 1 could be used as the destination track for the bounce.

|  | Intro | Verse 1 | Chorus 1 | Verse 2 | Chorus 2 | (Solo) | Verse 3 | Chorus 3 | Chorus 4 |
|---|---|---|---|---|---|---|---|---|---|
| Take 1 | 3 | 3 | 2 | 3 | 2 | – | 2 | 3 | 1 |
| Take 2 | 1 | 1 | 2 | 1 | 2 | – | 1 | 2 | 1 |
| Take 3 | 2 | 1 | 2 | 1 | 1 | – | 2 | 1 | 2 |
| Take 4 | 2 | 2 | 2 | 1 | 2 | – | 1 | 1 | 1 |

You will need to be aware of when there is too much difference between takes, especially with vocals. Vocal timbre changes as the session goes on, and the singer's position in front of the mic may change too. Apart from this reservation, 'comping' is probably a better technique than drop-ins, as you don't erase anything and the changeovers are smooth. Of course, you don't actually need to record the whole track each time. In our example, once Take 2 had been checked, Chorus 2 and 3 could have been recorded on Take 3 until they were right. Sometimes doing longer takes helps the performer's feel, sometimes it's fatiguing. Use your judgement as to what is best.

## Double-Tracking

Sampling, compiling and effects can all be used to fatten a performance with double tracking—as if two performers played the same part at the same time. This suits some styles better than others. It shouldn't generally be used for any parts with a lot of short notes or rhythmic components as it will be too obvious and may sound like a mistake.

In the above example, we could have mixed Takes 3 and 4 for Chorus 3 and Takes 1, 2 and 4 for the final, rousing chorus. This is the 'nicest' way to double-track, as it actually does involve several slightly different performances. Mix the best take loudest and err on the side of 'too quiet' for the others—doubles can be quite far back in the mix and still give a good effect.

With a sampler or effect unit, you will be using an exact copy of the best take. From a sampler, it may be best to trigger with the keyboard to give more feel, change the pitch by one or two cents, or use just a touch of LFO (low-frequency oscillator) to vary it from the main part. Be careful here. As with chorus effects, which work similarly, there is a risk of making the whole performance sound slightly out of tune.

To double-track with an effects unit, set up a short echo, a pitch shift of 1 or 2 cents with very little feedback, or a very slight chorus effect.

## MIXING

Let's go back to the start and declare straight away that the object of the exercise is to show how good your ideas are, not how good you are at working equipment. If the tune has a good vocal or lead instrumental part and has a good feel, then all you really need to do in the mix is showcase those elements.

Resist the temptation to mix at loud volumes. By all means play mixes back from the stereo at thundering levels, but don't work on the mix with the volume up, because:

+ You may press the wrong button or replug something or otherwise make a bad noise.
+ You will get fatigued and your hearing and judgement will worsen.
+ You will give yourself a misleadingly exciting impression of the track, instead of working to get a vibey mix.

Many people find it helpful to refer to a commercial recording which they think is close to how they would like their finished tune to sound. It's some-

times a bit of a leap of imagination to compare your portastudio stumblings to the output of a world-famous studio, but at least if you even begin to think you're getting there, you must be doing okay!

## Getting Started

Normal practice is to 'reset the desk' before beginning to mix. Before you do this, make sure you really are happy with all the recorded material and haven't forgotten to do anything.

Take all faders down, set all EQ flat and all effects sends off.

If you have spare desk channels, you may wish to think of a way of using them now. Often this means separating different MIDI sounds which have been coming from the machine's mono output, so sounds can be shaped and mixed selectively. If you don't use MIDI, you could route effects units to main channels instead of their returns, to give more control or more effects capacity.

Many engineers set the EQ and compression for each channel with only that sound playing, starting with each of the drums and working up through the mix one sound at a time. They then balance all the sounds, again working from the drums upwards, finally applying enhancing effects to specific sounds or to the whole mix.

## EQ

The gospel on using EQ is that you find an undesirable frequency range in a part and use EQ cut to diminish it. This is a fine approach, but it needs good EQ and good ears to work well. It's not very exciting and not very intuitive—many musicians when asked what's wrong with a sound when will reply, 'It isn't bassy/bright enough' and they will boost the relevant frequencies to compensate, rather than saying, 'The midrange is too forward compared to the top end' and cutting the mid till the top shines through.

Asking what, if anything, is wrong with the sound of the part is definitely a good way to start. It's quite okay to say that, within the overall standard of the recording, there's nothing wrong with a part's sound. After all, you presumably recorded it without cringing at the sound. If you have only bass and treble controls, with no frequency or bandwidth settings, do very little—try not to use bass boost in particular. Whatever your EQ facilities, don't try to make the part sound drastically different from how it was recorded, unless it's an experimental bit of some sort.

Using EQ boost is not a sin, especially if resources are limited. Here are a few, mildly sacrilegious, tips:

**Drums** (mixed to one track): add small amounts of 'upper bass' to give more penetration to the bass drum and body to the snare and 'upper treble' for liveliness. Purists may say this is the same as cutting the midrange, but it rarely is in practice.

**Guitar and brass**: boost midranges and treble quite heavily if necessary, but don't let the result get shrill.

**Vocals:** boost various midfrequencies carefully to push the vocal forward and give it urgency. Avoid 'nasality'.

## Bass Alert!

Many modern artists, the dance crew especially, might be tempted to put lots of 'bottom end' on their mixes. Don't! The bass you hear on commercial recordings is achieved with experienced use of EQ, compressors and special processors like Aural Exciters. Boosting bass EQ makes the lively parts of a tune struggle to be heard and gives a lifeless mix. Honestly.

# BALANCING AND PANNING

## Balance

The balance of different performances in the mix is very much down to musical style, fashion and personal taste. The only hard-and-fast rule is that the focal point of the recording—usually the vocal—takes precedence over everything else. Often the drums and bass are mixed at about the same level as each other. Check some relevant commercial recordings to see how the picture is built up for your musical style.

If a channel just won't settle down in the mix and is always either too loud or too quiet, listen to it on its own and look at its meter readings to see if there is a problem. If it does rise or dip drastically in volume, there are a couple of remedies:

+ Use a compressor if you have one available and spare—there might be one in a multi-effect.
+ Set different fader positions on its channel to compensate for different levels and move the fader when necessary.

With both these solutions, if you have a spare track, you can record the compensated version to it, either freeing the effects unit or giving you less to do in the final mix.

Often, though, just working away at achieving a well-integrated mix will make these uneven qualities much less noticeable.

## Don't Make Everything Louder Than Everything Else!

A common mistake when balancing the track is to increase the level of a part you think is too quiet, which then makes something else seem too quiet, so you increase its level and so on until sonic anarchy breaks out. Overcoming this is really a matter of experience, but you can take some precautions. Check sounds against other ones which should be mixed at about the same level—drums to bass, guitar to keyboards or backing vocals, lead vocal usually louder than any other individual signal. Or check that other parts with a similar timbre aren't cluttering the mix; maybe there's a bass synth and a bass guitar and a big kick drum all fighting for control of the bottom end, or three keyboard parts swamping an acoustic guitar. Try turning channels off to see if they are really making a difference. If in doubt, take it out.

## Panning

While you shouldn't mix everything dead-centre—it's boring and it can cause slight deadening of the mix—primary parts like drums and lead vocals should be at or near the centre. For other instruments, you can choose either to roughly copy your stage layout, if it's a fairly live lineup of instruments in the song, or to look for similar sounds and set them opposite each other, to some extent. Put lead guitar half-left and rhythm guitar half-right, for example, or spread backing vocals across the mix.

If you have recorded or bounced something as a stereo mix, you will normally pan the two channels hard over left and right. Otherwise, don't pan anything hard over unless you have a specific reason.

# EFFECTS

## Discipline

Once you have all the parts sounding as good as your EQ allows and nicely balanced, you can decide which parts need enhancement effects like reverb, echo, chorus and so on. This has been left until now because effects applied

DON'T OVERDO FX!

YEAH, I KNOW IT'S ALREADY COMPRESSED, FLANGED, ECHOED AND CHORUSED, BUT I NEED MORE REVERB!!

too soon can hide problems in the track and also make it harder to mix. You get used to hearing them and, even if you say 'I can give them up any time I want', it's not that easy. Occasionally, effects are fundamental to the part, but it's almost always best to suffer the dry sound, making it as pleasing to listen to as possible, then adding effects when needed. Another reason for leaving effects until now is that in most cases they shouldn't be used so emphatically that they require the mix levels to be changed. Effects should sit behind the parts they are applied to. They add noise as well and there's probably quite enough of that already.

## Application

The actual use of effects is subject to musical style and individual taste. Experiment, study and refer to commercial recordings until you are experienced. Such guidelines as there are include:

- ✦ Be careful with time delays on short notes—you have to get the timing dead right or it sounds bad and it tends to harm the dynamics of the part.
- ✦ Generally, don't use reverb on bassy parts; it sounds splodgy. If you must use reverb on a mixed drum kit, hack off low frequencies from the reverb signal as much as possible.
- ✦ Use pitch deviation effects like chorus very carefully, as they can make the part sound out of tune. If the part is out of tune anyway, especially a vocal part, don't use them and don't even use time effects in an obvious way because 'on' and 'off' notes may be echoed into a horrible mess. Use washy effects to hide tuning problems.
- ✦ And remember no one ever said 'I signed/bought/cherish that tune because of the fantastic use of effects'. Well, only people you wouldn't want listening to your music anyway.

## Transfer

Once you have decided the mix is ready, things are fairly simple. You need, of course, to be able to hear the mix while also sending it to the mastering machine. Record a quick take to a tape or disc before getting serious, to check

DON'T PUSH
RECORDING
LEVELS
TOO HIGH!

the transportability of the mix on as many different types of equipment as possible.

When you are totally ready, there are a few last tips:

+ It's not time to lighten up yet. Keep concentration high; don't chat and joke when the mix is going down. You may well be tired by this time and one lapse can cost you time you don't want to spend.

+ Within reason, try to get clean beginnings and ends to the tracks. Eliminate any count-ins, coughing or spurious noises, switching on things that cause sudden jumps in hiss and hum and so on. This helps when compiling tracks for duplication, but it's not going to change anybody's mind.

+ Make sure the meters on the mastering machine never stray into the red. Never! Recording hot is old analogue discipline, and what we want is a mix with no problems, no cracking up.

+ Log everything on the inlay card of the tape or disc very carefully and with comprehensible explanations—no matter how late at night it is. False starts, the lot. Won't you feel sick if you send the wrong mix to the duplication house?

+ Never take it for granted that a mix is captured in good order just because the last three were. If it's likely to be used, check it back.

# the recording studio

+++++++++++++++++++++++++++++++++++++++++++++++++++++++++++

## STU LAMBERT

Stu is a senior lecturer in Commercial Music at the University of Westminster. He is a multi-instrumentalist songwriter and programmer with many years of recording expertise as a member of a number of bands. Here he discusses the ins and outs of getting the most out of going to a recording studio.

### So what is the role of the studio today?

The recording studio was once just about the only place where artists could develop a piece of work beyond live performance. Its role changed dramatically around 1980 when the portastudio, home eight-track and MIDI arrived, and again around 1998 with home computers and affordable, powerful samplers, and still more in the late 1990s with full digital studio systems in the home.

Today, a commercial studio offers:

**Low start-up cost:** you have to buy a lot of equipment to produce industry-standard recordings without hiring a studio.

**Expertise**: the engineer is experienced in the whole of the recording process.

**Equipment:** quantity and quality—lots of microphones, lots of control over sounds, lots of effects, proper acoustics, low noise, low distortion and faithful speakers.

**Contact-making:** not vital, but still an improvement on the back bedroom.

A 'classic rock' recording uses only played performances, as do folk, jazz, blues and perhaps soul. In the studio, each musician is able to record their part separately until it is satisfactory. The recorder could be analogue or digital, tape or disc. When all the recording is finished, each performance is separately treated and balanced within the overall mix, which is then recorded to a two-track stereo

---

A STUDIO MIXING DESK LOOKS REALLY SCARY AT FIRST!

EEK!

recorder, ready for transfer to cassette, CD or vinyl for the consumer. Or converted to a streamable or downloadable format for a Web site.

A 'technological' recording uses a sequencer to make sound modules play the parts, which always give an identical performance and so do not necessarily need to be recorded. Each sound source is then treated like a performance from tape. A recorder can be synchronized with the sequencer, so that live performances can be used as well.

### How does the tape recording system work?

A multi-track recorder is like lots of tape decks in one box running perfectly in time, each able to record or play back independently of the others. The 'classic' format is a reel of 2"-wide analogue tape—equivalent to sixteen cassette tapes stuck together—which records twenty-four tracks. It is the industry standard for analogue recording and many people still think this is the best recording medium of all.

There is also digital tape, notably the Alesis ADAT format, which records eight tracks on S-VHS tape and which can link machines to give sixteen, twenty-four or more tracks. It's generally easy to transfer 2" or ADAT recordings between different machines and studios.

### And disc-based systems?

Disc-based digital multi-track systems are usually designed to look like tape decks, but instead of putting the signals to be recorded on a length of tape,

---

they store them on a data storage medium: Mini-Disc, Zip or Jaz cartridges, solid-state devices like compact flash or pen drives, or fixed hard drives.

It can be harder to transfer recordings between machines and studios than it is with tape.

## What about the studio layout?

A typical studio has a control room, where all the recording equipment is, with a window into a live room. The live room is where people go to do their performances, especially those involving microphones. It is soundproofed from the control room and performers communicate with the engineer via a headphone circuit known as talkback. Dance-oriented studios and production suites may not have a live room, though there is usually at least a booth for recording vocals.

A studio mixing desk, also known as the console or mixer, looks really scary at first—how could anyone remember what all those knobs and buttons do? But actually there are only a few types of functions on a mixer, each of which has to be separately available for each sound source. So a forty-eight–channel desk will have (at least) forty-eight of everything—tone controls, volume controls, routing controls—in a vertical line. All the channels feed the stereo mix. The mixing desk is the engineer's home ground and you should only get involved with it at their invitation.

✦✦✦✦✦✦✦✦✦✦✦✦✦✦✦✦✦✦✦✦✦✦✦✦✦✦✦✦✦✦✦✦✦✦✦✦✦✦✦✦✦✦✦✦✦✦✦✦

✦✦✦✦✦✦✦✦✦✦✦✦✦✦✦✦✦✦✦✦✦✦✦✦✦✦✦✦✦✦✦✦✦✦✦✦✦✦✦✦✦✦✦✦✦✦✦✦

## SHAUN HARVEY

Shaun is the proprietor of Fortress Studios in London. Fortress offers 2"/twenty-four–track and ProTools recording systems. Fortress is attractive to acts that need to go beyond their home recording capabilities for the first time.

### Why use 2"?

A lot of bands prefer the sound because you get tape compression, a warm valvey feeling. Lots of producers record to ProTools, record on to 2" after. But 2" is £170 a roll, which only lasts seventeen minutes. I still get the thrill from using a tape machine!

## Fortress Studio Client List

- The Go-team
- The Subways
- The Kills
- Gomez
- Cinematic Orchestra
- The Scissor Sisters
- The Killers
- Interpol

- Funeral For a Friend
- Hell is For Heroes
- The Duke Spirit
- Keane
- Coldplay
- Tom Jones
- The Libertines

**We've got a band that has gone through this book, done a few gigs and saved the money, recorded themselves at home and decided to pay for a studio for the first time. Let's start with a standard lineup rock band. How long should they allow to do drums, bass, guitars, keyboards and vocals and mix for three songs?**

Two days to record and mix. You can do it in a day, but they probably won't be happy with the mix. You should get all your backing tracks done on day one, Next day, solos, extras like tambourines, and the vocals. Then, on to the mixing, where you should allow about three hours or so for each mix.

### How should the band work with the engineer?

For first-time bands, it's important that the engineer doesn't work as an overbearing producer-type, but will gently prod, make suggestions for the good of the session. Even to the point of commenting on an arrangement which is too long or complicated.

Half the battle of working in a studio is communication skills. If your engineer can get the confidence of the band from the moment they walk in the door, he will be able to 'suggest that they make the right decisions', without being patronising or making the band feel he's taking over their session.

Problems can arise because a musician with a certain amount of recording knowledge can be more dangerous than if nobody has any knowledge. He may come into the studio and take what he thinks is a producer role, but if he only has a home setup it will be nothing like this. He'll make wrong decisions and waste time because his knowledge doesn't apply in this situation. The engineer will bury his face in his hands and say, 'Part-time producers—I hate 'em!' So the band should be happy to seek advice but not be bullied.

## Do you think it's a good idea to bring someone experienced along with you to the studio?

No, I don't think so. The important thing is to have a good house engineer and achieve a good rapport with him, and that the band is really well rehearsed. They've got two days and they know what they've got to do by certain times, they don't start arguing amongst themselves, and they keep the whole show on the road so it's a happy, positive environment. If they start arguing about arrangements and lyrics in a first-time, two-day demo session, you've got problems.

Sort out everything beforehand if at all possible. Lyrics, arrangements, tinkering around with little ideas that someone's had: they need to have discussed it, arranged it and decided what they are going to do. Otherwise they get stressed and run out of time.

## Take us from the start.

We would set the band up as a live unit and then the engineer would concentrate on getting good headphone mixes for everyone, because it can be a bit daunting at first, playing on headphones when you aren't used to it. Sometimes we will put the vocalist and guitarist in the control room so they are listening to the speakers. The engineer is looking for a fault-free drum take at this point. The other parts aren't that important in the early stages.

Drums: if you are using your own kit, it's important that the kit's well tuned, with fairly new heads and no squeaks or rattles—and cymbals that aren't cracked! If you have a cheapish kit and the studio doesn't provide one, it's worth hiring a good snare.

Sometimes it will be suggested that drummers work with a click to keep them in time. If the drummer hasn't practiced with a click, it's not going to happen. A drummer who isn't used to playing with a click will have to practice for at least two weeks before they come in. There's an art to playing well to a click-track. People have wasted so much time and money trying to do that when it isn't going to work.

Lots of engineers and producers these days will just use one or two takes in ProTools and then put them together, using the best bits. My objective is to get a good take which is repairable, rather than sticking things together. It's been noticeable recently that bands have been coming to us to record because they want to capture the sound of a great live band. You should be spending the time getting a good take rather than sitting in front of a computer screen dicking around with parts. You usually know when you've got 'the one' and just fix the odd small mistake. But you also have to learn to be able to make a decision not to keep on recording because the drummer only has a limited amount of energy. You've got to know when to stop, otherwise they get weary and start making mistakes and then they start sulking.

Then you carry on, taking the bass and building the track. You may already have the bass from the guide; see if it's useable.

### Will you work with the bass player's usual setup?

I use a bass drum mic to their amp and also take a DI. Lots of compression—if you want a quick session, you can build your sound and bang it down, rather than recording clean and then treating the sound. I'd do that when I'm trying to get five or six songs done in a day, for radio sessions. Bass players all want a big, fat sound and they don't hear the big fat sound in the mix at the end of the day because you know that all the bass they put on will be dropped out at the end of it, because it won't fit sonically.

### With guitarists, do you encourage them to use their onstage effects?

Whatever makes them comfortable. Pedal effects are often better than the ones in boxes in the control room. If they're too noisy, they can be gated—gate it to [the record track] and gate it back.

### So you would advise that bands try and do things their way and rely on the engineer to cope with it?

Yes. They should do exactly what makes them feel as comfortable as they can. But don't get drunk. Have a drink but don't get pissed, don't bring your girl-friends or your mates.

### Vocal—when in the day is it best to do it?

Probably better in the evening, around 6 or 7 in the evening. But in a short session, you should be mixing by midafternoon on day two. So on the evening of your first day, if you've got the drums and bass and guide guitar, you can see if you can get a few vocals instead of leaving it till it's a panic to get them done in time to do the mixes by the end.

Stay straight—a lot of singers have a few drinks or have a smoke to 'prepare' for their vocal, but for singers particularly it's a disaster. They'll be out of tune and out of time and they will think they are giving the performance of their lives when really, it's crap. So drink loads of water.

### Do bands get a bit of a shock hearing themselves back in the studio, transferring from their live sound?

Yes. The engineer will make suggestions for that if it's needed, but yes, you should try out some new ideas, especially if they are simple and can be done quickly. Don't sit around discussing it, just bang it down and see if it works.

### What should performers do when it isn't their take? Should they be around or go away?

I think vocals should be left to the vocalist and the engineer. I don't like bands being around for that. If you do ask for their advice, they often aren't really listening so what they say can be a distraction.

Drummers should concentrate on their drum tracks and not hang around the control room too much. Bass players and guitarists can feed off each other and swap ideas, so it's good for them to be around during each other's parts. Singers can do things like write their lyrics in big marker pen, or maybe the project sheet, which is a good idea. Figure out everything you have to do for the sessions and write it down and stick it on the wall. Keep track of what you've done and what's left to do and how long.

### What level of involvement do you think the band should have in the mix? When should they get involved?

Tough one! I don't know an engineer who likes having the band in the room when they are mixing. They would prefer the band not to be there and to put their CDs in the post the next morning. Well, it's not gonna happen but the band should go for a meal or something while I get the basic mix sorted, patch in all the effects and get everything ready to go.

Don't start making suggestions for quirky production ideas while the mix is being set up. At the right point, the engineer will ask what you think and that's the time. Reference CDs are useful. It gives the engineer an idea of whereabouts the band is coming from sonically and helps them get the sound they want. You can also play the band's other recordings at the beginning.

Mastering—you can master to half-inch for more of that glorious compression. If you haven't got a big budget—it's £50 for a reel of half-inch—

then you can master straight to CD. On a self-funded session, the band shouldn't be trying to sound like their favourite albums; they should be concentrating on presenting their songs the best way possible. The important thing for an A&R man is to hear a theme—a tune, a hook—so they can give them a deal and go back and record it all posh.

Bands will often put the wrong tune on first. They'll put the one that they think is artistically the best, as opposed to the most instant one. Get to the choruses quickly and put the most instant one first. Again, your engineer can advise you this if you ask.

### How do you work with a performer who just can't get a good take of something they can play perfectly okay when they're not recording it?

Red-light fever—the classic one. I don't tell people when I'm recording. I just say give it a run through, play along. . . . It often works. If it's really not happening and you're on a tight schedule, maybe do some takes that need doing, a vocal retake or whatever, and then go back to the difficult part later.

✦✦✦✦✦✦✦✦✦✦✦✦✦✦✦✦✦✦✦✦✦✦✦✦✦✦✦✦✦✦✦✦✦✦✦✦✦✦✦✦✦✦✦✦✦✦

✦✦✦✦✦✦✦✦✦✦✦✦✦✦✦✦✦✦✦✦✦✦✦✦✦✦✦✦✦✦✦✦✦✦✦✦✦✦✦✦✦✦✦✦✦✦

## STU LAMBERT

### Stu gives more advice on making a booking and planning the recording sessions

Some studios work in 'slots' of ten hours or so, or have day sessions and night sessions. Many allow you to book fairly freely between about 10 a.m. and 1 a.m. These are useful boundaries—people tend to be slow getting going if they arrive before 10, while finishing later than 1 a.m. and then getting home not only leaves you below par the next day, but makes it harder to over-run to reach the logical point to wrap up the session. Owner-operated studios tend to run one session a day.

If the studio runs more than one session per day, it may mean that you will have to pack up your gear in good time to make way for the next client and then set it all up again at the start of your next session. It's not too much of a problem if you're well organised. You must be sure that all the takes you need for a certain part are completed during the day, because it's hard to set up again so exactly that a drop-in won't show. If you start a subsequent day by setting up gear while previous work is reviewed, the next moves are discussed, and the coffee is beind made, there won't be much time lost. The alternative is to book a 'lock-out'. This means that work stops when you leave and nobody else can use the studio. It doesn't cost as much as booking both sessions and has the obvious advantage that everything is just the way you left it. Ask the studio if they actually have, or think they will get, a night session booked after your full day. They will want to attract your custom and may offer a lock-out free or cheap if they don't think the studio will be earning during the night. Tell the studio owner or manager how many tracks you intend to do, to what level (demo/posh, demo/releasable master . . .) and roughly what performances are to be recorded. They will be able to give you an idea of how long it will realistically take. Try not to plan mixing in the same session as recording. The studio equipment configuration is different and the mental attitude is also different. If possible, leave some days between taking rough mixes of the recordings away and doing the mixes. You can recover your objectivity and make notes about the roughs to speed the mixes along.

## How should a band prepare for the studio?

If drummers can't drum and singers can't sing and guitarists can't play a note, nothing's going to change by being in the studio! The most annoying thing for an engineer is bands that aren't fully rehearsed—although being a little under-rehearsed is okay; it can give you a bit of an edge, and an over-rehearsed band can sound bored.

I worked with a band and they set up, started to play and they were terrible. It was a complete mess; the timing was out and everything. In my band, the second time we play a song when we record is not much different than the first; there's about 10% improvement. This band played its songs about eight or nine times and I've never seen anyone improve so much. It was about 90% better by the end. We had some good demos by the end.

Lots of bands don't work out arrangements for songs. This isn't to say you can't change them once you get in the studio but you need some idea of how they should go.

Drummers and bass players should practice together. The kick drum won't match the bass part if you don't. A drummer and bass player not working out can sound particularly bad in a funky or dancey band. If you're rehearsing in a hall, you often can't hear that you're not working well together, so take some time with just the two of you.

Most singers have to work hard. They should sing every week; you can't leave it for three months if you're recording. Singers often feel they don't need to rehearse, that they've got the voice, but they do need to rehearse. Singers have the hardest time.

Sometimes it's almost unbelievable. Guitarists will come in with guitar strings that are rusty! They haven't played in that long. Drummers come in with hundred-year-old drumheads—although some people do like that sort of played-out drum sound—Charlie Watts of the Rolling Stones used twenty-year-old drumheads for his distinctive sound!

Always bring extra strings, extra sticks and drumheads. Snare heads in particular get broken.

Type out your lyrics and make two copies, one for the engineer; it makes things easier for him. Writing the chords above the lyrics helps too, if you can do it—and if the engineer can read music.

## What about working relationships in the studio?

People suffer from studio nerves. It's important to feel comfortable; somewhere that's too clinical isn't good for musicians. It's the engineer's job to make the musicians feel like he is on their side.

## What recording tips would you give to new musicians?

*For live bands:*

+ Rehearse fully. Pay particular attention to the rhythm section; make sure the drum and bass parts fit together. Rehearse any overdubs that you have in mind.
+ Work out accurate tempos that you are comfortable playing at. If you plan to play to a click, make sure the drummer can do it.
+ Bring good drumheads and new strings. Don't leave your tuners at home.
+ Lyricists, finish that second verse before you leave for the studio.
+ Work out all the backing vocals in a situation where you can hear what is going on, not in a noisy rehearsal studio.

*For MIDI acts:*

✦ Check with the studio that all your formats are compatible; maybe even send your computer and sampler discs to the studio to make sure they load.

✦ Make backups of everything before you leave for the studio.

✦ If you are doubtful of the quality of the samples you have, take the original source to the studio and resample.

✦ If you are relying on finding sounds at the studio, take a suitable example to the studio so that the engineer or programmer knows what you are talking about.

✦ Make a list for the studio of all the sounds you are using, showing which sound is coming out of which output on which machine and on which MIDI channel.

*General:*

✦ Don't bring lots of drugs or alcohol to the studio. Although it might be good fun, you are unlikely to perform at your best when you are wasted.

✦ If they are not involved in the music, resist the temptation to bring your girlfriend or boyfriend. Sounds harsh, but you will feel you have to entertain them rather than concentrate on the music. It can also split your loyalties between them and your fellow band members.

✦ Be prepared to run over on the time (and hence the budget). This does happen!

✦✦✦✦✦✦✦✦✦✦✦✦✦✦✦✦✦✦✦✦✦✦✦✦✦✦✦✦✦✦✦✦✦✦✦✦✦✦✦✦✦✦✦✦✦✦✦✦

# THE SESSION

✦✦✦✦✦✦✦✦✦✦✦✦✦✦✦✦✦✦✦✦✦✦✦✦✦✦✦✦✦✦✦✦✦✦✦✦✦✦✦✦✦✦✦✦✦✦✦✦

## STU LAMBERT

Stu Lambert has a list of sundry things to bring:

✦ At least two DAT tapes, preferably sixty minutes or longer each

✦ At least two blank CD-Rs, if the studio has CD writing ability (most have)

- ✦ Money to pay the studio, unless you have another arrangement (bring a bit extra in case you need a DAT or tape from their store)
- ✦ Cassettes, either for home reference or of suitable quality for sending to commercial contacts
- ✦ Any portable cassette players you can, for checking mixes
- ✦ Spare 'media' (discs, cartridges) where applicable
- ✦ Fruit, snacks, drinks
- ✦ Undemanding things to do—books, magazines, hand-held games, letters to write
- ✦ Cushions and blankets

### Can you take us through the process, from the start of the session?

At the booked start time, the studio should be absolutely ready for you to begin. There's scope for a little crossing-over time while you get your gear in and set up and have the first brew-up of the day. If you're not working within half an hour of arriving, you should arrange extra time or less money. If you're

---

not punctual, that's your problem. Only the kindliest studio manager will give you a late start if it's your own fault. Running late is no substitute because you're tired, and it messes up the engineer's already tattered lifestyle. Unless you've only booked one day, it's a problem for your next day too. The engineer should be given a quick play of the rough demo, the lyrics or format of the tune and the initial list of parts to be recorded. He or she can then begin planning where to record each track, which is their responsibility (though they will probably want to get stuck in right away, getting a drum kit sound or getting all the MIDI up on the desk). Play some examples of commercial recordings you think are relevant to what you're doing, so they understand your perspective and can help you. You'll need these again when mixing. What actually happens next is similar to the process outlined in the home recording section. The drum part is laid down—perhaps on six or eight tracks—with any necessary guides. Then the performers each add their contribution on separate tracks, either in the live room or in the control room, but usually recording on their own.

It's more pleasant and convenient to record in the control room, which is possible for direct-injected performances (no microphones). These are usually keyboards (including sampled drums, etc.) and bass.

## What are the differences between studio recording and home recording?

There is a skilled person who not only works the studio equipment but makes the decisions about how the recordings are managed. You may be consulted, but it's their job to record and preserve everything you want to a high standard, within the capabilities of the studio equipment. There is more pressure to achieve high quality, as the studio process shows up problems which the demo process conceals. Each performance must be as accurate as possible while remaining lively, and extra parts may have to be added—perhaps even written on the spot—to give the necessary depth to the track. The greater facilities, such as the number of available tape tracks, mixer channels, MIDI modules, sample libraries, percussion instruments, etc. allow more scope for high achievement in quality and in innovation. It's easier, for example, to keep several takes and compile them together as you did in home recording, and it's easier to do successful drop-ins, because professional tape formats respond more quickly. Double-tracked vocals or sub-octave-tracked synth parts can easily be accommodated to give depth to the arrangement.

## What about the communication process during a session?

There are several different communication problems in recording sessions:

### Communicating Ideas

Don't be shy! Music can be very hard to describe in words, so use any words, no matter how strange, which get your idea or feeling across. If the best you can say is that something should sound more 'rubbery' or 'alien' or 'like throwing a dustbin down car park stairs', then say it!

### Communicating from the Live Room or Booth

There are some simple things a studio can do to make this easier, but some don't. It's perfectly easy to set up a separate microphone which feeds the control room speakers but doesn't get recorded. The performers can just talk any time and be heard by the others. Less easy, but very useful, is to have a squawk-box speaker in the live room, which is linked to the engineer's talk-back circuit. Then the performer can hear what's being said, whether they've got their headphones on or not. Simple.

### Communicating Between the Client (You) and the Engineer

It's often best to have a 'spokesperson' for the act—perhaps the person with the most studio experience or technical knowledge. It's much more efficient to agree on what the artists think first, then put your suggestions, observations or criticisms to the engineer. Try to wait until the engineer hasn't got his or her hands on the controls for a moment before raising something with them. Be patient with your fellow-musicians. Even if they are extremely well prepared, the studio imposes different demands. If someone's having trouble with a take, your engineer should be able to advise you on the right balance for your kind of music, of accuracy and feeling. Be careful, though—it's amazing what little errors can slip by until it's too late and then annoy you every time you hear the track. A simple arrangement well played is usually better than shaky playing plastered over with production.

## How do you decide when a recording is finished?

No engineer should ever let a take be approved without hearing the recording back. Even if the last ten takes went down okay, this one may have some problem with it. People doing live-room work often waste time coming out to the control room then going back to the live room. Players in the live room should only come out if the people in the control room are happy and want the

---

players' agreement that it's 'the one' or if discussion is too complicated to hold over the talkback circuit. Recording can be a long, fragmented and boring task. If you're not involved in what's going on, you should try and rest your mind and your ears. You may not be able to go out, though it's a good idea to if you're absolutely sure you won't be needed to okay decisions. But try and go away from the control room, to the reception or an unused room. You might find a quiet place where you can practice, which is an ideal way to kill some time and be really confident when your moment comes. If you can't do that, bury yourself in a magazine or something. Save your attention for playback of takes that need to be approved before moving on.

Another point concerns visitors to the session. It's nice to have some guests drop by to ease the tedium, but conversation can easily build up to a level where it distracts the engineer and leaves the poor soul in the live room feeling left out and struggling to communicate. Maybe it's time for a proper break or a return to serious musicmaking.

## What about MIDI recording sessions?

The flow and timings of a session with few performances or none at all is quite different from recording live performances. More of the session time is spent on the mix and much of the remainder is spent, for less experienced acts, in working with the sounds used in the arrangement that was brought in on disc to make them 'gel'. It's often a problem, when bringing full MIDI and sampled arrangements into a studio, that the sounds seem to stand apart from each other, scattered around the soundscape. The first thing to do is to get your sequencer file running from the studio's sequencer, which should be no problem because you checked that it all worked beforehand, didn't you? Then, if you are using the studio's sampler, get those samples loading and start working progressively on the other sounds. Engineers usually like to get the drum sounds sorted first. When the instrumental mix is roughly there, it's time to record any performances you need, which is just the same process as conventional recording. After that, you could check out the MIDI stuff in the studio rack to see if the sounds you came in with can be improved upon. Generally, I would recommend doubling your own sound and a new one, rather than substituting. Your track evolved with your sounds as its foundations and removing them can affect the integrity of the arrangement. As always, you should keep in mind the total time budget for the recordings, their priority (e.g., single, filler . . .) and maintaining the vibe. The mixing process is the same as for conventional recordings, except that most or all the music is coming from MIDI equipment, not from tape, so changes are possible at any time until the final mix is on two-track. You should save working copies of all data whenever significant changes have been made. You should definitely save copies of all data whenever you finish working on a track. It's best to save to fresh media, so you always have the version you came in with to fall back on if it all goes horribly wrong. (Like when you save Song 2 over Song 1 by accident.)

## How about mixing in the studio?

When you are all sure that the raw materials are good enough for the needs of the session, it's time to build the final mix. Be very sure—any reconsideration now is time-consuming and therefore expensive. Desk settings and routings will be reset and it may be impossible to get a good drop-in, meaning the whole take will have to be done again. You need to decide which song to mix first. You probably have one you think's strongest, but get the engineers' opinion; they have an idea of what will sound good out of this studio. Conventionally, the strongest track is mixed first, but there are problems with this. The first mix takes the brunt of all the distracting tasks, like plugging up effects and getting routings and broad levels. Once sorted, these are usually good for the tracks to come. Hearing a track played back lots of times blunts the ear and the mind, which is a shame for your strongest tune. And though the first track gets the freshness, by the time you mix the second, everything's in the groove. This is a good opportunity for the artists to get out of the studio! The engineer shouldn't need you for a while, as he or she will have lots of basic tasks to do before any comment on the mix is required. Ask them how long they think they will need to put a decent first pass of the mix together and run it to two-track—it should be long enough for you to go out for some food and fresh air. When you come back, the engineer can take a decent break while you play the mix a few times and gather all your notes and thoughts about where it's going. Even if you're running short of time, the chill-out time is well worth it. Brief the engineer before you go. Play the commercial tracks which are like what you're doing. Describing music is hard, so go for the big concepts—'pumping', 'mellow', 'raucous', 'ambient'.

## How do you know when you have got the final mix?

Well, for your first six visits to the studio at least, this is very easy. I recommend that you normally accept the mix the engineer is happy with. Of course, it's your lovingly created music and you have strong feelings about it and an important investment in it. Successful music depends on the expertise of many different people along the way. They're not always right—they're not always even the right people—but those are the cards you're dealt. Your engineer has mixed loads of tracks for loads of acts, in that room, on those speakers. Just tell them what you want and say, 'Give it your best shot'. And all those sessions where, red-eyed, you quibbled over the hi-hat level or whatever were really a waste of time. Showcasing the talent you put into the song and the arrangement feel is 95% of the job and all the rest has serious diminishing returns. The mix you hear while the engineer takes a break isn't 'the one', of course. When they return refreshed, they will start refining it and should sometimes check that you're happy with the way it's going. Unless you're really unhappy, just say, 'Yeah, yeah, it's coming on nicely', which gives them the confidence they need to make decisions on your behalf. There's a temptation, even among engineers, to spend too long mixing the first song at the expense of the rest. It does have the setup time mentioned above, but try and keep things in proportion. Plan for this. Take the number of hours you have left, less one hour for setting up the first mix and doing tape copies at the end. If appropriate, take off break times as well. Divide by the number of tunes you want to mix, assuming they're all about the same length. Voilà! To sum up, the main things you should check on a mix are that it sounds reasonably like the commercial examples you played and that it still sounds like that when you play it on different equipment. Before approving each mix, make a quick cassette copy and play it on anything you can. Different things show up different devices: a Walkman isn't very reliable, but it is good for spotting detail problems and it will show if the mix is harsh or toppy; a car system will probably react to aggressive bass signals; and so on. Studios have different sets of speakers to try and imitate this and engineers will switch between them, but the good ones go and play cassettes on the office hi-fi or in their car. You only need to hear about a minute, when the track's at its fullest, to know if there's a problem. Here is an example of a typical mix budget:

+ Session: 11 a.m. till 9 p.m. (ten hours)
+ Lunch and supper breaks: thirty minutes each = one hour
+ Setup half-hour and tape copies half-hour = one hour
+ Four tracks to mix: eight hours = an average of two hours per track

## Anything else an act needs to know about recording?

Yes, you need to copy and back up your work. Before CD writers were available, it was vital to get a few cassettes made at the studio, unless someone owned a DAT machine, to cover the gap until you were ready to use a tape duplication house. Now, all you really need is a decent-quality copy—preferably

a CD-R, failing that a MiniDisc if someone has a MiniDisc recorder. If neither is possible, you need to arrange to have two or three cassettes run off either while you clear away or during 'dead time' in the next few days. The DATs may have a lot of stuff—unused mixes, false starts—which you don't want to distribute, so it may be best to make one copy of the whole DAT and one 'greatest hits'. You certainly need to back up the DAT. Some engineers do this as they go, either recording to two machines simultaneously or doing a digital transfer once the mixes of a track are finished and the next mix is being set up (my preferred method). If not, then either a CD-R or another DAT is essential. If there's only one DAT machine, perhaps the DAT can be transferred to a computer and back out to fresh tape. Again, this doesn't need doing right away, but it must be done within a few days. Back up any data which have changed since you arrived. Last but not least is paying for the session. The studio is entitled to keep the masters until you've paid, unless you have an account arrangement. If you're unhappy about any aspect of the service you have had from the studio and the engineer, this is the last time you can expect to negotiate for a reduction on that basis. If you pay the full amount, you are assumed to be satisfied. It may be easier to negotiate for more studio time than to reduce the payment. Make sure you get something on paper indicating what you have paid, and keep it safe.

✦✦✦✦✦✦✦✦✦✦✦✦✦✦✦✦✦✦✦✦✦✦✦✦✦✦✦✦✦✦✦✦✦✦✦✦✦✦✦✦✦✦✦✦✦✦✦✦

## BEN GRIMES

How do professional musicians approach that expensive studio time? See what Ben Grimes from US rock group Golden Republic has to say.

The Kansas City, Missouri, rock group Golden Republic consider themselves to be primarily a studio band, despite their extensive touring schedule. Spending every moment they're not on the road in the studio, the four-piece have a full home recording studio which they use to prepare material that will be completed in a professional studio. By 2005, these recordings had been issued as an EP, *People*, and an eponymous LP on Astralwerks. Vocalist Ben Grimes takes us through various aspects of studios and recording.

### What is the role of the studio today?

The recording studio used to be where you captured the essence of the band. Now the studio is where you create the essence because people go there to put stuff down but also tinker with it. It used to be if you were an amazing band you

would go in there, set up microphones and play all your stuff. In a day you would record your whole album. People would go see them live and the sound would be the same. There's a whole science of recording now where you can make a band sound a hundred times better than they really are.

Nowadays, they can take okay bands and put them in the studio and create technical wonders and the band has to live up to that once it's done.

### What's the difference between a professional studio and home studio recording?

Nowadays, the technology is out there so that you can spend $1,000 on a piece of equipment, take the time to learn how to use it well, and make a really great recording at home. At this point, I have a $300 piece of equipment at home that is state of the art and as good sounding a recording device as all of those top-notch recording studios in the Sixties were.

Usually a home recording won't have the polish and sound as cohesive as a studio recording will, but sometimes that's what bands are going for. By recording solely at home, you also miss out on the advantage of having other people around to guide you along and help you get through the different technical aspects of what you can do. Having somebody else to take care of that so you can focus on creating your music is a great thing to have. It empowers you  to make your creation the best you can without worrying about where some track you just recorded has disappeared to and spending hours looking through your manual.

### What does a commercial studio offer?

It provides you with a place where you can take your song and really peel it apart, strip it down, and take it any direction you want to. There are endless possibilities for different variations. But you have to have the right people working on it and who know how to use all the stuff.

### What are the roles of the various people in the studio?

If it's a commercial studio, you'll have an engineer who is the person that controls and runs all the equipment and knows how all that works. Usually, if you're doing an album for a record label, you'll also have a producer, who is the person who helps creatively to shape the sound and guide the recording process.

### What does the average studio look like?

An average studio is several different rooms all centred and conjoined around the control room. The control room is where you have the mixing board that all the signals are run through. You have a performance room to catch the actual performances where a lot of the instruments are set up. There are also smaller rooms called isolation booths where you would record vocals, certain guitar tracks, and things where you need a more confined sound.

### What are the different recording systems?
Analogue, which is recording to tape, is multi-track. That means you can record the different instruments, sounds and vocals each on a separate track, so that once you've laid them down you can tinker with them all separately and decide how you want to use them and mix them together.

Digital recording, which records the music you're creating as digital information can be tinkered with much in the same way as multi-tracks on a tape, except there are far more possibilities because it's in a computer. The only drawback to digital recording is that a lot of people feel like it doesn't sound as good or organic as analogue recording.

### What is the best way for a new band to approach recording in a studio?
The way you play live is the truest expression of the band that you are. Don't use the studio as an excuse to try and reshape that; rather, try to capture that. The way your instruments sound in a room is the way your instruments are supposed to sound, so bear that in mind as you go for it.

When you go into a recording studio, the best way to approach it is one song at a time. Lots of times people will record the drums, the bass, the guitars and the vocals for every song—do them all almost factory style. If you approach it a song at a time, you're able to perfect each song as you're going rather leaving it until you get to the end to look at everything and try to make all these minute changes.

### What can musicians do to prepare themselves?
Practice the songs over and over and over until your eyes bleed and your head hurts. Put everything into it so you can know those songs inside and out. Know them so well that it's sick. Get really good at playing them so that once you get in the studio you don't waste time messing up your parts. You should get in there and nail it out like you've been doing in weeks and weeks of practice. Don't try and write in the studio. If you have millions of dollars to spend on a studio, then you can write in the studio. If you are a new band, don't even think about writing in the studio.

## What are some of the starting steps in getting ready to go to the studio?

You need to get in touch with the people you're going to be working with at the actual studio. It's good to talk music with them. Talk about some of the albums that sound the way you want your recording to sound, and make sure they've heard you before. Make sure everybody's on the same page as far as what you want to accomplish. Always be on time. Bring with you every imaginable thing you could need in the studio. You'll spend a lot of time with your instruments' setup, doing mike placements and moving your amps and drums around inside the room and seeing what works best because there are endless possibilities of how a room will sound, good or bad.

## How long does it take to get everything ready?

It depends on how you want to do it. If you can get into a studio where you can get all your equipment and mic it all up, you can spend four or five hours getting mics set up and everything ready. Once it's ready, just start playing your songs and get them on to tape. For a new band trying to get recordings, that's a great way to do it. A lot of times it sounds much truer and more exciting to hear than if you go up and do it instrument by instrument. You can do an entire album in no time that way.

Personally, I tend to start with the bare minimum of acoustic guitar and vocals and build from there. A couple of guys in my band, the way they work is to do as much stuff as possible and then peel back the layers until it feels like it's not too crowded and that's when it's right. We end up in the middle and it works.

Once you go through to the end of the process of recording, if you're mixing it there in the studio, you'll go through all the songs, get a rough mix and do final edits. Make sure everything is cleaned up, get rid of all the extra little tracks that might have gotten left on there that you didn't want to be there. Once you've cleaned that up, you'll start on the final mix.

## What happens in the mixing process? How is that different from mastering?

Mixing is the process of making sure all the volumes are correct but also making sure that you got effects on the stuff you want effects on—tweaking the sounds to make sure everything has the right tone you want. You should mix one song at a time, too. Recording and mixing are both situations where you want to approach it a song at a time.

Once you've got all that set and all your levels are good, if you're really happy with that sound as an album, from there you'll send it off to somebody

---

to master it. All that means is that they'll make sure the album as a whole sounds together. Mastering is largely about making the album sound cohesive. They'll make sure all the songs are the same volume and the overall EQs, so there's nothing that's too piercing on the record. They'll make it sound nice and pleasant and ready for consumption.

### Are you involved in the mixing process?
It's something I like to leave to the professionals. I find my ear gets confused the more I listen to mixing. It gets to where they'll change something in the mixing and either I can't tell what they did or it doesn't sound any better, it just sounds different.

Whenever we're in the mixing process, I listen to what we've got and I tell them what I think needs to be done, then I leave. I let the mixing engineer process what I said and do his translation of what he got out of what I said. I'll go back in and listen to it again. I say what I think should be different and leave again. I never stay in the studio when they're actually making changes.

### How do you know when you have the final mix?
When it feels right. You kind of know how it's supposed to feel from the get-go and once it feels that certain way you can tell. Ultimately, it just needs to capture the energy of what that song is intended to be.

Technically, it's really different from song to song. If it's a really aggressive rock song then you want to get your guitars loud and your vocals as high as you can. A lot of times you'll add effects, reverbs and whatever, in the mixing process to bring the most out of that sound. At the same time, you can be in a little room with a tape recorder and an acoustic guitar and you're singing your song and you're done. Technically it's impossible to say. It depends on the song.

### What are the logistics of scheduling in the studio?
Usually a professional studio has what they call their 'B room', which is not the main studio, but the other studio in the same complex. It usually has a more affordable engineer, sounds almost as good, and will oftentimes be half the price. If there's a band recording, they'll record from 9 to 5 or 6 or 7, do it during the daytime. A lot of times if you talk to the studios, they'll let you get in there from 7 p.m. until midnight and have those five hours for a way discounted rate.

There's a studio here in town that's $1,500 a day. Friends of ours have gone in there and done the 7 p.m.-to-midnight block. That whole time cost them $150. The studio wouldn't be making any money if they didn't give that studio time to a band. For engineers, there are interns who are unpaid but need experience, a certain number of hours behind the board for credits for school. If it's an intern the studio trusts, they'll give them the key.

## Do you have suggestions on how to communicate in the studio?

Communicating in recording is a funny, difficult thing. A friend of mine was in a recording session with someone who didn't like the way the guitar sounded. The way she described it to him was the guitar sounded like chickens and she wanted it to sound more like marshmallows. After you've been in the studio for a while you get a sense of that and understand what that means. It's really hard to describe sound verbally, to pick up a phrase that sums up what something sounds like. It's almost like describing colour. It's too abstract. Having a lot of records on hand that you can reference is really helpful. Usually, if you have an idea and you can think of something that somebody did on another record that is similar to the sort of sound, you can play it for the engineer. That's a lot easier than trying to say, 'I want it to sound like cement' or something.

When you're in the isolation booth, you can't see whom you're talking to and they're talking to you through your headphones. When you're singing, a lot of times they're sitting in the control room listening to you sing without any of the music, just your vocal, which is naked and awkward-sounding. When we're recording, I hate listening to the playback of just my vocal, but you have to.

## How do you treat working relationships in the studio?

The big thing is to be really open to criticism. In the studio, you're going to get it from your bandmates and you will want to give it to your bandmates more than anywhere else. That's where you're making this lasting impression of what that song is. Be open to criticism and ready and willing to accept it. Decide ahead of time that you're not going to let yourself get mad because somebody's going to say you sang something off-key. Don't take that personally. They want the album to sound as good as you do. Talk about it ahead of time. Make sure that everybody is prepared to not take offence.

Similarly, if the engineer and producer hear something that bothers them they must be able to say so. Especially if you're a young band in the studio, the producer almost all the time is going to have way more experience than the band does. Taking criticism is a useful tool. You just have to be humble enough to use it.

## Any other nonrecording tips for being in the studio?

Bring tea and honey for your throat because you're going to be singing a lot.

Bring mindless distractions for when you're not working on something, so you can veg out and not think. Time in the recording studio when you're not actually recording is some of the most mind-numbing hours you can spend. Be prepared, but more than that, keep your spirits up and keep things loose and fun. It's more important to enjoy the recording process than to really fret over it and freak out and worry that you're going to fuck it up somehow. Recording can be stressful, and it usually is to some degree, but it doesn't have to be so bad. It can be a really fun thing. When you make it fun and make it an enjoyable, creative process in and of itself, it can be a great time.

✦✦✦✦✦✦✦✦✦✦✦✦✦✦✦✦✦✦✦✦✦✦✦✦✦✦✦✦✦✦✦✦✦✦✦✦✦✦✦✦✦✦✦✦✦✦✦✦✦

## RECORD PRODUCER

A record producer takes a direct role in the recording studio working with the musicians and the engineer to help create that perfect track. The role includes working on sounds and arrangements, engineering the recording through to the final mixes, sometimes even writing the material. The job varies considerably from project to project and artist to artist, depending on the level of production required. Many record producers started off in the studio as sound engineers; others were musicians and moved into production.

✦✦✦✦✦✦✦✦✦✦✦✦✦✦✦✦✦✦✦✦✦✦✦✦✦✦✦✦✦✦✦✦✦✦✦✦✦✦✦✦✦✦✦✦✦✦✦✦✦

### TOPHER MOHR

Guitarist Topher Mohr is a producer and session arranger at the Manhattan Producers Alliance, a network of composers based in New York City. He started out in Detroit as a contemporary of Eminem and Kid Rock, and later toured the US

with Top 40 pop band Custom ('Hey Mister'). He often collaborates with songwriter Wayne Cohen (see p. 314), putting tracks together for a variety of artists, and he still gigs regularly with hip-hop and R&B acts in New York.

**How did you get into production?**

I was hired to play guitar and sing backup with an artist that Wayne Cohen was developing. Through that, he heard some of the things I was working on and hired me to do drum programming. The more that he could see what I was able to do, the more he hired me for other things. I do a lot of string arrangements, because songwriters are now more concerned with having a master-quality sounding product. It's not as polished as something going on a record to be released, but it's as good as they can get without having to hire a bunch of extra musicians. Being able to handle that has gotten me a lot of extra work.

**So you mostly work on the arrangements of a track yourself rather than calling up musicians to play on the track?**

Yes, it's pretty much something I do on my own. I can handle the bass and guitar stuff and I can do the drum programming myself. If I need other instruments, I can do that with virtual instruments on the computer. Then, if the person I'm working for decides they want a real drummer we'll hire one, but that's not really my job.

**What sort of material are you given to make an arrangement of?**

I'm usually given a really rough vocal and maybe a rhythm guitar, just so I know how the song goes, and that'll give me an idea of what they're trying to do stylistically. Sometimes they'll have good ideas, but you do have to learn how to tell people that something may not be a good idea at all. That's part of the gig too, the psychology of it. I'll send mp3s of my progress on a track to the person and they'll send me back comments, such as they like the drum track but not the strings, and I'll keep working on it until it's something that they like.

**What other skills do you need to be a good producer and session arranger?**

You've got to know your technology and be proficient in which programme you like best, whether it's ProTools or Nuendo or Apple Logic or Propellerhead's Reason. It doesn't hurt to be proficient in several of the main programmes because different people use different things. Basically, you have to be able to get your ideas into something tangible. That was a skill I wasn't really into but over the past couple of years I've developed it through necessity.

**Why did you move from regular gigging to production?**
While I was playing in Detroit I got an offer to audition for a band in New York City, fell in love with the city and moved out here. Since then, I've been doing session work as a guitarist, but I also realised that I needed to diversify to make a living. So I got into production and taught myself to do drum programming and things like that. I've become a little too old to be a sideman in Top 40 pop groups—I'm twenty-seven—but I'm young as a producer, and that helps me a lot. People want my young ears.

**How do you get work as a producer or session musician?**
The biggest thing is putting yourself out there. You can be the best player in the world but if you're sitting in your room waiting for the phone to ring, it'll probably never happen. You must do something every day to put yourself out there. It's something I have to remind myself of all the time. Go to open-mic nights and jam sessions and meet other musicians in your area. That's really who gets you work, other musicians. Do something that'll make people want to have your number. If you played with a drummer on something and he likes your playing and then he has a session and somebody asks him if he knows any guitar players, he's going to recommend you.

✦✦✦✦✦✦✦✦✦✦✦✦✦✦✦✦✦✦✦✦✦✦✦✦✦✦✦✦✦✦✦✦✦✦✦✦✦✦✦✦✦✦✦✦

# putting out your own record

This section looks at the decision to produce commercial quantities of your recordings for sale and at making copies for promotion.

## GOALS

You are ready to put out your own record when you are confident that you can reach a wider audience with a product which already has proven sales potential from DJ play or gig sales (using small-run copying to establish this). You may decide that Internet sales or press coverage of gigs or white labels is enough to go on. The goals are:

+ To make a direct profit from sales
+ To bring your music to the attention of the media and of possible backers, including record companies
+ To be a good start in founding your own record company

## STRATEGY

### Market Testing

Before you even investigate mass-production, take your music on CD-R, cassette or test pressing to people who can give you an opinion which will be roughly in line with what will be said by the people whose support you will need to succeed.

Independent record shops can tell you whether your style is popular in their shop and whether you offer something which would sell against the competition. They can also advise you as to which distributors are good at handling your kind of music.

Distributors know what shops will buy and, to an extent, what publicity you can get. (See 'Distribution', p. 249.)

### Do Preliminary Costings

Work out how much it will cost you to end up with five hundred copies of a saleable product. (See 'Manufacturing', p. 265.) Put funding in place for this. You will almost certainly be asked to pay cash in advance at first, and even if you arrange an account facility, it's best not to rely on getting money from sales to settle the whole account. As you work through the promotion phase, you may become sure that you will sell more than five hundred.

### Secure Distribution or Enough Retail Commitment

You don't absolutely have to have a distributor, especially for dance records. If you can guess that you will recover costs of perhaps £750 from expected direct sales to shops, you have a viable product. No distributor will guarantee you sales, but in theory they won't take it on unless it is likely to be profitable for you.

### Make Copies for Promotional Use

Discuss what release formats to use with your distributor. In general, you will promote the product using the main format in which you anticipate selling records, once the promotion has given you confidence to go ahead. If your market is for 12" vinyl, the people you're promoting to need to use it in that format, so you will have to absorb the cost of lacquers at this stage. (You could do acetates or 'dub plates', but these are generally not cost-effective at this point.) If you plan to release on CD or 7", you can use formats which have a lower start-up cost—CD-R or cassette. CD-R is the better option, as it looks more 'committed' and is the format used for most record company product.

## PRESS AND PROMOTION

### PROMOTING THE RECORD

Promotion covers advertising, press, radio, club promotions, TV and remixing. For new artists, press (editorial coverage), radio and club promotions (if you do the latter yourself) and good old word of mouth are your best bet.

At this stage you can forget advertising, because it's just not worth your while and it's too expensive, and national TV, because there's no way (unless you've got some extremely influential friends or one of your relatives is a video producer) that you're going to be able to afford a video of the quality they now expect. The days of ruff 'n' ready, cheap 'n' cheerful videos seem to be over—although there are internet opportunities to broadcast (vlogs) on sites such as YouTube. And trying to get on and play live is equally impossible. Getting a live slot on shows like *Parkinson*, *Jonathan Ross*, *Later with Jools Holland* in Britain and *The Late Show with David Letterman*, *The Tonight Show with Jay Leno* or *Jimmy Kimmel Live* in the US is hard enough for relatively famous bands with chart hits to brandish, let alone a band just starting out. (See what Mark Jones of PIAS/Wall of Sound says about this on p. 297.)

Club promotions can also be quite expensive if you use a specialised promotions company. Your best bet is to find out which clubs are playing your music, get to know who the DJs are and give or send them the records yourself. If you're doing the right thing, they'll soon be approaching you to be on your DJ mailing list. And watch out: given that many DJs still want vinyl, a big mailing list is a very expensive thing to keep up. It's not cheap sending out vinyl records around the country.

### Word of Mouth

Never underestimate the power of chat. Word of mouth sells a high proportion of all records. People like turning others on to music they love and it's a big influence on sales. But don't leave everything to chance; you can help your-self along here. If you're a DJ you will be clubbing either for enjoyment or play-ing out. You cannot help but meet up with people who are interested in your records and will pass on the word; likewise, many of them will also be DJs and will hope you will do the same for them.

Bands meet other bands on the gigging circuit and recommend music to fans, the press and the industry in general. They may want to release an-other band's music on their own label. This was the case for Emperor Sly. When the band first set up Zip Dog Records, they got distribution and re-leased a few singles. Emperor Sly toured to promote their records and met many other bands and DJs on the gig circuit doing similar music and were looking for a way of getting their music out. So before Emperor Sly even made their first-artist album, the band did a compilation album of people they had been gigging with or who they had met through being part of a scene.

One of the aims of the compilation—which had a combination of 'names' and little-known or unknown artists—was to try to broaden the awareness of Emperor Sly's first-artist album by releasing a compilation which had the band itself on it with other acts that people around the country and abroad would know. Emperor Sly were part of a scene that included a lot of people who were not releasing on commercial labels, so putting them on a compilation did them a favour and helped the band too. Unlike some other types of business, one of the key features of the music industry is helping each other out when you can. It's that all-important contacts issue again.

Last but not least, word of mouth costs nothing!

<hr />

++++++++++++++++++++++++++++++++++++++++++++++++++++

## DAVID GLEDHILL

UK act Gledhill worked hard on its own promotions as an unsigned band. Vo-calist and band founder David Gledhill explains why publicising yourself is so important—whether going it alone or going for a deal.

David started by recording songs in his bedroom, and his homegrown demos got him a record deal and an unsigned demo landed him play on BBC Radio 1.

### When did you first get into music?
My father was a music teacher and went to the Guildhall Music School where he trained in classical music with people like John Lord from Deep Purple. So

from when I was born up until I was sixteen, I grew up listening to classical music. My dad used to practice four hours a day and tried to get me to do

it, but I wasn't interested! My parents also used to play the Beatles, Beach Boys, the Stones, and listening to them I knew I'd rather play pop or rock. By the age of six, I was writing songs, and later, for me, there were only two careers: to be a rock star or play for Liverpool football club—as I'm not good enough at football, it had to be a rock star!

**Is Gledhill your first band?**
No, I started off in a band called Slo-Mo, signed to a little indie label called Circus. This was more underground Beck-type music using a lot of samples and I recorded the album in my bedroom. It was a good learning experience for me, being signed to Circus—finding out about press and promotion, about licensing and, perhaps the best experience, finding out how much sampling cost! Then it all fell apart as Circus went bankrupt. But there was amazing press. The best one was an American journalist, Robert Christgau for the *Village Voice* in New York, who raved about the album—and this from a journalist who reviewed all the big bands.

It was a very cult thing. A track from the album went on to a Sony PlayStation 2 game called Driver 3, one of the biggest ever driving games, which sold eight million copies. I still get weird e-mails from people in Japan wanting to buy the album—which goes on eBay for £30 to £40! It's nice, but I'm not into going over old stuff.

**How did you get the Circus deal?**
It was through the manager I had at the time. Circus was a label belonging to Bernard McMahon, who was press officer for lots of big bands, like Garbage. My manager passed him a tape and he was on the phone that day wanting to

sign me. It was a small label and didn't have much money and it was a good experience for me to learn how much pluggers cost and press people—how expensive everything is. I've learned from this how Gledhill can avoid this trap—that everything that gets spent is ultimately paid for by the band. The record company may pay for it now, but the band will eventually pay for it. It's a lesson people need to learn; your royalties are miniscule compared to what record labels earn. George Michael was right! As far as I'm concerned, a record label is like a bank, willing to take a risk and offering you a high interest rate! When I was eighteen I had no idea about all this. Ten years later, I do know! Now if we want to do a video or a photo shoot, I want to know how much it costs. The business has really changed. You have to be much more savvy as an artist. You have to be able to multi-task; record companies expect you to do so. You can't just sit back and think all you need to do is write songs. You have to understand the business, too.

### How and when did you form Gledhill?

During the Slo-Mo period I became good friends with Nigel Heywood at Universal. He loved the music and that was how Gledhill started. I started writing and recording—I did it all, bass, guitar, vocals, etc.—and he thought the demos were fantastic and said I must put a band together. He also came up with the name for the band. I couldn't think of one, and I've always thought someone's name sounds a bit arrogant, but he thought it was a good name.

I'm from Sheffield and I put a band together from all the best players in the city. I am the vocalist and play rhythm guitar and the other members are Tom Jarvis, lead guitar; Julian Gallagher, bass guitar; Tracey Wilkinson, keyboards/backing vocals; and Liam Oliver, drums. Our sound is a development of a 1980s sound and we're all 1980s freaks—we love albums like U2's *Joshua Tree,* which is timeless—you can't date it. It was never our intent to be underground with this band. My philosophy is to play the sort of songs that will get us as huge as possible. Some bands want to be achingly hip but it's easy to go out of fashion: here today and gone tomorrow. This is not for us.

### When did you make your first recording. How did you pay for it?

Because I did Slo-Mo, there was a demand for tracks. For the first Gledhill record, we worked with Owen Morris (Oasis), paid for by a small label called Nomadic. We recorded in London and it went okay but Nomadic wanted to sign us and we weren't sure.

Everyone said the track 'Resurrect Me' was really good, so I decided to test it out by sending out an unsolicited demo. I've always really looked up to Simon Williams, who runs the Fierce Panda label. He's like a God to me—he put out the first singles by Coldplay and Keane when everyone else passed on them loads of times. He's done so many singles from good bands. I sent him an unsolicited demo and didn't hear anything for a while. This was because he was on holiday in Sussex. He was driving in his car playing my demo when his wife asked him if he'd phoned us. When he said no, she asked why not! He stopped the car and phoned us up.

We went into the studio with Andy Green (Keane) and it turned out to be the most expensive single Fierce Panda has ever done! Although we made one of the cheapest videos probably ever to be played on MTV! This guy did it on a camcorder for £150 and it got a few plays on MTV2—so you can do things on a budget and get them to work.

I then found out that all those big bands that Simon gave a chance to have never given him any points—he's never done a contract with anyone. I thought it only honourable to give him half a point [half a percent out of the artist royalties]. So we drew up a contract so he would get half a point if we signed a major deal.

### As an unsigned band, how did you get a demo played by BBC Radio 1's Zane Lowe?

We were talking to a plugger called Stuart Bridgeman and he gave it to Zane. Circumstances meant we couldn't go with Stuart, but we really liked him. At the time, we were unsigned and it was a great thing to get played on Radio 1. We got a lot of reaction from people, just from that one play.

### What were the next steps in your recording career, leading to being signed to your label MX3?

It was through Nigel Heywood. We had other labels after us, but Nigel put together a good deal and he believed in us. The label is backed by Sony BMG, although it operates as an independent label. So it's like being on a small label but with big-label advantages, like distribution.

### What advice would you give to bands starting out?

The most important thing is networking. When I was eighteen and starting out I had no clue but after Slo-Mo I put together a list of contacts and now I spend 75% of my time on the phone or e-mailing contacts, 10% of time on songs and 15% on the band. Frustrating but it's paid dividends. I have a friend in Sheffield who says 'Shy bands get nowt' and it's so true. My main criticism of unsigned bands is they think their music is good enough not to have to spend time networking but they're wrong. You can be great but still not get anywhere if you don't put the effort in. It's the biggest lesson I've learned over the past two years. Keeping in contact with pluggers, label people, salespeople, studio people, it makes things so much easier. They'll help you out and tell you things you'd never find out otherwise. I can't stress networking enough. My life has changed because of it.

If you're a songwriter, you'd be mad not to join MCPS and PRS [for more details see page 402]. So many new musicians don't realise they will get paid for being played on the radio if they are members. I get something like 3p for every record sold! So you can see that a lot of your income can come from other sources.

Try and enjoy yourselves in case it doesn't last. Most bands get dropped, so enjoy it! It's such good fun, the best thing I've ever done, and even if we do get dropped I'm glad I had this experience.

✦✦✦✦✦✦✦✦✦✦✦✦✦✦✦✦✦✦✦✦✦✦✦✦✦✦✦✦✦✦✦✦✦✦✦✦✦✦✦✦✦✦✦✦

## Press

If you are happy with your record, it might be worth approaching some specialist music journalists, asking them what they think of it, whether they think they could get reviews printed and whether they know any press companies that they feel give a reasonably good service to your area of music. Then you can approach the press and PR (public relations) companies and ask them if they can get a relevant spread of press coverage for your record. This is all before you've done anything but make CD-Rs. So all you've invested in is a few pounds and some time.

What a press or PR company can do for you will vary with the type of music you are making. If you are making dance singles, you will start by getting your tunes to DJs in clubs—these DJs often also review singles for dance magazines or have radio shows. If you are a live band, you should probably get yourself a PR person at the early stages of your gigging career, bearing in mind rock PRs are generally A&R-orientated and can give you a boost up the slippery slope if you want to get signed to a record label. Rock or pop or alternative PR is more of an all-round service than dance PR. Whether you want to make it independently or you want a record company willing to spend lots of money on you, you have to get yourself noticed first.

A PR can help you all the way through your career because a good PR person won't just know journalists, they'll know DJs, club people, venue people and so on, and a good PR will fit the strands together.

PR can also be a good way to get into the system, to meet people in the music industry. So if you want to be a DJ, for example, try dance PR or promotions so you can meet people; if you want to be an artist, then try doing PR for the same reason. It's a great way to make contacts. Be warned though, it's long hours and hard work!

When you decide to use a PR company, always ask them how busy they are. Try to find out if they have any retainer deals—deals where they work on a long-term basis for a company. If a PR company has major projects, those projects will be the ones that get most attention. You need to know what else you are competing with—what else your PR handles—and be aware of where you stand in their list of priorities. Always ask for weekly reports—if you're not getting access to your PR, the chances are they're too busy.

With smaller labels, a PR company will do targeted projects. Ask for a press plan—which magazines or newspapers they're going to approach. Demand press updates—you should get photocopies of your press cuttings or ask your PR to buy two copies of the magazines in question and bill you.

So, if you think you are ready to go professional on press, Stephen Emms in the UK and Wendy Weisberg in the US further demystify the press for you.

## STEPHEN EMMS

Stephen Emms worked for some prestigious independent PR and press companies before taking the plunge and starting his own PR company, Emms Publicity. He has been successful in promoting a wide range of acts, from newcomers to established acts, ranging from indie and rock bands through to hip-hop, soul and dance. He highlights the importance of PR in the industry process, from getting valuable press to getting signed.

### How did you get into press?

While studying for a degree in English Literature at Newcastle University, I started doing work experience for various record and PR companies in the summer holidays. I did a stint at Virgin just as the Spice Girls released their first single, but the company I did the most unpaid work for was Poole Edwards, the previous incarnation of the Outside Organization. At the time, they looked after artists like David Bowie and Norman Cook, so it was exciting for a twenty-one-year-old like me! I also worked for free on magazines, including *Attitude* and *TOTP*. Then when Poole Edwards split in 1997, I was lucky enough to be offered a job as junior press officer at the Point Publicity.

## Why did you set up your own company?

At the Point Publicity I worked on various artists, from established stars such as Nik Kershaw and Charlie Watts through to indie bands and DJs like Paul Oakenfold, but after four years at the com-

pany—two of which I had been head of press—I decided that it was time for a fresh challenge. I asked a couple of clients if they fancied coming with me, and they said yes, which was a stroke of luck. I never expected Emms to be successful though—I thought it would just be me on my own in a tiny office somewhere, working one account at a time. Now, four years later, I'm really lucky that I've got the best team and some brilliant artists, ranging from indie and rock bands through to hip-hop, soul and quality dance acts.

## Would you recommend PR as a good way into the industry for musicians and DJs?

It's a certain way to make contacts, so in that way, yes. However, I think you'll succeed better in music PR if your heart is really 100% in it; that is, in maintaining an open mind about music, trying to get inside what makes a band tick and also having impeccable writing and communication skills. At Emms, we are a creative PR agency, so we also place additional emphasis on the artist's visual presentation, from art directing photo shoots through to styling and brand consultancy.

## I'm a fledgling artist, I've just done a few gigs or got a record out. Why, in your view, should I go for an indie PR company. How will this help me, or should I do it myself?

If you have no budget at all, the best thing to do is mail a four-track sampler to a few PR companies that you like the look of. The best way to find the right PR company is through either personal recommendation or on the Internet. If a company is slow to get back to you, call them once or twice, but generally

Warren Suicide

Akala

Nate

Suicide Sports Club

they'll respond only if they feel it's a project they can take on, particularly at an early stage in your career when they may be working the project at cost level or even for free.

A PR company will help because it can generate the first initial buzz of press, from mags like *Music Week* to the *NME* or *The Fly*, which can lead to a band getting signed or played on the radio. It's as simple as that: nowadays, the best PR companies play a key A&R role, where they're constantly on the lookout for new bands and can be instrumental in getting them signed. As major record company A&R scouts can be followers rather than leaders, they often call PR companies for tip-offs about what acts are hot at the moment.

So, getting in with a PR company is probably the best thing you can do if you are a fledgling band.

### Will PR companies take on new artists for little or no fee to help them?

Yes. We work with all sorts of bands at different stages in their career, but I only take on a band for little or no fee if I think they're good enough to generate press coverage and/or get signed. Recent artists we've worked with from an early stage in their career include the Berlin-based electro-rock trio Warren Suicide, which had never played in the UK before we started working with them—by the time we had finished their album campaign they had four-star reviews in the national press and 9 out of 10 stars in NME!

Another is alternative UK hip-hop artist Akala. He's in an interesting one because we believed in him from the start and worked him in specialist urban press for free, and as a result were employed to do press around his debut single and subsequent releases. We ended up securing a great feature in *The Observer Magazine*, as well as new talent slots in titles as varied as *Metro* and *Blues & Soul Magazine*.

We also work charity projects for little or no fee. Last year, we did press on an album that was recorded by thirty-eight kids in Nairobi to overcome poverty in the slums, and secured the front cover of *G2* magazine. We also currently work with a Brixton-based charity called the Good Samaritan Music Project, which aims to get kids off the streets and into music. In such a context as this, it's all about using our contacts positively.

So, really, it depends on the artist and whether we feel they're right for Emms. If we do take an artist on at an early stage, I would put in a clause in the contract which would mean we would retain the contract should everything go well and the band go on to get signed.

---

## What do you want an artist to bring to you to get your interest?

Songs. The best songs ever. Songs that grab you, that stand out, that feel different from the mountain of CDs we get sent, some of which are at best average, and at worst terrible. We're looking after a fantastic Sheffield-based five-piece band called Gledhill and they stood out when we first played their demo simply by having genius songs. Every single track on the five-track demo sounded like an instant classic; it really was songwriting of the highest order, so it was obvious that once they were in a studio with a proper producer the tracks would blow your mind! They recorded their debut album with Owen Morris, who produced Oasis's *What's the Story (Morning Glory)* and the Verve's *Urban Hymns*.

A band also needs to have a striking visual image, or at least the potential to look good. Music is aspirational and bands need to tap into people's imagination; they need to fill a hole in people's lives. As I said, we're a creative company so we can advise here and make recommendations about visual presentation (if necessary), although we prefer the band to have at least some feel for how they want to look. We're working with another great band called Suicide Sports Club, who came to us with ideas, but nothing concrete. We discussed it all and, with the help of a photographer, came up with a very striking visual image.

Last, a good story is preferable, although this will grow as the band gains in experience and history. Some artists or bands come to us with a story that we just know will excite the media (the aforementioned Akala, for example, is Ms Dynamite's brother), and with others, well, you know you have to dig a bit deeper to try and piece it all together in order to write something that will generate interest. Sometimes we have fun with a band's story—for a certain band on Rob Da Bank's Sunday Best label, we created a load of 'myths' around them to let journalists create their own story.

## What should you look for in a PR company?

A band should look for genuine enthusiasm and make sure that the company's roster isn't full of acts at a similar stage in their career. After all, a company can only break so many bands at any one time. A band should also check that they feel the company has the right vision, genuine contacts and understands their needs and what makes them tick. The boss of the company should also be personally involved and passionate about making the project work. It's all about connection at the end of the day: you have to feel that they are on a similar wavelength as you.

## How do you persuade journalists to take notice of a record?

We set up meetings with key journalists to discuss priority releases, and we might encourage the band to play live to a selection of key tastemakers, or aim to get one key publication on board at an early stage. Using the Gledhill example again, my aim was to play the debut single, 'Remain', to the editor of *NME* as early as possible and certainly before anyone else had heard it. This is important, as key journalists expect a certain level of exclusivity.

Other ways to get the media interested in a new band or record is to feed them news and 'behind-the-scenes' pictures of video shoots, recording sessions or tours with or without other known artists. With Gledhill, we took pictures of their recording sessions with Owen Morris, as we thought stills such as these would generate interest in itself, such is Morris's reputation in the industry.

With established artists, our job is easier and there is normally a level of interest preceding a release anyway, so in that situation we have to manage feature exclusivity and organise press days and trips to secure the maximum editorial in the hardest-hitting publications at the best possible time. This is particularly important with famous or very established stars. When I worked with the Rolling Stones's Charlie Watts, we did a mere handful of interviews: with *The Observer*, *Dazed & Confused*, *Loaded* and *The Times* (and that was more than enough for Charlie!). Similarly, when I worked with Chrissie Hynde last year, we simply did a handful of phone interviews with titles like *I-D*, *Sleaze*, *The Independent* and *The Times* and one face-to-face interview with the *Evening Standard*.

Often, we are knocked back initially by a publication when we are pitching a new artist, so we trickle them a steady stream of information to a point where we eventually nail the editorial—and thereby succeed in raising the artist's profile. This happened recently in the case of a rising soul star we look after called Nate James—I'd been pitching him hard at national newspaper supplements until finally, after two months' hard work, we secured a feature in the *Mail on Sunday's You* mgazine, which sells three million and is perfect for his audience demographic.

So there is no one way to make journalists listen to our artists, and much of the time we really do have to make sure you stay on them until we get some kind of reaction, but if it's a band or artist we believe in (which goes without saying!) and we start a campaign armed with the right tools (a great song and/or album, a striking biog and press release, unique press shots, and a tight live performance), then we get results—simple as that. Ultimately, we use our contacts, reputation and passion for both the band and what we do to encourage the broader media to sit up and listen.

✦✦✦✦✦✦✦✦✦✦✦✦✦✦✦✦✦✦✦✦✦✦✦✦✦✦✦✦✦✦✦✦✦✦✦✦✦✦✦✦✦✦✦✦✦

## WENDY WEISBERG

Wendy Weisberg runs her own boutique publicity and Internet marketing company, Hello Wendy. Among its clients have been Johnny Marr and the Healers, Paul Westerberg, Eric Clapton, Fleetwood Mac, Red Hot Chili Peppers, Morcheeba, Sir Mix-A-Lot, Senses Fail, Tweaker, and Michael Franti and Spearhead. Wendy has been involved with publicity and public relations at several labels and at various independent PR firms since 1992.

### How did you get started?
When I was in eleventh grade in high school, I had an internship at *BAM Magazine* [a Los Angeles bi-weekly free paper]. They asked me to fill in as a judge for

a battle of the bands contest. That really got me interested in the music business and how it works. When I went off to college, I wrote for student newspapers. I joined the college radio station. In the summers, I worked as an intern at record labels. When I came to my fourth year of college, I started speaking to my music label contacts, asking if I could send out a résumé. At that point, I didn't know exactly what publicity entailed but I wanted to do something that involved some sort of writing. I got a bite from IRS Records when I was attempting to set up an interview with one of its artists and had to go through an intern who screwed it up. I spoke to the boss. When he sorted the interview out, I said, 'Can I send you my résumé. I'm looking to find a job when I graduate'. He offered me a three-day-a-week position. The pay was low. But I knew I was going to be living at home. I thought, screw it, this seems to be an entry route into this business, so I took it.

### How did you move from that entry-level position to a more established one at IRS?
My boss was in a really horrific car accident so he needed to take several weeks off. I started coming in five days a week to help out. They said, 'We're going to make you full-time and pay you a full salary'. My boss really let me get on with it. I was in Los Angeles; he was in New York. He would come in every two months or so. He started off by having me do record reviews and

try to get record reviews placed in publications. Then I helped with tour press and helping him set up publicity for albums.

## Do artists need to know about how publicity and PR works?

Absolutely. I think artists should really make an effort to find out how the machine works. I get artists coming to me who are not ready to hire a PR professional yet because they don't have the funds or they don't have a full-length release or they've got an album that they're only selling out of the back of their car. They need to learn how to construct a letter to media to pitch their product. They should look at, say, a publication like the *LA Weekly*. If a music editor is listed on the masthead, they should definitely send their record to that editor. Depending on their own type of music, they should check out the writers for the magazine—who's previewing DJs coming through town, who's previewing the Puddle of Mudd show, who's writing about a good massive happening or about Paul Van Dyk coming through town. That's the sort of thing people should do, to help get their name out there, because otherwise no one is going to know about you.

## Why would a new artist with a few gigs and who is putting out their record themselves take the independent PR route?

I've had clients who don't have a record deal but who are putting out something independently with decent distribution or are going to sell the record via CD Baby or Amazon.com, and I've gotten press for clients who are only putting out their records via these Web retailers. Press coverage is the only way their name is going to get out there. It's free advertising essentially. If you take out an ad for your gig in the *LA Weekly*, it's going to cost you a boat-load of money. It's probably a better long-term career investment to hire someone to get you this free advertising by getting a plug for your show.

## What if the artist already has a record deal? Should they still go for independent PR?

I've worked both sides of the fence. When I was at the record labels and artists wanted to hire outside publicity, I'd get very angry. But here's the deal with how the record machine label works. Records have a limited lifespan—unless they pick up a lot of steam and there's a lot of money being poured in and there's a lot of stuff going on. Typically at the record label, we would plan an album campaign to last for two, maybe three, months. If nothing's happening after that, a lot of times the artist gets dropped or their album is no longer a priority because the label constantly has new priorities shuffling through the system. So your record might be only worked, I would say maximum, if things are going decently, for five to six months. You're going through a machine. If you're not a top-selling artist, you're going to have, on average, three to four months. If you're touring a lot, the label will let the publicist work on those tour dates.

But if you're doing tour dates and you've got other things going on that don't operate within the record label's time frame, I think it's important to have an outside person like an independent publicist on your side. It might be costly for you, but in the long run expecting the record company to take total care of you is not being a willing participant in your career. You have to promote yourself and that means hiring a team of professionals around you and understanding what they do and how they can work for you.

### If an artist is approaching you to do some PR for them, what do you want them to bring to you in order to get your interest?

I want there to be something I can create a story from? Do you have an interesting background? Has your independent music been played on KCRW [National Public Radio, tastemaker station based in Los Angeles]? Have you been gigging? Do you have a booking agent? Booking agents are the hardest things for new artists to latch on to. If you don't have a booking agent, I at least want to see some kind of effort on your part. Have you booked gigs outside of your hometown? Do you have a decently written bio? Do you have a few press clips you've gotten from your local media? That's the kind of stuff I'm looking for. And, is your music good? Does it stand out? Is it something that stands out within your genre? Or speaks to me?

### Will a PR company take on a new artist for little or no money?

It depends on the company. The bigger companies have several staff members, so they usually can't because they've got a lot of overhead costs. It's a bit different for me, as I work from my home. Nevertheless, this is my job and I have to pay my mortgage or my rent and I have to pay my bills. A lot of artists don't realise this when they say, 'Oh but I'm paying for this PR out of my pocket'.

When I first started out doing this, people said, 'Well, I only have this to pay' and because I needed clients I had to take it. But there is a lot of negotiating, especially when you're an individual. I don't have a boss to say no; our standard rate is $4,000 a month. I don't have three other publicists besides myself to work on an account where I can command four or five grand a month. Am I going to take jobs that pay me only a grand a month? Hell no, although

I might make some exceptions. One of my clients said, 'I have x amount to spend. Work on it for as long as you feel comfortable'. But I like him and I've been working longer than that. He said to me, 'I want to give you some more money because I want to work on this longer' because he likes me. He has his company, but he also has me because he knows the company's going to have to stop its promotion because they've got the next product in line.

It's very unrealistic for a young band to say, 'Oh I can pay someone $500 a month to do a PR campaign for me'. Not going to happen. Unless it's a very specific thing that you're hiring someone to do: 'Do publicity for my LA and San Francisco show'. Occasionally I'll take those one-offs. I don't like to. I'd rather work on someone's full campaigns, rather than simply getting them in the *LA Weekly* and the *Times*.

## What should an artist look for in a PR company?

Look for someone who feels honest. Someone who doesn't make empty promises like, 'Oh your music is great. We'll totally get you TV. We'll get you radio'. Anyone who says they can absolutely get you something is full of shit. Totally watch out for that. By the same token, if they're unprofessional, some artists or people will come to you and say, 'I'll give you a bonus if you book me on such-and-such' or 'I want to pay per placement.' What a lot of people don't realise is that publicity is more effort than it is results. I've had records from independent artists that I've loved, the clients are fabulous, they're great, and I just can't get them arrested at press. It's just the way it works. Times are probably better than ever for independent artists but it's also tougher. There's so many records released a year that if they don't know your name and they don't know anything about you and you haven't gotten any clips of any sort, it's going to be tough.

I provide my clients with a weekly update. I want them to know what is pending, meaning what looks really good, what could possibly happen, what is confirmed, who I'm still pitching, who I'm trying to reach, and who has passed on your record.

If I were an artist, I would ask the PR company to send me over a proposal. You want to make sure they've listened to your album. They get what kind of genre you are and your story. You want a publicist who can go in and be tenacious, but not a pushy asshole, who will really give it their best shot. They don't get a response from an e-mail, they'll follow up with a phone call. It hits a point where if you're not getting response from the press, okay, they're not interested. But you don't want someone who sends one e-mail and that's it. That's not effort.

**How do you persuade journalists to take notice of a record?**

I try to pull out what's interesting about the acts. I'm fortunate in that some of the acts that I've been working of late have been artists people have heard of. You have to tailor the pitch for different people. If I'm pitching an indie rock band to *Remix Magazine,* I would talk about how they beefed up their electronic side of it. You have to think what their magazine is like. You're lucky if you have an artist that has many facets. It's the best kind of situation.

✦✦✦✦✦✦✦✦✦✦✦✦✦✦✦✦✦✦✦✦✦✦✦✦✦✦✦✦✦✦✦✦✦✦✦✦✦✦✦✦✦✦✦✦✦✦✦

## Radio Plugging and Promotion

In North America, it's called promotion and in Britain it's plugging. But whatever name you use, persuading radio stations to play your records is regarded by most people in the business as the key to success as a recording act. Once, this was restricted to the BBC, commercial stations and student radio; now there's a plethora of places to go with the explosion of Internet radio stations—many genre-specific—and also satellite radio in the US.

At whatever level you start, at first it's best to do a bit of radio plugging yourself. Send the record out to a few key people. In the UK, these would probably include Radio 1's Zane Lowe, Jo Wylie or one of the evening specialist shows/DJs; BBC 1Xtra for urban music or the more open-minded, independent radio stations like XFM in London or Vibe FM in Essex or the specialist dance shows on stations like Kiss FM or Choice or rock stations such as Kerrang! With no national radio in the US, you will be focusing on your local college radio and any stations in your city or state that already programme the type of music you produce.

But don't do an organised campaign at this point, spending serious money on it. If you think the thing's going to be a gift for a particular show, then send it in. If it's local radio, look for angles to give someone to pull your record out of that pile of records and stick it on.

In America, radio promotion is a very competitive and often cutthroat business. Most promotion is done in-house by employees of the label that is releasing the recording. There are many (probably hundreds) of independent promotion companies as well, however, and a large number of artists who do their own radio promotion (DIY).

Ideally, regardless of the amount of promoting that's done around a record, the quality and artistry of your music should get through to the key people in radio. Unfortunately—and unsurprisingly—this is seldom the case. There are so many labels, indies, DIYs and so forth sending out their music that it's not unusual to receive over one or two hundred different titles in a week at a radio station! The point of saying this is not to overwhelm you, but just to give you an idea of how necessary promoting to radio is to shed light on your own masterpiece. No matter how big or small the act, just mailing or delivering the record to the station is not sufficient. There will need to be some sort of follow-through for the record to gain the attention of the music director or programme director. America, unlike the UK, has literally thousands of local radio stations and because it's over two thousand miles from coast to coast, promotion is handled in a very different way (unless of course you want to be arriving in a radio station in Los Angeles two thousand radio stations and six months after you left a copy of your album in New York City).

One of the other important differences (possibly the most important) in American radio is the existence of college and noncommercial radio.

Commercial radio in the US is similar to UK radio, both listening- and business-wise. However, it is more tightly formatted than in Europe and it is extremely difficult for anything left-field or quirky to gain airplay, although this is changing with satellite radio. A small number of corporations own most of the commercial stations, of which about eighty are considered vital for breaking a record.

In contrast, college and noncommercial radio is often as unpredictable as it is impressive—and it's where new and up-and-coming artists go to get a name for themselves (think Pavement, Stereolab, Gomez). Because there are no big 'higher-ups' determining the format and playlist of these stations, they have the ability to play almost anything they want at any time they want. WSPN, the college station where Matthew Moore works (Matthew contributed to the first edition of this book), has two- and three-hour slots where the DJ or DJs play whatever their hearts' desire.

It's not uncommon to hear jazz, funk and rock in the same programme at some stations. If sometimes the mix seems disjointed and unappealing, there are many instances where a programme will just have that special something that surprises and delights its audience—unlike the often sterile and predictable environment of commercial radio.

The important thing about the huge variety of programming and the freedom enjoyed by noncommercial radio is that they are able to play anything—so if you're a new, unheard-of band, a Goth-dungeon alt-rock band or a new wave jazz artist, there is a place for your music on college radio.

You also need to know that many US stations do employ formatting, some even strict formatting, but most do have flexibility in their playlists and their charts. Some stations will play only punk or only metal, while others will play only hip-hop and rap—wherever your album fits in, it will be especially beneficial for you to find these speciality stations and wow them with your work.

There's also the rise of satellite radio: Sirius and XM boast over a hundred channels each (commercial free) which broadcast a range of musical genres, from Christian rock to dance.

## Getting in Touch

There are many lists and listings with radio station contact information available in both book and Web form. Some Web sites have impressive compilations of stations, even giving detailed listings of their wattage, audience profile and so forth. If you are sending out the album DIY, you should address all phone calls and mailings to the music director at the station or, in rare instances, the programme director. If your album is in a special genre, it often will not hurt to address your mailing to 'Music Director: Punk' or 'Metal Rock Music Director', etc. Many stations will have separate libraries for their different genres of music, and many will request that you send an additional copy if you feel your album should be in two libraries—for instance, the Chemical Brothers would be eligible for both Top 100 radio airplay and RPM (dance) charts. The best thing is to get in touch with the station, find out to whom you should direct your work and do so by name and title. Find out what their office hours are and call them at those times to check up on your album.

One valuable tip in approaching radio is to look through the charts over the past four to six months to find albums that did well and have some sort of similarity to yours—be sure to mention them in your press release/bio and your phone conversations. Although it may sound corny and/or limiting to your sound, it often helps to get your album noticed. Embarrassingly enough, Matthew once listened to a horrible album that was sent to him by a label that compared it to My Bloody Valentine—a connection that, frankly, he would have never dreamed of but it did get him to listen to that album!

## CMJ Charts

College radio stations report airplay information to *CMJ* (*College Media Journal*)—a weekly magazine that lists the charts of each station and the overall charts of each category, and has reviews, interviews and profiles on artists, industry personnel and radio stations. *CMJ* is available online at www.cmj.com.

*CMJ* publishes eight different charts. Top 100 is the overall chart, containing the most popular albums at the time from all genres. Core is similar to the Top 100 but it is comprised only of airplay data from a select few college radio stations across the country.

Among the specialist charts, RPM covers dance—anything from trance to drum 'n' bass to industrial; Beat Box is for rap and hip-hop with some R&B; Triple A is for adult alternative music that is usually a bit on the softer side of the spectrum, for a more mature crowd—Tracy Chapman would fit well into Triple A. The other three charts—Jazz, Loud Rock and New World—should be self-explanatory. If your music will fit neatly into any of these speciality categories and you're on a limited budget (which by this point you most likely are), find out from *CMJ* which stations report to your specialist chart and do a limited mailing to these stations.

## Using an Independent Promoter

One tremendous advantage of working with independent promotions companies is that they already have a complete mailing list, a means for mass mailings, contacts at all the radio stations and the knowledge of what has and hasn't been working at college radio—without needing to review old charts—and, of course, they are well versed in all the lingo and ins and outs of phone promotion. Of course, it is always important to choose your company wisely because, while they will have already established a working relationship with the radio stations, it is not necessarily a good relationship.

Eventually, you or your record label will probably be able to afford to hire a professional to deal with radio. Next we hear from two such professionals: Nelson Wells from the US is followed by Tony Byrne of the UK.

✦✦✦✦✦✦✦✦✦✦✦✦✦✦✦✦✦✦✦✦✦✦✦✦✦✦✦✦✦✦✦✦✦✦✦✦✦✦✦✦✦✦✦✦✦✦✦

## NELSON WELLS

Nelson Wells co-founded the radio promotion and PR company Team Clermont, in 1993. Before that, Wells and his partners worked as artist managers. The company's roster of label clients has included Chemikal Underground, Beggars Banquet, Tomlab, Sonig, Domino and Warner Brothers. Team Clermont has promoted releases from such acts as the Flaming Lips, Sigur Ros, Mercury Rev, the Polyphonic Spree, and REM.

**Why is promotion so important, and how much impact would you say that radio has on the general listening and buying public?**

In today's day and age, promotion is the only route by which music gets on radio. Back in the Fifties, an artist could drive from station to station handing out their records, and they could get some airplay from DJs right then and there. Things have evolved since then and have become much more controlled by money. The bigger record companies have typically had more money and so their artists have gotten far more exposure on commercial radio stations, which have also become much more concerned with the bottom line. The majority of stations that Team Clermont deals with are public or college radio stations, leaving commercial stations as one-fifth of our entire list. These noncommercial stations are very valuable to a young artist's career. Even with the growth of pod-casting, satellite radio and file sharing, the impact of radio on the record-buying public is still great. Radio is something the listener can just turn on and let it do the work for them or introduce them to music they haven't heard before.

**When is the best time for a new and upcoming artist to try to break their album?**

This is a question I talk with our clients about regularly. Smaller clients with newer or younger artists can sometimes take advantage of slower times of the year to release records. In other words, they should not release records in the first month or two of university classes or the dead of spring. There are simply far more records being released at these times, adding more and more competition for the young unknown artist.

**What's the normal life cycle of an album (i.e., breaking/adds, charts, peak, dropping, etc.)?**

At radio, there seems to be a well-established life cycle for a record. The lead time or prep time for a record prior to it being sent to radio is usually a couple of months. This is the time the promoters are reviewing the music and finding room for it in their schedules.

A record is sent to radio a few weeks prior to the release date (the press is sent the disc three months prior) with an 'add date' being close to or just before release date. The add date is the date the promoter asks the stations to add the record into rotation. During this add date week, the promotion company is trying to rally all the stations it has relationships with to get behind the record and start playing it.

On average, a record stays in 'current' rotation for six to eight weeks before it is moved to a 'recurrent' rotation, or 'the library'. During this short life, the promoter sees to it that there is forward momentum for the record at each station, asking for more plays, DJs' feedback, and for a chart position that reflects that airplay. Each station has its own chart of top-played records, whether it is a Top 20, a Top 40, or a Top 100. A promoter typically works with the label and artist to achieve more exposure by appearing in these charts.

**What recommendations would you make to a band or individual artists trying to promote an album in the US? Would you use an indie promo company?**

Well, since you are asking a radio promoter it will sound biased, but asking a band to release a record without a radio promoter or publicist would be like asking a band to go on tour without a bus. You need all the pieces of the pie to be in place if you are going to release something in a country the size of the US, or everything could be a big waste of time and money.

**How do you find the right indie promotion company for you?**

I am so glad this question is being asked. It is very important that you find the right company for your records for both radio and press. You need to do your homework, but here's a hint: in the US, there are many college radio promoters but there are five that matter. Research them, ask around about them, and check their rosters to make sure you want your record represented by them. Then contact them and send them the music. You must follow up, however. You cannot expect a busy promoter to listen to an mp3 on a Web site somewhere and follow up with you. Send a disc and a link and call back.

**How many indie promotion companies does a label need to use?**

A label needs as many promoters as it has genres of music. That's it, no more.

**If you were to do a limited mailing to radio stations, what markets would you make sure to target?**

The exact list of markets that should be hit in a limited campaign depends on the style of music. An alternative rock band that wanted to limit its promotion to major markets might decide to hit KCRW in Los Angeles, for example, but it would most likely be wasting its time and discs. This is why an independent promoter is so valuable. They will help you choose the appropriate markets and, more important, stations for your record.

## What tips, hints or shortcuts do you have for getting an album in the charts?

Ah, now if a promoter gave away his tips and shortcuts he would be out of a job! Seriously, the most important things in order are: find the right promoter and publicist; trust them to do their job; and follow up with them to make sure you are on their mind regularly. Then, once you have support from radio, reach out to them as an artist and show that you appreciate their support. Write letters, postcards, and e-mails to the station music directors and just let them know that it means something to you. Send them a care package if the promoter thinks it's a good idea. A good promoter will share with you the information that helps your record succeed up to a certain point. Like any relationship, being a successful artist requires work. And the link between the artist and radio or the artist and magazine writers is just that: a relationship. Treat them as such.

## What's the most important thing to remember while promoting your album?

Humility. You are not the only artist out there releasing their own personal material to the world. There are many others working just as hard and pouring out their souls just like you. Always respect them and know that they are trying just as hard to do the same thing.

## What have your biggest successes been?

Our biggest success has been in launching virtually unknown artists to new levels of exposure. We added unique promotion campaigns to remarkably creative recordings.

In each case, the artists also had a label behind them that was very supportive and helped to choose the right promoters and publicists to make these records stand out the most.

✦✦✦✦✦✦✦✦✦✦✦✦✦✦✦✦✦✦✦✦✦✦✦✦✦✦✦✦✦✦✦✦✦✦✦✦✦✦✦✦✦✦✦✦✦✦✦✦✦

✦✦✦✦✦✦✦✦✦✦✦✦✦✦✦✦✦✦✦✦✦✦✦✦✦✦✦✦✦✦✦✦✦✦✦✦✦✦✦✦✦✦✦✦✦✦✦✦✦

## TONY BYRNE

Tony Byrne, of Single Minded Promotions, has been running a successful independent promotions company for over twenty years, plugging a range of artists to radio, from the Pulp to Liberty X and Ian Van Dahl. Tony was born

---

and brought up in Liverpool and moved to Chester in his teens. He played in a number of punk bands around 1978 and then went to university, where he gained a degree in computer science and business. Tony moved to London in 1982 and got a job with the Independent Record Labels Association, which represented indie labels like Two Tone and Stiff. He says, 'Mick Hucknall came in to have a meeting one morning and brought his first ever record, the Frantic Elevators's *Searching for the Only One*, on his own label. I was actually a fan because I'd recently seen them playing at the Futurama Festival in Leeds only a few months before and had really liked them. I promoted the single, which was very successful at radio. However, the Frantic Elevators soon went their own way and Mick formed Simply Red and the rest is history!' Tony soon left the Independent Record Labels Association and went freelance and set up Single Minded Promotions in 1984.

**What sort of music were you promoting when you began your company?**

From 1984 through to about 1987–1988, the main thing I loved and was into was the whole post-punk indie scene. London was really buzzing and I was promoting new bands like Southern Death Cult (who later became Death Cult/the Cult), Sex Gang Children, and Sisters of Mercy, as well as bands like the Men They Couldn't Hang and Pulp (getting them their first Peel sessions on Radio 1!). I worked on the early releases of labels like Illuminated, which represented much of the early Manchester and London electronic scene, like 23 Skidoo and 400 Blows. I was also promoting the first releases on Creation and bands like the Blue Aeroplanes. I think by the late 1980s, I got disillusioned by that whole 'shambling sound' and it all started becoming a bit one-dimensional to me.

At about that point, I started getting involved with the whole computer side of things. My main ambition had been to try to combine music with computers when I had been at Uni, but I never succeeded. Then Cubase and the Atari and sequencing started making it possible for people to create music easily. As with the punk ethos, which maintained that you only needed to know three chords and to pick up a guitar, now people were using a keyboard and a MIDI sequencer to create music in much the same way.

White label culture started happening and there were loads of cool labels starting up again everywhere, much like the punk scene of ten years earlier. The dance music scene was starting to happen. I just jumped on that because it was younger people with lots more creative ideas—for me, it was the most exciting thing since punk rock. I felt I had a lot of experience to offer small labels, and there were a lot of labels that were just starting up—F2 Records, Champion Records, Rhythm King, Kickin' Records, Suburban Base Records, Production House Records, plus hundreds of others almost being spawned weekly. As well as the one-off singles, there were new artists coming through which I had started to work closely with, like Baby D, D:ream, Acen, Messiah and Adamski and A Guy Called Gerald. All these new artists and labels were starting up and wanting to put out records.

**How hard was it to promote this new sound to radio?**

We had a lot of success with these records because not many people were even aware of the market at the time. Radio 1 would phone me on a Friday afternoon and they'd say, 'Tony, there's this record—"Shut Up and Dance" or "Baby D"—we can't get it, it's not in HMV, we don't know who the label is; it's just a white label and it's gone in at number twenty-two in the charts. Can you tell us who they are?' And it's quite funny because I'd phone up and speak to the label, be it Production House or Shut Up and Dance, and they'd say, 'Tell Radio 1 they have to go out and buy a copy' or probably more colourful language from some of them, and I'd say, 'Come on guys, why don't you just send them a free copy?' And they'd say, 'No way let them go out and buy it'. They had a real anarchic attitude, which at the time was really refreshing but seemed a bit of an uphill struggle nonetheless.

**Do you think your plugging was instrumental in these people getting signed to major labels?**
Undoubtedly, yes! I think so. Back in the drum 'n' bass scene, shows like One in the Jungle on Radio 1 were very important. Underground music is a sort of barometer and has a big effect on how radio looks towards programming certain shows. For example, with the drum 'n' bass scene, there were no shows on national radio and I remember talking to Trevor Dann, who was the head of Radio 1 at the time, at a meeting of all the record companies and pluggers. At the end of the meeting, he was saying Radio 1 was looking for new ways to appeal to youth and keep Radio 1 as a cutting-edge station. He asked if anyone had any new ideas to appeal to people, and people were putting their hands up and saying, 'Well, maybe we should have another reggae show' or maybe it should be this or it should be that and at the end I went up to Trevor and said, 'There should definitely be a jungle show, a drum 'n' bass show, because that's the show that's really missing on Radio 1'. Next, I started getting phone calls from Radio 1, saying they wanted my advice in starting their own drum 'n' bass show, which became One in the Jungle. I put them in touch with all the labels I was looking after and ended up getting all of them as guest mixers on the show and even put an album together with Radio 1 to promote the show and the genre at that time.

**You then moved on to promote trance and garage. Why?**
Many other styles of dance were crossing over from the underground into the charts—house, trance, garage, uplifting stuff. So I moved on from drum 'n' bass for the reasons I mentioned before; I didn't want to take money from people and not be able to get their records on the radio. At the time, I worked on records like the 'Sweet Like Chocolate' and 'Doolally', singles by Shanks and Bigfoot on the independent dance label Chocolate Boy. 'Sweet Like Chocolate' started off as a white label, which nobody was interested in. I remember initially playing it to people and, even though it was a big record on the streets and sold a fair quantity on white label, there wasn't such a demand that it looked like it would crossover. I really felt strongly about it and I went out on a limb in pro-

moting it. At the time, I was also looking after the dance producers Ruff Driverz as remixers and we got them to do a house remix of 'Sweet Like Chocolate' and DJs started playing their mix on radio. Then I asked the then Kiss head of music, Simon Sadler, to listen to the original again because I thought it was the strongest mix. He did and he warmed to it. Then Dave Pearce (Radio 1) picked up on it about the same time—I played it to him in the car—and he really liked it and started playing it and Pete Tong started playing it also on Radio 1 and suddenly there was a real buzz about the record.

We planned a video (I had started producing videos for record companies) and offered to produce it and bring in the right directors for Simon, who ran the Chocolate Boy record label. He said, 'Okay, I've got a budget, can you make that work? We're not sure what we want to do'. I told him I had an idea of using the [television soap opera] *Coronation Street* chocolate animated trailer and said, 'Why don't we do something like that, like a Willie Wonka's Chocolate Factory meets *Coronation Street*' and he said he thought it was a great idea. A year later, when the song had gotten to number one, it was nominated for MTV Video of the Year and MOBO Best Music Video.

## What other dance genres have you worked over the past few years?

We had a lot of success with the whole drum 'n' bass scene with lots of artists from Adam F, Roni Size, UK Apache, Shy FX, T-Power, Aphrodite, M Beat, A Guy Called Gerald—a lot of the underground acts—and crossing them over to the mainstream. A lot of those artists were getting signed to majors and we stayed involved with some but not all of them. Then, although I still really loved drum 'n' bass, the market slowed and radio, for its own reasons at that time, stopped playing drum 'n' bass. There were fewer and fewer shows at Radio 1 and [London dance station] Kiss FM able to programme it. It's really difficult to take on a record or a label if you know that radio isn't going to playlist those records on daytime radio. So I decided at that time to move slightly away from the drum 'n' bass scene and more to the uplifting house, trance and garage scene. This was quite fortuitous, in that the Ibiza scene at that time was starting to become more commercial and I was promoting out there 'rinsing it' with lots of artists and international DJs, most of whom were running their own successful labels; I was working alongside them. Looking back on that particular time in dance music, the genre had become very commercial and I was working with some fantastic labels in that scene and promoting some milestone moments in dance. Classics like 'Café Del Mar' by

Energy 52 and 'Greece 2000' on DJ Red Gerry's Hooj Tunes Records and 'Bullet in the Gun' by Planet Perfecto and 'Resurrection' by PPK on Paul Oakenfold's Perfecto label, as well as 'Castles in the Sky' by Ian Van Dahl and 'You're a Superstar' by Love Inc. on Radio 1 DJ Dave Pearce's Nu Life label. Ibiza in itself was also a great way of finding the hottest new tunes.

## What are you promoting at the moment?

We have had big successes in the charts and at radio and TV with Freemasons 'Love on My Mind' and Gadjo's 'So Many Times', which started life in Ibiza clubs. Also, a great example was our number one, 'Take Me to the Clouds Above', by LMC V U2, which had originally started life in Ibiza the previous year as a moody cut-up bootleg which I heard and snatched up as a white label—making sure I was going to be the guy who plugged it to radio and TV when it finally got cleared by the publishers and released by the record company.

## Has Radio 1 always been key to your promotions strategy?

What used to happen back in the mid-1990s was that Radio 1 would put together the Top 40 on a Friday and they would look for four or five copies of a record and they would generally phone up the pluggers who were representing those labels and singles and say, 'Oh, if we haven't got copies, make sure we have four copies of the next Take That single' or whoever it might be. Obviously, with the new dance records coming out on white labels, they didn't know who to ask, so the producer on the show would phone me up and say, 'We've got another one of your records, Tony' and ask for more information and I'd say, 'It's so and so on such and such a label' or one of the labels that maybe I wasn't even working with but that was making that kind of music at the time.

If they hadn't phoned me, I wouldn't have known the chart positions until the Monday, so in a way they were kind of doing me a favour as well. It was, 'Well, you should get some copies over to Radio 1, otherwise you might not get your record played in the chart on Sunday'. So that was very helpful to me in a way at that time.

## Which other stations do you think are key radio outlets?

Because radio and dance always worked hand in hand, if that style of music is to crossover, the next landmark for dance was when Kiss FM started in 1991 in London. Between doing my rounds seeing producers at Radio 1 and Capital,

I spent about four years hanging out, more or less living at Kiss, on a day-to-day basis. Five years on, most of the people who had worked at Kiss FM had moved on to Radio 1. Luckily for me, I'd done a lot of promotion on the early dance music scene and became good friends with all the people there. These people moved on to key positions within the industry as dance music acts became household names. Looking back now, it was strange because Alex Jones-Donelly, who at one time was the Music Librarian at Kiss FM, went on to have one of the most powerful positions in the music industry as Head of Music at BBC Radio 1.

Since the early days of Kiss FM the radio environment has transformed, in that many UK radio stations have centralised or joined forces with major publishing groups. For example, Capital now has a major share of the radio market after its merger with the GWR Group, becoming the GCap One Network. Kiss FM also is now part of the EMAP radio network. Other key networks now include Galaxy and the Scottish Radio network, amongst others. This in a way has put greater emphasis on these networks in shaping future hits. So Radio 1 and all of these networks monitor each other when deciding which new artists and records they will playlist on their stations.

### When, how and why should you use a plugger?

It depends on the style of music. You've got to decide where your market is. Whenever I listen to a record to decide whether I want to plug it, I've got to decide first and foremost, do I like and feel the record; and second, how hard a job is it going to be to get radio to understand it? Is it very, very niche—like I was saying about drum 'n' bass in the late 1990s, where there were very few shows I could go to on radio to make a record work. If there's only, say, three shows on radio for this style of music, I'm not going to turn to the record company and say, 'Give me your money' to some guy who's just spent a grand and a half on a white label. If I thought I could only go and play it to three people and that he had no chance of crossing over to daytime radio, there's no way I'd want to promote it and take his money.

On the other hand, if you just stick a record in an envelope and send it to a radio station and just hope for the best, you may end up getting somebody like Judge Jules on Radio 1, Tall Paul on Kiss or Justin Wilkes on Capital picking up on it and thinking the record's fantastic. But whether it's mp3s on the Internet or white labels crossing over to radio, I still think you need promotion and marketing and somebody who feels strongly enough to take it into radio and convince somebody who's got a thousand records on their desk or five hundred things to do in a day to listen to it.

## if you didn't want to plug it, what would you tell the label or artist?

I might give him or her some good advice on what to do with it—with some records, it's best to go the club route first of all, or give it to some record shops—see if it sells through in some specialist shops or advise them go to their local HMV and see if they can sell five or ten copies and then come back to me if they sell a thousand in a week. If there's no demand for a record out in the street, then it's not really worth taking it to radio. Sometimes radio fuels the demand at shop level, but it's like if you're playing in a band and you're out there doing gigs and nobody's coming: it's no good starting to get someone bigging you up at radio if you haven't got a fan base. In my opinion, if I hear a record and I think it's got potential at radio, I'd want to get involved at whatever level.

I get sent lots of tapes, CD-Rs, CDs and mp3s and I do listen to everything. I've got a CD player in the car with twelve CDs in and I listen to CDs constantly just in case I might spot something that stands out from the crowd. But some guy who's not a major label or who doesn't have big money behind him might come in off the street and say, 'I've got this little single' and I'm as interested in doing deals like that as I am with the big major record labels.

## So, would you work on the record before it's released, then?

Definitely. I started working the 'Sweet Like Chocolate' record in July and it didn't get released until the following year. Things like that do take on a life of their own. The Ruff Driverz's 'Dreaming' started life as a white label and was around for seven or eight months just building and building. Some records are just like that; they just build and build and then the right time comes for them to be released. More recently also we had a single called 'California Soul', by Riot Act, which was a big record on radio but we built up the buzz on radio on that before they were signed to EMI. Even when we worked with Mis-teeq we were involved in promoting their first two singles at radio before they had a major deal. I have also set up my own publishing company, Single Minded Music, with the sole aim of signing new artists, producers and songwriters and one-off tracks to take them to radio with the main aim of getting a deal once we have built a buzz. The first of these that I signed was a track called 'Space', by Slipmatt, which we signed on and it sadly just missed out on the Top 40 charting at 41 but did well on airplay and we also got it on lots of compilations.

## What is the reason for radio edits?

As well as just plugging, I started putting together compilations and tried to learn a lot more about the industry. I also got involved in doing remixes and radio edits for a lot of record companies. We've done radio edits for hits by Moby and loads and loads of different dance artists.

When the whole dance thing was just starting up, there was not really such a thing as a radio edit. I heard a 12″ single on Suburban Base called 'Back Again', by Run Tings, which was two and a half minutes of break beats and then at the end there was this amazing riff with a vocal and a great hook at the end of the track. The record label obviously thought that if I took it to radio I would be able to get it on the playlist, but it would never have got on.

I told the record label that I'd like to do something with the record specifically geared up for radio. They were happy for me to go into the studio and do my own version. I went in and did a 7″ radio edit—and until that point nobody was doing radio edits of 12″ dance singles. I remember at the time Mark Goodier of Radio 1 played it as his record of the week and I was thinking, 'God, it worked!'

I started thinking to myself about what radio wanted, mixed with what a record label wanted, and put them together to get the edit. Just changing or getting rid of a sixteen-bar intro—manic drums, for example—would make a single much more radio friendly. It seemed so simple and so strange that nobody had ever thought of it. A lot of people have started their own little companies out of ideas like that.

With Moby, his track 'The Next Is an E' had come in from the States and we changed the title and changed the format of it and lo and behold it went in. I remember playing it to Alex Jones Donelly, who was working at Kiss at the time, and I asked him what he thought of it. I said, 'Don't you think having a title 'The Next Is an E' is gonna kind of give us a problem at radio?' and he agreed. I said, 'Well, I was thinking of doing one of my radio edits and changing it and changing the emphasis and maybe moving the choruses and even renaming the song if we can get Moby's permission'. He cleared it and it became a hit. It got into the Top 20 and it was the first thing Moby had done chart-wise since *Go*, and then we did more edits with him on the next three or four singles.

When someone like Dave Morales does a mix in the studio, he doesn't think about radio first and foremost; he thinks about what's going to work in the clubs. I only think about what's going to work on radio. I listen to a record and I might hear it in the clubs but when you hear it in the cold light of day, you think, 'What's a radio station going to think of it and how are they going to programme it into their format for the next six months on the station?'

✦✦✦✦✦✦✦✦✦✦✦✦✦✦✦✦✦✦✦✦✦✦✦✦✦✦✦✦✦✦✦✦✦✦✦✦✦✦✦✦✦✦✦✦✦✦✦

# Remixing

One way of promoting your records to a different audience is to get other people to remix your tunes. This isn't true only of the dance world. It was the Fatboy Slim remix of Cornershop's 'Brimful of Asha' that sent it rocketing to number one in the UK —the band had been a fairly trendy indie band before that on Wiiija, a medium-sized independent label, which, while it got mentions in the press, made only modest sales. A couple of years ago, Zip Dog commissioned a drum 'n' bass remix for one of its records: Roughcut's 'Come Out'. The original was a slow groove, hip-hop–based tune. It wasn't really a club tune but the drum 'n' bass remix went down a storm with DJs and got airplay on BBC Radio 1.

While it's unlikely you can afford someone like Norman Cook or Paul Oakenfold to remix your records, if you check out the dance magazines you can get a good idea of who's starting to get a bit of a name, and if you can catch them early enough they won't charge you too much for doing a remix—and as they are likely to be a DJ, they'll very kindly play it out for you, thus spreading the word about your hot tune! Make sure you listen to their music first, though: it's no good getting someone to do the mix and then hating the result because you just don't like the way they make their own music.

Listen to a few producers in each style and see whose tunes stir you the most and approach them. Don't choose someone just because they're fashionable; if they're not right for your artist, it'll come across in the remix and it'll be a waste of money.

Another good idea is for you or your artists to remix other people's records. If the mix goes down a storm, you'll have lots of free promotion and other requests for you to remix will come in and you should be able to start earning from this. If you're completely new to this, ask around to see if anyone's willing to let you have a go. Offer to do it on spec—that is, you get paid only if they use the remix. Obviously, this is worth doing only if you have a decent home studio or can get hold of some free or reduced studio time. And even if the mix doesn't get used, it adds to your portfolio of work and makes a nice little line in your artist and label biography.

Remixers Gabriel and Dresden from the US explain why remixing has been a boost to their musical career.

## GABRIEL AND DRESDEN

Josh Gabriel and Dave Dresden, better known as Gabriel and Dresden, have taken the art of remixing to a new level with their prolific hand at the craft. The San Francisco, California–based duo met at Miami's 2001 Winter Music Con-

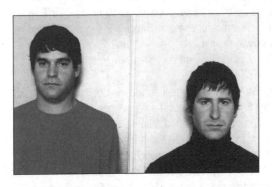

ference. It all happened during the transfer of music: burgeoning producer Gabriel's track 'Wave 3' went straight into DJ Dresden's well-connected hands. As a scout for Pete Tong, Dresden got the track to Tong and soon after it was played on that DJ's BBC Radio 1 program.

When presented with an opportunity for a remix by Tong, Dresden enlisted Gabriel to collaborate with him on it, and the partnership was established.

Since that time, they have done remixes for the likes of New Order, Depeche Mode, Britney Spears, Annie Lennox, Evanescence, Sarah McLachlan, Dido, Jewel, Dave Gahan, Tiesto, Paul Oakenfold, Weekend Players, Way Out West, and ILS, among many others. In addition to their remixes, the twosome have a mix CD called *Bloom*, and they have created music with vocalist Jes, under the moniker Motorcycle. They have had more than a dozen number one hits on the *Billboard* Club Play Chart Remixes, as well as a UK Pop Chart hit with their Motorcycle song 'As the Rush Comes'. In 2004, they won Best Producer and Best Dance Single at the International Dance Music Awards as Motorcycle, and Best Breakthrough DJ at the 2004 Dancestar Awards. Most recently, they have started up the Organized Nature imprint, focusing on creating floor smashers using traditional instruments.

### How did your remixing career get started?
**Gabriel:** Dave got offered a remix of New Order from Pete Tong as a thank you for all the work Dave did scouting music for him. Being more of a DJ and less of a studio guy, Dave went to go find somebody. My song 'Wave 3' was one of the songs he had scouted for Pete so Dave knew he liked my produc-

tion. He called and said, 'Do you want to work on this remix together?' We did, and never stopped working. It was a spec remix and I don't think anybody expected us to turn in anything anybody would like. It ended up that the band really liked our remix and that helped us out a lot.

### Did you start out as remixers, or as musicians trying out remixing?

*Gabriel:* We became known for doing remixes, but we got our biggest from doing Motorcycle, which is original. But I would say that we've been remix-heavy.

### What are the main things you are looking to do in your remixes?

*Dresden:* We want to make the best possible version of the song that we can.

*Gabriel:* We listen to the spirit of the vocals, the lyrics, what they're saying, what the tone of the voice is, and what kind of track it will fit best in.

### What are some of the essential elements you bring into a remix?

*Dresden:* Our love of 1980s music. It has to have that emotional ride; that's the most important thing for us.

---

**Gabriel:** A lot of times we'll rearrange vocals to give things slightly new meaning. Some things need to be different in the context of a remix than they do in the original.

### Is the clubbing aspect very important?
**Dresden:** Absolutely. That's essential. We're being hired to do a dance remix. We definitely want to put it front and centre.

**Gabriel:** I think that goes hand in hand with our DJing. I don't think you can make really good dance remixes and not be a DJ. You have to understand exactly how things are going to work.

### How do you approach a vocal-driven tune when remixing?
**Gabriel:** We put all the vocals on a CD, listen to them and try to find what parts move us. Especially in a track that has a lot of vocal parts, maybe there are some harmonies in the original that don't necessarily work for us. We try to find the vocals that do work for us so we can focus in on those.

### How much of your remixing is actually rewriting?
**Gabriel:** We would say all of it. A lot of the time, we're just given a vocal and we're creating a track from scratch underneath it. Even when we're using parts from the artist, we're mangling them beyond belief, sometimes changing chord progressions and song structures. For our Dave Gahan remix, we created new harmonies, which didn't exist, by pitching his vocals up and down different ways.

### How important is having the latest gear?
**Gabriel:** Not important at all. We have a Macintosh G5 computer, a bass and a guitar. We use Logic 7. We use some virtual instruments, not a lot. It's more processing.

### How has remixing affecting you as artists?
**Gabriel:** Making music always gives you experience. Doing remixes is like musical weightlifting.

**Dresden:** It exercises a certain part of your creativity. Writing songs is a different part of your creativity. DJing is another part of your creativity. Remixing is one of those things.

**Gabriel:** I think our sound has affected the remixes more than the other way around. We have a sound, or we've been told we have a sound. If I listen back to all our old stuff, even though we think everything sounds different, there's definitely a consistency to it and that's what I think we affect remixes with. Our remixes sound like they're coming from the same people that our original tracks are coming from.

## Is there a time when you feel you have too many remix offers?

*Gabriel:* Maybe too many bad offers. You can never have too many good offers. We've been offered a lot of things where it's a song that you can tell is not from the heart. The song is created in a factory, sung by somebody who doesn't give a shit, by a label that couldn't care less and they want you to turn it into something. That's not what we're about.

## Who takes care of your business arrangements?

*Dresden:* Our manager, Guy Ornadel. I've known Guy for years, when he used to run the DMC office [in New York City]. He came around right when Josh and I had started, three or four tracks in, asked if we needed representation. I looked at his roster. I figured, if those guys are there I want that.

## Is he instrumental in getting you work?

*Gabriel:* People's ability to network definitely affects their ability to get jobs in remixing. You're only going to get hired for a remix if somebody is aware of you in the first place. Dave's deep, longstanding relationship with the dance music world has helped us get remixes. People are aware of him, but through knowing him as Dave. He already had a bunch of people already aware of him that he didn't have to go make aware of him. A lot of the remixes have come from those relationships that he had before we started making music together.

## What are some things fledgling remixers should know?

*Gabriel:* If somebody is trying to make something and get it out there, the two things they can do are make sure they understand the music that it's going to fit in with, and the DJs who play that music. If they don't know what DJs play that music, then they're not really making music for anybody. If there are no DJs who are going to play it, they're not really communicating anything. If they know what DJs are going to play it, then it's not that hard to get stuff to a DJ. That's a way to get your stuff out there for no cost at all.

## Is it as simple as that?

*Gabriel:* We get handed tracks to play as DJs, and if they're good, we'll play them. We have a lot of radio shows that are broadcast all over the world. If you can get something from somebody and play it, they're going to get exposure and a lot of people are going to hear it, so it's a quick way out there. We're just one DJ; there are hundreds of people who have the same coverage. If you find the right niche, there may only be two DJs who are interested in your track, but your key is finding out which two DJs they are and going right to them.

### How do you find those particular DJs?

*Gabriel:* When people are producing, they need to be aware of the world that they're in. One of the biggest mistakes people make is not listening to the other music that is going to be played around the music they're making. They may think it's great but they don't know how painfully bad it sounds when it's played in the set that they think it should be played in, simply because they haven't listened to the music. A lot of people start making music, copycatting in their brains what they think people want to hear, but they're not really in the world they want to be in yet and the thing that gets you there is listening to lots of music.

✦✦✦✦✦✦✦✦✦✦✦✦✦✦✦✦✦✦✦✦✦✦✦✦✦✦✦✦✦✦✦✦✦✦✦✦✦✦✦✦✦✦✦✦✦

## SELLING YOUR RECORDS YOURSELF

Retail is still an absolutely critical part of the chain, despite mail order and online sales, and it's an often-neglected part. You can have press and all those other things, but for one reason or another, it goes wrong at the shops. And shops are one of the places where the people with the money are. Yes, they read the *NME* and all those things, but it's no good if they can't buy the product because it's not in the shops. Sarah found this out at Zip Dog. The label may be distributed by a national distribution company in the UK, and in other countries too, but of course it's at the discretion of each shop owner to decide to take a chance on your product cluttering up his or her shop. Zip Dog had people who loved their stuff but wrote in complaining that they couldn't buy the records.

Because artists and labels ignore shops a lot of the time, shop managers don't get hassled like journalists or radio DJs. This means they will often be a lot friendlier and more helpful than people farther up the chain. See what they will do for you. But be sensible. If you ask them to put some bloody great A0 poster up they'll say, 'No, we've only got so much space and we're going to put up a big-name poster there'.

There are many ways of selling your own records, and even if you have found a distributor willing to sell your records into the shops (see below) this should not stop you from doing it yourself too. Some musicians don't even bother with traditional sales outlets any more and rely only on mail order, the Internet and tour sales. Many are very successful.

If you are a signed band, you can also sell at gigs, festivals and by mail order or the Internet, but you will need to check with your record company first to see whether you are able to do this yourself over and above what the record company sells or whether your record company has sole rights to sell your product this way. Most record companies have quite sophisticated Web sites and mail order services and sell a reasonable amount this way. They may also sell your product through specialist e-commerce sites. When it comes to gigging, they may sell at the gigs for you or allow you to have a certain amount of merchandise to sell yourself. A band with its own label can obviously use all these methods to sell. Like bigger record companies, it will usually also have a deal with a distribution company to sell its product in the home market, and either export deals or licensing deals with companies abroad.

## SPECIALIST RECORD SHOPS

If you have pressed up some white labels you can approach your local shops and see if they are interested in trying to sell a few for you. They are not interested in any other merchandise unless you are a 'name', although you may be able to persuade them to put a poster up to advertise your record—if you have one.

## MAIL ORDER

You can sell by mail order. You can get cards or catalogues printed up with the details of the record(s), its price and costs for postage. Most independent record companies in the UK usually include postage and packing in the price within the UK and an extra charge for outside the UK (check with the Post Office for weights and prices). You can distribute the cards to shops. Put one inside each record so people can get in contact with you, hand them out at gigs, festivals and clubs.

## OVER THE WEB

If you have built your own Web site (see p. 275), then you will need to include a mail order page with a form that people can submit to buy your records. You also need either to have a secure way for people to pay by credit card over the Net (a bit difficult this at first, unless you can link up with another company willing to process payments for you, or you could sign up for PayPal, a secure method used by eBay buyers and sellers, though you can use it for your own product too), or ask people to send in their form with a cheque or postal order for the right amount of money. Do not send out their records right away—you will need to bank the cheques first and make sure they clear before sending out the records. Occasionally, people's cheques do bounce and you want to make sure it doesn't happen to you!

## TIPS ON SELLING YOUR OWN RECORDS

### KEEP GOOD SALES RECORDS

It helps to keep good records at this point: when you receive the cheque, when it was banked, the date funds were cleared and the date you actually sent out the records. Sometimes, for whatever reason (and the Post Office isn't keen on taking the blame!), the records never reach the person who ordered them. They will get back to you and complain and ask for more records. Tell them to wait for another twenty-eight days and that if they still haven't turned up you will send some more. If they are trying to pull a fast one and get extra records for free, this often seems to put them off. If they do get back to you and want more, and if you get no joy with the Post Office, then you'll just have to send them again.

### COMPLAINTS

Some people complain that the records have arrived damaged or won't play properly. Ask them to send them back so you can check them. Sometimes it's just their record deck or CD player, so you can send them another one and keep the original one to sell to someone else, but sometimes faulty records have been shipped by the manufacturer so you're stuck with the dodgy one. Another tip: send everything second-class mail—it's surprising how much money that saves in the long run! And keep all your postal receipts and receipts for packaging materials, receipts for manufacturing merchandise, etc.—you'll need them for income tax purposes.

## PACKAGING

Be very careful with your packaging, especially with vinyl records. They get damaged easily in the post and some people buying records seem to value the cover as much as the disc inside! Buy proper 12″ vinyl mailers and padded Jiffy bag–style envelopes for CDs. If you're sending more than one CD to someone, it's worth using some extra packaging material inside the Jiffy bag around the records, as the plastic jewel boxes can scrape each other in transit and may not arrive in the best condition. With vinyl, it's worth putting in an extra piece of cardboard to strengthen the packaging, as vinyl records seem particularly prone to damage in transit.

# distribution

Distributors are the middlemen between you and the shops, and they take around 30% of dealer price—the amount the shop pays for each record. You give them the records, they sell them into the shops, either by telesales or by a sales rep, and they physically deliver the bought goods to shops around the country. There are various deals they have with shops, but normally to persuade retailers to take records by newer artists, they will give the shop a free copy for every five records the shop buys.

## JOHN KNIGHT

John Knight is partner and co-owner of Southern Record Distribution (SRD), one of the UK's biggest independent distributors. SRD, which is based in London, distributes a wide range of styles, including rock and guitar music, reggae and all forms of dance music. The company is always interested in taking on new artists and John explains how it all works.

### How did you start SRD?

I'm a failed musician really—I started to make my final steps away from playing and into the industry side of things around the time punk rock took off in 1977. I started work delivering records for Fresh Records, Miles Copeland's label (Copeland was the manager of the Police). Fresh distributed labels such as UK Decay and Illegal Records. I persuaded Our Price—the leading retailer at the time—to buy from the independent network. So I started from selling records from the back of a van and ended up selling Joy Division to Our Price.

In 1982, the guy who owned Fresh dropped out of the music business. The four of us who were left formed Jungle. We had Johnny Thunders and other ex-Fresh acts and some UK indie labels. We continued to supply Our Price and ran the labels.

The distribution side of things failed in 1986. Another independent distributor, Rough Trade, forced Jungle out of the distribution side of the business. I had to resign, as there was no job left for me—I did the honourable thing and walked and left the others with jobs. I spent a year driving Edwin Shirley trucks. (Edwin Shirley transports stage equipment and sets on tours.) Then in 1987, I met John Loder, my partner in SRD. He was working with labels like On U, Adrian Sherwood's label, Crass, and Blurg. They were all finding it hard to get proper distribution. I said he should start a distribution company and a couple of days later he phoned and said let's do it.

We set up SRD in 1988, starting in his front room with a couple of records. I phoned up Our Price and asked if they wanted to take independent records again. They said yes, and we also sold to all the independent shops. So off we went.

## What is a good way to find out if product is ready for distribution?

Take copies of your 7", 12" or CD into the specialist shops in your area and get advice from people who are supposed to sell it. If you are in a guitar band or have a guitar label, I'd recommend any band having problems getting distribution should take your record into the Rough Trade shop in London. They are still a tastemaker shop and if they pick something up and recommend it, a distributor will notice that.

Otherwise, send your music into a distributor—it's worth sending it in even if you are on your first 12" single, as it may be so good it will get picked up! Independent distributors such as ourselves, Cargo or ShellShock will all listen to anything sent to us that's decent and in a genre that we deal with.

We'll always listen to 12" pressings and white labels, but if someone sends in a CD-R with no supporting information, we won't listen to it. If someone sends in a test pressing, there's a commitment there.

Be careful what you send in. Nowadays, with so much coming in on CD-R, the temptation is to put too much music on. If there's too much, it probably won't get listened to at all. Just send three to five tracks on a CD-R—that's enough. It's hard enough for label managers to get through everything as it is.

## When approaching a distributor, how does an artist or new label find the right person to contact?

You need to find out who the right label manager is before you send things in. Phone the switchboard and they'll point you in the right direction. At SRD, we have house/techno/trance label managers, drum 'n' bass, breakbeat, indie and left-field, reggae/dub and happy hardcore. You need to get the right one. The label managers are all very busy.

## What should an artist send into a distributor to get a distribution deal?

It helps if you can go into a distributor with your 7", 12" or CD and a book of press clippings or live reviews. We do pick up one-offs, but generally we're into developing stuff. A one-off can be from a label not just a band.

Always make sure your music is totally finished. There's no point in submitting things if they are not mixed down correctly or you have no ideas for artwork, for example. We want to hear what the punter is going to hear.

We normally look for ongoing projects, like a label idea. Send something in that looks like you've got longer-reaching plans than just releasing one 12" single. Sending us a 12" single is fine if the label is using it as a trailer to a forthcoming album. It's also good if we can see the roster of artists and singles leading through to an album.

We have picked up a couple of labels recently. We know they'll only sell around five hundred but it's a sales-and-build profile. One such label is Sketchbook. We picked up the label when they had only one or two releases out. They had no massive release schedule but knew what they wanted to do. We had faith, and now they're selling ten thousand albums. Resonant is another label—it has experimental and eclectic Icelandic acts on it—we know sales won't be more than one to two thousand units at the moment but will be more later.

## What next?

You must go in confidently when trying to get distribution. You may get knocked back, but the distributor will give you a few words of advice and keep the door open. We are effectively A&Ring—the second stage of A&R. If it gets past us, the public is the next A&R stage.

If you have connections in the industry—use them. For example if your record has been produced by someone who has previously produced a big-name band or up-and-coming band, say so. Explain that your record has been produced by so and so who produced 'x' band's album. Give a succinct explanation which ties in a stronger aspect.

The label should mention if it has approached a press agent or radio plugger and at what stage the negotiations have reached. For example, if you are using Zzonked for radio plugging, say so. But be truthful. We'll phone them up and find out if you're not! If you've got specialist Radio 1 play, that's good to hear.

Phone the label manager a day or two after sending product in. Remember that each label manager gets five to ten records a day. That's around twenty-five a week and a couple of hundred in a month—so don't wait four weeks because the manager won't remember it! So you must always follow it up; it's no good sending things and not doing that. It's amazing how many people just send things to us and expect us to listen to them but they never bother to phone and find out what we thought. If we see you're keen, then we'll listen to it.

If you phone up, we'll make sure we listen to it.

So make contact as soon as possible—but be careful how often you phone; the label manager won't want to feel hounded. I tell label managers to get enquiries out of the way as soon as possible. This allows the band/label to get on with things.

## If a distributor takes on an artist, what information do you need with releases?

It's crucial to make an impact. You have to fill us in on how the year's going to go—how many singles, albums, what club dates or gigs the artist is going to do, and how big it's going to go. Anything to raise awareness.

With a brand-new project, it takes a couple of weeks to sort out basic administration and then it takes six weeks after that to get the stuff out there. This is the same time as it takes for a press and radio campaign. Journalists need time to write copy and get it into magazines and papers. There's a lead-time they have to work to and this kind of thing must be taken into consideration when planning a release.

Bear in mind that there are some differences between rock and dance product. Dance is a DJ-driven market so the records will mostly be bought either by working DJs or bedrooms DJs aspiring to be working DJs. Often when dance music is presented its destiny is set. It's been out there on white label, test pressings and so on, making people dance. There'll be two to three thousand people who want it; whereas with guitar music, you enhance the build up by getting retail on board and aiming for good response from the press.

Dance music needs to be tried and tested. So we ask the label to come in and meet us to go through everything that the label needs to do. We go through a timescale for working a single and an album—for example, six weeks for a single and eight for an album. What happens every week during that period? We explain that indie shops will want a 5 + 1 deal, or sometimes 6 + 1 for albums. This is a way of getting a new label noticed. With a new label, shops have to risk taking the deal. When you're six or seven records down the line, the shops are willing to entertain them. The sales tend to go up then anyway.

If it's an album release, we expect fifty copies of sales and marketing notes and the same amount of promos. In the notes, you'll put things like whose doing the press, radio plugging, and club promotions, any press cuttings you've already had and a list of press coming and a breakdown of the artist or the tracks if it's a compilation.

Packs should be well presented and follow the guidelines in the sales and marketing notes we issue. We get back to the label and give an order for quantities based on what the shops have told us. Then it'll be ten days to two weeks for pressing and another week for shipment.

Artwork is quite crucial to help sell albums and we like to be involved from the start. We want to see rough artwork to see if it will work. For example, the label may have run the lettering right across the top, and if it's racked at HMV, the way they display albums the lettering will be hidden, which isn't much good. We may say the lettering should be in the middle and not right across. Or maybe there should be a statement raving about the music. If it's a compilation, you have to have the information in the right place. The list of artists should be at the top, not the bottom where nobody can see it.

### Do you do pressing and distribution (P&D) deals?

We do offer P&D deals but we prefer the label to do its own manufacturing. It's a quality-control thing. If we are in charge of manufacturing, we may not know if a record has been pressed correctly, if the sound has been re-created properly, or whether artwork is right. Only the label knows the answer. However, we will offer P&D if it helps with cash flow and if the label is reasonably well established.

### What about digital distribution?

We are also moving into digital distribution. In the last nine months, we have soft-launched our digital distribution network and have a dedicated new media dept. My personal belief is that in five years' time, considerable revenue will be derived from it. I think prices will come down to irresistible levels—if twenty thousand people want a particular track on 12" at the moment, then there may be another sixty thousand who will buy it as a digital download. Downloading is definitely beneficial to music. We're uploading as many tracks as we can to all the major digital retailers. We started with Real in the US and now we're with all the major retailers. We're doing it in the indie fashion—just supplying a range of music that retailers want and downloaders want and in an efficient way.

✦✦✦✦✦✦✦✦✦✦✦✦✦✦✦✦✦✦✦✦✦✦✦✦✦✦✦✦✦✦✦✦✦✦✦✦✦✦✦✦✦✦✦✦✦

✦✦✦✦✦✦✦✦✦✦✦✦✦✦✦✦✦✦✦✦✦✦✦✦✦✦✦✦✦✦✦✦✦✦✦✦✦✦✦✦✦✦✦✦✦

## STEVE 'WESS' WESTMAN

For a US angle on distribution, here are the views of Steve 'Wess' Westman. He has been involved in the distribution side of the music business since 1990. He runs the Los Angeles–based MRI (Majestic Recordings Incorporated). MRI distributes dance and indie CDs to independent shops and major retail chains such as Tower and Virgin, from such labels as Illicit, Ball of Wax, LAX and numerous one-offs from artists without a label.

## How should a new artist approach a distributor?

If you have made your own record and you've got finished product that you want to get distributed, you could approach me directly. In a lot of cases, I pick up records for distribution through other bands that I've put stuff out for. New bands approach that band asking them how to do it and that band refers them to me.

## Is that all it takes?

I have to be positive about the product from an artist. But I can only offer them distribution. They have to come up with their own money for marketing. It's better for me to pick up people who have more than one artist and one record, such as labels with an entire catalogue. However, I've got several bands that I'm distributing records for now. None are super-successful, but this is a building block for the band because they've never had anything out before. A couple of them are Los Angeles bands and we concentrate mostly in the LA marketplace. You can put it in the stores, but that doesn't mean anything unless the band has a little bit of a fan base. Nobody else is going in there to buy it, especially if the CD is by a new indie band.

## Don't you make a loss that way?

Yes. That's one of the problems, because not everything is returnable. But in a lot of cases, I'm not on the hook for anything—especially with a couple of my labels that do their own pressing and everything and they're merely giving me their records and I'm putting them through the system. I work with [a larger distribution company] Navarre now—they take my product to the stores.

## How does that work?

My deal with Navarre is that they do the physical distribution. I used to do dance vinyl releases and I would drive out to stores with the records. But with CD, it's really hard to be a small independent distributor because you can't get good deals with Tower or Virgin. Companies like Navarre like doing deals with companies like mine because it brings them more labels and more product coming through their system. If a band with a one-off CD wanted to go directly through Navarre, Navarre wouldn't do a deal with them because they're not into having one-off projects and they would pass them down to me to handle it with the smaller projects. There are so few large independent distributors out there right now and they only want to handle labels that are going to have twenty to thirty releases a year maybe. If you're a band or even a small label which is going to put out one or two records out a year, it's not of much interest to companies like Navarre.

## Do you do pressing and distribution deals?

Yes. I can arrange for the pressing plant to ship as much as we need, directly to Navarre, so we don't have to overpress. And it's all recoupable back to the label or band. Usually, all the bands I have form a label and we do a percentage deal with the labels.

## Typically, what is that per cent?

It can vary anywhere from 25% to 35%.

## What are some risks of being a smaller distributor?

Especially with one-off band items, you can get it pressed and into the stores but nothing happens. So there's not enough money being made off the record to recoup even the pressing costs. You could lose money that way; that's really easy to do.

When a bigger project with bigger expectations doesn't pan out, you might ship twenty thousand units and then find out the record only sells three thousand. And all the unsold stuff's going to come back to you from the stores.

There are co-operative deals with retail. The distributor has to pay a little money to participate in some program for a chain to even stock your record. You might spend $3,000, or something like that, for Tower to bring in a whole bunch of your CDs. They may also put your CD in a listening post or something. The cost of the co-op deal is recoupable from the band or label. But if the product doesn't sell, there's nothing to recoup from and I'm on the hook for it!

✦✦✦✦✦✦✦✦✦✦✦✦✦✦✦✦✦✦✦✦✦✦✦✦✦✦✦✦✦✦✦✦✦✦✦✦✦✦✦✦✦✦✦✦✦✦✦

# manufacturing

Manufacturing is where the music and artwork come together to make a saleable record. There are lots of agencies around that have deals and contracts with manufacturers and will handle all this for you. If you shop around, you can find competitive prices, and this is another area where personal recommendations from other labels or artists is very helpful. And it's not always about getting the cheapest price. It's about someone who'll deliver on time; it's about the quality, making sure the cover is the right way up and so on.

Preparation is very important for manufacturing, for a smooth and economical process. If your music and artwork have been prepared properly, in an acceptable way for manufacturers, it will go fairly smoothly and should come in at the price you were expecting. But if it's not, if in some way you haven't prepared it properly, you can almost guarantee there will be delays and very probably surcharges to correct the faults. Remember, the artwork must include a bar code. If there's one thing we've learned about manufacturing, it's getting it right at every step of the way. Ask advice all along the way—it's usually free.

## CUTTING AND MASTERING

Before you can manufacture your record, you need to be able to present it to the pressing plant in the correct format.

### WHAT IS MASTERING?

Mastering is the process that takes your studio master through to a production master. It's about tweaking and massaging the track to squeeze the very best out of it (very sophisticated equalization, compression, limiting and leads that don't go *buzz*!). What you can do on a PC yourself now is quite extraordinary compared to just a few years ago, but ultimately if you want the best, then you go somewhere where they've spent thousands of pounds on a mysterious little rack unit with no knobs on it at all that makes things sound great in some indefinable way. The mastering studio uses special equipment you don't get in the recording studio.

### IS IT EXPENSIVE?

It can be anything from quite cheap to extremely expensive, in excess of £100 per hour, and to a certain extent you get what you pay for. Some studios and CD duplicating houses which also do mastering for CD only are usually midrange on price and equipment. It all depends on the depth of your wallet. The golden rule is to get price estimates first.

## WHAT CAN MASTERING DO FOR YOUR SOUND?

Mastering can't really sort out a bad mix, although it can make some corrections. What it can do is add a bit of sparkle, get the bottom end right and do all kinds of other things to a track to make it more transportable to other systems and generally sound better. It will make your tracks sound consistent in terms of level and sound.

## DO YOU NEED TO PREPARE MUCH?

Preparation beforehand will save you time (which equals money) and save you having to take snap decisions that you may live to regret. Rehearse the running order for your music. Compile as much as you can on to one DAT or CD so the mastering engineer can just play it straight in, rather than spool up and down various DATs emerging from your plastic bag. Think about fade-outs, fade-in or if you want the tracks to overlap. Hearing all the tracks together and in context may highlight flaws that you want corrected in mastering. Finally, keep an eye on the total running time and make sure you are under the limit. For CD, it's seventy-four minutes, although you can squeeze a bit more in. Before you actually go into the mastering session, find out what format your manufacturer wants your production master in. Generally, CD-R is good enough but you should ask. Then tell the mastering engineer that's what you want. At the outset, you need to inform the mastering engineer, at whatever level studio you go to, whether it's for CD or vinyl or both. The mastering for vinyl generally has less bass and different treble on it because of the CD's ability to handle a bigger dynamic range than vinyl.

## HOW MUCH INVOLVEMENT SHOULD YOU HAVE WITH MASTERING?

The mastering suite should have its monitoring sorted and the engineer should have his or her ears on your mixes and be able to get the best out of them. That's what you're paying for and, by and large, you should let them get on with their job with occasional guidance and explanations about any given track.

## SHOULD YOU TAKE A SAFETY COPY OF YOUR MASTER?

When your tracks are finished and your music is mastered and compiled and everything's sorted out for your production master, it's worth the additional expense of taking at least one DAT or CD copy. It's your reference; it's your safety copy. If the production master gets lost or damaged, at least you've got a copy of what you paid for—much like coming out of the studio with more than one copy of your mixes.

## WHAT ABOUT VINYL MASTERING AND CUTTING?

Studios able to cut vinyl are quite rare nowadays. There are lots of small studios around offering low-budget and reasonable-quality mastering for CD. Vinyl requires a cutting lathe, which is a much more expensive investment and, as a consequence, there are a lot fewer mastering studios that do it. Once you've got your track sounding right, the engineer cuts the track on to a disc lacquer, which is the template for your vinyl production process.

## HOW DO YOU GET THE BEST RESULTS?

It's worth noting at this point that to get the loudest result from vinyl you should have it cut at 45 rpm and keep your track under six minutes for a 12″. The longer the track, the closer the grooves and the quieter the record, no matter what the engineer tries to do as far as compression goes. If you want a longer track, then you can have it cut at 33 1/3 rpm but it'll end up a bit quieter. It's a specialist skill, getting good-sounding vinyl that's loud but that doesn't jump tracks. It's a bit of an art, and studios differ in quality. Try and go somewhere that's got a reputation and check out what they have done for other people.

## WHAT'S AN ACETATE?

Your lacquer must not be played on your record deck because it's soft and your stylus will seriously degrade it. If you want something to play out or play on your turntable, then ask for an acetate to be cut as well. It can be quite expensive, so ask about prices first. When you've got your production master, whether it's for CD or vinyl, you then send it off to your manufacturing facility.

## ARTWORK

Artwork is not really necessary for vinyl singles—and it's very expensive. But for all CDs and vinyl albums, you will need artwork, and this is a hurdle that

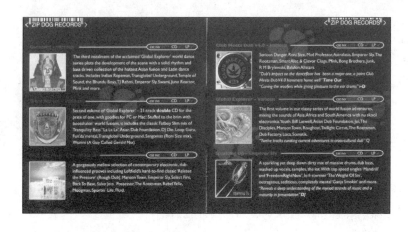

so many labels fall at. Not getting the artwork right or not getting it ready in time has been the cause of so many releases getting delayed and missing their scheduled release dates—and this is just as true for major record labels as tiny ones. It's amazing how artwork gets left until last, and yet if it's not right, the record can't go ahead. Make sure someone other than you proofreads the written copy too—it's so easy to make a mistake on the text and not notice it yourself because you were the one who input the data.

Artwork promotes your product—it could be one of the factors that persuades retailers to take your music and customers to buy it.

## WHAT ARE THE FIRST STEPS IN PRODUCING ARTWORK?

First of all, you need to decide who's going to do what. Getting the artwork done can mean doing it all yourself, or using friends, through to paying somebody else to realise your ideas or do the whole lot for you, including the creative bits. Whichever way you go, you should be clear in your mind what you want your artwork to actually say before any ideas are worked on. Try and look at it from a dispassionate point of view and consider what it's got to achieve from a purely marketing standpoint. It will help to know what formats you are going to release your record on: CD, vinyl or both. If you want to press up vinyl as well as CD, bear in mind that although visual ideas are largely translatable across both formats, it's generally more expensive to produce artwork for vinyl albums because of pre-production costs.

## WHAT ARE THE KEY STEPS IN THE ARTWORK PROCESS?

+ Coming up with visual concepts
+ Choosing and refining the best one and developing it to create the artwork
+ Adding all the other bits like additional pages, inlays, CD on-body artwork
+ Proofreading the text
+ Adding bar codes and catalogue numbers
+ Checking everything and making sure it's all okay
+ Handing over the digital files to your chosen manufacturer

Anybody with a PC or a Mac can create their own artwork. And now that CD production prices are so low, you can pretty much do full-colour artwork throughout without much difference in cost.

## WHAT ARE THE KEY THINGS WHEN COMING UP WITH ARTWORK IDEAS?

You need to think about the fact that your product is in the rack along with everybody else's. The artwork needs to get your message across quickly and effectively so that the punter who is likely to appreciate your music and is leafing through the racks picks it up, looks it over and buys it. If that happens, the first job of the artwork is done. If they get it home and like what they've bought on the strength of the artwork, then that's another tick in the box. If they buy subsequent releases just by recognition of your artwork, then you can't ask for much more.

## SHOULD YOU WORK ON ONE DESIGN OR MORE THAN ONE?

Whether you are doing it yourself or commissioning someone else to do it, it's always worth starting with at least two completely different concepts rather than plunging in and spending lots of time on one just because you suddenly get enthusiastic about it. The initial concept can be very simple. Sketch things out, even if it's sketching on the computer. Don't dive down into the detail too early on; concentrate on the core idea. When you've worked up some concepts to a stage that demonstrates largely what further developed artwork will be like, try and get some appropriate external feedback on them. If you've commissioned the artwork, the designer will come to you for feedback. If you're the designer, then get someone else's feedback. Brief that person on what you want to achieve and listen to both their initial reactions and then their more-considered comments. It's like a bit of market testing, so make the most of it.

## DOES MUSICAL STYLE INFLUENCE ARTWORK?

The direction for ideas really depends on the type of music—it's a bit like product branding. If you compare artwork on rock albums to dance albums or R&B to world music, you will see they are all very different at a basic level, with varying degrees of boldness, funkiness, sparseness, etc. If you're working on title graphics, for example, it doesn't necessarily mean it's got to be the biggest, brashest and boldest title. Some artwork succeeds by having a more minimalist and simplistic approach, where the very presence of space around the artist's name draws your eye to it; whereas a more messy or abstract approach portrays a completely different attitude. It's not that one's more valid than the other—it's a function of the type of music, the nature of the act and the contemporary style. You need to make your design as effective as possible within your area.

## WHAT'S THE NEXT STEP AFTER DECIDING ON THE ARTWORK?

If the artwork is a hand-drawing, painting, montage, photograph, etc., at some point it will need to be scanned at a professional bureau and it's probably worth spending the moderate fees getting it scanned really well rather than using your desktop scanner that you got with your PC—you'll see the difference. If you are doing this sort of thing yourself, make sure all the images are in CMYK format (cyan, magenta, yellow, black)—i.e., suitable for the standard four-colour print process—rather than RGB (red, green, blue), which is how most low-end scanners work. Also, watch out when using other people's photographs from magazines or whatever. It's like sampling, only worse—they may find out and come after you for payment. If you are doing it all yourself on your computer, take note of how you need to deliver your output to your chosen manufacturer. The standard computer platform for artwork is Apple

Mac, although PC-generated artwork is widely recognised, with the favoured computer programs being Quark XPress and Adobe Photoshop. If you are paying for all the design work, then it's the designer's responsibility to know all this sort of thing.

## WHICH PART OF THE CD ARTWORK IS THE MOST IMPORTANT?

The front cover is the key element, followed by the reverse (the inlay at the back), probably followed by the disc artwork and then, last, the inside pages of your CD booklet. It's all about packaging a product, and that's how you need to think about it. Music is a retail product, competing for shop space and punters's hard-earned money, so it stands to reason that record companies spend a lot on packaging and promotion. Just look at labels like EMI or the larger UK independents like XL and you can see that they spend quite a lot of money on their packaging. You have to compete with them but on a smaller budget.

## WHERE SHOULD YOU PUT TRACK TITLES, ARTIST INFORMATION AND SO ON?

On most records, the artwork at the back of the case (the inlay) is where people put track titles, artists' names, marketing message, record company information or any other message you want to sell the record. It's the recognised place for the bar code as well. The bar code—swiped by the shop assistant as with any product in a supermarket or other type of store—is essential for identifying sales of your record both for payment by the shop to the distributor and for chart purposes. [For how to get bar codes, see p. 267.] Once you've got all your artwork created, it's probably worth showing the files to somebody who has had experience in the area of delivering files for printing and manufacturing. Rerunning and reprinting faulty files can get expensive, as you may be charged for mistakes. So if you've got any contact to a professional who's done it before, use them.

## HOW DO THE COSTS STACK UP?

Before you go running away with extravagant ideas of elaborate packaging, pretty much anything outside the norm of a colour booklet and a jewel case costs extra money, and the more abnormal it gets, the more it costs. The cheapest additions are having a clear CD tray to see artwork through it, adding pages to your CD booklet or adding colours to the CD itself. Then there are more expensive options, like printed sleeves to go over the case, card-packaging, special inks like metallic or fluorescent and even using different materials. It's worth noting that from a distributor's point of view, extremely weird packaging is not looked on all that favourably because it is difficult to rack. The biggest thing you have to play with, without incurring runaway costs, is the fundamental cover design, and possibly adding stickers to it. Spend your time and energy first on the cover, then on the back of the inlay. You have to remember that when a punter picks it up you've got their attention for only a short while. If you don't get that, all the love and attention you gave to the inside pages of text and design doesn't mean anything, particularly if the CD is shrink-wrapped and the customer can't see inside anyway. You should try to avoid getting stung for extra costs because your artwork is not in the correct format for the production people or you've specified additional special colours. If you already know who's doing your manufacturing, ask them for a dimensional template for artwork dimensions and the print specifications. If you don't know who the manufacturer is yet, start ringing up people for prices and ask them for the template and the specifications along the way.

## WHAT MAKES SUCCESSFUL ARTWORK?

When Sarah's Zip Dog label put out the first volume in its Club Meets Dub series, there was a huge response from people saying, 'Great artwork'. Whether it's to your personal taste or not, it did the job— it sold the record and Zip Dog used it in one form or another for three more volumes. People knew exactly what sort of music they were buying because of the title and the cover artwork, and the

---

time spent getting it right in the first place paid dividends. From press to distribution to the public, if you've got a stunning cover, people notice it. Zip Dog even got it on MTV—not bad for a first album on a small, independent label.

On the other hand, for one of Zip Dog's early releases, the label commissioned an illustration of a natty DJ on the decks, thinking the illustration looked better on a plain white background and even better without the title on the cover—incredible! Not surprisingly, sales of the record weren't very impressive. The distributors weren't pleased and warned Zip Dog it might not do well because of the artwork. It seems extremely obvious now, but at the time it seemed like a bold move to show off the illustration that the label had paid out for.

## GETTING YOUR RECORDS MADE

### HOW DO YOU GO ABOUT CHOOSING A MANUFACTURER?

The first time you get records manufactured is the worst, as it's all new to you, but just be systematic; find out the deadlines and the costs for everything and don't be afraid to seek advice. Manufacturing is where the music and artwork come together to make a saleable record or CD. There are lots of agencies around that have deals and contracts with manufacturers, and if you shop around, you should get a competitive price. It's not always about getting the cheapest price. It's about someone who'll deliver on time; it's about the quality, making sure the artwork is printed correctly, the bar code is included, and so on. Personal recommendation is really handy or, failing that, visit the firm to see what sort of operation they are. Whatever, make sure you ring around and get the agency or manufacturer to talk you through the bits you need to do and give you the prices. It will educate you and make sure you've got a general idea about what each stage of the process should cost and how long it will take. Preparation is very important for a smooth and economical process. If your music and artwork have been prepared properly, in an acceptable way for manufacturers, it should come in at the price you were expecting. But if it's not, if something's wrong, you can almost guarantee there will be delays and very probably surcharges to correct the faults.

## WHAT'S THE PROCEDURE FOR MANUFACTURING CDS?

Manufacturing CDs is fairly straightforward. You can effectively split the project into the packaging artwork and the CD. For the packaging artwork, you need to supply the finished digital artwork files ready for print. The best approach would be to work with an agency that can do as much for you as possible, including running the artwork from your digital files. Just make sure you get a total price for everything first so there aren't any nasty surprises or an annoyingly excessive delivery bill. For the CD itself, you need the on-body artwork and the mastered music to give to the manufacturer. You can supply this on DAT or CD. Again, ask the company you are dealing with. They sometimes offer quite good package prices that include mastering if your music hasn't had that final treatment.

## WHAT ABOUT MANUFACTURING VINYL?

For vinyl, it's much the same sort of process but a bit more complicated. Your manufacturer will need two lacquers (one per side), disc label artwork, and cover artwork as appropriate. Twelve-inch singles often go in a plain bag—termed a disco bag. The manufacturer can cut the lacquers for you, for a fee, but you need to give them clearly marked-up masters to show what goes on what side and so on.

## WHAT ARE TEST PRESSINGS?

A certain quantity of test pressings [TPs] of vinyl is pretty much mandatory because, unlike in CD manufacturing, there's a point in the manufacturing process where you, the client, are given the responsibility of checking the production process. You will be given test pressings to check that the record doesn't skip and that it sounds how you'd expect. It's worth talking to your manufacturer about price breaks for test pressings.

## WHAT ABOUT WHITE LABELS?

White labels (or promos) are pre-release copies of your record to be given to DJs and journalists. As the name implies, white labels don't have any disc artwork on them; they just use a white label and minimal info on them. Sometimes you may have to put the information on them yourself—type labels, write on them by hand or get out the toy printing set from the loft! If you decided the TPs were okay and you're short of time, you could ask for additional copies to be made for use as white labels. However, making white labels on the same run as the TPs is a bit of a gamble because if there are any faults on the TPs your white labels will have them too, and there's nothing you can do about it. But it could save you a week or more and you may just need that extra time to get your promos out. If you've got the time, check and approve the TPs, get your white labels pressed, get the promotional activity working and then commit your money to the main production run as late as possible.

## WHAT IS THE BAR CODE AND CATALOGUE NUMBER?

In the UK, the artwork must include a bar code and a catalogue number. The bar code is something that you (or your manufacturer, distributor or agent employed to handle manufacturing) need to get from the Article Numbering Association, but the catalogue number is up to you. Manufacturers generally

work by catalogue number, not artist and title. They don't care about artists and titles; they just want a reference for the product. Simple is best. Zip Dog Records's are ZD1, ZD2 and so on. But if a record is in both CD and vinyl, you'll need to call them ZD3CD and ZD3LP, etc.

Once you've decided on your catalogue number, and the artwork, including bar code, is complete, then it's pretty much a case of handing over all the parts, telling them how many you want, writing a cheque and waiting for the records to show up.

## IS IT WORTH PRESSING ADVANCE PROMOTIONAL COPIES OF A CD?

You may want promotional items before you do your main manufacturing run but you must check out how much it will cost. If you want fifty or a hundred promo CDs before you even consider committing to manufacturing, it may be worth getting CD-R duplicates made. These will give you the mastered music and a relatively low-resolution cover image, which is often good enough for promo. If you're going to manufacture anyway, it may be worth getting manufacturing done and assigning finished copies for promo and putting stickers on them. It depends on your timescale, your budget and your needs. Also it's worth looking at the price breaks. CD manufacturing is a quickly changing market and you should look out for any deals you can get.

## DO YOU NEED TO PAY YOUR MANUFACTURER IN ADVANCE?

If it's the first time you have used the manufacturer, you can expect to have to pay upfront. As you establish a working relationship with a company that performs well for you, you can set up an account to give you credit for anywhere between thirty and ninety days, depending on how much of a wheeler-dealer you are. When you are looking at the price breaks, the thing to bear in mind is that it's not only about getting the cheapest price. You need to think about your cash flow. If you've paid for three thousand or five thousand CDs because you're confident of selling them, that payment's been taken out of your cash flow for all that time. You sell the first five hundred easily enough, but you've still got most of that initial order filling up your living room and obscuring your TV. Just because it might be a bit cheaper to buy more copies at the start, don't do it if you think you might not be able to shift them.

## HOW MANY SHOULD YOU PRESS UP?

If it's your first time and you're paying for it yourself, a thousand is enough. It's a pretty good economical order. If they sell like hot cakes, then you can afford to re-press because you should be getting the money in from the thousand you've just sold.

✦✦✦✦✦✦✦✦✦✦✦✦✦✦✦✦✦✦✦✦✦✦✦✦✦✦✦✦✦✦✦✦✦✦✦✦✦✦✦✦✦✦✦✦✦✦✦

## SCOTT POLLACK

Next, Scott Pollack, president of AtoZ Media, describes what a US manufacturer can offer a new independent label or an artist wishing to sell their own product.

## What is the role of an independent manufacturing company, and what services do you provide?

We're one of the unsung heroes of the music industry. I think we play an integral role in helping labels and artists achieve what they want to do, but at the same time no one really knows who we are or pays manufacturing much mind. We work with individuals, bands and smaller 'tastemaker' labels, which are our bread and butter, especially being in New York. We also work with a number of English labels.

In September 2005, we changed our name from AtoZ Music Services to AtoZ Media in order to encompass more services and embrace new clientele and to not get pigeonholed in only music. That said, we've been in business since 1994. We grew out of a company called AtoZed Music Services that started in London. It was one of the first independent CD manufacturers in the industry, going back to the mid-1980s. The company itself now caters mainly to independent music labels, artists and management companies. As the DVD market has come into play, we have increasingly embraced independent film companies and filmmakers—really anyone that wants to put something out on CD or DVD.

The basic premise of the company is that someone could walk into the office and we'll be able to help them—they may have their artwork created already, they may not; they may have their record mixed and perhaps mastered, they may not. We can extend as many services as the client needs and we do it on a case-by-case basis. That should be the strong point of any independent CD or DVD manufacturing company. Any prospective client should know that the company they're working with has their best interests in mind, they have flexibility and, ultimately, they're there to serve the client. For example, if someone comes to us and says, 'I need help designing my booklet intray', we have designers on staff that the person can sit down with. We try to create an open atmosphere that lets people get into a creative state and come up with cool artwork. Conversely, someone can walk in with everything already done. In that case, they just want to know the price and how long it's going to take from when they give us all their parts to when they can expect stuff delivered to them or to distributors and stores. We're basically a broker, and we make no bones about it: at the end of the day, we're not doing much of the work in-house. Everything is outsourced but it's getting outsourced to proven partners of ours, that we have years of working with, and they may be folks who aren't necessarily geared towards providing your particular individual needs. We can organise that.

## What mastering service do you provide?

There's mastering and there's glass mastering. At AtoZ we have reciprocal relationships with a number of very well-regarded mastering engineers here in New York and around the world. It's important to find a mastering engineer you feel comfortable with, who will work with you and understand your needs. We work with mastering houses that work with top major label recording acts, but you may not be best served there if you're a singer/songwriter on a budget. But we can find whatever it is that's more along the lines of what you're looking for. Typically, you'd probably need two mastering sessions, about six to twelve hours each. The engineer will go over all your work and put it into Pro-Tools. Each engineer has a very specific ear—you're looking for one that suits the style of music you make. There are some mastering engineers who specialise in hip-hop and some in rock. We work with jazz labels a lot and they use the top two or three jazz mastering engineers.

Glass mastering takes place after your master has been submitted. After the mastering engineer has provided the client with a reference CD that they are happy with, the client brings us the replication master. I would not advise that someone listen to the replication master; I'd just give it to the manufacturing house. We send the replication master to the facility to get it glass mastered. This is a polycarbonate stamper, a digital reflection of the master you've provided, and it allows the manufacturing facility to create, mould and replicate each of the discs being ordered, whether it's a thousand or a hundred thousand. The glass master is a more evolved version of the stamper process that vinyl manufacturing helped establish.

## Can the whole process happen electronically?

Even though the files on a glass master are digital, they can't be transmitted electronically because there is still signal loss. At this stage, it hasn't evolved into a completely digital medium in the sense that you mix and master your record and the engineer whams it over to the plant and they create a glass master from that. There still needs to be a physical master, which is in turn glass-mastered. Pure digital transference is around the corner, and that's certainly something we do with all our print packaging. That used to be done with films and matchprints and it was very expensive, and mistakes could mean a rerun, which could cost the client hundreds or thousands of dollars. To eliminate the physical master, the music itself needs a slightly fatter bandwidth and better security, but it's around the corner.

**Many musicians now have the capacity to burn CDs and print liner notes on their own, so why should they still come to you?**
The technology exists to let people master their own discs, burn a hundred copies themselves and print up their own artwork, but you get what you pay for. We're geared towards the artist who's beyond DIY and is really looking to make an impact in today's music industry. We're all for DIY, but you need to know where to spend your money. At the end of the day, a band should go to a decent mastering engineer and even a decent mixing engineer to really get their stuff to sound how they want it to. And as a manufacturing house, we make that record retail ready. However, we don't do distribution or marketing. Those are harder jobs than manufacturing.

**What kinds of costs are involved for first-timers and for more established smaller labels?**
The person coming off the street we call a 'one-off', and could be anyone making a thousand CDs, which is typically our minimum run, or up to fifty thousand. We treat the first-timer the same as someone we've been working with for fifteen years, because whoever comes through that door, they're bringing us their baby. Pricing is based on a CD or DVD and the packaging going into it, whether it's a folder, tray card, digipack, cardboard sleeve, whatever. The packaging makes up the basic differentiation in pricing. The CD or DVD manufacturing tends to be roughly the same price at similar levels, so if it's a thousand CDs, there's generally a price we charge, and there's a price at ten thousand and a price at a hundred thousand. The prices go down as you make more, and right now they've never been cheaper. With printing, you notice a much larger drop in price as you make more of them. The prices for CDs have dropped so low that anyone can make one for you, which is why we concentrate on offering a service to prospective clients.
Prices will be different depending on how many CDs you're running, how many units of print, how many pages make up your print, whether it's four-colour process on the inside and the outside, whether there's shrink-wrapping, a sticker. . . . All these things are what change your price. For established clients

such as record labels, we tend to work on a case-by-case basis and try to build relationships that last for years.

## So what's a rough cost for a basic one-off run, and how long does it take for the process to be complete?

For a basic run of a thousand CDs, three-colour silkscreen on the CD, glass mastering process, jewel box cases with your choice of black or clear tray, shrink wrapping and, let's say, printing of a four-panel insert card, tray card and retail barcode that we provide free, you figure about $1,000. Spending about a dollar and change per unit is a good ballpark figure. As for turnaround time, we have all of our templates on our Web site, all of our general artwork guidelines and all necessary purchase order forms. If it's laid out to our specifications or just needs a little adjusting (which we do generally for free), then we make a hard-copy proof that needs to be approved by everybody, and you sign off on that. This takes about a day or two, from you giving us your art files to running off the proof. Once it's proofed and we have your master, you should expect it to take about twelve to fifteen days to manufacture the CDs, do the print, handle all the assembly, shrink-wrapping and boxing it up. Then you should allow a couple more days for freight. We work with a network of partners spread around the country, so if we know where it's going to ship to we'll ideally set up your job as close as possible to your geographical location to cut down on costs.

## Are there differences between manufacturing in the US and the UK?

Printing is much cheaper in the UK, especially for specialty packaging. CDs run about the same in terms of cost, and they run them quicker too. There are English labels that we worked with for years, then lost when the pound became weaker against the dollar, and now we're working with them again because of the strong pound. We have to temper their expectations of the American market, because things happen a little bit slower here and can sometimes be a little more expensive, but they're saving money because the cost of freight has gone up tremendously. So instead of shipping over twenty-five thousand CDs, they can just send me a master and artwork and I can do everything here. So the cost savings are in the freight, even though it may be a little more expensive to make the CDs here.

## What about newer technologies, such as the Internet or DVDs?

In an obvious way, downloading is in direct competition to us, but then again it's not, because at the end of the day it's our belief, and our clients' and labels', that the packaged good is not going away. People want something they can hold and touch and feel, and there's a whole collector's mentality about buying music, especially independent music. The packaged good isn't going away, it's evolving. Major label bands are starting to put out multiple versions of their record, so you'll see a deluxe edition with the photobook and CD and DVD at a certain price point, then the CD/DVD in the standard jewelbox, and then there's just the CD. I see that happening in independent music as well, with more and more acts and groups and labels doing DVDs as part of their CDs and not charging for it. We're also seeing more music labels putting out DVD projects of bands that maybe don't have a new record planned for a number of years, so you bridge the gap between releases by putting out a DVD of the last tour.

Another new technology is the dual disc, which is a fantastic proposition. It's a full-length CD on one side, and a full DVD-5 on the other side. It offers a more unified vision of the band's work and is less prone to being copied. Also, the next generation of DVDs will be interesting for certain groups, particularly electronic labels. I think the next-generation DVD, whether it's BlueRay, DVD-hybrid or HD-DVD, will present a lot of interesting capabilities for visual as well as audio improvements, so fans can enjoy the music on another level. These are also not as copy prone, so the labels will be more excited about releasing them, and so should artists themselves. Right now, a dual disc is more expensive than a CD and DVD packaged together, unless you're making fifteen million copies. But the costs will drop soon.

❖❖❖❖❖❖❖❖❖❖❖❖❖❖❖❖❖❖❖❖❖❖❖❖❖❖❖❖❖❖❖❖❖❖❖❖❖❖❖❖❖❖❖❖❖

# the internet

No serious musician would be without a Web site. It has become a key way to promote music, whether to the public or to the music industry. A&R, press, pluggers, agents and advertising agencies will all expect any serious artist to have a top-notch, well-designed Web site to showcase themselves and their songs.

The Internet is also a key way to promote and sell your music to the public, either as a mail order service or as downloads, saving the expense of manufacturing.

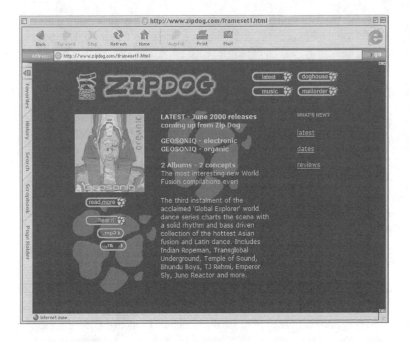

You will have noticed the Internet constantly crops up in this book as people mention checking out sites, developing their own sites, talking about the potential for marketing and so on. Indeed, anyone doing music cannot ignore the significance of the Internet, whether it's listening to other people's music, checking out new band sites—signed or unsigned—getting your own music on new band sites, or creating your own site. As a marketing tool, the Internet can open up the world to your music and it's virtually free.

On the other hand, the complications of copyright, piracy and who owns what are getting greater, and major record labels are getting more concerned and more demanding when it comes to their own artists putting their own music on their personal sites.

This section looks at the two major aspects of music on the Net: creating your own site to expose and most likely sell your own music, and getting your music on someone else's site with the objective of getting exposure and probably a record deal. We begin with creating your own site. Rod Lambert explains how the process behind the DIY Web site offers musicians the ability to sell their own CDs and digital downloads.

## ROD LAMBERT

Design software and new media director Rod
Lambert has lots of experience developing
Web sites as well as running a record label.
Here he takes you through the basics of de-
veloping your own site.

### How do you set up your own Web site?

The Internet is the cheapest means of worldwide promotion. You can pretty much say that
anybody who's trying to be something in a serious capacity should have a Web site. In fact,
even if you're not serious, you should proba-
bly have a Web site. The main things you'll need to do are get the content for
your site, build it, get it put up on the Web and then promote it. Promotion is
important because there are millions of Web sites, just like there are bands,
and finding a site can be like looking for a needle in a haystack.

The Web is so huge—it's almost like space! There are a number of ways
of getting your site on the Web. What's best for you depends on what you
expect your site to do (e.g., is it a brochure or a shop?), how much you want
control of yourself and ultimately how much time and money you are prepared to spend.

### Do I want complete control and ownership of the site?

Naturally, most people would answer yes. However, to achieve this, you will
need to register a unique name (called a domain, e.g., myunknownband.com)
for your Web site. This is yours as long as you keep paying the annual subscription to the company that registered it for you. But owning your own
domain means you will probably not be able to use the myriad of cheap or
free online Web site building services—like *www.myspace.com* or *www
.iwantoneofthose.com*; on the latter, go to the site and then search for Mr.
Site—this will take you to the relevant page. You don't get a lot of space
for the money with iwantoneofthose.com but it is a package that offers the
home users everything they need. Or you could use those provided by lots

of Internet Service Providers (ISP). To use these, your site will almost certainly have to be on their domain and so will ultimately be under their control. So your Web site will be called something like cheapsitebuilder.com/myunknownband.

If you want to dip a toe in and get started quickly, these are fine and offer very good value for modest amounts of money, although it's probably worth choosing where you can upload music files. The best thing is to find one using a recommendation or search engine and just get stuck in.

### How much am I prepared to do myself?

If you've never done it before and you've no personal interest in learning what goes behind a Web site, then get help from someone who has or find a commercial concern to do it for you. Before you start with anybody, ask to look at the sites they have built and ask them how much everything will cost, from setting the site up (registration and hosting fees, e-mail service, and any other facilities) through to design, building and updating it. Be very clear on what you get, what you actually own and what the implications are if you want to move your site later on down the line.

This is an area that is worth doing research on, seeking advice on, and looking at the fine print. The Web is a pretty stable business now, so if something seems incredibly cheap there is probably a catch.

There are an increasing number of companies offering a complete package of domain registration, design site setup and dedicated software that manages most of the site for you, collectively known as content management systems (CMS). These are great because you can easily change your site for free. Their downside is that they are usually of a pretty standard design, because they rely on templates—great for small businesses but maybe not best suited for your purpose. Again, look at examples, do some research and be clear on what you get.

If you really want to learn how to make a Web site, it's going to take you a while to get it together and looking right. Although there is also software to help, you'll have to learn at least the basics of hypertext mark-up language (HTML) and get to grips with putting your site on to the Web. To make your site look like professional music sites, then you will also have to get your head around animations and programs like Macromedia's Flash.

To take this on, you should be fairly computer literate. It will take time and you might not want to waste your life doing that sort of thing. If that's the case, get others involved, explore your network of friends or try colleges.

## Does it cost much?

As with most things, there's very cheap, not so cheap and expensive. Very cheap means you build the site yourself with software that's free or borrowed. Unlike many other kinds of businesses, there are lots of people working away in their bedrooms building Web sites so it doesn't need to involve ridiculous sums of money to get somebody else to help out—unless you're rich and don't care, of course!

If you pay someone else, it's probably best if they look after absolutely all of it for you and do things to an agreed specification. They'll look after site registration, construction and everything. You tell them what you want and they should deliver it. Before you sign up for that sort of thing, get them to show you examples of their work that are actually online and say things like, 'So how much will all of that cost me?'

## What do you want to use your site for?

Let's suppose you've found a provider, registered the domain myunknown-band.com, and you've bought some space with an ISP that offers good service, support and connection speeds. Part of the process should set up e-mail (maybe forwarding it to your private account) and a means of securely uploading your site on their system.

The next thing is to build your site, and part of that is deciding what you want to do with it. The two basic angles are one, promoting and marketing the act, and two, selling merchandise. Promotion and marketing is cheap to set up by comparison because it just relies on good content and your effort. You should try keeping your site up-to-date and changing it frequently because there are thousands of sites around that are never updated and people don't bother to go back to them. The Web is an increasingly important aspect of music distribution and promotion and it's much better to have something simple that you can work with up there now rather than taking months to get something complicated up.

## What should the site look like?

In terms of the site, there is the design (including navigation—getting from section to section) and the content. Whether you're building it yourself or someone's doing it for you, at the end of the day you're trying to improve your profile, so you need to pay attention to how the site looks and works and the quality of the content. As a rule, simple is best on the Internet. You can get really good looking, simple sites where a couple of tiny pages and some music do most of what you need. If they're simple, they'll work faster and be easier to build and maintain. They might not be as exotic as ones that have had lots of money and time spent on them, but start simple and get something up there because you can always change it later.

I get really frustrated with complicated graphics and animations on the opening page of a site unless they are really good. It's where everybody puts them, for obvious reasons, but I, and a lot of other people, find them annoying when visiting or spending time on a site. They give attitude but should not get in the way of the information.

Think about having buttons to click so the user can bypass any time-consuming pages if they wish. The counterbalance is that you do want visual interest in the site but it doesn't necessarily have to be complicated. It's good to deliver some level of funkiness, such as using applications like Macromedia's Flash that can generate animated sequences, including sound, with a relatively low overhead so long as you don't have to wait too long. It's something you should really test thoroughly online, not on your computer, to see how long it actually takes to get through it.

### Is there any easy way of getting design advice?
You don't need to work it all out for yourself. If you are trying to get to grips with HTML, there are a number of Web sites which will advise you on how to design your own site, such as webhelp.org, or you can visit other bands' sites and, with your browser—Internet Explorer or Netscape Navigator—use 'View Source' on your menu where you can see the background code they used to build it. It looks horrible at first but starts to make sense if you study it a bit. That's the great thing about the Web: so much is free if you take the time to learn about it. Time spent looking at lots of other people's sites, both good and bad, will give you a good feel about how to go about things—what's best to include and what to stay away from.

### Any other basic rules about building a site?
You need to think about how people will access it through their browser. You should understand the kind of base level of browser that you're aiming your site at, because more complicated aspects that will work in Microsoft's Internet Explorer (most PCs) may not work in Mozilla's Firefox (popular on Macs) and vice versa. There's lots of information about it on the Web and there are lots of books about it. The other thing on the browser side of building the site is that you really should check how your site looks and works in both. Try and use style sheets when you build the site, because they give much better control and consistency to how each page is delivered.

## How do i get music on the site?

As you get more ambitious, you can have music and video and all kinds of things. As yours is a music site, you should be looking to include audio as soon as possible because, naturally enough, people are going to be more interested if they can hear what you're doing. The most basic way is to offer audio files as some kind of download—people click on the file and it's downloaded to their computer and they play it when they've got it all. Mp3 files are universal, although keep your eye on size and quality when you convert your files (you will probably need special software for this).

Most people (but not all) now have some form of reasonably fast digital Internet connection. This is fine for mp3 files but video is still pretty demanding. If you are interested in this, then look at streaming services like Real.com.

## What information should you put on your own Web site?

Check out other people's sites to see what's included. There are sections in most sites which explain the artist or label's identity and give news of events, gigs, record releases; things that are changing; areas of musical, social or political comment; pictures; music; how to contact them; how to buy their merchandise; and links to other sites of interest.

## Why are links important?

Links to other sites are a promotional tool and help improve your placing in search engines. Contact sites that you think may be interested in helping you to promote yours—you have a link to your Web site on theirs and they have a link to yours.

To optimize your promotional opportunities on search engines is to make sure that you have good descriptive key words built into your Web pages in the right order because the search engines will pick up on these. If you make techno, for instance, the word 'techno' should feature high up in the key words.

Changing the content on your site frequently also helps with search engine ranking. This is an advantage of a simple HTML site that uses all text for words rather than making them pictures to look fancy. Search engines will ignore words that are made as picture files.

## How do you sell your merchandise through your site?

The other significant opportunity the Web offers is selling from your Web site rather than somebody else's (like eBay). Again, as with all Web stuff, go and have a look at what other people are doing. At the basic level, it's a mail order business. You display your product on one of your pages, list how much it costs and people post you a cheque using overland mail. It's simple, it should be effective but it's not really utilising the full resources of the Internet. Even at that level, you're going to need a bank account, and it might be an idea to have a P.O. box number rather than putting your home address up on the Web. If you want to get some kind of online transaction going, you're going to need to be able to handle credit cards and you should really be thinking of some level of security of the transactions. There are lots of companies (including banks) that will provide merchant accounts and credit card services for you and secure transactions, but you're obviously going to have to pay for it. Your site will need to hook up to their technology, so someone's going to have to know what they're doing. If you're the novice Web site builder, I'd strongly recommend you to get some advice on it. You've got to do some sums on how much business you expect to do and whether it's worth the investment or not. If you know other musicians and labels, there's no reason why you shouldn't think of clubbing together and sharing a facility. After all, it's partly about making things cheaper.

✦✦✦✦✦✦✦✦✦✦✦✦✦✦✦✦✦✦✦✦✦✦✦✦✦✦✦✦✦✦✦✦✦✦✦✦✦✦✦✦✦✦✦✦✦✦✦✦✦

## ONLINE RESOURCES FOR UNSIGNED ARTISTS

There is an abundance of useful online resources for unsigned artists. Many of them vary and offer good ways of helping to host, sell or distribute your music. As a band or artist, when you start building your fan base and creating awareness of your music, it is important to make your songs widely available so that as many people as possible can hear them. Most people within the industry, whether they are promoters, managers or A&R, will want to hear the entire track and be able to send them around to people that they think may be interested. This is why it is recommended that you do not offer just thirty-second samples of your songs on your Web site or songs that are protected using DRM (Digital Rights Management). DRM can make it impossible for certain songs to be playable on different types of mp3 player. A simple full-length mp3 with no copy protection is the best route to creating awareness of your music if you're starting out. If you have an album's worth of songs and are reluctant to give them all away, then just put two or three on your site and keep the rest for when you release the album.

## Hosting

If you want your songs and information about your band made public, there are a number of simple to use and often free services. A very popular one is MySpace.com. To sign up, follow this link—signup.myspace.com. Another site that offers free hosting for bands is uberlabel.com. Uberlabel offers more song storage then MySpace and helps you sell merchandise and CDs. Music-zombie.com also offers hosting, as well as many other very useful services for unsigned artists.

## Selling Your Music Online

Obviously, iTunes.com and Napster.com are the most well-known download stores and, thanks to CDbaby.com and Ideadistributors.com, it is possible for you to sell your tracks from these popular stores by following the simple instructions on their sites. CDbaby also offers you the ability to sell your physical CDs online and allows you to accept payments via credit card, a complex process if you are hoping to set this facility up yourself. They also fulfill the orders and inform you when a CD is ordered. (See interview page 284.)

Another good online download store is Tunetribe.com. This was set up by Tom Findlay of Groove Armada and offers a straightforward and effective way of selling your music online; all one needs to do is fill in some basic information and submit the songs. To quote from the site:

> 'It's free to join, you set the price for your music and manage everything online. You also get a much bigger slice of the pie—up to 80% of every track you sell. TuneTribe also markets and promotes artists, helping you reach new audiences'.

An alternative way of selling your music online is provided by Weedshare.com. This service allows people who buy your songs to make a commission if they introduce your music to a new buyer. That buyer is then able to make a commission from selling the track. This provides a good incentive for people to introduce your music to friends they may think will be interested in it.

## Information Portals

There are many very useful information portals that can help you find out about new music that you may not otherwise be aware of. Upto11.net indexes peer-to-peer networks and forms recommendations based on which artists have been downloaded by certain users. Another good resource is Allmusic.com. This site provides rich information on the history of certain artists and genres of music, as well as lots of other very useful information.

## Other Useful Sites

Sonicbids.com offers various tools to help artists with press kits, helping save money on mail outs. Starpolish.com offer artists a variety of useful resources and can hook them up with A&R reps from a broad cross-section of major and independent labels. Drownedinsound.com is also useful, with interesting news and features. Garageband.com offers hosting and allows users to submit their feedback on songs, creating a chart generated by the users themselves. Keeping your fans up-to-date with what's going on is important and Bandletter.com offers newsletter services to help you do just that. Other interesting sites for artists are Indiemusician.com, which contains good information and links, and Tourdates.co.uk, which hosts artist Web sites and songs as well as provides information on gigs and concerts. There are also some useful links in Musicbusinesslinks.com/directory.

## A Bit on DRM

Many of you may not be aware of what DRM is. DRM stands for Digital Rights Management. Many labels and musicians want their music protected from online piracy, and DRM, to a certain extent, can provide some of this protection. Without going into too much technical detail, there is much controversy surrounding DRM. Apple uses its own proprietary DRM, which is exclusive to the iTunes store and iPod mp3 player. Essentially, you can only play music bought from iTunes on your iPod, or music that is not protected with any DRM, such as music from CDs or downloaded on peer-to-peer networks. If you buy a song from Napster.com, it won't play on an iPod. Other players, such as those produced by Creative, allow you to play pretty much any music files on them (even ones bought from iTunes). The three main DRMs are provided by Apple (as discussed), Microsoft (as used by Napster and most other download stores) and Real Networks (as used on its own store). Unless you have your songs on iTunes, you won't be able to use its DRM.

Many labels and artists want to see a standard DRM so consumers don't need to worry about whether songs they buy are compatible with their music players. At the moment, it is a bit like going into Tesco's and the chain saying that any DVD you buy will only work on a Tesco DVD player. If you are going through most of the online music stores previously mentioned, they will provide the DRM encryption as a part of their service, so it is not something you need to worry about that much. If you want to sell your songs yourself directly from your site, you may want to use a service such as Weedshare, as this will allow you to protect your songs and offer a financial incentive for people who may buy them to forward them to their friends.

## What's the Catch?

There are a couple of problems with offering your music to a talent site. While you retain the rights to use your music—all initial arrangements are nonexclusive—you will probably give away your music to a potentially paying public. But this is the way things are going, and even acts that have international distribution are beginning to offer free downloads as a means of promotion (after all, it's much the same as those free CDs mounted on music magazine covers). Until you are quite successful, you give away quite a proportion of your music as promotion anyway and at least this way it doesn't cost you anything to do that! Some sites offer facilities for people to pay a download fee or make a custom CD, so you could be earning a bit from the Internet before you can fund a proper product release.

Compared to running your own site and getting as many people to hear your music as you would on a commercial site, you don't have nearly so much chance to gather an electronic database to boost future attempts to sell product or get people to gigs. But achieving high traffic on your own site is very difficult—how will you make people aware of what you're doing? If you go on to a third-party site, try any means necessary to get people to e-mail you—it's even worth giving up a bit of band biog space, if that's what it takes.

But don't abandon normal promotion in favour of the Internet—and get your act together!

So it is clear that there are an abundance of online services geared towards unsigned artists. They all vary greatly in terms of what they offer but the ones previously mentioned will most likely be of service in various ways, depending on your needs. The majority of unsigned artists should be more concerned about creating awareness of their music. There are literally hundreds of thousands of artist Web sites on the Internet, and having people find yours is a difficult process without a heavy marketing budget behind you. How do you choose? Here, two Web services, CD Baby's Derek Sivers from the US, and Indy.tv's Ian Clarke from the UK, describe what they offer.

✦✦✦✦✦✦✦✦✦✦✦✦✦✦✦✦✦✦✦✦✦✦✦✦✦✦✦✦✦✦✦✦✦✦✦✦✦✦✦✦✦✦✦✦✦✦✦✦✦✦

## DEREK SIVERS

Derek Sivers is founder and CEO of CD Baby, a Web site that offers musicians the ability to sell their own CDs and digital downloads via the Internet. Derek has been a musician for many years. He graduated from Berklee music school and also worked for Warner Chappell music publishing. CD Baby was estab-

lished in 1998 and since then has grown consistently, helping musicians to sell their music to a worldwide audience. So far, over $15 million has been given to musicians from sales of their music through the site.

### What motivated you to set up CD Baby?

Having put out my own album in 1997 and gotten college radio airplay, it got too much to just rely on selling my CDs at shows. I called up Amazon and other online music retailers and they asked me who I was using for a distributor. I realised that there was no service that would actually allow me to sell my CD online if I didn't have a distributor. I decided that I'd sell the CD from my own band Web site, so I went about getting payment facilities for all of that. It was a lot of work setting that up, so I went to my other music friends and told them I'd be happy to sell their CDs for them, too. Eventually friends told friends and it developed from this hobby into CD Baby. Because this was the original direction, the company DNA was shaped. The focus has always been about providing a proper service for musicians.

### How long ago did you set it up?

It was really in 1997 that it was set up, although at that point it was still just me selling my and my friends' CDs from my Web site. In March 1998, I got a new domain and CD Baby was launched.

## Did you need any funding to set it up?

No. It took me about ten days to actually build it. My startup expenses were about $500. CD Baby has always been profitable and in the black.

## Have you done a lot of advertising?

It's mainly been word of mouth. A CD manufacturer here in the US, Disc Makers, has helped to promote the service, which has been very useful. I never really bought any advertising or went out of my way to do any marketing. We just focus on providing a good service.

## How rapidly has the service grown?

Very slow for the first few years. It has roughly doubled in size every year since we started and has been at a manageable rate. Six months into it I was only getting three or four orders a week, but because I was spending so little, the company was able to grow steadily, despite not selling huge volumes in the first few months. After four years of CD Baby, we hit the million-dollar mark of payouts to musicians; nine months later, we were at two million; and four months after this, we were at three million. Currently, we have pay out almost a million dollars a month to musicians.

## Can you summarise what CD Baby could offer independent musicians?

CD Baby was founded to be a distribution-deal dream come true from a musician's point of view. When I started it, I thought what my ideal situation for distribution would be as a musician. The first thing I thought was that I would like to be paid every week; second, I want to know the full name and address of everyone who buys my album; third, I won't be kicked out of the system if I am not selling enough. Finally, there should be no paid advertising placement for musicians, as this would compromise the credibility of the service. We are here, from a musician's point of view, to get their music out to the world in a way that entirely treats the musician as king, in all ways: it's down to a transparent system that shows them the details of every single order and very open accounting that gives weekly account updates. We are also now the single largest digital distributor to all the different digital services, such as iTunes and Napster. We account for around 25% of the iTunes catalogue, so not only can we fulfill orders for your physical CDs but we get your music on all the digital services as well.

### How is the money divided between the musicians and CD Baby?

We keep a standard $4 cut per CD. For digital downloads, it is different: we take a 9% deduction.

### What are the day-to-day processes of running the company?

We have a system in place; it's all about managing the quantity of orders. We get around two thousand orders a day and a hundred new artists wanting to join each day. We're open seven days a week, with people working in the offices from 7 a.m. until 10 p.m.

### Where do you see digital music going?

It's very difficult to tell what the future holds for music. I try not to get too tied to any one idea or prediction. Right now, I am interested in providing a service that works well for musicians.

✦✦✦✦✦✦✦✦✦✦✦✦✦✦✦✦✦✦✦✦✦✦✦✦✦✦✦✦✦✦✦✦✦✦✦✦✦✦✦✦✦✦✦✦✦

✦✦✦✦✦✦✦✦✦✦✦✦✦✦✦✦✦✦✦✦✦✦✦✦✦✦✦✦✦✦✦✦✦✦✦✦✦✦✦✦✦✦✦✦✦

## IAN CLARKE

Ian Clarke is chief technological officer of UK company Indy.tv, the owner of a music discovery tool that helps artists gain global exposure to their music by placing it on the site for download by listeners.

### When did you start working on the Indy.tv music discovery tool?

We started thinking about it around August 2004 and then began developing it in December 2004. It started off with one person working on it full-time and then it grew from there.

### Was it your idea?

I had been thinking of something like this for a while. The idea is not new; it is based on a system known as collaborative filtering. A similar system is also used by Amazon to recommend books to people, based on their previous purchases.

## How does it differ from other similar services?

The closest alternatives are Last.fm and iRATE radio. I felt that the functionality of iRATE did not have a high standard in terms of usability and that with Last.fm, you don't get to keep the music. With Indy.tv, you always get to keep music you have heard on it.

Our service is a hybrid of pre-existing ideas, incorporating functions based on our own ideas that we feel make it better to use then the alternatives, either as a listener or artist. The beauty of the service is that it bypasses genres and preconceptions of what users think they might like. As a result, users are introduced to music that may be new to them and which helps their musical discovery. Because this system overcomes pigeonholing of music into genres, it can direct music that covers a broad range of styles based on what the user has rated. It considers other people's ratings and uses this information to help direct the right music towards the right people. The symbiotic way in which it works means that the more feedback you give, the more accurate it will be in delivering relevant music to you. We want it to become a pure meritocracy for music. Indy.tv can also expose music to niche groups more efficiently and cost effectively then conventional and more traditional forms.

## How did you start your service?

Indy.tv is an offshoot of Change.tv, which is a project backed by a Venture Capital firm.

## Who runs it on a day-to-day basis?

We have a team of Web developers and designers who are responsible for ensuring that the systems are working and can deal with the increasing usage volumes. I am the CTO (chief technology officer) and my brother is in charge of everything related to the coding. Steven Starr and Oliver Luckett played a substantial role in helping set it up.

## What's involved in running such a site—what are the practicalities?

The majority of the work we do is updating the service to make it work more efficiently, as the usage levels are increasing at a very high rate.

### Do you take any music?
The music must be freely available and be provided with the consent of the copyright holder.

### In what ways do you promote the service you offer?
So far it has developed through word of mouth. Originally a site called Boing-boing.net picked up on it, then Slashdot.org.

### Who do you seen benefiting from it?
Artists will benefit in terms of global exposure. Music lovers will benefit from it because it will help them seek out music that isn't necessarily signed to major labels.

### How many artists/songs are on it so far?
There are twelve hundred tracks on it and we have forty thousand in reserve. We also have around four hundred artists using it, which we anticipate to grow rapidly.

### The service is currently free for artists and users. Do you have any intentions to commercialise it at some point?
Yes, at some point; however, this will not affect the fact that it is free for artists and people who use the service.

❖❖❖❖❖❖❖❖❖❖❖❖❖❖❖❖❖❖❖❖❖❖❖❖❖❖❖❖❖❖❖❖❖❖❖❖❖❖❖❖❖❖❖

# running your own label

If you have had some success putting out your own records and you fancy the challenge of running a record company as a business rather than as a vanity label just for your own tunes, then this section gives you the information you need to make that next step.

# SETTING UP YOUR OFFICE

It sounds obvious, but you need a sensible workspace and a certain level of equipment to run your label efficiently.

You'll need a computer with office software. You can't work effectively without at least a Windows computer, a printer and a modem or broadband connection.

You can invest in some tailor-made bookkeeping software, but if you're really skint you can use an integrated multifunction package like Claris Works or those supplied by Microsoft to prepare something your accountant can use.

You must have at least a basic filing system. You'd be amazed how much paperwork gets generated—things like distributor statements, MCPS invoices and licences, artwork and delivery notes. Sometimes it seems endless.

You need to create a corporate identity. A good logo is essential to put on your records and on your paperwork, etc. When you send someone a fax, for example, you want the receiver to know that it comes from an established company and not someone they've never heard of. A good logo can help sales too. Some people fall in love with a label rather than any particular artist on the label and they'll buy everything the label puts out. Sarah and her colleagues have had a lot of positive feedback on their Zip Dog logo and it has certainly been an asset in selling the label's product.

In the UK, you need a subscription to *Music Week* in order to get a free copy of the indispensable *Music Week Directory*. The *Directory* comes out annually in January and costs a lot (£65)—so you're much better off getting *Music Week*, getting the directory free, and having the added bonus of reading about what's happening in the industry as well. The *Directory* is invaluable: it lists contact details (address, phone/fax numbers, e-mail and Web addresses, names of key staff members), the majority of record labels, distributors, manufacturers, press and promotions companies, agents, venues, rehearsal rooms, studios, merchandise suppliers, jingle producers, session companies—well, you name it; if it's about music it's probably in there. The only area where it does fall down is that of specialist retailers—there are very few listed—and a lot of the very small, underground labels. If you want your label to be in it—it's worth it and it's free—the details of who to contact and when are in the book.

A key point to remember is always, always, always write down useful information that you find out—for example, reviews editors or journalists' phone and fax numbers, magazine circulations, people who can do decent artwork cheaply—whatever.

Write everything down so you don't have to go back and find it again. Have a file or book called 'leads' and make sure everything goes in. It can be extremely frustrating to realise you need to get back to someone, like a journalist who really liked your last record, only to discover you've lost his or her number. Getting journalists' private telephone numbers is a real feat and they should be guarded like gold dust. Asking people for the number again usually gets the brush-off.

## RUNNING A RECORD LABEL

There are some things about conventional business that are not applicable to the music industry. In the UK, you may decide to get a government-backed business loan to start up your label, or money from a charitable source, such as the Prince's Trust. In regard to government funding, to be eligible for the money, you will have to go on a business-training course. However, such courses will not find it easy to advise you because music is such a varied and unusual product—no two records or artists are exactly alike (even though we may think so sometimes when we watch TV chart shows or listen to the radio) and the product arouses people's emotions—from love to hate.

Music is very much a personal aesthetic choice, even more so than clothes. But with niche marketing (which applies to virtually all indie labels), you don't have to check out High Street competition in the same way as companies in other industries have to. Indeed, independent record labels don't always see each other as deadly competitors.

The music business generally operates with different rules and there are only some things that apply to both music and other industries.

### Identify Your Market

This doesn't, however, mean that you shouldn't identify your market and not ask yourself, 'Who do I think is going to buy my records?' and 'Do these people exist and are they accessible as a group?' This isn't as daunting as it sounds. You may be a rock band and decide to put out your own records. You've discovered that a hundred and fifty people go to a certain pub every Saturday. You've found out from the musicians who play there that they play in twelve similar pubs. Do your sums and you'll discover that you've actually got a potential buying public of a couple of thousand people reasonably local to you. They won't all buy the record—if they did, you'd have a mildly successful first release—but some will buy it and play it to their friends, and if the record's good the word will spread and the next record should do better, and so on.

## Music Policy

The key role of the new independent label is to put out exciting music which hasn't managed to convince the main body of the music industry that if it gave it a go it would get its money back. It's as simple as that. The mainstream business today is run more and more tightly, and not controlled by people who can afford to be passionate about music. So there's a better case for new forms of music being put out independently.

If you've already been putting your own records out, you already have experience and some success in selling new and, in your eyes, exciting music to the public. Now you feel you want to branch out, put out music by other artists, but before you do this you need to look carefully at your music policy and make sure it is consistent and that your distributor, retailers, the press and the public know what to expect. It will only confuse people if you start putting out a variety of styles. If you've always released your own rock records and you suddenly start releasing house tunes, you'll need a different label at your distributor, or even a different distributor altogether. Shops won't know how to rack (display) your records, and any music journalists who like your rock records probably won't like the new-style house tunes and you'll disappoint fans of your label out there who expect only the best in rock from you—they may even despise house! So decide on your music policy, what style you're going for, and stick to it for now.

## Artist Relations (A&R)

Well, you can't have a label without an artist. This book primarily concentrates on you being the artist, but if you want to sign artists other than yourself, what do you do? And should you?

If you decide the answer is yes, then most people start by putting out records by people they know or by local artists and building from there. But don't rush to put things on a formal basis at first. The important thing is to let your relationship grow and to help the artists with their music. Many people who want to go into the record company side, who are not musicians themselves, want to go around being sticklers for everything and filling in the right forms. A quick dose of the record industry will cure you of that. And it's not in your best interest.

Another thing to bear in mind is that your record label, like any other record company or publisher, whether an independent or a major, will expect to recoup—or get back—the costs you've incurred on signing, recording and marketing an artist. Any monies spent on an artist are recouped out of the band's royalties; the band gets nothing until the record company has got all its money back first.

The way we feel you should proceed for your first release for an artist other than yourself is that it should be 'We're in this together. Let's take our knocks and see how it goes'. Try not to get involved with any contractual relations with them whatsoever. Unless they downright refuse to put the record out any other way, try to keep things on a matey basis and see how it goes. If that doesn't work, and if you're not comfortable with it, then probably the best thing to do (in the UK) is to get hold of the Musicians' Union guidelines and sort out whatever flexible terms there are between yourself and the artist. On the whole, contracts are only any use if things are going right. If the relationship doesn't work, then you're probably not going to be interested in putting out records by that person anyway. And they will not interested in being released by you because, for example, they think you didn't sell enough and they didn't get any money for their effort in the studio. So it's only if things go seriously right that you need contracts, in which case you're on a better footing to say, 'Well look, I sold lots of your records and I want decent terms on your contract'. (See p. 377 for more on contracts.)

At the same time as wanting your artists to give you the music without too many commitments on your part, you want to get the relevant commitment out of them. You would like them to support the record release in any way that they can. If they play live, obviously you might get involved in increasing the number of gigs they're doing and in having a presence at those gigs. Don't ignore the grassroots: go to gigs with the records and give them to the band to sell. If they don't play live, can they be persuaded to do so—because that will help. Do they go to environments where they can affect the future of the record? This may be a student union where they can get the record on to the jukebox; it may be the gigging circuit or they may be hangers-out in record shops. It's in their interest to get this record going, so try to make sure they help out.

If things go well, you will want some follow-up records, and one rule that you should apply to the early stages is that you want more of the same music.

You may not choose to release it, but it's comforting to know that you have a couple of tracks that are in the same style and it is a toss-up which one you do next. Because if the punters liked that first style and are pleased with it, they want the same kind of music the next time—if the band is adventurous and experimental, then they want the same adventurous and experimental music the next time, if not the time after. And that's why a lot of people get turned down at record companies: for not having enough focus. In the early phases, when familiarity is growing, people want a narrow thing to become familiar with. So that's how you should structure your artist relations.

## Marketing

The basic principles of marketing and promotion—press, radio and club promotions discussed earlier in this chapter—still apply, although you might want to spend more on them now that you've committed yourself to running the label as a business.

As your label becomes more established, it may start to become worth advertising its product. If you think so, then either use a media agency, which can get better rates than you because they buy so much advertising space, or negotiate with your selected magazines for deals. There are often deals going because a magazine may be just about to go to press and it may have a couple of slots to fill and it would rather fill them for one-quarter of the normal price than not have the ads.

In the UK, your distributor and shops will expect you to advertise in the press—preferably magazines like *NME* or *Q* or genre mags like *Kerrang!* if you're into heavy rock, or the dance press *Mixmag* if you're doing dance. This is very expensive and in our opinion does nothing for a new label or band—you'd be far better spending more money on press, radio and club promotions or helping yourselves or your band to get gigs. Sometimes your distributor will do group ads, where more than one label is included. This can be a good deal and might be worth taking up.

Radio advertising is pretty expensive and, again, it's not advisable at this stage, although you could try pirate radio stations, which are a lot cheaper. As they're illegal, it's a bit complicated to track down phone numbers and make payments but it can be quite effective, especially in the UK dance world, where there are specialist stations such as hardcore stations, drum 'n' bass, garage, etc. which play really underground tunes that the bigger stations rarely touch. They also tend to have a loyal listening audience, which, if you pick your station correctly, will be exactly the type of people to buy your records.

You could also try fly posting. Again, this is actually pretty expensive and doesn't work a lot of the time. Getting big enough posters is expensive and so is getting one of the fly-posting companies to put them up. Don't try it yourself; they really don't like it! And unless you pay a lot of money, your poster only stays up one week, which barely gives people time to notice it.

## Licensing Out

Licensing is the process where the holder of rights in a recording (the Licensor) grants a licence to someone else (the Licensee) who will market a product of their own containing the Licensor's work and pay an agreed fee for the use of the work. The main pathways for licensing are licensing a track to a larger label which has better ability to generate success, licensing a track for release in a foreign territory, licensing for use on a compilation album, or licensing it for media use.

The first two possibilities largely rely on an interested party contacting you. If that happens, take advice from all sources: your promotions person, distributor and other business associates, and official bodies listed at the end of this book.

If you think your release is likely to generate serious attention in any area where compilation albums are popular, you could start approaching people who release compilations. Compilations are made of chart singles, popular club tracks and, to some extent, notable tracks in genres like drum 'n' bass, hip-hop and rock. If your track is likely to chart, you probably will have people coming to you with licensing proposals. If your initial DJ reactions on a club track are good, discuss the licensing possibilities with your distributor. If your work fits a genre where compilations are popular, do some research in record shops, in magazines or on the Internet and approach the labels that release them.

Licences are usually nonexclusive, which means that you retain the option of using the track in other ways and on this occasion are just allowing a usage for a specific purpose.

The fees involved are often expressed as a proportion of a percentage of PPD (published price to dealer, or 'dealer price'), typically between 15% and 25% for each unit sold. Your payment would depend on how many other tracks are on the CD, because all licensors split the 15% to 25% between them. The PPD of CD albums in the UK in 2006 is £8 to £9, so you would receive the agreed percentage of this, divided by the number of tracks included.

The following is an example of compilation album royalties:

> PPD = £8.50
> Royalty = 16%
> Number of tracks = 12
> 16% of £8.50 = £1.36; shared among 12 tracks = 11.33p per track per
>     copy sold
> sales of one thousand gives £113.33

Another basis, used by small labels, is a 'net profit split', or '50/50 deal'. The label makes a statement of sales revenue and a statement of what it has spent on manufacturing and promoting the project, not counting its own operational overheads. The remainder is divided between the label and the licensors, each side taking half shares.

A fixed royalty is easier to compute and keep track of, as the amount that the label spends and the discounts it offers to retailers are not relevant. However, if a profit split is on offer and represents a good opportunity to get your material more widely heard, you should give it very serious consideration.

## LEGAL AND BUSINESS STUFF

So you've manufactured records that some people might like to buy. If you haven't already done so, you should register with all the relevant rights bodies, such as MCPS and PPL in the UK or Harry Fox Agency and Sound Exchange in the US, for permissions or payment of things you are owed. You will also need an accountant and a lawyer, and you may wish to join a trade group such as AIM. Some of the important things you need to do as a record label are listed here. (For further information on the various bodies and collection societies, what they do and who they represent, see 'Business affairs', p. 358.)

You have a legal requirement to register in advance your wish to mass-produce copyright material. In the UK, you must tell the Mechanical Copyright Protection Society (MCPS) what you're doing. MCPS acts on behalf of the composers and publishers of songs and tunes that are recorded. The composer and publisher are entitled to a 'mechanical royalty' on every copy sold and it is the label's responsibility to pay this royalty to MCPS, which then passes it on to the publisher or songwriter. The US equivalent to MCPS is the Harry Fox Agency.

If you are the composer as well as the label (something which often happens in the independent sector), make MCPS aware of this and they should waive collections when your compositions appear on your label.

Next, a certain amount of care is called for here from a small label because mechanical royalties do not have to be paid on records used for promotional purposes. MCPS has historically been a bit suspicious about promotional quantities, particularly once dance came along and the floodgates opened and people threw records around like confetti. You must make sure that you follow their rules and guidelines on marking your promotional material very clearly as 'not for commercial sale'—the pressing plant will be quite used to doing this; it's not a preposterous thing to ask for. You will not have to pay royalties for items that are not for commercial sale, so work out what kind of promotional quantities you need and why. Your distributor will often want to promo quite heavily for the first release. Although it's a bit of a punch in the gut, really they are doing you a favour.

So you need to give away at least a hundred and you might be only planning to press five hundred in the first place. You will need copies for the press, you may need copies for DJs, you may need some general walking-around copies. . . . Don't do too many, as you have to mark them in such a way they can't be used for commercial sale, but suss out from your distributor and promo people what they need, add a few for the band and general purposes and declare those to be a special item. Maybe put 'W,' for white label, on the end of the catalogue number. Consult MCPS: they're not averse to telling you what to do if you conquer your fear and ask the questions. It's like the taxman: lying low and saying nothing doesn't work in the long run.

In the UK, the Association of Independent Music (AIM) looks after the interests of over six hundred labels, from the large and well established, such as Beggars Banquet and Warp, to the newest startups like yours. The AIM website address and Web site are in the Toolkit section at the end of the book.

Because of the numbers of its members, AIM can represent indies in dealings with government agencies and various music industry bodies, such as Phonographic Performance Limited (PPL). PPL is similar to PRS in that it collects fees from radio stations, clubs and other venues that use recorded music. The resulting cash is split equally between labels and recording artists, based on the data PPL collects on what is actually played on the airwaves and in various venues. Of course, the lion's share goes to the major record companies and their top acts because their records get the most plays on air and on jukeboxes. But as PPL collects about £80 million a year, some trickles down to independent recording acts and labels like yours. Because US copyright law does not grant performing rights for record companies and artists, there is no direct US equivalent to PPL although Sound Exchange does something similar (see page 420).

PPL is a membership organization for record companies. As a label, you should join PPL and you should inform them of what you've released. And follow their guidelines about using the 'P' symbol that is included on the record disc artwork or CD and submitting details to them. PPL has an information pack for new labels and the PPL contact address is in the Toolkit section.

A record label will also be required to do proper bookkeeping, fill in tax forms, possibly register for VAT, retain the services of a lawyer and so on. These actions all fall under the section Business Affairs (p. 418).

So you've done it all! Let's hope you sell loads, but even if you don't, we hope you've enjoyed the process!

We leave you in this chapter with interviews with two independent labels, which will highlight many of the issues we have just been talking about. The labels concerned are the British dance label PIAS/Wall of Sound and the US indie label Saddle Creek.

❖❖❖❖❖❖❖❖❖❖❖❖❖❖❖❖❖❖❖❖❖❖❖❖❖❖❖❖❖❖❖❖❖❖❖❖❖❖❖❖❖❖❖❖❖❖❖❖

## MARK JONES

Wall of Sound is a UK independent label renowned for its ability to sign unusual, left-field acts and develop them into major successes. Röyksopp, Wise Guys, Propellerheads and Les Rhythmes Digitales are among its acclaimed top-selling artists. Wall of Sound merged with Belgian label PIAS in 2006. Wall of Sound founder Mark Jones explains how the label was born.

### Why did you start your own company?

I started by working for a record distributor called Soul Trader. I'd been involved with bands, and one of the things I did was visuals at clubs, just before acid house broke in 1988. I met a guy at the clubs called Marc Lessner who was selling records off a table. Then one day we met each other in a record shop in Kensington and he said his table with some records had become a distribution company and asked if I'd like to work for him. His company was Soul Trader. I started packing boxes and sorting out stock and eventually I learned about distribution, export sales and so on.

Marc and I set up Wall of Sound together while I was at Soul Trader. We

started doing pressing and distribution (P&D) deals for artists who didn't have a label but whose music we thought was good. This was how we found Kruder & Dorfmeister, Howie B, Pussy Foot, and Basement Jaxx, artists that went on to have quite a lot of success.

### What was your first Wall of Sound release?

One day I said to Marc, 'Why don't we do an album, a compilation album of all the music that we work with and material that we know people want and can't get?' And that was *Give Em Enough Dope, Volume 1.* I didn't have a big master plan; it was just a natural progression of the work I was doing and where I was working.

*Give Em Enough Dope* was critically acclaimed because there weren't really that many alternative compilations out back then. We put out a second volume which did even better and someone asked me what artists we had signed to the label and I thought, 'Oh yeah, we haven't got any!' So Marc and I went in the studio together and made the first Wall of Sound single, which was *E-klektik*, based around a phrase from Edmo Zarife, a famous Brazilian football commentator at the 1994 World Cup who shouts, 'Goal'!

We did a third *Give Em Enough Dope,* and artists were coming to me attracted by the compilations and the ideals of the label. We were a bit more brash and dance floor and alternative than Mo Wax or other labels of that time but we also had melody and hooks while a lot of the other stuff was more experimental.

We started signing artists, releasing records and I ended up getting a separate office. All of a sudden, I found myself surrounded by a group of people who felt the same way about music as I did. In the beginning, we didn't really have contracts; it was very primitive. Then the label kind of exploded around 1996 and 1997 with

## WALL OF SOUND DISCOGRAPHY

### ALBUMS

| | | |
|---|---|---|
| WALLLP001 | VARIOUS | GIVE 'EM ENOUGH DOPE VOL 1 |
| WALLLP002 | VARIOUS | BACK TO MONO |
| WALLLP003 | VARIOUS | GIVE 'EM ENOUGH DOPE VOL 2 |
| WALLCD004 | VARIOUS | THE FIRST X1 |
| WALLCD005 | ROOTLESS | ROTTEN WOOD FOR SMOKING BEES |
| WALLLP007 | HUSTLERS OF CULTURE | MAMEY STYLES |
| WALLPUSSCD1 | VARIOUS | WALL OF PUSSY |
| WALLCD008 | THE WISEGUYS | EXECUTIVE SUITE |
| WALLLP009 | LES RYTHMES DIGITALES | LIBERATION |
| WALLCD010 | VARIOUS | GIVE 'EM ENOUGH DOPE VOL 3 |
| WALLLP011 | DIRTY BEATNIKS | ONE ONE SEVEN IN THE SHADE |
| WALLCD012 | VARIOUS | DIG THE NU BREED |
| WALLCD014 | VARIOUS | THE SECOND X1 |
| WALLLP006 | MEKON | WELCOME TO TACKLETOWN |
| WALLCD015 | PROPELLERHEADS | DECKSANDRUMSANDROCKANDROLL |
| WALLCD016 | AKASHA | CINEMATIQUE |
| WALLLP017 | THE STRIKE BOYS | HOUSE IS NOT A HOME |
| WALLCD018 | VARIOUS | SELECTED FUNKS |
| WALLP019X | VARIOUS | BUSTIN' LOOSE |
| WALLCD020 | THE WISEGUYS | THE ANTIDOTE |
| WALLLP021X | LES RYTHMES DIGITALES | DARKDANCER |
| MAGICD1 | UGLY DUCKLING | FRESH MODE |
| PHAT002 | MEKON | PLAYS A VOLUME 1 |
| WALLCD022 | AKASHA | CINEMATIQUE THE REMIXES |
| WALLCD023 | E-KLEKTIK | WE LOVE YOU ...SO LOVE US |
| AMOUR 1CD | VARIOUS | MARACANA MADNESS REMIXES |
| AMOUR 2LP | SHAWN LEE | WE LOVE YOU ...SO LOVE US |
| AMOUR 3CD | 10 CENTS | THE WEIGHT |
| MAGICLP0 | THE CREATORS | BUGGIN' OUT |
| WALLCD024 | DIRTY BEATNIKS | FEEDBACK |
| WALLLP025 | MEKON | RELAX WITH MEKON |
| MAGICLP3 | THE CREATORS | EXTRA WEIGHT |
| AMOUR4CD | VARIOUS | SO LOVE US TOO |
| MAGICLP4 | JERRY BEEKS | THE CROP REPORT |
| WALLCD026 | MEDICINE | IRON STYLINGS |
| AMOUR5LP | I AM KLOOT | NATURAL HISTORY |
| WALLLP027 | ROYKSOPP | MELODY A.M. |
| MAGICLP5 | BLAK TWANG | THE KIK OFF |
| WALLCD028 | ZOOT WOMAN | LIVING IN A MAGAZINE |
| AMOUR6LP | THE BEES | SUNSHINE HIT ME |
| CAMPLP1 | JUNIOR CARTIER | TELLE COMPILATION |
| WALLLP029 | VARIOUS | BEYOND THESE THINGS |
| WALLLP030 | THEMROC | THE MECHANICAL FORCES OF... |
| WALLCD031 | MEDICINE | PROMISE OF LOVE |
| AMOUR7CD | ZOOT WOMAN | ZOOT WOMAN |
| WALLCD032 | VARIOUS | TEN YEARS OF WALL OF S... |
| WALLCD033 | VARIOUS | HIDDEN GEMS |
| HGCD001 | VARIOUS | WE LOVE YOU SO LOVE |
| AMOUR8CD | VARIOUS | DIALECT |
| MAGICCD6 | TWO CULTURE CLASH | TWO CULTURE CLASH |
| WALLCD034 | DIEFENBACH | RUN TRIP FALL |
| AMOUR9CD | BLAK TWANG | THE ROTTON CLUB |
| AMOUR10CD | DIEFENBACH | SET & DRIFT |

### SINGLES

| | | |
|---|---|---|
| WALLT001 | E-KLEKTIK | |
| WALLT003 | MEKON | MARACANA MADNESS |
| WALLT005 | AKASHA | PHATTY'S LUNCHBOX |
| WALLT006 | ROOTLESS | JACADELICA E.P. |
| WALLT007 | ZOOT WOMAN | THE MENTAL SPIRITUAL E.P. |
| WALLT008 | ARTERY | SWEET TO THE WIND E.P. |
| WALLT009 | THE WISEGUYS | THE DOLLAR (TEMP DEL.) |
| WALLT010 | CEASEFIRE | NIL BY MOUTH |
| WALLT011 | DIRTY BEATNIKS | TRICKSHOT |
| WALLPUSST | MEKON | BUGGIN' THE GAP E.P. |
| WALLT016 | WRECKAGE INC. | REVENGE OF THE MEKON |
| WALLT019 | W.O.S VS PUSSYFOOT | SALVAGE |
| WALLT020 | AGENT PROVOCATEUR | WALL OF PUSSY E.P |
| WALLT021 | THE WISEGUYS | RED TAPE |
| WALLT022 | LES RYTHMES DIGITALES | THE SOUND YOU HEAR/WE KEEP ON |
| WALLT025 | DIRTY BEATNIKS | KONTAKTE |
| WALLT026 | MEKON | SPANISHFLY |
| WALLT027 | THE WISEGUYS | BEATNIK BOUNCE |
| WALLT028 | ZOOT WOMAN | WELCOME TO TACKLETOWN |
| WALLT029 | AKASHA | CASINO |
| WALLT030 | AKASHA | GOTS PAREILA BETTER WORLD |
| WALLT031 | PROPELLERHEADS | CHASING CARS |
| WALLT032 | DIRTY BEATNIKS | BROWN SUGAR |
| WALLT033 | LES RYTHMES DIGITALES | SPYBREAK! |
| WALLT036 | WRECKAGE INC. | JACQUES YOUR BODY |
| WOW | PROPELLERHEADS | HISTORY REPEATING |
| WALLT037 | LRD | MUSIC MAKES YOU LOSE CONTROL |
| WALLT038 | PROPELLERHEADS | BANG ON! |
| WALLT039 | AVENGER | OOH LA LA |
| WALLT040 | CEASEFIRE VS DEADLY | EVEL KNIEVEL |
| WALLT041 | THE STRIKE BOYS | |
| WALLT042 | LES RYTHMES DIGITALES | THE RHYME |
| WALLT044 | THE WISEGUYS | (IF YOU) WHAT'S THAT SOUND |
| WALLT045 | PROPELLERHEADS | START THE COMMOTION |
| WALLT046 | AKASHA | THE REMIXES PT1 |
| WALLT047 | THE STRIKE BOYS | EXTENDED PLAY EP |
| WALLT048 | THE WISEGUYS | THE REMIXES PT2 |
| WALLT049 | AKASHA | JET SET |
| WALLT050 | THE WISEGUYS | COSMIC '78 |
| WALLT051 | E-KLEKTIK | REMIXES PT3 |
| WALLT053X | ZOOT WOMAN | REMIXES PT2 |
| CAMPT1 | AKASHA | MARACANA MADNESS (REMIXES) |
| MAGICT1 | DIRTY BEATNIKS | IT'S AUTOMATIC |
| MAGICT3 | LES RYTHMES DIGITALES | SWEET CHILD OF MINE |
| WALLT065 | THE STRIKE BOYS | SANDY & BUD |
| PHAT001 | JERRY BEEKS | ON AIR EP |
| WALLT056 | UGLY DUCKLING | HUNGRY |
| | PHSYCO COWBOYS | NOW! |
| | MEKON | EVERYBODY C'MON |
| | CEASEFIRE | COME ON DANCE |
| | | PLAYS A VOLUME 1 |
| | | CRUISING |

| | | |
|---|---|---|
| MAGIC18 | MEDIA 101 | MISCHIEF NITE |
| MAGIC19 | KING TEE FT PHIL | BACK UP |
| MAGIC20 | AYATOLLAH PRES. | WINDOWS OF THE WORLD |
| MAGIC21 | VINYL DIALECT | SAY NO NAME |
| MAGIC22 | JERRY BEEKS | FALLING IN LOVE WITH A STRIPPER |
| MAGICT22 | BLAK TWANG | KIK OFF |
| MAGICT23 | BLAK TWANG | TRIXSTAR |
| MAGICT24 | THE BEES | A MINHA MENINA |
| AMOUR14S | BLAK TWANG | SO ROTTEN |
| MAGICT025 | MEDICINE | WE'RE ON WET EP |
| WALLT076/77 | THEMROC | GOLD IS YOUR METAL |
| WALLT078 | ROYKSOPP | POOR LENO |
| WALLT079 | EASTWICK & HOLLOWAY | EPLE |
| WALLT080 | THEMROC | NUMBER ONE |
| WALLS091 | MEDICINE | BLOODLINE |
| WALLT082 | ROYKSOPP | I SMILE TO MY EYES |
| WALLT083 | ROYKSOPP | SPARKS |
| WALLT084Y | BLAK TWANG | DERRICK CARTER SO EASY |
| MAGICD026 | SCISSOR SISTERS | PUBLIK ORDER |
| WALLT085 | VINYL DIALECT | COMFORTABLY NUMB |
| MAGICT027 | THE GLORY HOLE | OUCH! |
| WALLT086 | PRASSAY | WALK THE NIGHT |
| WALLT087 | THEMROC | INTO THE LIGHT |
| WALLT088 | AMANSET | COME HOME BABY JULIE |
| AMOUR15T | ZOOT WOMAN | GRACE |
| WALLS099 | THE BEES | A MINHA MENINA |
| AMOUR16S | THE VISITOR | OUR LIPS ARE SEALED |
| WALLT090 | VINYL DIALECT | GEM |
| WALLS091 | VINYL DIALECT | D-FUNKTIONAL |
| MAGICD028 | MEKON | TAKEN IT ALL |
| WALLT092 | ZOOT WOMAN | WE LOVE YOU SO LOVE US ... 3 SAMPLER |
| AMOUR17T | VARIOUS | AS YOU DO |
| WALLD094 | MEDICINE | IKNOWYOUKNOW |
| VR95 | CASS & TOM MANGAN | HOW DO YOU LOVE? |
| WALLT095 | TWO CULTURE CLASH | MAKE YOUR MIND E.P. |
| AMOUR18T | DIEFENBACH | ZEBRA JEANS E.P. |
| AMOUR19T | THE GIRLS | YULE LOVE US |
| AMOUR20S | VARIOUS | RE-MAKE YOUR MIND E.P. |
| AMOUR21T | DIEFENBACH | LOVE GAME |
| WALLT097 | SHAKEDOWN | ...AND DANCE |
| WALLT098 | TWO CULTURE CLASH | KNOCK KNOCK |
| WALLT099 | TWO CULTURE CLASH | LOVE GUIDE |
| WALLT101 | TWO CULTURE CLASH | ENUFF 4 YOU |
| WALLT102 | BLAK TWANG | G.C.S.E. |
| WALLT103 | WEST LONDON DEEP | INSIDE MY HEAD |
| WALLE100 | THE INFADELS | REALITY TV/GIVE YOURSELF TO ME |

| | | |
|---|---|---|
| CAMPT2 | TRAINER BOY | NERVOUS BREAKDOWN |
| CAMPT3 | JUNIOR CARTIER | WOMEN BEAT THEIR MEN |
| WALLT057 | PROPELLERHEADS | TAKE CALIFORNIA AND PARTY |
| WALLT059 | THEMROC | FUZZY LOGIC |
| MAGICT4 | THE WISEGUYS | START THE COMMOTION |
| MAGICT5 | VINYL DIALECT | B-BOYS ROCK THE WORLD |
| CAMPT4 | CAGE | '54' |
| CAMPT5 | VIZIONS | FEEL OUR MUSIC |
| CAMPT6 | POUR HOMME | BORN THIS WAY |
| MAGICT6 | JOEY CALIGULA | THE FIRE |
| WALLT053 | THE CREATORS | THE HARD MARGIN |
| MAGICD6 | DIRTY BEATNIKS | NEW ADVENTURES OF SANDY & ... |
| WALLT061 | THE CREATORS | THE HARD MARGIN |
| AMOUR1S | PASCAL R | KILLING /FRECHTOUCH? |
| AMOUR2T | SHAWN LEE | EP |
| AMOUR 4S | 10 CENTS | BLOW IT UP Y'ALL |
| MAGICT3 | SHAWN LEE | KILL SOMEBODY |
| MAGICT5 | JERRY BEEKS | FLASH |
| MAGICT10 | 3582 | EARLY MORNING |
| MAGICD2? | UGLY DUCKLING | 86 5's |
| MAGICT11 | THE CREATORS | I DID IT LIKE THIS |
| MAGICT11 | MASTA ACE | THE MUSIC |
| AMOUR 5D | SKITZOFRENIKS | NOW U A MC |
| AMOUR6T | 10 CENTS | SLOW IT DOWN |
| AMOUR8S | SHAWN LEE | BUBBLE BATH |
| WALLT063 | MEKON | HAPPINESS |
| WALLT064 | DIRTY BEATNIKS | CALM GUN SHOT |
| WALLT065 | MEKON | DISCO DANCIN' MACHINES |
| CAMPT7 | THEMROC | WHAT'S GOING ON |
| MAGICT14 | VIZIONS | FROZEN |
| WALLT066 | THE CREATORS | EVERYBODY JUMP |
| WALLT067 | MEDICINE | KRONKITE |
| MAGICT15 | RED CLOUD | CAPITAL ROCKA |
| CAMPT8 | DJ PIERRE | SAINTS AND ANGELS |
| WALLT067 | DIRTY BEATNIKS | IN MY HANDS |
| WALLT068 | MEKON | WET DREAMS |
| AMOUR7S | VARIOUS | WHORES FREAKS SAINTS AND ANGELS |
| MAGICT16 | BLAK TWANG | RELAX |
| YOUR8S | JERRY BEEKS | WE LOVE YULE |
| ART003 | THE BEES | U KNOW |
| LS0669 | VARIOUS | BRONX SLANG |
| LST070 | ZOOT WOMAN | NO TROPHY |
| VR95 | MEKON | MEKON REVUE |
| T9 | I AM KLOOT | YOU AND I |
| T071 | DATALIFE | PLEASE STAY |
| T105 | ROYKSOPP | DARK STAR |
| T2 | THE BEES | PEAK |
| | ZOOT WOMAN | EPLE |
| | WEST LONDON DEEP | PUNCHBAG |
| | ROYKSOPP | LIVING IN A MAGAZINE |
| | TRAINER BOY | BO RUSH |
| | I AM KLOOT | POOR LENO |
| | ROYKSOPP | GET THE FUNK BACK |
| | ROYKSOPP | MORNING RAIN |
| AMOUR12D | THE BEES | REMIND ME |
| WALLT075X | ZOOT WOMAN | REMIND ME/SO EASY |
| | | YOU GOT TO LEAVE |
| | | IT'S AUTOMATIC |

Propellerheads and the Wise Guys and Les Rhythmes Digitales and the whole, for want of a better word, 'big beat' phenomenon. It was crazy! If I'd tried to plan the label in my mind there would be no way we could have known that those genres of music could be thrown together—hip-hop influences, rock influences and electronic influences, all mashed up together.

## How did you pay for your first releases?

We did it through the distributor, through Soul Trader. We were lucky because Soul Trader had accounts at pressing plants but we each put an equal amount of money on the table, which wasn't a lot at all, hundreds of pounds, definitely not thousands. At first, our costs were pretty basic and you can make money if you are delivering your records off a back of a van.

Still, it was a very tight ship, still is, and still has to be, even though now we're a little bit bigger!

## How did people find out about your releases?

We always pressed a few white labels for promotion but I don't think we ever had any marketing plans or ideas. The records were in the right shops, where we had a reputation for supplying good music. Obviously, we mailed some to DJs and magazines and put a mailing list together, and once we'd released six or seven records in a short space of time, magazines were ringing us up to do label profiles.

## Can a label still start out like that today?

Yes. I think that's the best way to start off, with that DIY ethic. Hit those key shops, those Rough Trades, Piccadillys, and make it work, whether you're a band trying to get signed by a bigger independent label or whether you have started your own label. That's the best way to do it, get into the street level. You can still mail stuff out, find out what journalists like in what magazines, find out who would like the music you're making and just get it out to them. Be in people's faces, get out there and ask questions.

We're in a visual age with the Internet and everything, and we know how important it is to get known. If you're going to produce sleeves for your records, why not spend that little bit more time, care and attention and make them look good? If you've got friends you can call on who are designers or people at art college, then do it. There was always a label identity with our records. We did a series of sleeves, the first ten were in one bag with one design, the second ten in another bag and the third ten were different again. And there were little things, like a quote that we came up with on the back of every sleeve. Those quirky little elements made people who bought Wall of Sound records feel like they were part of something. The sleeve designs and records were both collectable.

## Once the label started to get established, what sort of promotion did you do? How important is radio to you?

When I started, I didn't even think about the radio. We didn't care! And we've never had huge amounts of radio support because where we come from isn't a safe place. We always had specialist radio but not much daytime radio until we started to have success with albums by bands like Propellerheads or Röyksopp and radio saw them as safe, with no risk factor. But the chances of daytime radio playing your record early on are very, very minimal.

Press coverage is obviously a huge part of it. We have records that are really press-led in getting people's interest in checking them out. The artists I work with are never short of something to say; they're characters and that's the difference between us and a lot of other labels. I always wanted an identity for our artists, not just to be faceless DJs. That's why the visual element always came in.

Otherwise, we promote records through the usual means, getting the records played in clubs because a lot of our music is aimed at the dance floor. Through the years, we've had in-house pluggers and PR depending on what sort of roster we've got and we've used independent companies for promotion as well. You have to look at every artist individually in a long-term picture, because we have different kinds of artists, whether it's Blak Twang and hip-hop or whether it's Röyksopp, or more band-orientated acts like the Infadels or Diefenback. We have to find the best plugger individually for each act, as some are better in some areas than others. And you want someone dedicated and who believes in the act.

But early on in the life of a label, you can get around that. You don't have to be hiring pluggers, just deliver the records yourself or send the records out.

## When you started to become successful, did you get approached by major labels?

Absolutely. But not until you get that big key act, and mine was the Propellerheads, and we didn't even have a contract with the band at that stage. But you have to decide which route you want to go down. Whether you want to own a record company and own repertoire and spend years developing somebody or whether you say, okay, I want to move this along and sign this act to a mainstream company. With the Propellerheads, our mind was made up for us, as the band didn't want to work with a major!

The Propellerheads were confident of their ability and went and got a publishing deal and got funding there. They signed a separate recording deal for America and had pipeline income from it. They were self-sufficient, recording-wise. They didn't have to go into a big studio so they didn't need a large amount of money. If you've funded the record yourselves, why do you need to take thousands of pounds from an independent or any other company? Any band that's really smart and knows that they have a career and a future doesn't want advances from you because most of them will end up in debt.

### Do you license records, both in and out?

Occasionally. If it's licensing in, it's usually one-off dance singles. A label like PIAS/Wall of Sound is about catalogue, and for me it's about owning the records because of the hours and the years of work I've put into this. Licensing can work and we have occasionally done it.

You have to think of every act as different and this is the freedom you have as an indie. You couldn't really do that as a major label. I know there are a lot of hidden gems left in our catalogue that can be exploited in one way or another.

### How did you get your very first song on a TV commercial?

They rang us up and said they wanted to use it! We said, all right then, how much? It is like that; people hear things and want to use them. Creatives who work in ad agencies are the sort of people who buy Wall of Sound records and a lot of them are sitting at home looking for something and we're the first port of call they come to. This was around 1998. The first huge synch (synchronised music to an advertisement) we had was the Wise Guys 'Ooh La La' Budweiser ads. It was enormous. The record ended up at number two.

We also turn down a lot of syncs; there are things that we don't do. We'll do syncs as long as it doesn't compromise the artist's integrity or the label's. But television is a potentially massive way of getting your music across if it's done in the right way. And with our left-field specialist music we're not going to get lots of radio, so television can be very effective.

### Has synchronisation been a significant revenue source?

It's been huge. It's hard financially for independent labels and the kind of money that is offered for a lot of commercials really helps. And agencies often go for new music rather than more mainstream music because they know how influential it can be. When our music has gotten television exposure it has had a massive impact on sales.

## How did you become successful in getting syncs?
It's a combination of a lot of things. The music we've released in the past has always been a little bit different. Now we make sure that when we cut an album, we also cut an instrumental version so you've got those elements there to service the creatives.

But this is just one element. Other key things are the personal relationships you have with creatives, and if you've had one success it has a knock-on effect so that they'll come to you first next time. The personal touch is essential, making them feel special, making them feel that they are the only people. Lots of these people long to be a creative source as to where this music is coming from. They know if they get it right, music is one of the only ways *to* communicate with certain demographics.

What we do works and we're setting up a company to service music into ads and syncs as a whole. It'll be like a music library and we will only work with PIAS/Wall of Sound and catalogue from independents. People are queuing up for this service. I've already been approached by my fellow label owners on this.

## What are the essential things for an independent label?
To know what you want to do and believe totally in what you're doing. I think you should start a label with a certain feel. If you're too diverse too early, it's difficult for people to get a handle on it. You need to keep your overheads as low as possible in the early years. You can't compete financially with major labels if you're trying to sign a band, so you need to build up contacts and reputation and if you find a band with a vision you share you're much more likely to get them to work with you. In the beginning, you won't be able to afford a lawyer so you do a contract in the form of a one- or two-page document called a heads of agreement, but if you want to become a serious label, you will need to have legal advice and a good accountant's advice. There are people out there you can meet by going to different conventions or through the Internet or via AIM (Association of Independent Music), which all new labels in the UK should join.

## How should an artist approach a label like yours?
It's no good just mailing unsolicited records into a company like ours. First, you find a company which releases similar music to your own and believes in what

you believe in. You should find record companies and A&R men who appreciate what you do. To me it's about contacts. You find out who that person is and how you get hold of them and you hassle and you 'accidentally' bump into them in pubs or get to them via friends of friends. I'm much more likely to sign a band or an artist because I unexpectedly saw them at a gig or because a friend of a friend recommended them. Local studios or people like AIM are really useful or you can go online. There's ways of contacting people—if people e-mail our Web site and ask to send us some music, I'll answer it personally. We do listen to the music that's sent in, but the most important thing is narrowing down who those labels are. If you do send something in, make it different, make people remember it.

It doesn't work for all music, but there's a lot to be said for live venues. A lot of key A&R people go out to gigs, and record company regional people are always at venues looking for artists.

### Is the demand for physical records coming to an end?
The market is changing and has evolved dramatically since we started the label. Live music is huge and the Internet does hold the future but I think some people will never get over wanting to hold physical product. Yet even some DJs don't use vinyl any more. They use CDs and some have gone further than that. But I love vinyl and we always press a few vinyl copies of all our releases. And when the records come in, it's the vinyl copies I pick up and hold in my hands. I remember when the first boxes arrived from the pressing plant to Soul Trader and I took out a record and just stared at it for what seemed like an hour. That was the day I knew this was what I wanted to do.

✦✦✦✦✦✦✦✦✦✦✦✦✦✦✦✦✦✦✦✦✦✦✦✦✦✦✦✦✦✦✦✦✦✦✦✦✦✦✦✦✦✦✦✦✦✦✦✦✦

✦✦✦✦✦✦✦✦✦✦✦✦✦✦✦✦✦✦✦✦✦✦✦✦✦✦✦✦✦✦✦✦✦✦✦✦✦✦✦✦✦✦✦✦✦✦✦✦✦

## ROBB NANSEL

Based in Omaha, Nebraska, the Saddle Creek label evolved out of Lumberjack Records, which had been started by Conor Oberst, better known as Bright Eyes, as a way to get his own music released. In the past decade, Saddle Creek has become a notable label with a formidable roster of artists, including such critical favourites as Azure Ray, Two Gallants, Cursive, Orenda Fink,

Maria Taylor, and Bright Eyes. Label owner Robb Nansel recounts the history of Saddle Creek.

## Why did you start the label?

Lumberjack Records was formed in 1993 by Conor Oberst and his brother so they could release Conor's cassette. A bunch of our friends played in bands we all thought were amazing. Everyone was trying to get labels outside of Omaha to pay attention to our friends' bands, but nobody seemed to care about the music except for us. We decided we would pool our money together and press up some cassettes, 7"s and CDs to release on Lumberjack. There was no budget for the releases early on. By selling a hundred copies of each release, we were able to make and put out another record. Each release paid for the next. That's how the label functioned for the first few years.

By 1996, a handful of releases had accumulated and I wanted to make sure more people heard all this great stuff. I didn't want these records to get lost and not make it out of Nebraska. Mike Mogis, a producer with his own studio, and I took over the label and started seeking national distribution. We really started to promote the bands. I graduated from the University of Nebraska in Lincoln in 1998 and moved back to Omaha. Mike stayed in Lincoln with the recording studio and I took the label to Omaha with me. Along the way, we ran across Lumberjack Distribution and changed the name to Saddle Creek to avoid confusion.

## How did you market your first releases?

There was no marketing early on. By the time we changed the name to Saddle Creek and started to think about things on a national scale, the Internet was starting to have a real impact. We got a Web site up and started to get the word around about our bands through that. Between our Web site and the bands' consistent touring schedules we were able to spread the word.

## Have radio and TV been important tools, or are you relying on other forms of media to bring awareness to your music?

College radio has always been a focus for us. We send our records to college radio because they tend to play music that is a bit more interesting than what we hear on commercial radio stations. Independent, local video shows in regional markets have also been supportive since we have started to make videos for our bands in the recent years. But in general, commercial radio and mainstream television have had little to no effect on the success or lack thereof of our bands or the label.

**Did major labels start approaching you after your success?**
Yes, as soon as we started to sell some records the major labels started to express interest.

**Have you licensed material as well as being a licensor?**
We have licensed some songs to movies, television shows and commercials, but not a lot. We only do it if the bands want to. We also license albums to other labels in other territories of the world. We don't act as a licensee too often.

**How do you approach the international market?**
We have a person in the office who focuses on this. We have established some great relationships with some international partners and we use them for the release of our records overseas as much as we can. If we can't work with one of our international partners, then we seek out a new licensee.

**Do you ever encounter problems with your licensees?**
We have had some trouble getting proper accounting statements and we don't always agree with how they choose to market our releases, but those are common and expected issues. There is a huge cultural barrier in some territories, and we don't expect things to go completely smooth all the time.

**What do you think are the essential things for a record label?**
Good records and a competent staff.

**Is the demand for physical records coming to an end?**
It sure feels like it. The demand for digital downloads is definitely increasing. I am not excited about the coming of the day when you can no longer go out and buy a physical record because there is something about holding the whole record (artwork and all) that really excites me. It just isn't achieved with the digital format. But maybe that is just me getting old! I think I might just have to get used to it.

# SECTION 3

# OTHER STUFF

# introduction

**S**o far we've concentrated on the most familiar aspects of making music—gigging, touring, DJing and making records—as ways of becoming an artistic and financial success. But not everybody wants to be making records, gigging in bands or spinning tunes, although they do want to make music. This chapter concentrates on other ways of making a living out of making music, such as professional songwriting, writing jingles for commercials, TV idents and theme music, writing music for computer games, being a session musician and teaching.

## GOALS

Some people are happiest in the studio writing music as covers (songs to be recorded by other artists) or for use in the media, or they just love playing live and aren't that bothered about going into the recording studio. If any of these is for you, decide which is your area and get to work on getting in. If it is studio work, then your goal will be to set up a good home studio to work in and provide eager companies with just the right music for song covers, advertising, TV or film, or radio companies. If being a session musician is your dream, then getting regular recording work or touring dates is essential.

# professional songwriting

Although it's been the custom since the era of the Beatles and Dylan for most rock bands and solo acts to write their own material, there are still numerous pop acts who don't write or at least need the skills of a fully professional songwriter to give shape to their ideas for songs (think of Celine Dion, Robbie Williams or Beyoncé). And even among the rock fraternity it is now widespread for the band or their main writer to collaborate on a single with someone who has a track record in composing hits.

It can be very difficult to break into the song covers market, as professional songwriters Martin Brammer, from London, and Wayne Cohen, from the US, explain. However, once you're in, you can make a very good living at it, and the message here is to keep on plugging away despite the setbacks. Make it, and the rewards are great.

✦✦✦✦✦✦✦✦✦✦✦✦✦✦✦✦✦✦✦✦✦✦✦✦✦✦✦✦✦✦✦✦✦✦✦✦✦✦✦✦✦✦✦✦✦✦✦✦

## MARTIN BRAMMER

Martin Brammer hails from Seaham in the North East of England. He was the lead vocalist with top band the Kane Gang, has a host of successful hit songs for the likes of Tina Turner, Lighthouse Family and Rachel Stevens under his belt and an Ivor Novello award to his name. The Ivors are the UK's top prizes for songwriting. Here, Martin explains how he got into songwriting and gives some tips on what to expect.

### How did you get into songwriting?

I learned to play the bass guitar when I was a kid, and then I became a singer because that was what was needed in the bands I joined. I became better at singing as I went along! I was totally winging it to start off with, but it was right for my personality.

I was writing songs right from the start. My friend Dave Brewis and I were in a band together when we were about sixteen. At lunchtimes, we used to sit in the music room at school and write songs. We were influenced by the people we were listening to. We were very American-influenced at the time, bands like Steely Dan and the Doobie Brothers—adding a slightly arty British sense of humour to the mix.

As well as starting our own bands, we sometimes joined other people's bands but then got kicked out! They always wanted to keep hold of Dave because he was a great guitarist but they were not so keen on me!

We tried many different styles of music before we formed the Kane Gang and then we wrote one song that changed things: 'Brother Brother'. This was the first time I'd sang a song that felt like me. Before, when I was writing songs, I was learning the art of a songwriter, but with this song it was really me and it was this song that led us to our first record deal.

We signed with an independent label called Kitchenware, which also had Prefab Sprout; they were already good friends of ours. Via this deal, we signed with London Records and made three albums; two were released. We spent six months in New York recording the third one.

It didn't really work out with London Records. We never saw eye-to-eye and eventually we asked to be let go so we could take the third album somewhere else.

### When did you get your publishing deal?

We were also signed to Capitol in the US, and SBK Songs (which now belongs to EMI) was our publisher. We were persuaded to leave London by Capitol and SBK and we managed to manipulate our way out of our deal; then Capitol changed its mind about signing us for the UK and we had no deal. That was the end of the Kane Gang.

I'm passionate about what I do and this type of thing is very stressful. I learned that you have to take blows and criticism. I also learned the value of maintaining relationships: make sure you keep your lines of communication open with people you meet or work with along the way.

### When did you get your first song covered? Was it a hit?

After the Kane Gang finished, I saw my income grow smaller and smaller and I had to borrow some money off my friend to pay the tax bill! After some time, EMI Music let me go, as I was still unrecouped by a six-figure sum from the Kane Gang days. I was then offered a deal by PolyGram/Island Publishing (now Universal Publishing) via a guy called Tim Smith who had a subpublishing deal with them. I signed the deal at their Christmas party. It was there that I was introduced to an A&R guy called Colin Barlow, who asked me if I'd like to work with the Lighthouse Family. I said yes, and the first song I wrote with them was 'Lifted', which became a big hit.

Initially, the company looked after me very well; first, because of a great relationship with Tim Smith and then because I was having hits! But at the end of my days with Universal, it was not very good. They had a huge number of other writers to look after, so unless you had a current big hit or owed them lots of money (I was always pretty much recouped all the time because of my previous hits) they didn't spend much time on you. I'd never advise any writer to sign with one of the big companies unless they are getting lots of money or are really confident of the relationship with the creative person doing the deal.

Universal kindly let me out of my contract when my penultimate option came up. I rang Tim Smith, who was then at Zomba, and told him I was free and we did a deal pretty quickly because of our mutual respect for each other.

## Had you written your other songs already, or were they commissioned?

A mixture. Some songs I do on spec, some I write with the artist. But you can never be certain the songs will be used. I co-wrote two songs with my friend Gary Clark for Nick Carter of the Backstreet Boys. There were probably about forty songs commissioned for his solo album and about thirty got into production. We got two songs on out of the two we wrote for the album, which is really good. Often you waste your time; you write and record songs and then they are not used and no one pays you for your time or your studio time, which costs you money. You always feel like a bit of a cheapskate asking for money for studio time. Yet my studio, which isn't an expensive one, costs me £800 a month.

If you write with a new artist and it's a big success, it's not unusual for them to want to distance themselves from the person they wrote with. They want to prove it's *their* success.

Although I really believe in having a good time when writing, there are times when a certain amount of tension or pressure helps the whole creative process. It's not always your best friend you write best with.

## What is the creative approach like for you? Are you a methodical writer or an inspirational writer?

I'm quite a logical person. It's a good idea to have some ideas to bring into a session. I have a notebook which is full of spare ideas: a list of phrases I think are quite interesting. Some might be quite mundane but they are useful if you are trying to write the first line of a song, even though we'll probably change them later. I also have phrases that might be in the first-person or third-person, which I'll use depending on the landscape of the song. I get phrases from all kinds of places—newspapers, magazines, movies, books—they're then changed and made more like natural, believable lyrics. I like plays on words but sometimes they can seem too overtly like *songwriting,* which often gets in the way of emotional truth.

I am quite methodical, at least I thought I was until I went to Nashville to work with writers there! There'll be between two and four people in a room and they write in a short session. They are incredibly methodical; they've done it so many times that the quickness with which they work is amazing. It's like a computer programme. They've a kind of ready reckoner that decides which chord should follow next, which changes, which lyrics and so on. It doesn't often lead to much mind-blowing inspiration but it's something to admire. It can get you out of a tight spot.

### What are the golden rules of songwriting?

First rule of writing is there are no rules. Some people say get a story, the story is king! I quite like to start with a title and then let it flow from there. It's not too unusual to decide halfway through the song to flip the whole plot the other way round.

### Do you prefer to collaborate as a writer or write on your own?

Virtually all my songwriting is a collaboration. I do write in isolation but I don't really enjoy it. I prefer to have a two-way approach. I like to bounce ideas off someone else and it helps if that person is decisive. I write both melody and lyrics. I have no preference for major or minor keys; it's mixing them that's interesting. The hardest songs to write are up-tempo, major key, happy songs!

Collaborating can be fantastic, coming up with chords and ideas and sharing them with someone. But you have to be able to listen, to be honest with people without upsetting them and not to take any offence if you are criticised. Be open and generous in spirit. You need to be slightly chameleon-like so you can handle different situations and personalities.

### How do you get around writing blocks?

I don't have blocks; I have periods when I am more inspired than others! It's inexplicable why it happens. I had a friend who had a writing block and I advised him to write anything, even if it was something bad, to get the crap out of his system. I tend to work well under pressure. If it's an occasion where it's important that a song be great, I will usually up my game.

### Do you have a singer in mind when you write a song?

It's rare to write a song without someone who could sing it in mind. That is one of the most difficult things to do. It's often helpful to have the singer there, to have their vibe when you are writing the song. I have had songs used that I did not write for that specific person. The Tina Turner song 'Open Arms' was written seven years previously for someone else. She recorded it in 2004 in the UK and it charted both in Europe and US.

### Do you think songs should be written with just a vocalist and an instrument, or using technology?

Technology can quite often get in your way when you are writing a song. One of the biggest hit songs ever, Wet Wet Wet's 'Love Is All Around', was written by the Troggs' Reg Presley on a bass. He just wrote the melody and lyrics. There's a certain naked purity in writing like this. However, a song like 'Can't Get You Out of My Head' does need its bass line to work, as it's more of a dance song.

### What advice have you got for young writers? How should they present songs?

Never send in more than three songs. No one will listen to six—and if you haven't begun to convince them by the first three, you never will. I had a conversation with an American A&R man and he said if he got two CDs, one with six songs and one with three, he'd listen to the one with three and never bother with the one with six on it. They haven't got time to listen to them. If you're not sure which are the best three to put on, play them to other people—it's surprising how often other people agree on what's your best song and it's often not the one you thought was the best! Your choice might be right in the end, but not for that first listen. It's initially about making an impact, grabbing someone's interest.

It's really difficult to go straight into being a songwriter. One of the commonest routes is to be in a band first; people get to know you and you see the links in the chain. It helped me enormously having been in a band first. It means I've met people along the way like A&R men and managers who remember me and offer me work and because I've been an artist I understand how they work and I am on their side—without annoying the A&R man of course!

### How hard is it? What are acceptable rejection rates?

About 95% to 98%! Don't get depressed or disheartened by it; it's the way of the world. The most successful writers in the world get most of their songs rejected.

### If someone wanted to write a song for someone, say, Madonna, how should they present it? Should they get someone to sing it who sounds like Madonna?

Yes. You should try and get the best singer you can to sing your songs. It may not be easy and there's a financial consideration. You may have to pay the singer, and the better they are they more they cost. But with rejection rates they way they are, you can't afford to pay too many!

## How easy is it to make money from writing songs?

Unless you get airplay, it's hard. Record royalties are pathetic. For example, on Tina Turner's *Greatest Hits*, which sold 2.5 million, there were thirty songs. I wrote my song with two other people, so I get a third of the royalties for just one song—not very much! The same for a song on Beverley Knight's album. The album sold 250,000 and I wrote a third of a song, an album track, and I'll get £3,000 tops. And that is a success! The economics are not good unless you get airplay: you need singles, singles, singles! With Lighthouse Family, I wrote three songs, all singles and all hits that got airplay. That's the ideal situation.

✦✦✦✦✦✦✦✦✦✦✦✦✦✦✦✦✦✦✦✦✦✦✦✦✦✦✦✦✦✦✦✦✦✦✦✦✦✦✦✦✦✦✦✦✦✦✦✦

✦✦✦✦✦✦✦✦✦✦✦✦✦✦✦✦✦✦✦✦✦✦✦✦✦✦✦✦✦✦✦✦✦✦✦✦✦✦✦✦✦✦✦✦✦✦✦✦

# WAYNE COHEN

Wayne Cohen is a multiplatinum-selling hit songwriter and producer. His first success as a songwriter came with five co-writes on the debut album by Cur-

tis Stigers, who was signed to Arista by Clive Davis, an industry legend and early champion of Wayne's work. Cohen's further success includes his multiterritory hit song 'Just a Step from Heaven' (which broke UK girl group Eternal through Europe and Asia), as well as hits and cuts with several US, UK and European major label artists. He has also written music for feature films and television. Cohen has made staff songwriter deals with Sony, Windswept and EMI, and currently publishes himself through administration

deals he negotiated on behalf of Wayne's World, his publishing company. He has also finished a collaboration with Sophie Ellis-Bextor at the studio of his New York production company, Stand Up Songs.

## How did you get your start in songwriting?

I've always been infatuated with the three-minute pop song. When I was nine years old, I heard a song and thought, 'Yeah, I could do that. It's easy'. But it's not so easy. It's a challenge. Basically, I've spent my whole career developing a way of crafting pop music; it's a cumulative process that never stops. I started by being in rock bands, and after studying jazz and music theory in college, I was fortunate to work in the advertising music industry as a music producer. In college, I played bass with lots of pick-up ghost jazz big bands and was on and off the road, but always had my ear to pop music. I didn't think I had the talent to be a player, but I had an overview of how pop music works. That was what excited me.

I spent eight or nine years as a journeyman music producer in advertising and worked with some of the best producers, musicians, singers and writers on the planet. Jingles and underscores, every kind of music you'd hear in ads. In those days, from 1980 to 1988, there was a very fertile live music scene, and before MIDI came in, everything was done live. I would spend anywhere from four to twelve hours a day in a recording studio. It was a great way to learn to deal with every stripe of musician, singer, engineer and clients, to understand how business is done, how there are so many more concerns beyond what a particular musician or singer thinks about or even what a particular song or score is about. Music fits into the firmament of pop culture, whether it's advertising or film or pop music. We're all cogs in the machine, and that's not a bad thing, it's just the way it is, so I've always tried to keep that in mind.

### What steps would you recommend to a person today with similar impulses to the ones you had?

Write from your heart and write what you believe has a universal emotional truth. Listen to the radio: pay attention to it but ignore it at the same time. Don't worry about fitting into current genres, because at the end of the day, it's all about breaking through with something different. It's something of a cliché, but everyone in this industry is looking for something that stands out. But it also has to have that universal emotional truth, and if it has both of those things, then you're in business. I'd tell all the people who might be interested in songwriting that they should not lose heart or be cowed or intimidated by the industry. It's just about coming up with something that sounds hot. So you have to go with your gut. All the breakthroughs in pop music, and pop culture in general, have come from people wanting to tell a story and finding a fresh way to tell it.

### How are you inspired to write? Does it make a difference if you write songs for yourself or for a client's brief?

It happens all kinds of ways. It can come as a commission from a particular artist or manager, or it could come from a newspaper article, something on TV, or something that happened at home. For example, I was inspired to write two songs in two days with Sophie Ellis-Bextor, which came through Sophie and her manager Craig Logan. Generally, the inspiration comes from an artist, but I do write for myself too. Sometimes when I wake up it's just there, a title or phrase or subject. It took me a few years to realise this, but I don't write because I want to but because I have to. Frequently, I find that initial inspiration for a song is not the final vehicle for a song, which is okay as long as I get a great song out of the inspiration. I like to think of something Sammy Cahn, who wrote a slew of hits for Frank Sinatra, said when he was asked which comes first, the music or the lyrics. He said, 'The phone call'.

### Let's say you have a bunch of songs you've written. How would you go about getting them exposed, or whom would you try to send them to?

It depends on if you have a network of contacts to start with or not. If you don't have a network, people think that you have to do all kinds of crazy things to get noticed. This is not a good idea because it irritates people. It's really all about building relationships. You may not be able to get the person to listen the first time you meet them, whether it's a manager or producer or A&R or whatever, but you must try to build a relationship with them and give them something of yourself that's potentially of value to them, even if it's just a tip on a cool band you just heard.

To me, the whole Internet and e-mail world has fostered this atmosphere of passivity in how you reach out to people. It's good for some things, but you need to figure out a way to catch someone's attention. You can turn up at an office unannounced or send a CD and follow up with a phone call. Don't bother to leave a voice message because you're only adding to the noise they have to deal with. It comes down to persistence, and there's nothing sexy or fancy about that. It's just the way life is. I would suggest getting the songs you really believe in to artists, producers, A&R people, music publishers, managers, PR people, anyone you know associated with artists you want to be associated with. Even today, I spend at least half my time marketing my work and the other half writing.

### Any other essentials?

Just expose your work live as much as possible. Having a Web site is also a really good thing, although I wouldn't spend a lot of time on how it looks. It has to be functional, and it has to be easy for people to access the mp3s or the streams without taking lots of load-up time. It's really about persistence and believing in your songwriting. Try every possible way to collaborate and build relationships that work, with anybody you think is closer to where you want to be. Reaching out to a hero of yours is okay too, as long as you're not stalking them. Creative people respect talent and it doesn't matter where it comes from.

### Does your song have to exist as a recorded piece already, or can you send people written music and a lyric sheet?

If you're trying to convince someone to work with you, like a co-writer, you could send them lyrics. But people in the industry don't really have time to deal with anything that isn't coming through a pair of speakers.

### Does that mean that as a songwriter, you need a high-quality recorded version of your song to pitch it?

A good A&R person will be listening for a breakthrough lyric idea that says the same old thing a fresh way. They'll be looking for amazing hooks, melodies that lodge themselves in your brain, but not necessarily a perfect recording. Having said that, there are lots of A&R people who are looking for copycat artists. For example, when Avril Lavigne hit, lots of labels went out and tried to get their own version of her. Sometimes you can make that work for you, but you have to be careful because as an artist you have to be true to yourself.

### What professional associations should new songwriters consider joining?

I'm a big believer in ASCAP because it's a performing rights society that is basically run by writers; a big collective with good, smart people and a good network. It's probably the best association to join when starting. It's not going to get you work, but it may help you get some showcases or co-writing opportunities. But still, the challenge when you're getting started is getting someone who makes decisions to pay attention to you. It's true that we're living in a corporate world, and if you really want a breakthrough record you need to be attached to one of the four major labels. But if you want to hone your craft as a songwriter or recording artist, the important thing is to just keep writing, performing and recording and not worry so much about that. Performing is great because you get immediate feedback from people about which songs are working and which aren't. The Internet is a great leveller of public opinion. But to sell a platinum record you generally need a big machine behind you.

## What skills do songwriters need?

It's useful for songwriters to have basic instrumental skills, minimal music theory knowledge and basic notation. The important thing is to be able to communicate your ideas, lyrically or musically, in a cohesive way. But it's by no means necessary to be a really well trained musician. In fact, I've noticed that the first ten years of my training was about the craft of being a musician, and it took me another ten years to forget about all that and actually get to the core of it, which is finding that universal idea that's going to move people.

## How does collaboration work? How do two people write a song together?

It's a bit like blind dating: you never know quite what you're going to get. There was a period in my career, when I was signed to Sony, when I was writing with a new person nearly every day for about a year. After that time, there were maybe two or three people I struck up good relationships with that felt complementary. Basically, you bring to the table what you do best, whether it's a strong melodic or lyric sensibility or really good technical skills. You can't be too worried about not being able to do everything. I think the future of songwriting in America will be collaborative. To make a hit record these days you need a great lyrical idea, great hooks, *and* a hot track, and then marketing. It's definitely possible to do it yourself but it's a lot more time-efficient if you can do that as part of a group.

## How does a songwriter get paid?

There are three streams of income. The first is the mechanical royalty for record or Internet sales, which would be halved if you co-write a track with someone, and half of your half will go to a publisher if you have one. The second is performance income, which comes from radio, which is paid through ASCAP, BMI or SESAC in this country and PRS in the UK. That's basically it, so the game is to get a song on the radio that gets played a lot, and/or once the song is promoted through radio that people buy the record. I prefer to concentrate on songs that engage radio, because that's a more reliable source of income than record sales. The third stream is synchronization licenses for songs in films or TV, but that's ancillary income, so I tend to concentrate on the first two.

## You've worked in the US and the UK. What do you think are the differences between them?

The UK marketplace today is generally more pop-driven, although that may be changing at the moment. I find that the UK is much more open to eclecticism when it comes to pop music styles, and labels and people in the industry are still not afraid to state their opinion on whether they like something or not. Here in the US, it's such a huge financial risk for the companies to mount something that they have to be completely convinced that it's a sure-fire hit before they even spend the money on it, and it costs a lot of money to break an act here. You can get things to happen more quickly and more reliably in the UK than here. In the American market these days, you basically have to write in one or more categories to get cuts: pop, urban, rock or country. But in the UK, if it sounds hot and it has a great hook, you can do it.

◆◆◆◆◆◆◆◆◆◆◆◆◆◆◆◆◆◆◆◆◆◆◆◆◆◆◆◆◆◆◆◆◆◆◆◆◆◆◆◆◆◆◆◆◆◆◆◆◆

# writing for a music library company

Demand for music for TV, films, commercials or computer games is growing but the market is still competitive. Music can be short jingles (commercials, TV idents or signature tunes) or longer pieces for film or games music. There are various routes to take. One is to approach a library music company, jingles company or games company that will place your music for you; another way is to start your own company and place the music yourself.

Library music companies are often a good way to get paid for making music. When you work with a library company, you record full albums, which are then taken to advertising agencies, video production firms and a whole host of big and small TV production companies worldwide. They pay you when they use it and the library company takes 50% of your fee.

To work for a library you must first send them a demo of your music. If they like it, they'll ask you to come in and see them. If they still like you, they'll give you a budget for your album. It's not so much an advance as a budget to cover the costs of your recording.

Making the demo is a similar approach to making a demo for a record company. Make sure it's as well presented and professional as it can be. Try to be original: don't listen to music on TV or on the radio and try to copy it; they've obviously got lots of stuff like that already. The majority of this type of music is instrumental, so don't send everything with vocals on it. Also, bear in mind that the TV company will often only want around thirty seconds of something, so give them things of this length so they can see if it will work in an ad or for TV incidental music. In Britain, think of TV shows like *The Bill* and you'll get the idea. *The Bill*'s music was written by Charlie Morgan and Andy Pask and started life as a piece of library music. The show's been running for years and years—and every time the music gets played, a nice wodge of money enters their coffers.

# writing for advertising

There are many ways of making money out of music other than producing records or playing live. Getting your music in TV, radio or cinema advertisements or commercials (known as synchronization or sync rights) can be quite lucrative. Leap Music is a company that specializes in helping artists and songwriters do just this.

✦✦✦✦✦✦✦✦✦✦✦✦✦✦✦✦✦✦✦✦✦✦✦✦✦✦✦✦✦✦✦✦✦✦✦✦✦✦✦✦✦✦✦✦✦✦✦✦

## LEAP MUSIC

Leap Music was established in April 2003 as a joint venture between Richard Kirstein and London-based advertising agency Bartle Bogle Hegarty (BBH). It was the first music publisher inside a UK ad agency; it is a publisher member of MCPS, PRS and the Music Publishers Association with global administration through Bucks Music Group. A major focus for Leap is working with unsigned talent, publishing individual compositions in return for exploitation within commercials. Leap works with many agency clients around the world: past projects include Levis, Audi, Lynx, Vodafone and Bacardi.

Founder/managing director Richard Kirstein and his team—Ayla Master (music services manager), Simon King (A&R/music researcher) and Susan Stone

(music services co-ordinator)—explain what they do and how the company operates. For more information, check out their Web site: www.leapmusic.com.

## How did you get into the music industry?

*Richard Kirstein:* I played in bands, studied music to degree level, did some record production, and composed music for ads—which I got by knocking on many doors in the late 1980s/early 1990s with demo tapes. Then I joined Zomba Music Publishers in 1994 (at the time, the world's largest independent music company) setting up its film and TV division, which I ran for nine years. I signed composers, managed sync licensing (for commercials, films and TV programmes) and struck publishing administration deals with broadcasters, film and TV production companies. From that, I created a plan for how an ad agency could get into the music publishing business for commissioned scores and existing unsigned songs. Leap Music was the next step.

*Ayla Master:* Prior to working in advertising, I managed private recording studios and independent dance music labels. Then I decided to get into doing music for television, starting with music supervision for BBC, then *RI:SE*, the Channel 4 breakfast show. I'd heard about Leap and thought it was an interesting prospect, but at that point it was just Richard and his laptop. When we met, there wasn't a job available at Leap; however, the company was doing so well that Richard called on me soon after to help him. I mainly work with classical music and sourcing licensed music.

**Simon King:** Like Richard, I also started my career in a band. I began working for the management company that my band was signed to, moving on to set up my own management company. I then jumped around a bit, working for BBC Television and then trying music PR for a while, moving over to work as an A&R Manager in music publishing and eventually starting my own label. After closing my label during rough times, I then did some consultancy for a few people on syncs and helping out small indie labels. I saw Leap's ad and got the job as A&R/music researcher, finding unpublished bands for song placement in commercials and searching for music for specific projects.

**Susan Stone:** I moved to the UK from the US and met Ayla through my husband, also in the music industry. The timing and fit was serendipitous really, as they were looking for someone whilst I was looking to continue my music career in London. My background includes music licensing, music programming and youth culture marketing, working for organizations like DMX Music and Groovetech.

## What does Leap Music do for unsigned artists?

**Richard:** Leap offers new acts a direct path to leading advertising agencies that want to hear and use their music. Instead of new bands seeking a label to launch their careers, Leap builds on the many past examples of commercials breaking new artists. New bands wishing to gain exposure through TV ads can use Leap to promote their material to agencies on the basis that we publish any title successfully placed. We are involved with about 90% of the TV commercials produced at BBH that feature music, in addition to our work for other agencies. As a result, we can provide great opportunities for bands.

**Ayla:** Leap does quite a lot of work with classical composers as well, which I usually handle because of my background. One of my jobs is to supervise and executive produce classical recording sessions in Eastern Europe.

**Simon:** I do a similar sort of thing but on the dance, rock, pop, hip-hop level, generally. I'm out there all the time looking for unsigned bands, which often only look at record companies and conventional publishers as the only way to get into the music industry. We are an important alternative route. Getting into commercials can get them exposure and provide a good chunk of income as well.

## What is the process of getting music in an ad through Leap Music?

*Richard:* What happens is we receive a script for the commercial and then we draft a detailed deal memo which spells out exactly how the music will be used and the terms of the contract. Then, we provide a detailed creative brief, deal memo and script to our writers and music contacts. The music is brought in or created, and the ad agency decides if it wants to use the music we've put forward. If an unpublished track is chosen for the commercial, we then publish the individual track, working on a 'single song assignment' basis. We don't represent the whole catalogue of an artist; we pick individual titles. We're very above-board in explaining that we won't sign a song unless we sync it with an ad. If we do acquire a title, but for whatever reason it isn't used in a commercial, the rights revert to the songwriter/composer. We don't take entire catalogues like traditional publishers and labels do.

*Simon:* We are trying to be fair to the artist. We are not tying them up.

*Richard:* Exactly. That said, we do have some artists that we've worked with more than once. The final decision on which track is used lies with the client and the agency.

*Simon:* We've got a massive catalogue of unsigned artists, which I'm constantly building, so we can very quickly do a creative search to pitch tracks we think the agency would be interested in.

*Richard:* In addition, we produced a twelve-track CD compilation of unpublished acts called *Leap Unsigned,* which we distributed to agencies we work with as an introduction to our catalogue of unsigned material.

*Simon:* We also went a step further and launched an event called Leap Live, putting new and unsigned bands on at events in Soho to showcase them to the BBH creative staff. Our first one was at Madame Jo Jo's club—we had a good turnout from BBH and it gave them another opportunity to hear talented bands, hopefully sparking ideas for using their music in commercials.


## Has any of the music you have placed in ads gone on to be hits?

*Ayla:* We had our first Top 20 hit single in 2005 with Studio B's 'I See Girls (Crazy)'. The original song was on a Lynx deodorant ad and we published it. Tom Neville did a remix and Pete Tong caned it on Radio 1's Essential Selection. The ad planted the seed of the song in people's minds and it grew from there via a brilliant remix. The track was in the charts for several months and on various compilations, including some with Ministry of Sound.

### How do you find unsigned tracks?
**Simon:** A lot of the music we find is through word of mouth, through people we know in publishing, at independent labels, managers and lawyers. I also go to conferences and gigs to find new, unsigned artists. We have a big catalogue of music but are always looking for new talent, as you need a wide variety of music for the ad industry.

### Are you also signing recordings as well as publishing?
**Richard:** We have launched Leap Masters, which is a subsidiary company with which we acquire master rights. Effectively, it is a digital record label. This route is for some bands where we believe there is an opportunity to release a download, realtone, or a full track download off the back of the ad. We will acquire the master and the publishing on an individual-track basis if the track is placed in a commercial.

### What's the best way to approach Leap Music to try to place music in ads?
**Ayla:** Try to make your music stand out. We get a lot of unsolicited music sent in, so include any previous work you've done (demo reels, press cuttings, interest from the industry, gigs, etc.) that shows your determination. We look for something different.

**Simon:** Send a strong selection of your best work. Then gently hassle for feedback, keeping in mind that it can take a while for us to listen to everything that comes in.

**Susan:** Take the time and effort to make a good first impression and make it as easy as possible for your audience to learn about you and your music. Clearly provide your name, contact details and track information, including the basic genre details for your tracks. Add digital title/track/artist info for those of us who listen via iPods and computers. It can be frustrating to be interested in a track and then not know which one it is or how to get a hold of you!

**Ayla:** Unsigned bands have lawyers and managers. Those bands worth their salt have got managers who pay for quality recordings. It's so competitive now.

**Simon:** I've also dealt with some artists who didn't have representation or who might have been signed a while ago and who are now free of any recording or publishing deals. It completely varies, but the quality of music we work with is always high.

## What advice would you give on entering the music business?

**Richard:** Total belief in what you do, *but* a clear understanding of what you can bring to the market that isn't already on offer. You have to demonstrate your unique selling points.

**Ayla:** Absolutely. When I came to work for Richard, I had a lot of the skills for placing music in TV, but I didn't have experience in advertising. I had to show that my TV experience would work just as well in advertising.

**Simon:** You have to demonstrate that you can offer something different. What makes you stand out from the rest of the crowd.

**Ayla:** When I first came to London from the US, I didn't have a work permit and I had to convince employers to sponsor me, which was tough enough, let alone convincing the UK government I had the right skills. You really need to have determination, an incredibly positive attitude and not get fazed by the knock-backs.

**Richard:** It helps to be able to handle a variety of roles. The job we do is a mixture of creative and legal. We're not lawyers but we do a lot of business affairs work. I spend most of my time reading and negotiating sync rights and contracts. We interpret briefs and then bring them to the songwriters. We bring the songs back to the agency for them to present to clients. It takes a lot of effort and a broad set of skills to explain everything at each stage.

✦✦✦✦✦✦✦✦✦✦✦✦✦✦✦✦✦✦✦✦✦✦✦✦✦✦✦✦✦✦✦✦✦✦✦✦✦✦✦✦✦✦✦✦✦✦✦

# writing jingles

One of the most powerful aspects of TV and radio commercials is the music that accompanies the film clip. Think of numerous products, and the music is probably the thing you remember better than the pictures.

Some ads use sound bites from existing records; others use jingles. Jingles are short pieces of music written specifically for TV, radio and film commercials. A jingle is tailor-made to fit the product it is helping to advertise—if it's a soft drink, it'll be bright and breezy and fun, to attract children and young adults, the product's biggest market. If it's for chocolate, the music is likely to be softer, more romantic sounding, as the main target market for chocolate is women and this is what advertisers think women like. Mood is a key component to writing jingles—study TV ads and you'll soon see how the mood changes with the type of product.

The best jingles are specially commissioned for each product or to fit a film, although a lot are taken from library discs or records. The profile of each jingle is defined by the client and the ad agency. The standard length is thirty seconds, but pop it in the sampler and you can offer any length that's required, whether it's thirty seconds, fifteen seconds or ten seconds. Interpreting mood and getting it right is what jingle writers excel at. Many musicians turn their hand to it. Next, some tips from a leading jingle writer.

+++++++++++++++++++++++++++++++++++++++++++++++++++

## DAVID YORATH

David Yorath from Surrey Sound is a musician and has sold records worldwide, as well as having written and sold many jingles. He explains the ins and outs of jingle writing.

### How did you get into writing jingles?

I looked at the big brands out there and made up jingles and sent them in. The first one I did was for a Burger King advert a few years ago. I set this dreadful rhyme to music. You have to think laterally; you have to go out and get work.

You might send things in and they might not want it but they might like it anyway and you could get something later.

### How do you find out what people want?

It's not too difficult to decide what advertisers want. One way is to pick up a copy of *Campaign* every week—this is the bible for the UK advertising industry. It tells you what campaigns people are working on and which companies have won what contracts. With the Burger King advert, I looked at the slogan—it was probably out of date by the time I looked at it—but I wrote something around it and it went from there. You only have to look at the television to get ideas. Often the first ad is part of a campaign, so you'll get a run of work.

## What should you send in?

When I started, we sent things in on cassette, which was a bit difficult. Nowadays, it's easy: send things in on CD. It's just like sending in things to record labels, really: don't send in more than three bits of music; any more and it doesn't get listened to. It puts people off. After all, that's what advertising is all about—trailers are short. They're just a sound bite, maybe thirty seconds or less. In some ways, they're great because they are short. If you see a particular advertising agency has won an ad campaign, get in there quickly before they've gotten going or had ideas. Your idea could be the one to start the whole campaign, the one they write the campaign around. It doesn't matter whether it's a radio or TV campaign; the ideas and the music they want don't differ.

## Is it hard to get your music used by an ad agency?

They're not as bombarded as record companies but they still get a lot of music sent to them. One thing they're not interested in is deals, or people offering to do things cheaply. They can afford to pay more for the right thing; they're going to go for the best to impress their clients. Everything you do adds to your portfolio. If you start to get known, people will ask you for your show reel, so put everything on it. If not, you could do a show reel of mood music, to show different moods.

## What do you earn?

Payment depends on the client. Rates vary and many ad agencies pay by 'buyouts'—that is, they pay a one-off payment for your music, no matter how many times it gets used for that ad—whether it's one TV showing or a hundred, you just get that one payment. If they want to use it for another ad campaign, they'll negotiate another payment.

## Are there any drawbacks?

Jingle music is creativity of a kind but it can be very restrictive. Ad agencies and their clients often have a strong idea of the kind of music they want, citing a specific record, but they don't want to pay the money. So they'll play you the record and ask you to come up with something similar—they say they want something like that and it doesn't cost them as much. People have been sued a lot over this, because of plagiarism.

✦✦✦✦✦✦✦✦✦✦✦✦✦✦✦✦✦✦✦✦✦✦✦✦✦✦✦✦✦✦✦✦✦✦✦✦✦✦✦✦✦✦✦✦✦✦✦

# writing for tv

With the expansion of terrestrial and satellite channels, there's a growing demand for music for TV and film—although satellite channels do not pay as well as terrestrial. This televisual explosion uses lots of library music, so the library music business is doing very well. Additionally, there may also be the chance to write for new programmes.

Although everyone dreams of writing the theme to a successful drama, dramas tend to be the hardest to get and the competition is very high so you should set your sights lower to start with and work upwards. You will be expected to work from video and have the right equipment to sync your music to the pictures well.

To get into the field you, need to make contacts and know your stuff. There are a lot of programmes out there: watch them, listen to the main themes and come up with new themes. Record them. Make sure your new themes are not too cluttered, and leave space for the voice-over. The voice-over needs to be able to duck in and out. Satellite is not as precious as terrestrial TV—on terrestrial every second counts!

Look for something to represent the style of the programme. If it's a sports programme, it should be dramatic; if it's drama, it might be ambient. Cartoons are more upfront. Making cartoon music can be a good way to express yourself. Make sure the pieces of music are not more than a minute and a half with thirty-second, fifteen-second, ten-second and sometimes even five-second stings.

TV and film composer Flipper Dalton lives, appropriately enough, in Tinseltown. He will open your eyes to the realities of composing for celluloid.

✦✦✦✦✦✦✦✦✦✦✦✦✦✦✦✦✦✦✦✦✦✦✦✦✦✦✦✦✦✦✦✦✦✦✦✦✦✦✦✦✦✦✦✦✦✦

## FLIPPER DALTON

Flipper Dalton is based in Los Angeles where he has created music for film (*The Beach*), television shows (*Nip/Tuck*) and advertisements (Pepsi, Esso and others). Starting in the field of dance music in the UK in the late 1980s, he worked with the Prodigy, Sasha, Moby and his own project, Twelvetrees, whose album *The Boy on the Cloud* included the hit 'The Lost Tribe'.

### Is the world of film and television music difficult to get into?

Yes, it's hard to get into because the film and TV people go for composers who have already proven themselves. When I first moved to Los Angeles, they definitely tested me by giving me one scene in this film, one scene in that film. It was a while before I said, 'You know I can orchestrate if you have something like that'. The main things are that you deliver and that you deliver on time. If the main client is not into it, that's fine as long as the people who commission you are into it. If they aren't, you can spend $100,000 of their money on a three-minute piece of music with a thirty-two-piece orchestra, the best engineers, the best guitarists and the best pianists, but the director might turn around and say, 'You know what? I kind of just want someone to play the banjo'.

### Is there a certain thing that everybody's looking for?

People are looking for something different all the time. But it's always something similar to something that's already out. It's always, 'Well there's this Radiohead track that's been temped on it [used as a temporary soundtrack for the scene in the film]. We want something on that vibe now because we've gotten used to it'. They always want you to relate to some temp piece playing rather than writing whatever you feel. Film people don't take risks like that.

### What do you recommend if you're trying to get into film and television and you don't have any track record to speak of?

If you live in Los Angeles, it is easier. You need to get out and meet these people. There are plenty of functions where you can meet film people, music supervisors and agents. Even if you haven't got a track record but you've got a CD of shit that's hot stuff, when you meet these people, you can say, 'I'll send you a CD'. They are open to listening to stuff. But, at the same time, a lot of ad agencies are getting really commercial and they want an actual band that's really happening now, not a composer who can write in that style.

### Do you recommend sending stuff in or going in in-person?

Most people won't listen to stuff sent to them unless they already know the person who sent it. There's got to be some kind of handshake in the middle.

### Is it better to write original music for film and television, rather than licensing existing music?

I licensed some stuff to Neophonic for the *Nip/Tuck* series, although I prefer to write something original rather than have something licensed. There's no

---

challenge when something's licensed—you've already written it. If you write something new, you're creating something for the scene rather than someone trying to find a scene to fit something you've already written. It's like a jigsaw puzzle. I'd rather do it that way.

**How do you find out exactly what it is they want from you?**
They usually tell me the kind of vibe they're looking for. They usually, in fact they always, have a temp piece of music underneath: 'We're looking for something in this vibe', so that's what you do.

**How does working with an ad agency compare with working for film companies?**
I found the ad agencies less reliable, less consistent.

**How does the payment work? Does your agent take care of that side of things? And is it a one-time payment or do you get residuals?**
I send them an invoice and sign a release form. I have an agent. They take their cut. Most of the time it's a one-off payment.

**Are there any drawbacks?**
No, I haven't found any. I did a Pepsi commercial that I got paid for and I didn't even have to do the music. The music was there. They just needed a series of drums to be added that I synched. It took me a couple of hours.

It's not really hard work. In this town they don't say, 'Can you count to a hundred?' Most people are asking me if I can count to five. 'Yeah, I can count to five'. 'You're sure you can count to five?' 'Yeah'. 'Really sure? Because we're trusting you here. Can you count to five?' But you can count to one hundred just as easily. I think the most I've had to count up to is twenty-three. But the Pepsi job, it was definitely a five. I've probably had a lower one, where this guy played me a bit of *Scarface* and it's a one-note hit from an Oberheim keyboard. 'Can you do something like that?' 'Let me see now, that would mean me holding one key down on a keyboard for thirty seconds, hmmm, without doing anything else. You've got me there. It's a tough one'. It's a two. I even knew the preset that the guy was using. For me, to count to a hundred would be writing a whole score out in notation on the piano for a sixty-piece orchestra and conducting the orchestra. Then I'd be happy.

✦✦✦✦✦✦✦✦✦✦✦✦✦✦✦✦✦✦✦✦✦✦✦✦✦✦✦✦✦✦✦✦✦✦✦✦✦✦✦✦✦✦✦✦✦✦✦

# writing music for computer games

With the rapid rise in the popularity of computer games played on consoles like Sony PlayStation, Nintendo and Xbox, there's a growing demand for soundtrack music to set the games against and add excitement. While much games music still relies on licensing records by artists like Fabolous, Beenie Man, Petey Pablo, Blur, Fatboy Slim, Crystal Method and so on—and inclusion on a computer soundtrack not only brings in revenue but can give you wide exposure—lots of music is commissioned and written specifically for games.

To put the games market into perspective, recent research showed a major hit game can sell more than five million units worldwide, and although only a handful will achieve this in any given year, a larger number of hit games can be expected to exceed one million unit sales. The research also showed that 40% of the respondents said that after hearing a song they like in a video game they then bought the CD; 40% of those responding learned of a new song or band from a game and 27% of those went out and bought that CD; and 92% of respondents remember the music well after they stopped playing the game.

As well as commissioning exclusive tracks, when using existing songs, many games companies include album covers where possible on the game, giving instant recognition and making it easy for players to find out details and go and buy album. Games companies very often release games in unison with records, combining marketing efforts with the record company, and they sometimes release game soundtrack albums.

✦✦✦✦✦✦✦✦✦✦✦✦✦✦✦✦✦✦✦✦✦✦✦✦✦✦✦✦✦✦✦✦✦✦✦✦✦✦✦✦✦✦✦✦✦✦✦

## SERGIO PIMENTEL

Sergio Pimentel has had a varied career in the music business, including several years' experience licensing music for computer video games, culminating in working for Sony Computer Entertainment Europe. Here, Sergio, who is a big computer game fan himself, explains how he chooses music for games and what he is looking for.

## How did you get into games music?

I was working in PR and was approached by CouchLife, a leading music consultancy working on video game soundtracks exclusively. As I am a big video game player and music lover and I was DJing and promoting parties in London, it was the perfect match! I began as new business manager, working with the top games publishers and developers and, through interest in the sync side, got involved in licensing music. After three-and-a-half years, I was approached by Sony Computer Entertainment Europe, which was setting up an internal Music Licensing Department. The rest as they say is history!

## Do you take finished tracks, do you commission, or both?

We license finished tracks and we also commission producers and artists to write music for our games—it depends on the game. On SingStar, our highly acclaimed singing game, we usually license profiled pop tracks. On the Getaway; Black Monday we commissioned musicians to do a score for the cinematic cut scenes and commissioned some of Ninja Tunes's stable of artists to remix the jazzy orchestral score for use in-game.

Artwork courtesy of Sony Computer Entertainment Europe

## What kind of deal can you expect to get? For example, if it's your first year of writing or supplying music for games, what's the most you'd expect to get out of games companies?

It varies, as music budgets on games are based on overall development costs. I would say that it is unlikely that if you are new to music for games you would be given the bigger projects but fees can vary from buy-outs to royalties—it depends. Usually when music is commissioned it will be a flat fee.

## If a musician sends in a demo, should it include visuals as well as music, or should you just stick to your own music?

Stick to the music, but if the composer has experience in sound-to-picture in other media, it might be worth sending in a show reel. Since this is an art in itself, it will show the games company that you have those necessary skills.

**Is there a similar style to all games, or do different genre games require different genre music? For example, you don't hear that much games music with vocals (apart from exceptions like games with tuneable 'radios' in them)—is this still the case, or are things becoming more varied, the more games there are?**

This has changed over the last few years with mainstream games such as SingStar and also the Eye-Toy range of games. Before, it was usually rock or dance that was heard in games, with the exception of the games with the 'radio station' idea. Now we can use many different genres, from pop to chill-out.

**As in other areas of music, is it best to have some kind of track record before approaching a games company? Perhaps a successful club tune or a track picked up for TV or film?**

It always helps if you have a good track record within another media.

Artwork courtesy of Sony Computer Entertainment Europe

**Do you think people should be dedicated games music providers and develop that as a skill, or should they continue to make music for other fields? If they want to be dedicated, can they expect to make a reasonable living at it?**

It is very competitive and there are many out there trying to break into games. I'd say it's worth working across a number of different media, as this is likely to ensure that the skillset is broad and musicians will then show that they can do a range of things.

**If you are successful at games music, will record companies or publishers come knocking at your door?**

We certainly hope that in the future artists will be broken by having music in games—watch this space!

✦✦✦✦✦✦✦✦✦✦✦✦✦✦✦✦✦✦✦✦✦✦✦✦✦✦✦✦✦✦✦✦✦✦✦✦✦✦✦✦✦✦✦✦

# STEVE HOROWITZ

Computer games composer Steve Horowitz is based in New York. Steve has made a living composing music for video games for a decade now, as well as

for film, TV and cartoons. He started on guitar at the age of seven but found his instrument when he switched to bass in high school. He attended the California Institute of the Arts, and at age twenty-four decided to go to music school, where he 'got into weird classical music' and for the first time saw computers used for music, though more for recording (and playing games) than composition. After setting up a recording studio business in the San Francisco area, Steve was set to 'write weird music and die poor and that was cool' until a new offer came his way.

Steve explains how he entered the field and provides advice for anyone interested in entering the music-to-animation domain.

### Once you had your recording studio business set up, how did you move into computer games?

A friend of my cousin's, who had a company working on console game titles for the Sega Genesis (known as Megadrive in the UK) and other cartridge-based systems, told me I could make a living writing music for games. This was in the early 1990s. So I started to write music for him and all kinds of companies. At the same time, the CD-ROM boom was happening, so we had people coming to us going, 'We're doing Dante's Inferno and we want you to do the sound'. This meant the music, the sound effects, recording it all—everything. And then another company would say, 'We're doing two games this year, and eight next year', and it was just blowing up. So two games came out in which the animated sections I'd scored looked great but the game-play was terrible.

I moved on to the Netherlands for a while and started to become interested in Web audio after I saw the Beatnik audio engine. When I moved back to New York in 2000, I interviewed with Nickelodeon Online, and they were opening a music studio. They knew the Web was coming of age then, so I was in-house for a while; now I'm a vendor to them. I've spent the last five years focusing on kids' games, doing preschool games with Nick Jr., hundreds of titles for on-line games and interactive cartoons for on-air broadcast and Web-casting.

## How do you write a piece of music that changes according to the actions of the player? How is it different from scoring a TV show?

That's a good question because it gets down to the heart of the debate that's going on within interactive audio and the game world. One paradigm is the licensing of existing tracks for a game like *Grand Theft Auto*. These are games just with pop music in them. In that case, it's not particularly interactive—not that they aren't effective games. Another paradigm is something like a *Star Wars* game, where you take John Williams' music and repurpose it by cutting it up. Then there's a group of people who are very committed to what's called 'adaptive scoring' for games. You work with DLS banks (downloadable sounds) and create MIDI that applies itself adaptively to the score. The companies that do this have their own proprietary engines for the tasks and then, depending on who their audio director is, that person will work with the programming group to define what the parameters are of this engine, of what it can do and how.

I think that about a quarter of game scores are orchestral recordings, often using orchestras in Seattle or Eastern Europe. This can be exciting and cool but at the end of the day you cut that score up and talk to your programmer and figure out how to make it as adaptive as possible. Then there are adaptive scores that are built from the ground up, and these are the state-of-the-art of game scoring. When you score a TV show or cartoon, you're basing everything on producer direction and visual clues. Within a game, it's the same except you can base the structure and dynamic of your music on a lot of things, like the health of the player. The interactive triggers and tie-ins to these games can be based on these variables, and that's where it gets really interesting. You work with a pool of loops—every time a character gets into battle, their health level changes, or they enter a new stage and you have a pool of loops and they'll all work against each other. The challenge is to create loops that can work interactively and be triggered at any time. Now, you set it so that loop one to three works on Level One in the game, and loops four to seven on Level Two. So you have these pieces of music that work together and with gains in health or weapons or whatever it is, the music is going to adapt accordingly and expand and retract. The difference in gaming is that there's an

---

added dimension of real-time feedback and action, and that opens up many different challenges.

### If someone is interested in writing music for games, how would they get a foothold in the field?

When I started, the industry was not as developed as it is now. It's important to have an interest in technology. As I said, a quarter of game soundtracks are orchestral, so there's a chance to come up as a composer who only writes symphonic music for games. That's cool. On the other hand, there's the more conventional ProTools with every plug-in, or Logic, or a digital setup with a sample bank—or best of all, a combination of live musicians and samplers. One of the things that's been nice about the game business for me is that, for the most part, you're left alone. The programmers have their idea and then you go away and produce a lot of music. Movie or TV jobs tend to be more micromanaged.

Then there are the smaller platforms. What's coming up now is Casual Gaming based on Flash, which I'm doing with NickOnline. It used to be that games on the Web couldn't be over 500kb, from the audio to the graphics and everything in between. Now games in Flash are being delivered in 5Mb to 20Mb. You can get a lot in that and make some very compelling games. Another step down is the mobile phone market, and that's an industry that's only on its way up in terms of needing music. And it's at a weird arcane stage with the technology right now; it feels like the dark ages but that's how the Web felt and it's going to change pretty quickly. Then there's the path of sound design and sound effects, if you prefer that angle. So there are many different niches now. There's a lot of competition, and breaking in is always hard but you just have to apply itself.

### What are the differences between the US and European games market? Do you really have to be in LA or San Francisco to work on game music?

In the US, it's pretty California-centric, which is a source of debate because there are a lot of British games music composers, and I think there's a cultural gap there. The European games market is very large, of course. The Game Audio Network Guild (www.audiogang.org) is quite LA-oriented. The Interactive Audio Special Interest Group (part of the Midi Manufacturers Association) and the International Game Developers Association (www.igda.org) are good in terms of bringing groups of people together working to produce white papers and research for the industry, and it's a way for composers to talk directly with developers. I think it's as wide open in Europe as anywhere. I live in New York, and if I wanted to do console games exclusively, I'd have to go to LA or Austin or San Francisco. In New York, there are toy companies and media institutions like Viacom, which is where I do most of my work.

✦✦✦✦✦✦✦✦✦✦✦✦✦✦✦✦✦✦✦✦✦✦✦✦✦✦✦✦✦✦✦✦✦✦✦✦✦✦✦✦✦✦✦✦

# session work

Another route into the making of music is becoming a session musician, or, another way of putting it, a freelance musician. Many people prefer their independence rather than being in a band or orchestra and this is a popular route to making a living out of making music.

Many people pick up session work through the people they know, so use those music college/school contacts or music industry contacts like mad. There's a huge variety of work, from miming instrumental parts on TV shows such as *Top of the Pops* (but this isn't as easy as it sounds!) to going on a months-long tour with a major artist.

If you want to make a career out of session playing, you have to be dedicated and be willing to work very hard. Most musicians are not like this! You have to be very disciplined. You can be on tour for six months with a famous band and you can earn lots of money but then you may not work for a year. It happens a lot. People think it's glam, and it is, but it's hard work, too. You need to be versatile, able to get on with people and it's better if you can sight read, though not mandatory.

Session musicians Shannon Harris from the UK and Jonny Cragg from the US explain how the how it all works.

✦✦✦✦✦✦✦✦✦✦✦✦✦✦✦✦✦✦✦✦✦✦✦✦✦✦✦✦✦✦✦✦✦✦✦✦✦✦✦✦✦✦✦✦

## SHANNON HARRIS

Shannon has had a varied experience as a working musician, from being asked to join successful US rock band Wheatus, to forming his own bands, writing music for TV and being a successful session musician. Here he reveals all.

## When did you first learn to play a musical instrument?

I learned piano at home when I was a kid, at around five or six years old. I was obsessed with music and had lessons early on and passed the classical music

grades. I always liked classical music but I had a problem, as my hands were too small. It got to the point where the teacher told me I wouldn't get any further, as I would never be able to play parts of the classical repertoire.

## When did you start playing jazz, pop and rock?

When I was growing up, I only listened to classical music. My Dad was very into classics and he thought pop music was a lower form of culture. He was very strict with me. I had to be up at six a.m. and practice for two hours before breakfast. I went on with this until I was around sixteen and then I heard jazz for the first time. I heard a guy, a teacher, playing blues in the music department and it blew my mind. I burst in and asked him to teach me. It devastated my Dad! I stopped playing classics and began playing boogie-woogie. From there, I got interested in pop music and then at university I got into Brazilian music, funk and other genres.

## When did you first join a band?

I had a band at university and when I left I went on the dole and practiced eight hours a day and did this for a year and a half. Then I started earning a living playing jazz music for a couple of years. I was a gigging jazz musician and I played at all sorts of places. I played seven or eight times a week, getting back late every night and making around £30 to £40 a gig. I was living in Oxford and got to know everyone on the jazz scene—I hung out in jazz pubs and clubs. After a couple of years, I got fed up with it and realised that although I liked jazz I wanted to do something different.

I became a member of a rock band, Vitamin. It was great fun, as this was the time when Oxford was really buzzing—it was the time of Radiohead, Ride, and Radio 1 came to Oxford with Sound City. There was a real vibe that every rock band from Oxford was going to make it big! Lots of young musicians were coming to Oxford and there'd be lots of lock-ins in pubs and we'd be locked in with Radiohead and Ride, so we got to know them all. I had an absolute blast for a couple of years, wearing loads of makeup and trashing things. Then the scene died down and I got into writing music for TV. This was through a guy I met in Oxford who was a sax player and a music writer for TV. I wanted to learn how to write music on computer and he taught me all the software. I did that for a couple of years and at the same time had a jazz residency at a club.

### When did you get your first work as a session player?

I was also in a band called Shuffle and one night someone came up to me and told me that his brother was in an Irish band called Relish and the band was looking for a keyboard player. I talked to them but wasn't ready to leave Shuffle and go to NI. A year later, Shuffle had broken up and I talked to Relish again, sent them a demo of my stuff, they liked it and I went on to work with them as a session player. By now, Relish was signed to EMI Ireland in Dublin.

I was with them for two years and we did loads of festivals and tours and big TV promotional shows in Ireland and I recorded part of their debut album, 'Wildflowers', which reached the Irish Top 10. We supported U2 at Slane Castle, V2001 and T in The Park 2001 and I met Wheatus—this was the year of their big hit 'Teenage Dirtbag'. Steve Harrison, Relish's manager, who also manages the Charlatans, got us a support tour for Wheatus. They loved our demo and we ended up playing thirty dates with them on their theatre tour.

### You became a member of Wheatus; what made you decide to go back to session work?

Brendan (Brown), the singer from Wheatus, asked me if I'd like to be the keyboardist on the new album. I agreed, as I'd had enough of being a session player. He wanted me to be a full band member. I joined them in March 2002. I moved to New York and lived with their parents in the granny annex! We made the record, their second album, and it took ages. We did loads of tours and I witnessed the decline of the band. Although I was a member of the band, I was not part of the creative process. It was rather a one-man show. We made the third album during 2004 but I got pissed off with not having enough creative input so I decided to leave and I returned to the UK.

It was hard at first, as many of my contacts had grown cold. I started working on my own projects and decided to do well-paid session work to keep me going. I heard about the session fixer, Sue Carling, and sent off my details. I didn't hear for a while then she got me a gig on Parkinson with Rod Stewart, which was great fun. He was really nice. Then I did promotional stuff with Jem and *Top of the Pops* with Tyler James and I have been to auditions with bands such as Razorlight.

In the meantime, I have my own band, Urban Myth Club, a sort of ambient electronic Zero 7 and I play Brazilian electronic music and we played Glastonbury and the main stage at the Big Chill festival. I also work with a band in Oxford doing breakbeat and work with DJs and VJs doing live percussion and still do a little mixing and production for TV.

### Is it hard to get pay out of people?

It can be hard to get paid. I did a TV show with Jem which took nearly six months! With Relish, EMI were very slow and it took months to pay me.

Even with Wheatus, even though I was a band member, it took ages in the beginning. I was promised a regular wage, which took a while to come through. It got to the point where I couldn't take money out of the bank and had to borrow from friends! It wasn't the band's fault; it was the way it went through the system.

It's partly my fault for not being more insistent about money. I've learned a lot from these experiences and I've gotten better since then. I've learned that people are selfish about money and want to minimise their costs so you've got to be tough and insist on payment.

### What advice would you give someone wanting to be a session player?

It really helps if you have a flexible schedule; this is really crucial. Lots of stuff you get offered is tomorrow—or even today, sometimes! You have to be willing to go for work at the last minute. If you don't go, there's always someone else out there who will. And it's an opportunity to get to know well-known bands. Loads of things can lead from it. It's a way of meeting well-connected people and furthering your career. So do it, and don't be too precious about it!

You have to be really friendly; you have to get on with people. It's okay for me because I like meeting people. What I don't like is that session players have quite a low status; many of us don't care because we have our own projects, but you can't let it worry you. You are there to do a job and do it well. You can't have too much of an ego. You've got to get on, be versatile and get known around as someone who is reliable and does a good job and you'll get more work. When you turn up, you need to do the work quickly and accurately; people are paying for the time, and it's expensive. You need to be able to play different styles of music and come up with parts that fit the song, sets it off, probably something simple with the right inversions and melody. You've got to be a team player.

++++++++++++++++++++++++++++++++++++++++++++++++++++

++++++++++++++++++++++++++++++++++++++++++++++++++++

## JONNY CRAGG

Drummer Jonny Cragg has been a professional musician since he was fifteen years old. Originally from Leeds, he now resides in New York City. As a session musician, Cragg's work can be heard on advertisements for Doritos, Budweiser, and Gogurt, as well as on albums from Spacehog (*Resident Alien*), Morley (*Sun Machine*) and Cantinero (*Championship Boxing*).

**Why did you pick the drums?**
It's very visceral and physical. There's a lot of instant gratification that comes from playing the drums. If you hit a drum, it sounds like a drum. If you blow down a saxophone, it doesn't always sound like a saxophone. You certainly need to know your way around the fret board a little bit before you can make a guitar sound like a guitar. With the drums, there's something instant there that can be built upon. It's a very primal instrument.

**Did you ever take lessons?**
For years. I keep going back every now and again just to get out of bad habits or learn something I don't know. Or just to try and improve.

**When did you first start playing any kind of live show?**
I was fifteen in Leeds in a pub. I played in a Goth band.

**What was your first proper job in music?**
I'm still waiting for a proper job, but my first professional gig with a cabaret band playing chart covers at the age of seventeen. We played in the work-

ingmen's clubs of Northern England. It was an apprenticeship into playing properly, the kind of thing that, if you do it for too long, you become too comfortable appropriating the styles of other drummers, but if you do it for a bit, it helps you become a proper musician. It was like running away and joining a circus.

## How do you approach doing session work?
Session playing is all about adapting quickly to somebody else's style and what they want. You have to be sensitive and ignore your own wants, desires and gratifications because you are serving somebody else.

## Do you try to get session work often?
My thing with session playing is neither trying nor not trying—I'm just there. I've never found that trying to get session work culminates in getting it. It's always that I'll get three calls in a week then I won't get anything for three months. I'm always looking to meet people and be available. If there's money involved, there's seldom a situation I'll turn down.

## Is it hard to get paid?
I've never had problems getting paid. On a more casual level, people will pay you cash. If it's small-time people and they're working on a project and they want some solid rhythm track but they don't really want any involvement from you, sometimes the money is a way of them defining the relationship. I found that a lot in America, whereas people expect favours a lot more in the UK. There they will ask you to play on their stuff, but it won't be clear what the terms are. The one thing that's clear or at least implicit is that you're not going to get paid. What you are going to get instead is never really discussed. It seldom ends up being creative control.

## What are some benefits/downfalls to being a session musician versus being in a band?
If you're a successful session musician, you're working in different environments every day. It never gets boring. Some gigs are better than others. You're not locked in with a certain set of people and you can operate with a certain amount of autonomy. The downside is that it's not always that creative and it can end up being a bit of a job. You can fall in and out of favour on a whim without really having done anything wrong.

**Is there anybody you would want to work with regularly as a session musician?**
Someone like Prince would be a dream come true. I can't imagine there'd be much input there. I would love to be told exactly what to do by someone like Prince.

✦✦✦✦✦✦✦✦✦✦✦✦✦✦✦✦✦✦✦✦✦✦✦✦✦✦✦✦✦✦✦✦✦✦✦✦✦✦✦✦✦✦✦✦✦✦✦

## Session Fixers

Many session musicians find work through specialist agents called session fixers. Sue Carling explains what's required.

✦✦✦✦✦✦✦✦✦✦✦✦✦✦✦✦✦✦✦✦✦✦✦✦✦✦✦✦✦✦✦✦✦✦✦✦✦✦✦✦✦✦✦✦✦✦✦

## SUE CARLING

Sue Carling runs a successful session fixing agency and places singers and musicians in a wide range of session work, from TV shows to tours to fronting major label projects. Here, Sue explains how she started her company, what she's looking for in a session musician and gives useful tips on being a success in the field.

### What was your experience before starting your company?
I went to school and college in Cornwall. I moved to London with a couple of friends and got a job initially at Sony Records as a secretary. I moved from there to WEA records (Warner, Electra, Atlantic). I worked in production and then moved on to the Atlantic Records office working for the label manager. I then spent a year in LA, where I gained a lot of valuable experience in the music business.

When I got back to the UK, I got a job in a small label in press and promotion, working on a variety of acts, ranging from Don Williams, Ace, the Four Tops and one of the first punk bands, the Adverts.

My experience from there ranges from working with a small record label (Real Records—the Pretenders and Johnny Thunders from the New York Dolls)

---

to Logo Records, working on the Tourists (members: Annie Lennox and Dave Stewart) and the Q-Tips (singer: Paul Young).

I then began my own management company signing acts to WEA Records and EMI Records.

## How did you start your company?

I met an established and successful music director. He is the person who puts musicians together, arranges the music, rehearses the band and so on for any live work for artists who tour, showcase, etc. We set up an agency together with the aim of supplying musicians for anything from live work to TV promotion to recording.

We worked together for a couple of years and then mutually agreed to go our separate ways. Initially, I took the TV promotion route, but the company grew and diversified. We still work together on some projects.

My job is to supply and organise musicians. I have to be organised and my musicians have to be organised. You have to do a good job.

The industry has changed over the last few years. Major labels have merged, and the work pressure is enormous. I hope to help take away some headaches and provide, co-ordinate and organise musicians to fit record company briefs and needs.

It is because of this that I have to provide an efficient service. My musicians represent my company when they work for me, so they have to be talented, professional and reliable.

## Who needs session players?

There is a wide variety of work.

Some agents specialise in providing session musicians for studio work, others represent musicians/singers in tribute bands, some hire out function bands or place singers or musicians on cruises or in clubs, and some work for the theatre and provide musicians for touring productions or shows in the West End.

My area is the music/recording industry and I work to specific briefs supplying musicians for casting directors, musical directors, management companies, production companies, television companies and record companies.

For example, TV promotion departments in record companies have solo artists who often need bands for their promotional campaigns, or existing bands which need a string section or a Spanish guitarist, percussionist, a brass section, backing singers and so on.

UK-based artists need musicians and singers for all aspects of promotion. Often, American artists come over to Europe and cannot bring their musicians with them, so they require musicians and/or backing singers for their promotion.

Television companies need musicians for their entertainment shows. They give me the brief and I put people forward.

## What type of work is there?

It's very varied and ranges from a day's work to whole tours, sometimes lasting months. There is touring, TV promotion, radio promotion, music videos and castings for TV commercials, TV and film.

Management companies and musical directors contact me to let me know they are auditioning for musicians or backing singers for a tour and I send along people who I think might be suitable. Tour managers also call, or put management onto me if the band they are working with are looking for extra musicians or singers. Casting directors call me to advise that they are casting for a music video or a TV commercial.

On occasion, I am approached by record, management or production companies on a consultancy basis to source musicians or singers to front a particular project. Some of these people will then go on to sign a record deal themselves, and hopefully enjoy a successful career.

Record company promotion campaigns can go on for months, and involve everything from TV promotion, to road shows, radio promotion, showcases and tours.

Whatever work I get for my musicians and singers, all the liaison comes through my office. I negotiate fees, deal with contracts, invoice and provide itineraries and travel details.

For example, for road shows, there is generally a central pick up point where musicians are picked up by the tour manager, transported to the show, and driven home. I will liaise with the tour manager or record company and let the musicians know what the pick up time is, what time they arrive at the venue, onstage time, what tracks are to be performed, clear time, and so on.

If it's a long day, catering is provided onsite, or a 'per diem' is paid, which is an amount of money you have for daily expenses (i.e., food, phone calls, etc.). This is normally only paid when a musician is working away from their place of residence.

In tour situations, there is usually transport provided to the rehearsal venue, or to meet up with the tour bus. Any flights and hotels while on tour are paid for by the company commissioning the musicians, as are any per diems. In some cases, per diems are not paid daily but incorporated in to an overall fee.

Sometimes, musicians will be needed for European promotion. When Mary J. Blige came to the UK, she used my musicians for her promotion in the UK, as well as in Italy for festival appearances.

Music video directors often need extra musicians for videos; they hold castings and successful musicians get several hours filming. You get paid *and* great experience.

### Have you worked with TV talent shows like *Pop Idol*?

I've worked with *Pop Idol* winners. I organised the strings for Will Young's summer festival tour last year, and I have provided musicians and singers for TV promotional campaigns for Alex Parks, Gareth Gates, Michelle McManus, Alistair Griffin and Steve Brookstein.

### What qualities do you need as a session singer?

Whether you are a singer or a musician, you must be good at what you do. You must be able to perform well in any situation. Be confident. And above all, singers—do your vocal exercises *every day*, work on your breathing and take care of your voice. All the best singers do, and you will harm your voice if you don't—not to mention hinder your performance ability.

And my performers must be professional and reliable. I won't recommend anyone for TV work, for example, if I get the feeling they are lacking in confidence and need a bit more experience under their belts I won't use them— it's not compatible with high-pressure situations!

Be realistic. It may take a while to get work once you've sent your details in. Session fixers have many, many musicians on their books so it could be some time before we get back to you.

The thing to remember about being a session singer or musician is that it's not about you—it's about the producer, the director, the record or television company, or the artist you are working for. You do a good job for *them*. If you do, you very often get asked back.

### What do you ask prospective session musicians to give you?

A CV and a good photo—and from singers, a demo. If necessary, I request a demo from musicians farther down the line.

Prepare a good CV. Say what you play. Sometimes people forget to include that, believe it or not! If you play guitar, is it bass, rhythm or lead? Do you play any other instruments? Do you do backing vocals?

Make sure your phone number is on the CV and your name and contact number is on the CD supplied, if you've sent one (I only ask singers to send in

CDs initially). Remember, CDs get separated from CVs and you may have an incredible voice but it's no good if I can't phone you.

It's amazing how often I think someone looks right for a project then can't phone them because they've left off their number!

Keep your CV brief and to the point—people don't want to plough through your entire school history before getting to the details they need: you might be at music college or recently graduated and you're probably in a band which has played some gigs, so you'll have a little experience but not much. List which venues you've played—this will show you have live gigging experience. It doesn't have to be with someone famous!

Always add a couple of referees at the bottom of your CV—people who can vouch for you, your ability and your reliability.

Keep people informed of changes of address and phone numbers. It's recommended you keep the same mobile number—there is nothing worse than trying to contact someone to find their number doesn't work any more.

Make sure you include a good picture. It doesn't have to be a professional one; it could be taken by a friend with a digital camera. It must be a head-and-shoulders shot—action shots seldom work well. In many situations these days, the photo is what will get you to the next stage, whether it be for auditions or TV work, so you must look good and *turn up for work looking good* not like you have just fallen out of bed!

You have to be ready at a very short notice because when a session fixer does contact you, the work often requires you to be available almost immediately. You must be flexible and accommodating.

If you get the work, you must be very professional. You must always be on time—in fact, I'd advise getting there at least half an hour early—then you can have a relaxing coffee instead of arriving out of breath and harassed. TV companies cannot wait for you; neither can rehearsals, tour buses or shows.

Be prepared, as in knowing the song. Even if it's for rehearsals, you will usually get a CD sent up-front.

Pay attention to the dress code. This is the outfit you will be notified of and are expected to provide for stage or TV. It's advisable to bring a small selection of clothes that fit the brief so that the stylist can say which they prefer. Sometimes, measurements are required and clothes provided.

You are usually requested *not* to wear clothes with logos—however small! No logos means no logos!

If you are working, don't ask if you can bring a friend or boyfriend or girlfriend. You are there to work.

And never ever ask for autographs either of the person you are working for or of other artists who may be on the same show. Don't give them CDs of your songs, or promote yourself—be professional.

There are also some other unspoken rules of work. When working for television, don't chew gum on camera or wander off without the production staff or record company person knowing where you are.

You can be at some TV shows for a long time with run-through, camera rehearsals and dress runs. If you are told you are on a break, check before going out for a breath of fresh air and keep your mobile with you in case you are needed back quickly.

### Can someone make a living out of session work?
It depends on the area of work they choose.

There isn't enough work out there for all the people on any agency's books. However, saying that, in the record industry, if someone is very, very good and meets the right people, it's possible.

If you are playing with a very successful established artist, they often like to keep their musicians/singers on a retainer so that they are always available to that artist. This is very expensive and so few people do it.

It is possible to make a living if you are a musician interested in playing in the house band at theatres. There are many theatrical companies that tour and their productions can often end up in the West End and run for years.

A lot of session musicians have other means of earning a living. Some have their own creative projects and are developing their own band or their own act and have residencies in clubs around town. Some are in function bands and do weddings and parties; others are in tribute bands and still others do cruises.

There are many options to be explored!

✦✦✦✦✦✦✦✦✦✦✦✦✦✦✦✦✦✦✦✦✦✦✦✦✦✦✦✦✦✦✦✦✦✦✦✦✦✦✦✦✦✦✦✦✦✦✦✦✦

# education

Another career you might consider is going into teaching. This doesn't have to be teaching guitar or piano to reluctant school kids or inept adults. There are a number of opportunities to teach enthusiastic students at colleges and universities in anything from songwriting to being a DJ—and in many cases you don't even have to read music. Or you could take on private students who want to learn an instrument on a one-to-one basis. So all you self-taught musicians out there, read on!

✦✦✦✦✦✦✦✦✦✦✦✦✦✦✦✦✦✦✦✦✦✦✦✦✦✦✦✦✦✦✦✦✦✦✦✦✦✦✦✦✦✦✦✦✦✦✦✦✦✦✦✦✦

## HELEN REDDINGTON

Helen Reddington (aka Helen McCookerybook) is a musician who started off in a punk band and later recorded as Helen and the Horns. She still writes and performs music but she also teaches songwriting. Here she explains how it all happened.

### How did you get into music?

I started at art college in 1977, when punk rock happened. I lived in a big squat in Brighton and there was a band that lived in our basement and they were really, really noisy and we decided to get them a gig and they chickened out of it. So we formed a band to play the gig that we got and we wrote the set in an afternoon—something like seven songs! We wrote the songs by looking in newspapers. We bought the *Sun* and stuff like that and read about things that were happening that day and wrote songs about them. I did have a guitar but I couldn't play very many chords and it was a band with blokes and they got me to play

bass. They said, 'You play bass. It's easy!' And I borrowed the bass from this girl and it was actually the Buzzcocks' bass guitar! After that one gig, we got more and more, which was really strange because we only put the band together out of spite!

### How did your career as a professional musician develop?

Gradually things mutated, the band mutated, members left and we ended up being a three-piece band. We signed to a record label in Brighton called Attrix and became part of a scene called Brighton Rock, around 1980, but we didn't really like it, so we moved to London. Then we were signed to Graduate Records, which was UB40's company, or at least UB40 were signed to them, and it was obvious they weren't going to let us make an album so we split up, because unless you get an advance for an album, you have trouble making a living. Next, I got asked by some friends to write some music for a television programme. I thought it was a joke, party talk, and I said yes, I'd do it, but then I got the money from Channel 4 and that was my first big royalty.

## Did one of the people have contacts at Channel 4?
No, Channel 4 was throwing out nets at the time, looking for people, like all these digital channels are now. They want people with strong ideas. It was when almost everybody was being asked to make a programme and this lot were, and I think it's a very similar situation now with all the satellite channels.

## How did Helen and the Horns come about?
The guy from Rough Trade, Geoff Travis, gave me some money to record a demo. I recorded a demo with a full band on it and I tried to get some gigs but the drummer said, 'Every time we do a gig, I'm going to need five quid for a taxi' and I couldn't afford to pay that so I just rehearsed with the horn section. I ended up being given a gig with just myself and the horn section and it went down really well. We got offered loads more and that band eventually signed to RCA. We were together for about three years as Helen and the Horns. I was a member of the Performing Right Society and they collected all my radio royalties and it ended up being quite a lot, really; it was enough to live off. After various problems with RCA, my band formed their own label with me, and we recorded our own album *Hell Hath No Horns* and released it and distributed it independently. Well, after that we decided to split up. A record company, Near Shore, approached me and, in 2005, we released a lot of those songs again, and I've been playing live to promote the CD and playing lots of new stuff too. In the intervening years, I seem to have acquired a Japanese audience, and even an Argentinian DJ has been playing my stuff!

## What did you do after the band split up?
I started writing music for theatre groups. I just started saying yes to anything because I wasn't sure what to do next. I'd gotten very fed up with the business and so I wrote songs for the Inner London Education Authority youth theatre and all sorts of other things like that. It was paid work and I really enjoyed it. You had a very direct relationship with the people who were performing; you'd actually hear someone singing or meet them and the director would say, 'Can you write a song for them?' It was a very personal kind of thing—work-

ing and running music workshops on how to do songwriting with people who weren't musicians. It was incredibly fulfilling because people found they could do things they didn't think they could. With things like that, funding is always difficult to get, and eventually I started coming to the University of Westminster as guest lecturer. Parallel to that, I'd done an MA at Middlesex University in performing arts and for my final show there I did a song cycle based on the seven deadly sins, and I did a run of that at a theatre just off Tottenham Court Road—my West End run! It's a theatre that holds forty people! It's great to do the same thing night after night. So I kept working as a performer but on a much smaller scale. Gradually, I started doing more work at the University of Westminster on songwriting and then eventually ended up working as a full-time teaching academic as well as production work. I cut back on my teaching because I wanted to do more performance.

I wrote a song-cycle called *Voxpop Puella* and invited some of the film-makers I'd worked with over the years to contribute film shorts; I got a grant from the Arts Council of England to tour this in arts centres throughout England, running songwriting workshops alongside it based on the central idea, which was the seven ages of woman. It ended up with a week at the Edinburgh Festival Fringe and I got to sing a song live on the BBC World Service. I've also always had this relationship with various videomakers, where they can't afford to pay me and I do the music anyway and the next time they get a budget they'll pay me or do art for titles for my projects. It's a trading system, trading art for art!

### How do you write your songs?

I used to write them on guitar but I got a grant from the Arts Council to learn how to use programming packages, so I do a lot of programming now because then you can have a complete orchestration and, as I don't read music, you've got all the sounds there straight away. And then you can always get people in to play them if you need to. So it's a boon to people like me.

### Do you have your own equipment?

I have got some of my own and I use a lot at the university. I do a lot of programming and I've got a computer and I've got a sound module and I can make broadcast-quality stuff at home, but I don't make broadcast-quality songs because I think you need to go into the studio to record voices.

### What TV or radio work have you done recently?

The last thing I did was for a BBC animation which was shown on BBC 2.

---

## What helped you get into teaching at the university?

Partly, the community work, partly the MA and also partly having had a deal and having my own band—that kind of thing. Also my other teaching, because one of the things I do outside the university is devise and run songwriting workshops in schools and other community organisations. I had started this before I came here, but since being here I've been PRS Composer in Residence at a group of South London Schools (the children wrote songs with me from scratch for a performance in front of hundreds of parents) and also worked as a songwriter in youth clubs and with elders as part of the *Voxpop Puella* tour, with autistic children and young people with learning difficulties. I now apply for funding to run my own workshop series in local schools, always with songwriting at the centre of the workshop. It's very real and down-to-earth; if the people you're working with don't like something, they let you know straight away, with a degree of honesty you don't find in the music business! But I have found that these workshops have a knock-on effect on my own music; you learn not to be precious about lyrics and the creative process in general. I sometimes mentor students and ex-students in this, if they seem to have an interest in it. I have now had a lot of experience in this type of songwriting— it's really fulfilling to create unique songs with groups of people who didn't see themselves as creative beforehand. Within the university, I try to encourage songwriters as much as possible—a couple of years ago, I helped the Musicians' Benevolent Fund devise a songwriting competition for university music students, and this is now an annual event.

## What advice would you give for learning songwriting?

I think the most important thing is to be able to tell the point at which you're getting satisfaction out of what you're working on and whether it's more important than making a lot of money. Because some people are blissfully happy doing something like country and western compositions with a band on the south coast somewhere and having a job as a computer analyst and they'd be miserable if they tried to flog their songs and got nowhere with it, and other people are terribly miserable and cynical, despite having a lot of money from writing chart hits. It's very hard. The songwriters who I teach are very torn between whether they think they ought to be going for the big bucks or just sitting at home, and some of them have got such strong singer-songwriter identities that I just have to advise them not to change. Because the way they sing and the way they perform is so tied into the songs they write that if you imposed anything on them it would be destructive. Whereas with others, I think if they bumped into the right person at the right party and said the right things they'd have a publishing deal straight away. I say to them, 'When you go to a party, tell everybody that you're a musician because you never know who might be there'.

I think one of my biggest breaks was writing the music for television programmes, and that started off as a kind of fantasy, sitting down and chatting after a party and suddenly it was there.

### Should songwriters aim for the charts?

I do say to the students that it's all right not to aim for the charts, and that's purely because a certain aspect of songwriting might completely stop if showbiz—boy/girl band writing—is all that's acceptable. If people are just writing to make hit records, the innovation will stop. I like being where people haven't got a songwriting voice and giving them the opportunity to be expressing themselves without commercial considerations. It's quite a shock for the students to hear how, if they write for a famous artist, the famous artist takes a percentage of the royalty. We had a publisher in to speak to the students who runs a very small company and he won't do deals with artists like that; he'd rather not bother.

### What's one of your own favourite compositions?

One of the best things I did was write some music for a documentary about Millwall football fans. They asked me to go down and I recorded the football crowd chant and then I wrote some ambient music and put the chant on top of it. So instead of sounding really rowdy, it sounded really beautiful. Working with a choir of ten thousand people was amazing.

### Did they like it?

Apparently they did, but *Private Eye* magazine took the piss out of it. I was absolutely delighted because I always wanted to be on *Top of the Pops* and never managed to, so getting *Private Eye* was like a really good second-best. But that was such good fun. I had to be in The Den (Millwall's stadium) with all the roughest fans who were the best singers. I think I went to about six or seven matches to get the best weather and sound conditions for recording outside. I remember sitting outside the studio thinking, 'This is really going to work'.

### Is it hard getting paid?

People say you've got to be tough about being paid but almost always the stuff I haven't been paid for has led to something I have been paid for. Sometimes, the things I get paid most for just go nowhere and things I don't get paid for do really well. There's no logic. It has always been really important to me to balance the buzz I get out of being creative with making sure I remain a professional, not an amateur. Songwriting opportunities often come from strange quarters—my next project is with Routemaster bus crews and taxi drivers in London, and I'm having to think laterally about how I'm going to fund that one!

✦✦✦✦✦✦✦✦✦✦✦✦✦✦✦✦✦✦✦✦✦✦✦✦✦✦✦✦✦✦✦✦✦✦✦✦✦✦✦✦✦✦✦✦✦✦✦

✦✦✦✦✦✦✦✦✦✦✦✦✦✦✦✦✦✦✦✦✦✦✦✦✦✦✦✦✦✦✦✦✦✦✦✦✦✦✦✦✦✦✦✦✦✦✦

## JEFFREY JAMPOL

Jeffrey Jampol has been a lecturer in the Entertainment Studies and Performing Arts School at University of California, Los Angeles since 1995. With thirty

years of experience of music business marketing, branding and management, Jampol manages the Doors and is consultant to a number of record companies and estates, including that of Janis Joplin.

### How did you get started in the music business?

I was a passionate music junkie from when I was a tiny kid. I was a real loner with low self-esteem. Rock music was my road to sanity. Through the lyrics and the meaning and that visceral palpable feel of the presentation, it gave meaning and context to all the things I was going through. When I got to college, I started working in college radio and managing bands. I had no clue what I was doing and was making every possible mistake one could make.

### How did you get started as a music lecturer?

I was asked by UCLA to come in and teach a course. They were referred to me by a couple of people in the industry. I've spoken on several panels and I've been the keynote speaker in several different music industry events. Once we started the UCLA curriculum, it just grew from there and led into a whole different series of courses. They say, those who can't do, teach; and if you can't teach, teach in the music business!

### What are the courses you teach?
Personal management for the recording artist, breaking a career artist in the music business now, artist development for artist managers, and the music business now, which is the people and events that influence it.

### Why would someone want to take your classes, rather than learning by experience?
I think everybody has to learn by doing it. But the music business is like a secret society that is very hard to penetrate. It's a relationship-based business and there's no real curriculum for it so we wanted to set out to change that, first, by introducing students to the key business people and decision makers, and then planting a seed so our students can grow a relationship. And also to expose them to a lot of the footwork we all did over twenty to twenty-five years. There's no use reinventing the wheel. Why should they make the same mistakes we did if we can point out areas of danger or concern or something they may want to follow, or not follow?

# SECTION 4

# BUSINESS AFFAIRS

N the previous sections, the focus was on your creative activity onstage and writing and in the studio. Now it's time to consider the various professional support services used by most full-time musicians. Although it's necessary to understand what copyrights, contracts and accounts are, many musicians don't have the time or inclination to take care of this business themselves. So in this section, we'll try to explain the role of managers, lawyers, accountants and collection societies and how to find the right business support when you need it. We start with the manager—and the all-important question: do you really need one?

# artist
# management

## DO ALL BANDS HAVE A MANAGER?

Most bands start life without a manager. The exceptions are 'put-together' or 'manufactured' bands like the Spice Girls, Westlife or those put together for TV shows like *Pop Stars*. The members of these bands have usually auditioned to be in a band that was being put together by a manager or music industry high-flyer, and they are usually already dancers or actors or have media experience.

It's not essential to have a manager. Some bands, even successful bands, prefer to look after their own affairs, feeling that their lawyer, accountant, record company, press agent and so on can look after things adequately on their behalf, thereby saving themselves the 20% of their earnings that managers generally charge. After more than a dozen years together, the US indie rock band Superchunk is still self-managed. The band's Mac McCaughan explains.

✦✦✦✦✦✦✦✦✦✦✦✦✦✦✦✦✦✦✦✦✦✦✦✦✦✦✦✦✦✦✦✦✦✦✦✦✦✦✦✦✦✦✦✦✦✦✦✦

### MAC MCCAUGHAN

**How long have you been managing yourselves?**
From the beginning.

**Why did you choose not to use an outside manager?**

For one thing, it's another person taking a share of the money you're working hard for. And because our focus was really making records and writing songs and touring, and these things aren't things a manager should be helping you with, it just never made sense. Also, the longer you're around and the more managers you come into contact with, the more you realise they're not generally the kind of people you want to hang out with. Not all, but most.

**What are the day-to-day duties of management?**

I don't really know, as we've never had one to take whatever these duties are off our hands. I think that, in general, managers organise your life for you, which can actually be what some bands really need. They also probably pitch you to people for God knows what.

**Speaking from past experience, would you recommend that new artists, either solo or groups, attempt to manage themselves, or would you recommend hiring a manager and focusing on other aspects of their careers?**

It really depends on how organised and efficient and energized you are as a band or as a person. Like I said, I think some bands can probably do what they do a lot better with a manager taking care of all the organizational duties. Also, bands that have no head for business or negotiations can use their manager as a 'bad guy' in sticky situations and as someone to do deals, if there are deals to be done. Again, I feel like I'm talking about something I don't know a lot about.

**If you were to look for an outside manager, what would you look for?**

Someone who's honest and seems to understand what you're doing and what your goals (not theirs) are.

✦✦✦✦✦✦✦✦✦✦✦✦✦✦✦✦✦✦✦✦✦✦✦✦✦✦✦✦✦✦✦✦✦✦✦✦✦✦✦✦✦✦✦✦✦✦

## SO WHY SHOULD YOU HAVE A MANAGER?

You may feel you don't need a manager now, but if things start to take off you'll be amazed at how the tasks multiply. No longer are you just making music—being musicians; now you've got to rehearse for gigs, go on tours, give interviews—and these can be for press, radio and TV—negotiate with the record company, look at contracts, sign things and approve requests for interviews, licensing of your tracks, or placing your music in ads or in films and on TV. The list just goes on and on.

Suddenly, you realise that all the peripheral things are taking so much time that, not only are you finding it hard to fit the music in, but you're not getting any rest either. Writing and composing top-quality music is a process that requires rest and time off, and you get less and less of that as you get more and more famous.

When you are struggling to make it, the idea of touring, TV appearances and lots of press interviews sounds fantastic. You can't imagine how anyone could object. However, when your records start to sell and you become famous, you'll find it gets very tiring and sometimes becomes an imposition when you're constantly being badgered to do this interview or that and rarely getting a day off for months on end.

This is often when many bands decide to go for a manager, despite the expense. A manager comes into his or her own in taking the business affairs work off your shoulders and protecting you from unnecessary encroachments on your time. A good manager will fight on your behalf with the record company, which may well be trying to load as much on you as possible with scant regard for your time off.

## YOU'VE GOT A MANAGER; WHAT'S NEXT?

It's common to sigh with relief when you sign a management contract and to turn your attention to the thing that made you become a musician in the first place—the music. Unfortunately, this is unrealistic and a close watch should be kept on your management affairs. A poor manager can foster bad relations with your record label without your even knowing. A poor manager won't keep on top of media attention—you could be losing out on vital press for your new record or tour. A poor manager won't be on top of your financial and legal affairs.

This is as true of managers a band has chosen to work with as it is for those bands who are manufactured. The Spice Girls's falling out with their manager is perhaps the most famous recent example of this type of manager–artist breakdown, but it happens constantly.

## SOME BAD EXPERIENCES—AS A JOURNALIST

One of Sarah's experiences with sloppy management was in trying to fix up an interview with a band which wanted to do the piece with her but wanted her to organise it through their management company. This was the right thing for them to do—the management company holds the band's diary and knows what they are up to and when things can be slotted in. This particular company was inefficient and continually failed to get back to Sarah with a date to interview the band—and this was for a pretty big feature spread. Numerous phone calls and explanations that the band wanted to do it failed to have an effect, and eventually they missed the deadline, so that the band missed getting some prestigious press coverage that they actually wanted.

## SOME BAD EXPERIENCES—AS A BAND MEMBER

Sarah has also experienced bad management as an artist. Her band's first manager had also ran a PR company and he pressed up a white label and then expected his press team to work it—sending it out to the media and to DJs. Unfortunately, he didn't check what they thought of it and whether they were doing a proper job. They weren't, and the record languished. Then he had problems with his major artist and no longer had time to look after Sarah's band—a common scenario. You should always check how many bands your potential manager or management company is looking after and what sort of priority you're going to have. It's no good having a manager if they never spend any time on your affairs at all. It's worse than having no manager, because you think things are rumbling along happily only to discover months (or even years) later that you are in exactly the same position as when you signed with the manager—right at the bottom. You'd have been better off doing it yourself.

The second manager Sarah's band had was a very enthusiastic but naïve woman who worked for a distribution company. Her company had distributed the band's first record and she loved it so much she asked if she could manage them. After this was agreed, she wanted to bring in a business partner with lots of management experience. This turned out to be a disaster similar to the experience with the first manager. The partner came to see the band play, liked them, but spent all his time with a high-profile boy band. In the meantime, the band was advised not to put another single out right away and to work on an album. They ended up, months later, with no single out to capitalize on the success of the first, and no manager either, as the experienced manager decided to concentrate on the boy band.

## LEARN FROM YOUR EXPERIENCES

Sarah's experiences led to the decision by the band to learn how to manage themselves and to start a record label to get its records out there. This led to putting out other people's records too. But be warned: managing yourself, running a label and trying to make your own music is immensely time-consuming and is probably best undertaken as a means to an end. Building your profile to the extent either you sign a major label deal for the band or, better still, sign a licensing deal with a major label which will generate lots of cash for projects but will allow you to retain a measure of independence.

Next, we hear from two successful artist managers, Seven Webster in the UK and Keith Cooper in the US.

✦✦✦✦✦✦✦✦✦✦✦✦✦✦✦✦✦✦✦✦✦✦✦✦✦✦✦✦✦✦✦✦✦✦✦✦✦✦✦✦✦✦✦✦✦✦

## SEVEN WEBSTER

7pm Management is the brainchild of Seven Webster, who has had a long industry career, including spells as 'failed musician', promoter, DJ and music

journalist. His management roster of DJs and producers has encompassed some of the biggest names in the UK dance scene: Carl Cox, Sasha, John Digweed, Stonebridge and Danny Campbell. He explains the pros and cons of management and just how detailed the job can be.

### Things are changing rapidly in the music industry. Where do you see the music industry going in the future?

The music business across the globe has receded enormously unto a point where there are now only four major labels. Sony and BMG have become one, SonyBMG; then there are Warners, EMI, and Universal. Within these remaining four labels, it is still likely that at least two of these could still merge over the next few years. One industry figure joked that in a couple of years we might only be left with two: the 'Blues' and the 'Reds'. Basi-

---

cally, these industry giants are increasingly becoming distribution and marketing houses for a decreasing number of the biggest-selling acts and there-

fore they are primarily only looking for acts already with a fan base and a story or projects with a TV show or angle attached. This, in turn, is easiest for them to achieve by acquiring (gobbling up) smaller credible independent record labels that they can then plug into their global marketing and distribution infrastructures and accelerate their global sales of their company's artists' albums.

The A&R departments of major UK labels are definitely suffering from all of this change, as they rely more and more on paying premium rates for acts that have already A&R'd themselves into a position of success. It is increasingly an A&R-by-accountancy policy, with only a few labels still in the business of signing and developing. The upside of the industry is via the digital revolution that has enabled young artists and bands to build followings and database via the development of their own Web sites and hands-on relationships with their fan bases. It is also much easier for agents and labels to check out artists' Web sites and see for themselves what is happening within their own online communities. It is also helpful when an artist is trying to interest A&R departments, if the A&R guys see that ten thousand people already on that artist's Web site. If they see this, then they know they can achieve chart positions if a percentage of these people were to buy this artist's record in the first week —thus eliminating the A&R man's chance of failure!

Personally, I see this as being the time of DIY. The more an artist or a band does for itself, the better. The band can also create income streams by selling their music via download using sites like TuneTribe, iTunes or other online sites. Even Universal has an active online distribution company that is fast seeking out new acts to distribute—thus bridging the gap in fail-safe A&R. I am sure that if they see an act selling loads of downloads, they will be the first to offer these acts a proper deal through one of their many acquired labels. It's another example of fail-safe A&R. Other companies, such as CD Baby in the US (see p. 284), are also great for selling mail order copies of finished CDs and driving sales and income via their online store. Basically, bands just need to see themselves more as businesses and treat their Web sites as shopfronts and get out their and do it for themselves. Then, if a major likes what it sees in their shopfront after seeing a great live performance, they too can offer the band the chance to be distributed by the Reds or the Blues.

Obviously, the other key thing to remember is that the acts need to have talent and great songs. This, for me, is an abbreviated view of the modern industry as I see it.

### Who are you working with?

I tend to work with producers and solo artists rather than bands. I was heavily involved with DJ culture from the start, with DJ/artists like Sasha, Carl Cox and John Digweed. Lately, I've moved away from that, but I've kept a couple who I wanted to work with and who are still in-spiring me musically. One of the producers we manage is Stonebridge and we look after all he does, whether it's remixes—East 17, Another Level or Melanie C—or putting together his own branded label, Stonebridge Recordings, which, again, reflects his musicality. We have a credible producer with a story to tell, a pedigree and a credible label.

### What is the manager's role?

Basically, the role of the manager is to protect. The best managers are people who are failed artists, like myself! We've been through the industry and worked in the industry. A lot of management is not just the idea but the experience: how to deal with corporate takeovers as well as how to deal with the nitty-gritty of marketing a record, doing hands-on press and publicity and promotion of a record. Good management is to be able to anticipate, drawing from working within the industry over a period of time, always thinking about what is going to happen next. If you find a new artist, you want to be able to anticipate what the next two years are going to hold. As for when an artist needs a manager, it's when they feel they can't do anymore themselves and they need someone with this sort of expertise and contacts.

## How do you find a manager?

Finding a manager can be a problem, as the good ones are almost too busy—you have to go on gut instinct. When I was an artist, I asked a number of A&R men who I had had meetings with and played tracks to if they could give me a list of the top ten managers in the country. So they all jotted down lists and I went and knocked at doors. You'll probably get it wrong a lot of the time but you've got to go to people who you like, who you get on with and believe in you, who you feel can take your career further. If you think he's a hard-nosed bastard who's going to take you all the way and get record companies to listen, then fine, but I think that people are more likely to feel happy about people they can sit in a room with and get on with.

## What are some of the jobs a manager does for his or her artist?

When I first started managing people, the first thing I wanted to do was to manage acts on a number of UK labels—I wanted to see if I could learn from working within those different communities and obviously learn about which labels I would enjoy working with the most—which were the least and most stressful. You complement and build upon the basic things that a record company structure will do: pressing, manufacturing, marketing and distributing your record. You work with the label to ensure all the other crucial things that are going to happen: that your records are going to get into the shop, posters are going to go up on the date they're meant go up, adverts and artwork are spelled right, and that the shows you've put together will tie in with it—all the basic fundamental principles of putting a record out. For a manager, if those things are handled well, half the battle is done.

My idea of management is never putting your hand in your own pocket. The idea is for other people to pay up. I usually look to see if you can get this artist a living because you've got to—otherwise it's mismanagement, in my eyes. Many artists have been signed by a management company whose basic premise is they've got 20% of the artist's career whether they do jack shit or not. These artists then have to look for other management and give away another 20% of their money and take legal action, and it's very sad. It's harder as a rock band, as there are fewer avenues to go down. With dance, you build up the remix thing and create a story around it—I did this with Blue Amazon and with Sasha. I arranged for Sasha to do several remixes at around the same time, which gave him an international face: twelve different record company press departments were using him as their selling-point story. You have to put it into place by writing the story.

## What sort of work do you try to get for your artists?

If you're going to have an artist–management relationship over many years, you have to know them a little bit before you sign—both ways—it's a two-way street. When you see someone who is fantastic, of course you want to work with them, but I do think you have to feel you can guarantee that person a living or let them go. You try every aspect: remixing, TV, film and ad work. I got one of John Digweed's *Bedrock* tracks on the *Trainspotting* soundtrack, for example. I take a marketing approach to it all: every two or three weeks, we write a story. It's not enough to know you've done the remix of whatever it was; you tell the story to the press and let the press run riot with it. You put out the stories and they get used. I put them out myself, and if you've also got six press agents working with you because the DJ's done all that work, it becomes easier to do. We tend to create the angle and come up with the story. Marketing an act can be, at the top level, getting Neneh Cherry to do a duet with Michael Stipe to try and get it into America; or at the bottom level, try and write a little story to get the act mentioned in the *NME*.

If the music's great and the record company believes in your belief, then it's down to the public: whether they want to buy it or not. Beyond that, it's about how creative you are when you market and distribute the record. To get through that maze, you need someone to help you do that and deal with all those different departments, someone who has a grasp and understanding and enough experience within the industry to say to someone, 'What you're saying about sales isn't exactly right, maybe we should try and do this'. You're working alongside the record industry and you need to be able to offer those people different angles and advice. I've learned from being hard-nosed at times exactly what happens when you go in. Sometimes an A&R guy can get resentful when a manager comes crashing down and says, 'Actually, you've got this wrong'. However, there's a bit more respect within certain companies, so you'll always be drawn towards placing your artists with them.

## What's the relationship between a manager and A&R?

I think what you try and gauge as a manager over the course of time is what all the different A&R guys like, what makes them tick musically. If a guy at Columbia loves R&B, you are not going to send him the new thrash metal, indie or dance act; your personal knowledge of what they individually like and what makes them tick is something that you can only build over the course of time. It's another reason why artists need good management. A good manager should be able to hear a piece of music and say immediately that it would be good for this or that person at that company and get it to them. It's a quick result, rather than heaving it around the industry for the first two years just to find this out.

## What do you feel about signing an artist to a major label?

Even if I'd signed an artist to a major label I'd be happier to see them come out on an associate or affiliate label. The public doesn't have to know that it's actually funded by a major. You can sign your act to a major label or deal but be clever about how you do it. That's good management. When majors sign an artist, their biggest mistake is putting them on a major label. It's almost imperative that records do come out on independent labels first. Even ones signed to major labels find that they have to go back to square one and say, 'Well, we know we've signed to Polydor but we have to put this out on an independent, subfunded label just to give it a fan base'. Not to do that is like building the second floor of your house without the first; it's never going to work.

Major label A&R has become more and more redundant: it's less about development. Certainly, in the UK, very few major label A&R people would ever sign anything off a demo tape; I don't think that happens any more. Now they just sign labels; Sony signed Skint Records because it's got credibility. Whichever is the label of the given moment, it's more likely they'll go and pick up the label and retain that credibility.

✦✦✦✦✦✦✦✦✦✦✦✦✦✦✦✦✦✦✦✦✦✦✦✦✦✦✦✦✦✦✦✦✦✦✦✦✦✦✦✦✦✦✦

✦✦✦✦✦✦✦✦✦✦✦✦✦✦✦✦✦✦✦✦✦✦✦✦✦✦✦✦✦✦✦✦✦✦✦✦✦✦✦✦✦✦✦

## KEITH COOPER

Express Entertainment
Artist Management & Music Publishing

New York + 1 212 222 8760
Cell + 1 917 971 0145
London +44/07771 654 223
E-mail: keithcooper@expressent.com

Keith Cooper has been in the management game since 1990 with his company Express Entertainment. Stereo MCs, Ian Brown, Dot Allison, PM Dawn, Aphrodite, Jungle Brothers, Finley Quaye, Lily Cushman Culhane and Dead Combo have been among his clients. Originally based in the UK, Cooper is now a resident of New York City, where he functions both as US representative for British artists and as worldwide representative for selected US-based artists.

## What is the manager's role?

To focus the artist's career on all levels, from creative to business to marketing and promotion. It's an all-encompassing role. And you're the conduit to their partners in the music business: the record companies, the publishing companies. And you're a conduit with the outside world. All the dealings come through you, get filtered through you, and organised through you.

## What are some specific jobs the manager does for an artist?
It's a different role when you've got a new artist who isn't signed, compared with what you do for an artist who is signed. Sometimes, you decide to release things on your own but traditionally a manager will get the new artist to a point where the record company will be interested in them and want to sign them. And that can be in a multitude of ways.

When you're managing an artist that's signed to a record company, that's obviously not a part of your role. Then you're working with the record company to advance the artist's career.

## In the case of the unsigned act, what are some of the things you would do?
You help shape the artist's music. That might be putting them with different producers, might be getting the music to radio programmers, might be working with marketing people doing some on-line marketing, perhaps getting them shows through an agent or yourself, getting them on support tours, raising the profile, putting a record out yourself through your own means. It's an ever-changing landscape for the manager—as the marketing picture changes, so you adapt. Ten years ago, you wouldn't have had to do any Internet marketing, or you wouldn't have been able to. You're just trying to get them noticed. Trying to build their fan base. Supporting the artist, encouraging, trying to plan, trying to budget.

## What are some of the specific things you do in working with a label?
When you're working with a label, you've got to plan releases, which means getting the material ready, planning when it's right to release it, what territories, making videos if that's what's appropriate, touring if that's what's ap-

---

propriate, radio promotion, television appearances, balancing all that stuff out—liaising with all the different departments of the record company, motivating all the different departments and being the focal point for everyone so that everything can sit together properly. It's quite a broad task. Some managers will do it totally differently than others. There's no right or wrong way, which makes it hard sometimes because you don't always know. Each artist will require a different set of tools because the music requires that. The type of artist, a rock band as opposed to a soul singer, will require a completely different approach.

### How does one go about getting a manager?
I think managers are probably the hardest ones to find because they aren't always in the phone book. It's a personal relationship. You have to like and trust your manager. You have to respect your manager and feel that they understand what you're trying to do with your music and have enough time to give to you. It's best to have someone with experience, although often that can be a hindrance. Their enthusiasm for your music and competence is probably the most important thing. The best place to start, for a new band, is to find an artist where you like the way that artist's career has been handled, then go to the person who's responsible for them. It might not be a similar genre, but it might be an artist who has had a great career. They've had a great way of interfacing with the world. Their press is well handled. Their marketing is always good. They don't oversaturate themselves. Shows are really good. The tickets aren't overpriced. They always come over well. If, as an artist, they seem to be doing what they want to do, it's probably a lot to do with their management.

### How do you see the relationship between management and A&R?
This relationship should be the easiest relationship because it's not as cluttered as all the other relationships in the business mechanics. The A&R person is generally the first person who's brought the artist into the label and has probably the most direct relationship with the artists. In marketing and promotion, the manager has to balance. It's sometimes difficult to navigate because there are often times when a label will want an artist to do something they don't want to do and that's a situation that the manager has to handle diplomatically, and it's not always easy.

**How do you feel about signing an artist to a major label?**
There are pluses and minuses to all those situations, and you have to go in with eyes open. Be aware that with a major label you've only got one shot. You've been given a chance to play the game, but it's a short game and you've got to win. No one has a second chance in the developmental stage.

**What are the differences between management in the US and the UK?**
In the UK, managers mostly have that all-encompassing role. In the US, there's often a division of labour in terms of personal management and business management; therefore, there's often several managers involved in an artist's career. There's big management organizations in America where managers group together and are almost mini-record companies. In the UK, you get a lot more of the one-man-band manager. But, as I see it, something of that is coming in here in the US. There are a lot of people who come out of the major label system, A&R people, in particular, who have been laid off from downsizing, and they've become managers. I think there have been a lot more people trying to become managers in the last few years than ever before.

✦✦✦✦✦✦✦✦✦✦✦✦✦✦✦✦✦✦✦✦✦✦✦✦✦✦✦✦✦✦✦✦✦✦✦✦✦✦✦✦✦✦✦✦✦✦

# tax and accounts

## DOING THE BOOKS

It goes without saying that to run a successful—or, just as important in some ways, an unsuccessful—career as an artist or as a record label you need an accountant, and one who's familiar with dealing with music business matters. You can find them listed in industry directories like the UK's *Music Week Directory*, or ask around if you have friends in the music industry already.

Record label accounts are not complicated to run when you are the only artist. But once you start putting out records by other artists or, if you're a real masochist, putting out compilation albums, then life can get complicated.

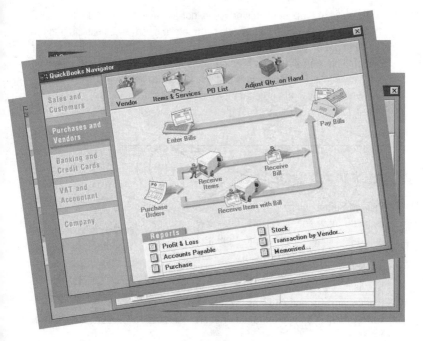

There are many aspects of running a record label properly. As well as the normal books detailing income and expenses from things like sales and manufacturing, you will also have to pay artist royalties, for instance. Royalties can be quite complicated to work out. They are based on record sales and are usually paid every six months. Each artist gets a statement detailing their income and they invoice you for payment. You will also have to cope with mechanical royalties that are due to the songwriters and publishers of the songs recorded by your artists. Generally, these will be paid to a collecting society representing writers and publishers, such as MCPS in the UK and the Harry Fox Agency in the US. Their activities are explained later in this section.

If you license tracks for a compilation album, you will end up with twelve or so artists to pay royalties to, many on different deals and having received advances. If you license tracks or records out to other companies, you need to make sure you find out what you're owed and invoice promptly every six months, especially if it's a major label—some can take forever to pay up.

---

If you've got lots of money or you've got a willing friend to do the books, then giving them all the paperwork, contracts, etc. is the easiest thing to do. Let them get on with it. Most of us, though, have to struggle on and do that side of things ourselves. This is where you may want to invest in special record company bookkeeping packages like QuickBooks to help you.

Two music business accountants, Richard Soltes from the US, and London-based John Smith, tell us about their experiences.

✦✦✦✦✦✦✦✦✦✦✦✦✦✦✦✦✦✦✦✦✦✦✦✦✦✦✦✦✦✦✦✦✦✦✦✦✦✦✦✦✦✦✦✦✦✦

## RICHARD SOLTES

Richard Soltes has been an entertainment industry accountant for twenty-five years. After acting as a partner in an accountancy firm, in 1999 he formed his own company, Soltes Accountancy Corporation. Among his clients are leading Hollywood film and television players, including John Eisendrath Productions, Greenlight Films, Skinny Nervous Girl and cinematographer Robert Fraisse.

### At what point should an artist have an accountant?

Any time you start a business, doesn't matter what it is, I would have an accountant from day one. They can give you the right direction, how to keep records, what type of business entity you should be: in other words, are you going to be a sole proprietor, are you going to be a corporation, are you in business with somebody else and do you want to be a partnership?

### At what point should an artist declare their gig earnings?

The official answer, what the Inland Revenue Service would say, is that any money that you make should be declared income. The unofficial is quite different. If you're just making a couple of grand, and it's cash, don't tell me about it.

### What sort of accountancy books should an artist keep? Should they retain every receipt?

It's very important for artists to do so because they tend to buy things with cash. If you're starting a business, you're generally going to be losing money in the first few years so you're going to be showing losses on your tax return. If you're ever scrutinized or subject to audit, you need to have those things available.

### What advice would you give if somebody wants to start a record label?

In any kind of business, one of the first things I would do is to meet with a qualified accountant to determine what the requirements of the business are and what type of entity should you be.

### What are some of the things you can claim against tax?

In terms of the rules about what you're allowed to deduct, basically the IRS says that, for a business, your expenses have to be what they call 'ordinary and necessary'. Let's say as a musician you decide that you must have a $5,000 bird that sings to make you feel good so you can be creative. That would not be regarded by the IRS as an ordinary expense. But the essential question to ask yourself is, do you have to spend this money in order to conduct business? It's something of a grey area but it can get you a little leeway in claiming a deduction.

✦✦✦✦✦✦✦✦✦✦✦✦✦✦✦✦✦✦✦✦✦✦✦✦✦✦✦✦✦✦✦✦✦✦✦✦✦✦✦✦✦✦✦✦✦✦✦✦

✦✦✦✦✦✦✦✦✦✦✦✦✦✦✦✦✦✦✦✦✦✦✦✦✦✦✦✦✦✦✦✦✦✦✦✦✦✦✦✦✦✦✦✦✦✦✦✦

## JOHN SMITH

John Smith (not his real name) has been a music industry accountant for many years, both for major labels and now running his own company. He also runs a small, independent record label, so he is well placed to understand all the intricacies of music business accounting.

### What should you do immediately?

The first thing an artist or band will have to do if they're gigging is get a bank account. They will probably not need an accountant immediately, depending on how their initial gigs go. It they start earning money, they will have to inform the Inland Revenue. There is a procedure to informing the Inland Revenue, which they will explain to you, and there is a set date for registering, which they will tell you, because you have no backup for it. Anything at all for

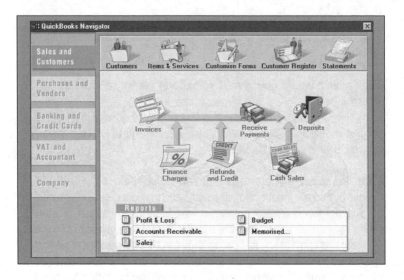

an artist, the strings, the tapes, the records, the CDs, the microphones, the wiring, anything to do with their business is deductable.

**What advice would you give when starting a record label?**

Record labels are very difficult. Most young people think that it's very easy, but it's not. You need money. If you don't have money to start a label, you're wasting your time. How do you promote it, how do you market it? Then you have to have somebody do the record, pay for them to do the record, mix it, master it, then you have to promote it. That costs money. Then you have to have street teams; it all costs. Most people think they can do it with $25,000 to $50,000—they're in a dream world.

**In terms of tax and accounts, what are the differences between the UK and the US?**

The UK tax season starts 6 April and ends 5 April. The IRS is 1 January to 31 December. For the Inland Revenue, for any money earned in the UK you have to file a tax return. But you can be a nonresident by not being there, and if you don't earn any money in the UK you don't have to file any tax returns. For the IRS, if you're a US citizen or a resident alien, you have to pay tax and have a Green Card. Any place that you make money, you'd have to pay tax on it here in the US. But if you paid tax in Australia for something you earned in Australia, you could get a tax credit on it here.

## Is it best to do it yourself, or would you advise getting professional help?

I personally would get an accountant to prepare everything for you or give you advice on how to do it at the point when your musical activity changes from a hobby into a business. If you are planning on running a record label, I would definitely advise getting both an accountant and a solicitor.

For musicians, one vital reason to get professional advice is to deal properly with tax and national insurance issues. You could go to the Inland Revenue yourself if the band's not earning a great deal. They will help you complete your returns. But you will have to do this before 30 September, after the end of the relevant tax year. The Inland Revenue has an entertainment division which reads the music press, so as soon as you get your first review they will be aware of you, but they will probably only be interested in you once you sign a deal. Many bands get a mention in the press, but don't make enough money to affect their tax status.

Accountants and solicitors experienced in the music business will also give advice about the appropriate legal and financial structures for artists or bands, such as sole trading, partnerships and/or limited companies.

## What if members of the band are unemployed? Can you still claim benefit if you are gigging?

If the members of the band are unemployed, you can still claim benefit, but if you do start earning money from the gigs, you will have to inform the local Social Security office, which will decide whether you can still claim benefit. You will have to declare these benefits to the Inland Revenue as well, as they form part of your taxable income.

## How do you log your earnings and expenses?

You will need a cashbook to record income and expenses and to log your cheques and any other receipts or earnings. You must also keep any paperwork relevant to your earnings; for example, keep your contracts from venues saying how much you've earned from each gig, royalty statements and distribution sales statements, etc. Record labels also need a sales daybook and a purchase daybook. Or you can buy a specialized accountancy computer package such as QuickBooks, which is very good. You must also write in your expenses. If you're a musician, these can be van hire, equipment hire, various gig expenses, session musicians, etc. A record label will have many expenses, such as office expenses, manufacturing, promotion and so on.

You will need a petty-cash book to show any small payments, such as buy-

---

ing stamps, magazines, office supplies and so on if you run a label; food, drinks, guitar strings, etc. when you're touring. And if individual band members spend their own money, this should be noted as well, and the amounts kept separately in a different book.

### What about VAT (value added tax)?

If the band or label does turn over a reasonable amount and exceeds the VAT limit, which is currently £51,000 on turnover (but it changes every year in April), then you have to apply for VAT registration. Depending on the nature of your expenditure and your income, it may also be beneficial to register even if your turnover is less than this, so that you can claim VAT on expenses. You can get your accountant to do the registration, or call your local VAT office, which will give you the forms.

### What about collection societies?

Individual members of the band who are songwriters should become members of the Performing Right Society (PRS). They get these forms from PRS and they're quite easy to complete. As a record company, you would have to register with MCPS and PPL. You might have to account for artist royalties if you are signing other artists or putting out compilation albums.

✦✦✦✦✦✦✦✦✦✦✦✦✦✦✦✦✦✦✦✦✦✦✦✦✦✦✦✦✦✦✦✦✦✦✦✦✦✦✦✦✦✦✦✦✦✦

# legal matters and lawyers

A music business or entertainment industry lawyer will become more necessary as your career builds. If you are running a label, in the early days you can get by on using a simplified contract for your artists (perhaps based on the criteria recommended in the UK by the Musicians' Union). But as they become more successful, and if the label becomes so successful that you are licensing your artists' tracks or licensing in tracks yourself for compilations, a lawyer becomes essential. Again, drawing up contracts with artist royalty provisions, advances, packaging deductions and so on can be a tricky business.

If you are on the other side of the table, as an artist or even an artist manager, a lawyer will be needed for negotiations on recording and publishing contracts. In fact, most record companies and publishers will insist that an artist has independent legal representation. In the UK, this is partly because of several high-profile court cases in which lack of such representation caused judges to find in favour of artists who were sueing companies over unfair contracts.

✦✦✦✦✦✦✦✦✦✦✦✦✦✦✦✦✦✦✦✦✦✦✦✦✦✦✦✦✦✦✦✦✦✦✦✦✦✦✦✦✦✦✦✦✦✦✦✦✦✦

## KIENDA HOJI

Kienda Hoji is a London-based lawyer and university lecturer with music business experience on both sides of the Atlantic.

**Are there any types of agreements that an emerging talent might be offered where you would say legal advice is essential?**
My attitude about agreements is that there is not a single agreement that is not worth getting legal advice on. In the music industry, talent is exploitable well before getting a record deal. Artists are going to be offered all sorts of agreements before then. For example, you might hire a publicist or an independent promoter or, more likely these days, an Internet distribution agreement. This is very common nowadays. Sometimes smaller agreements can be more important than the bigger ones you may be offered later on because they are less likely to be scrutinized and more likely to be restrictive agreements or contain restrictive clauses.

By rule of thumb, anything involving exploitation of intellectual property or any other rights definitely needs scrutinizing; looking at clauses involving publishing, record company, agents, etc. means securing a lawyer on an ongoing basis.

Any agreement lasting for any length of time, rather than one-off agreements, should be scrutinized. It's well worth the cost of the legal fees. One-off agreements include agreements for pub gigs or similar single events. It would obviously be pointless to go to a lawyer for things like that.

## Would you give the same advice for musicians in the US?

Lawyers in the US have become more central to the music industry—in the US, you can't operate without a lawyer. Now this is starting to happen in the UK. Record companies are starting to demand that not only do you have a lawyer but that he or she is a good one. This is opposite to the way they behaved years ago.

Record companies nowadays understand that ensuring that the artist has the proper legal advice before signing will help to avoid future litigation. In a way, it is as if they are protecting themselves and their investment.

## What are the main principles of merchandising agreements?

The basic idea is that an artist or group license the right to someone to use their image or logo on items of merchandise.

A merchandising agreement uses much the same kind of exclusivity rights as other agreements. At the start of an artist's career, these rights may not be worth a great deal, but later on, if the artist becomes famous, these rights could become very valuable and it could be very hard for you to exploit your merchandise rights if they have already been signed away. Such a merchandising agreement could be for two or three years. The merchandising rights could be exercisable by the licensee and those rights can vary in value between individual artists. But whatever they are, not having access to those rights could be a real problem later on for the artist.

## And Internet agreements?

The Internet has become a very important place for the distribution and sale of music. In many ways, the Internet has become more important than traditional sales channels. It is important that artists understand the implications of signing online distribution deals early in their careers. On the one hand, securing good, early Internet distribution is a good way of getting profile. On the other hand, cyberspace is still a place fraught with all kinds of copyright problems.

When companies offer to exploit your music on the Internet, those agreements have to be carefully scrutinized. There could be complications with record agreements later on. If a record company can't get an artist and all their rights, it reduces interest in the deal. The artist has less to offer and might not get a deal at all. Record companies tend to want everything.

## How do studio agreements work?

Independent artists may be offered a deal by a studio, or an artist may want to acquire studio time. A studio deal can be a positive thing.

An independent artist is able to negotiate deals with the studio where the artist is given recording time in return for points [a share of royalties from record sales]. So you don't have to pay upfront for studio time. This is a studio production agreement.

These agreements generally say that the studio will undertake to provide you with tapes and studio time in return for giving them a few points. All studio costs will be paid when you sign a record deal, plus points. The difficulty arises when a studio wants reimbursement from source. This is really important when it comes to albums. If the agreement doesn't specify the number of tracks, then the studio may ask for royalties on all tracks on the album. You need to specify in the agreement whether it's two, three, four or however many tracks you recorded in the studio. You have to make sure the agreement says exactly the percentage on singles or on an album, or whether it's dependent on the number of tracks recorded in that particular facility.

## What about production agreements?

This is another issue. A single artist or even a band may be offered a production deal by a production company. The artist then has an obligation to the production company not to release material but to allow the production company to seek a distribution deal through a record company. The artist signs to the production company and the production company signs a deal with a record company. The production company needs to earn its money, so it takes a royalty split and earns its money by taking a percentage off the top.

## And management agreements?

Things have developed over the past twenty years where the culture of the manager offering agreements is linked to aspects of production deals. Those kinds of agreements should be carefully scrutinized. A manager should be looking out for the artist and the artist's interests, but there may be a conflict of interest if the manager is also the owner of the artist's production company. The artist will have to pay the usual 20% manager's fee plus a percentage of money from the distributed material—so essentially the manager gets two bites of the cherry.

This phenomenon of managers doing multiple deals with artists has increased over the years. This increase seems to be fuelled by the 'reality TV instant fame show' craze, where the manager ends up being the production company, manager and label for the winning artist.

## Can lawyers negotiate for the company side to give or advance legal fees to the artist side?

This is a controversial one. Agreements that are negotiated with a new artist can include an undertaking where the record company pays for legal advice and specifies that the legal advice must be independently sought. You can't use the record company's lawyer; this would be a conflict of interest. You must have independent advice and the artist must not have any influences from another party.

The artist may have to face the reality that the record company may not agree to do this.

I find this condition difficult to accept as a lawyer. I try and get the record company to pay the fees whether the artist signs or not. It's very difficult to get record companies to do this. After all, they're also accountable to someone for the money they spend.

My advice to independent musicmakers is that you should push for record companies to pay for the legal costs. As a compromise, some record companies may be prepared to fixed contribution towards the artist's legal fees.

There is an element of risk for a record label; they know they may not recoup.

As they know they are in a risk business, they should take risks, and one of them is paying artists' legal fees. If they are sure the agreement is sound, then they should be prepared to do so. So independent advice is essential.

One thing to remember about the entertainment and music industries: they all know each other; they're all friendly with each other. I saw a recent case of a band which had gotten quite successful with Top 10 hits and they had a problem with their recording agreement. The deal had been made between the record company lawyer and their lawyer. Not only did the two lawyers know each other, but they'd both worked in the same company at one point, one had actually given the other a job. The agreement was not in the band's favour.

Lawyers are supposed to be beyond that. It doesn't happen often but it is something to be aware of, not to get paranoid about. I do battle with a particular lawyer in the day and we play squash at night, but it doesn't affect how I fight for my client. Independent legal advice is critical.

### What does hiring a lawyer typically cost?

There's no real straight answer on what it will cost. In the UK, you can have a lawyer at the bottom of the scale who will charge £70 or £80 an hour, and it ranges up from that. If you go to a top practice, it could be £250 to £300 an hour.

City firms cost more than street firms. In the States, dare I say it, lawyers tend to get paid rather more than in the UK, particularly the practices based in big cities like Los Angeles and Atlanta.

The important thing is that you must choose a lawyer with expertise in the music industry. In record company recording agreements, there is usually a clause saying that the artist must have chosen a lawyer who specializes in the music industry.

People have learned over the years that the music industry can be full of all kinds of legal pitfalls that may result in the collapse of deals, sometimes years after a deal is done. It is for this reason that experienced people in the business will now consider not doing business with you if you do not have a lawyer. I've seen people not get legal advice with disastrous results.

Sometimes, artists trust their record label and decide not to bother with legal advice. Later they regret it. Record companies will get artists to sign and say they have sought legal advice and artists will sign and say they have even when they haven't. If they do this, it can be a big problem for them later.

If you are a record label, even a small one, you should be very, very wary of this. It's not straightforward. Courts recognise the fact that the artist is not an expert in law so they will find in the artist's favour, even if it was the artist's choice not to take legal advice on the agreement. This can rebound badly on a label.

Hiring a specialist music industry lawyer is usually very expensive. This can be a big issue for an artist. One way of containing legal costs is education. It's important for an artist to understand the basics of the law, such as what copyright is, how it works, and what you can and can't get away with when it comes to intellectual copyright. Knowing these things is useful in reducing costs.

I use the analogy of the owner of a car being taught to drive a car but who doesn't understand how it works. They don't understand the principle of the combustion engine. If the car breaks down, they take it to a mechanic. He looks doubtful and says, 'Leave it here; I'll look at it'. A long time goes by and then he fixes it—it was something small—at the last minute and gives it back to the driver with a big bill. But a driver who knows what's wrong, who diagnoses the problem, even though he or she can't fix it themselves, but takes it to the mechanic and says, 'Can you fix this problem?' will pay far less.

So it's best to have lots of discussion with the person offering the agreement. If the artist has a manager, then the manager can negotiate with the record company and go through all the early steps; this saves time later with the lawyer. The small points don't need to be dealt with by the lawyer. This can reduce costs.

### Should an artist expect a free initial consultation before committing to a lawyer?

A free initial consultation is something an artist should demand. Lots of legal firms will do this. You can't have someone in your office and then find you don't hit it off. There are agencies that provide free legal advice—like the Musicians' Union in the UK. It's a good idea to be a member. In America, there are various organisations like Volunteers of Legal Service for the Arts.

In the initial consultation, the artist can't expect to take an agreement in and get it done for free. The initial consultations are usually quite short and it's more a process of seeing if you can work together. An artist may hand an agreement over and ask how much it will be but cannot expect each clause to be gone over.

Having said that, some big firms do free work on the side. But artists shouldn't expect this. I know people who haven't a penny but who have powerful lawyers.

The music industry is full of lawyers who are involved with artists they think are talented so they are willing to do their legal work for free, expecting to get paid for the work when the artist is successful. Some law firms are quite egalitarian and do free work for the Musicians' Union. It's the nature of the industry, and it's the same in the US.

It's important to remember that your relationship with your lawyer should be more than a legal one because you're dealing with intellectual property, cultural interests and creative talent. The lawyer has to be more in tune with the artist, with the stresses and strains of the artist.

I think when people aspire to be music lawyers, they should think what they need to become one. It's not like other branches of law. Being a music lawyer is 75% knowing the music industry, and the remainder is knowing the law. This balance is crucial. The lawyer has to know how people in the industry think and what they expect.

### How does an artist select a lawyer?

The lawyer must be someone who's experienced—so the artist should investigate his or her work. Make sure the lawyer has a track record in the industry. Who are the lawyer's other clients? Speak to the other clients in person if possible.

Another good way of finding someone is through word of mouth. Someone recommending a person is always a good way of finding someone good who you can work with.

Look at sleeve notes on CDs where they mention a lawyer. Look in the music press for cases where they mention a lawyer's name. Look in *Music Week*, *Billboard* and the other music industry press. It's not adequate to just look in the *Music Week Directory*; anybody could put an ad in there. Look at written material on the Internet.

It's always worth ringing the Law Society. They have lists of people who specialise in entertainment and media. Sometimes it's good to go and see a friendly lawyer—which you can do without committing yourself. Get advice from the Musicians' Union. You need to find someone you like and feel comfortable with.

Use as many of those methods as possible before choosing someone.

### Are there any other checks you should make on a lawyer?

There's often a potential conflict between artist and lawyer, so make sure to conduct any checks regarding potential conflicts, for example, corporate tie-ups.

There's a potential problem where the lawyer works in a firm that represents the other side. Both in the States and the UK, the rules of conflict are very strictly controlled.

### What kind of service can the artist expect?

Services are very varied now. The standard service is commenting on agreement agreements, negotiations, conflict resolution—where issues between two partners need resolving—disputes and litigations. Contrary to what you read in the press, things rarely get to court; it's more a matter of settling out of court.

Intellectual property (IP), or copyright, is now one of the most common areas of work for lawyers. This is largely because of the increasing use of technology in the music industry, like sampling, the Internet and computer software.

File-sharing peer-to-peer networks are the most controversial and legally contentious area of music law. Recent case law in the US has caused many lawyers to become involved in high-level technology rights-management issues. This is a growing area of a music lawyer's workload.

There's a range of other things too. Some lawyers take an interest in new artists. This is very much the case in the States, where lawyers find bands deals. Getting your demo recordings to a lawyer can be far more important than getting it to an A&R person. The reason this culture has arisen in the States is because they know everybody—lawyers know lawyers in the record labels and speak to them about the recordings they've got and it goes from there. This is not the traditional A&R route but it's becoming more and more important—it's often lawyers making stars these days.

Music lawyers are not like other lawyers. They have playback facilities in their offices and nearly always look trendy, maybe wearing jeans. You can always spot the music lawyer in a practice. And because of those things, and because they are into the music, they understand what's required of a lawyer working in the music industry. This means that with some lawyers, additional services may—and I repeat *may*—be available. These services could include introduction to record labels, managers or agents, or advice on routes through the industry or business advice.

In some cases, I will have an artist come in with a record agreement, and after talking to them, if I find they are self-sufficient and have their own studio and so on, then I might recommend that they start a production company and do it themselves rather than sign to a record company. Or I'll make introductions and move things along outside the legal process.

When someone brings me an agreement that turns out to be an absolute disaster, this can be a difficult thing. This may be an artist who's struggled for years, playing in small pubs and so on, and earning absolutely nothing. Then someone comes out from the crowd and gives them a card, says they'll be in touch, and then gives them an agreement very quickly, which is a very exciting moment for the artist. Then they show the agreement to me and I have to advise that they don't sign it. Some artists sign anyway, because they feel they're getting somewhere at last, but I would advise that you don't ignore your agreement for short-term success. So many artists regret it later. When artists come to me in this situation, I like to be in the position of offering some way out as a means to soften the blow. I can sometimes offer studio facilities or help with promotion and marketing.

It's very important not to believe that the size or success of a record company is an indication of the integrity of the company. You can get bad deals from big and small labels.

### What can you do if you are unhappy with the service your lawyer has provided?

The important thing to remember is that the lawyer acts for you. The relationship is one where the lawyer provides you with a service—and you pay them for it. So you can change your lawyer when you want to, although you need to be sure you've paid up before moving to another lawyer. Changing your lawyer involves changing your files, which can be difficult.

If you feel your first lawyer doesn't understand you, this is a different sort of unhappiness than believing your lawyer has harmed you by, say, creating a situation of massive financial loss. In that instance, you might have to write to the Law Society and make a formal complaint.

If you sense that your lawyer is involved in any kind of conflict-of-interest situation that results in them not looking after your best interests, then it might be worth considering changing them.

## Is there any point in retaining a lawyer, or should you consult them on an ad hoc basis?

This depends. If you're setting up a corporate entity—that is, if an artist decides to start a label or production company requiring a corporate structure—then it's best to go to a lawyer. They'll set up a file for you, which will be a record of all your dealings, and for this purpose you need some form of consistency. With the whole management of intellectual copyright you really need the same lawyer. They'll remember what you've given in previous agreements and there won't be any conflict. They won't offer rights to someone for a recording or publishing deal that has already been given away.

Opinions really differ from one lawyer to another, which gives them a different angle on things, and this can cause serious problems if you move from one lawyer to another.

In the US, many lawyers ask for a retention fee. The retention fee is offset against your bill. It happens quite a lot and it does mean an artist has consistent, clear advice. The more consistent the advice is, the more it affects the agreement, which in turn affects the artist's life long after the agreement has expired. It can affect the artist's earning potential. It's rather like a manager: using a manager means you are supposed to receive consistent advice and management. Using a lawyer on an ad hoc basis makes for an unstable life.

## What are the conditions for paying your lawyer?

It's important that an artist gets proper, clear bills. Billing is a difficult area. For example, I might take hours to draft an agreement but in many practices, cutting and pasting is done in most agreements. They're drafting agreements all the time, and many of the clauses in one agreement can be used in another, so they just cut and paste them. They're drafting agreements that could make or break an artist but they may not spend much time on them.

So an artist should always ask for itemized billing to see how long the lawyer has spent on drafting agreements, on the phone, in discussion and so on. These notes are called attendance notes and are attached to your file. All are computerized now. Effective note-keeping leads to more accurate billing, which allows you to spot the differences and can make the difference between spending a couple of thousand pounds or a couple of hundred. With an itemized bill, you can question items and raise issues about how much you have been charged.

### What crucial differences are there between US and UK law?

In the States, you have to be careful because of state laws—differences between one state and another. It affects aspects of agreement law and some ancillary issues.

It is worth noting that there are huge differences in copyright law between the US and the UK. It is often copyright law that's at the heart of many legal issues in the music industry. It is therefore worth getting expert advice on how these differences between countries might affect you.

At the end of an agreement, it will always say that the agreement is subject to the laws of whichever country or state it was drawn up in, for example, California, or it will say 'Subject to the laws of the United States'.

So if you're doing a trans-Atlantic deal and you live in the UK, because your agreement was offered in the US, you will be covered by the laws of the state it was drawn up in. If there is a dispute, it will have to be fought in that state and you will have to have an American attorney in that particular state. This can cost you more in one state than in another.

### Should you be meticulous in record-keeping?

Keep copies of absolutely everything you sign—even informal agreements. Don't do any work of any kind for anyone without something on paper. If someone wants you to do a track, write a song or do some backing vocals, don't do it until you get some sort of an agreement. If the track becomes successful and you feel you're owed money, you won't get anything without having something down on paper. You've got to get agreement in advance; you can't get it afterwards.

Even if it's a two-paragraph letter saying how much you're going to get paid and when you're going to get paid, it's worth getting. Keep records such as which studio was used and on what days and how long you were in doing the track.

### Final words?

The lawyer is their client's best friend.

✦✦✦✦✦✦✦✦✦✦✦✦✦✦✦✦✦✦✦✦✦✦✦✦✦✦✦✦✦✦✦✦✦✦✦✦✦✦✦✦✦✦✦✦✦

# publishing

*'We are our own publishing company, and though we do have some-
one who administers our songs overseas (collects publishing money),
they do not own any part of our songs; we do.'*

Mac McCaughan, Superchunk

Most people consider that music publishing is one of the easiest jobs in music! Basically, the job of a publisher is to administer the catalogue of songs written by its roster of songwriters and composers. Until about fifty years ago, selling printed music was a major part of the music business, and publishers needed all the marketing skills now required by record companies to sell CDs. Today, the amount of activity by a publisher on behalf of a writer is highly variable. Songbooks still exist but they are marketed by specialised companies like Music Sales and Cherry Lane, while the biggest element in most writers' income—royalties from performances and recordings—is collected by specialist agencies like ASCAP, BMI, the Harry Fox Agency, PRS and MCPS. Their role is explained later in this section.

The most proactive publishers today are those that get covers for their writers' songs on albums or singles by nonwriting or co-writing performers (as described by Martin Brammer on p. 309 and Wayne Cohen p. 314) and those who actively promote their writers' works to all the audio-visual media, including advertising, film, television and games. In return, they take a percentage of their writers' earnings. For the performing rights fees paid by ASCAP, BMI and PRS, the amount is fixed by the agencies' rules. For other income, especially the so-called 'mechanical rights' income from record sales, the split is negotiated. A typical deal for a new writer with a record deal might be 70% for the writer and 30% for the publisher. The publisher would pay something as an advance against future royalties, and larger publishers will sometimes pay for a home studio for promising newcomers—not as a gift but as another advance against royalties. At the superstar end of the scale, it used to be rumoured that a top British rock act had a 100%/zero deal with his US-owned publisher. The publisher made his money from the interest earned on royalties he received in between the twice-a-year payments his firm made to the star.

If you don't want this kind of help with your songs—maybe you are content to record them yourself and earn from performing and recording them only—then you may not need to sign to a publisher. As with a label, it's quite possible to start your own publishing company to publish your own songs. That way, you get to cop the royalties, although you will need specialist help to run the company, probably by paying an existing publisher to 'administer' your publishing. Administration means that they take care of the accounts from the collection societies, tax, etc. But they don't get to own any of your writers' works.

And if you don't fancy getting involved in publishing at all, you don't need to. Songwriters can join the societies without having a publisher, and record companies will list songs on albums as 'copyright control' if they don't have a publisher.

---

## DENNIS COLLOPY

Dennis Collopy of Menace Music has worked in the music industry for thirty years, mostly in music publishing, either as an independent with his own com-

pany, Menace Music, or for other independents, such as EG, or for major publishers, such as BMG. He has been running Menace as both a publishing and management company for the past thirteen years. His roster of artists is eclectic, covering rock and dance. Some of the artists Menace has looked after include the All Seeing I, Lisa Millett, I Monster, Virginia Astley, Mark Van Hoen and Locust, Steve Edwards and Mojave 3. Dennis says his criteria for choosing which artists to work with are that he likes their music and he can relate to them personally.

### Why should a fledgling band get a publisher?

If you're a new band, you probably need management initially more than you need publishing. To be brutally honest here, I'm sure publishers will say, 'Yeah, you've got to come to us', but until very recently, publishers had become totally reliant on the efforts of record companies, especially as far as artists who wrote

---

their own songs were concerned. The record company signed the act, sold the records, and the publisher might then have been able to do something on top. This was especially true for the most successful pop acts and rock bands. Now the stakes have become so much higher, especially if the band could become a future multi-million seller. Most publishers have become far more conservative in their deals. These days, they sign fewer acts but these often involve far more money and thus greater risk. The idea that a publisher could and would get a record deal for a band is very much the exception rather than the rule.

This certainly applies to the bulk multinationals and major companies. I honestly think that if you were Lennon and McCartney and you walked into EMI or Warner Chappell with a collection of songs, they'd say, 'If you haven't got the deal, if you haven't got any interest, we're not really sure where it's going to go'. I don't think you'd get a deal. I don't think many publishers in this day and age will take a chance on that kind of writer. That said, some publishers have realised they have to change the way they sign acts—especially because they are having to pay such big advances and thus incur greater risk. A couple of the major publishers have been more proactive in helping to develop new acts (e.g., Coldplay and Keane) and then help the bands secure good record deals. But overall, the number of new acts being signed seems to have dropped.

**Isn't that why an artist would go to an independent publisher, because you take more time and have the kind of contacts that get you signed?**
I'd say in the modern world a band isn't going to achieve much just by being with an independent publisher. I wish it weren't the case but the fact is, apart from money, the resources needed for an unsigned band aren't really appropriate for music publishing. At the outset, what you are focusing on is playing gigs and trying to get signed. That's basically it, and unless the publisher in question has a very strong relationship with a certain set of A&R people, it's unlikely a publisher can do much to help.

This is why our company developed what I call a management-based music publishing service, whereby we provide management services to the acts we publish.

There are other exceptions in Britain, including Windswept Music and Perfect Songs. The latter, for example, was very good at spotting talent very early on and had good relationships with A&R people. They discovered Mark Morrison and Gabrielle. But most of the other independent publishers spend a lot more on producers and production and generating exploitation through co-writing, placing productions and marketing. What is clear is that you cannot rely on the traditional ways of working: by signing talented songwriters and getting their songs covered or by signing a band and hoping to get a record deal. You have to use a lot more imagination.

## When should someone go for a publishing deal and why?

Bands should do it when they've got a record deal and when they can maximize the value of that. When you are about to sign a record deal, and when there's lots of competition for the band, the publishers' creative staff usually follow the record label A&R men around—hunting in packs. So if Parlophone, RCA, XL or Polydor are all vying for an act, you will find their associated publishing companies and many others will be in there and creating a bidding war. The manager has to judge whether it's the right time or not. Ironically, this is the best time because you're dealing with hype or fantasy—you're dealing with a band which the A&R crowd or pack have wound themselves up into believing is going to sell a million records or whatever. When you've released your album and you've only sold 15,000 units, that is clearly not the best time to do the act's publishing deal. For a manager, there is almost a sleight-of-hand about the whole process.

On the rare occasions that you've got a band that's got real potential but don't seem to be getting anywhere finding the right record label, then clearly publishing is the next step. But the first call was always finding a record deal and making sure you have a good manager. Then do a good publishing deal and that's where the band will make some decent money, and that's how the manager buys his Mercedes. Seriously, that's how almost everyone treats publishing, and the majority of record labels see that as justifiable. They can pay a band less money initially and say, 'Do a publishing deal, that's how you'll get enough money to live', and the industry seems to function on that level.

I did a very good publishing deal for the All Seeing I; indeed it was one that I, as a small publisher, could never have afforded. They signed with Chrysalis, who really showed quite staggering commitment to the act and I have nothing but admiration for them and can only say positive things about them as publishers.

Another common scenario is that an act needs a record deal but needs some help to get it. That's really when the managers, especially the young managers, might come to young small independent publishers such as us. They think, 'I'm not going to be able to do it right the first time myself. I need some help'. That seems to be the appropriate level for independent publishers to come in.

### What would you do for this young manager?

Well, a lot of it comes down to advice and providing the manager with the benefits of my contacts and my own experience. You might say something like, 'You're looking at the wrong labels'. It could be a timing thing, such as being a guitar band at the wrong time. A few years ago, we had a guitar band and we were on the verge of getting three or four recording contract offers—it suddenly went very quiet and we thought, 'What the hell's going on here?' Suddenly the industry seemed to have lost faith in guitar music, and the obvious places you'd look at—Mushroom, Nude, Creation, those kind of labels—were not signing anything new. Each label had a surfeit of guitar bands and very few really lasted the course!

Let's say you as a manager still have faith in the band and you want some money at such a stage to continue recording—perhaps the tracks you've done aren't good enough—and you need to get a producer involved. This is when you would look to a small publisher to invest some money into recording. This is something all publishers have done at one time or another. I think we were the first (when I was at BMG) to do this with the Mission, when we funded a white label—paying for PR, the pressing, the whole setup. We gave the act their own imprint, through an independent label called Chapter 22. We also did this for All About Eve. They both had number one singles on the independent chart and along came the major record deal.

### You did this in the 1980s. It would be harder today, wouldn't it?

Yeah. Much, much harder. I have to say if someone came here and said, 'We're the best thing since sliced bread, we're really good, etc.', I'd have to wonder why they're here and why they're not at EMI or Sony, given the way the industry works. The industry doesn't work overall in favour of independent publishers, which is why each of the successful independent publishers has to find its own niche. We're good at dealing with people who are writer-producers and that's why we do both publishing and management: because they work very well together. You can sign someone, you can establish co-writes, you can find singers, you can do tracks, you can license those and I see it as a spectrum between the kind of publishing we do and the kind of management we do; they're very directly related to each other.

### How hard can it be to get record companies to understand what you are trying to do with a band?

Sometimes it can be very hard. I used to manage the All Seeing I, which had a recording deal with London Records (now part of Warner Music). The band's debut single, 'The Beat Goes On,' was a big hit in the UK in early 1998 and they were approached six months later by Jive Records, who had a new artist called Britney Spears. They wanted the band to do a version of the same song with Britney.

I saw the video for her first single (which had not yet been released) in September 1998 and I sent it on to London Records because I thought, 'If this is going to be big, I might as well get London involved with it'. But they really didn't see the potential for collaboration at all. I had discussed a possible plan that would benefit everyone, where London would release the new version in Britain as the All Seeing I Presents Britney Spears and Britney's label Jive were going to put it out in America, as Britney Spears with the All Seeing I. Jive was incredibly confident and was saying, 'We are going to sell millions of records', to which my natural reaction was one of great caution, like, 'Well, I've heard that one before'. But once I saw the video to the first single, 'Baby One More Time,' I knew she was going to be successful. But London just could not grasp what an opportunity this was.

So we agreed to get involved, but only as remixers, which got us out of our re-recording restrictions with London. And of course once the track appeared on the massively successful Britney debut album, we were able to retain all the money we made from the remix. I got the band a good deal because they were essentially giving up their chance to have any further success with their version of 'The Beat Goes On'. The main point was that the band needed money to survive—they needed the money from doing the Britney remix, especially as they were still 'signing on'.

London, as record companies still try to do, were desperately trying to get hold of the All Seeing I's publishing rights. They made us several terrible offers, which I just kept turning down—I ended up saying, 'I'm not giving you the band's publishing for £20,000'.

However, the label then tried another gambit—they told us they would not give the band any further money under the record deal and would only give us money for the publishing rights. The best our A&R man could offer for the publishing deal was £20,000 on signing and maybe another £20,000 when the album came out—an unbelievably small amount in comparison with what I knew we could get for the band by hanging on to the rights. So I turned them down and then agreed to do the Britney remix. I did the Britney deal the same day we turned down London's final publishing offer.

For me, it is all a matter of making sure the act can survive financially, and retaining control of the publishing enabled us to do make more. The act had a poor recording deal with London Records; they were still signing on and had no money. That was why the publishing was so important. In the normal scheme of things, a publishing deal is so much the cornerstone in financial terms of how an act survives before they can start making money through a record deal. In the modern age, you can sell half a million albums and still not be making any money. You might have made an expensive album, a couple of basic videos, you've got the cost of the whole touring setup plus all the tour support, and of course you've got to pay a manager, the lawyers and the accountants. So you can get through half a million pounds before you actually make any money at all very, very easily. A good publishing deal gives you a lump sum of money to enable the members of the act to live reasonably comfortably. It's the financial cornerstone for most new bands.

### When you were offered £20,000 for publishing, what would have been fair?

The All Seeing I had only had 'The Beat Goes On', which they did not even write; we hadn't had any other success but I wouldn't have accepted a deal for less than a £100,000 because they had to split the money between them, pay off all of their debts and budget enough to live on for at least eighteen months to two years—they had to pay commissions, you've got to pay lawyers and accountants and of course set aside some to pay tax.

That hundred thousand isn't even £100,000 for the band, is it? You've got to work out what everybody needs to live on and you've got to be realistic—you're going to need that money to last for more than a year. The gap between recording the first album and the option which comes with your second album, which might get picked up by the record company, could be as long as two or three years. So it's about planning, and I think that's why, when professionals are involved, they are going, 'Well, you really do need a lot of money—you've got to pay for us, you've got to plan, you've got tax, you've got touring and live setup costs'—and most musicians have got debt by the time they've got to a record deal. The only thing that you can tap into to give you that independent source of income is a publishing deal. Artists also get trapped into making records too quickly, before they're ready for it.

## How should you negotiate with a major publisher?

I negotiate for all our clients because obviously I've done publishing deals and I know my way around it, but I think it's usually down to the band's lawyer. But it's very important for me, and everyone we deal with, that everyone's happy with the choice of publisher. Some people obviously just go for the cheque; although I know some people who've been in the position to take really big money but have taken less and gone with a company they think can offer them something special. Something like synchronization work, where in a band there's one guy who really likes to work with other people and wants covers of his songs. For producer-writers, you look for a company that is very creatively driven, where perhaps they'll put you together with other acts and can get you further work.

I would say, if you sign a record deal and you've got a measure of success it's certainly not a good idea to sign to the same publishing company that is associated with the record company. There are some good reasons why you can, and you can do well out of it, but as a general rule it's not a good idea. If the record label is uncertain about you, that uncertainty will translate, will be fed through to or communicated to the publisher at some point. So your two main relationships could both be compromised just because one A&R guy's got a crisis of confidence in his act—the last single only got to number twenty-four and only got on the Radio 1 C list and that was it, and suddenly it's 'Oh God!'—because the pressures on A&R people today are extreme. So you want a different publisher that is supportive, as Chrysalis was with the All Seeing I and Universal was with Lisa Millett.

## How would you advise a new act to get a publishing or recording deal?

When I first started, bands could break relatively easily because there was a decent live scene. Today, it doesn't work that well, now that promoters and agents are every bit as conservative as A&R men. Many bands have major record deals and substantial publishing deals but still can't get an agent. Some of the most conservative people I know at the moment in the music industry are agents. To get an agent, you've got to have something really going for you.

Sending tapes and CDs in to A&R people is a waste of time. Most members of the MPA [Music Publishers Association] don't accept unsolicited material. The industry works mainly on personal recommendation. If it comes from someone I know, I'll take much more notice of it.

I take material and I play it to people. It's the only effective way of doing it. I don't just send things out. If the material is only in demo form, put only three or four of the best songs on a CD-R (never tape) and don't send long-winded letters or reams of lyric sheets. You must make it easy for people to listen and react positively. Remember also that each area in the country has got someone who is a designated A&R source—it could be the manager of a locally successful band, a local record label, recording studio, venue—these are often the source of tips for major label A&R people.

In Sheffield or Leicester, for example, we knew to chat with the manager at one of the local studios or the main local venue—London-based A&R people would come to them and ask what was going on in the area. Bands coming down to London to play at venues like the Garage on a Monday night—its new-band night—is usually just wasting time and money, as A&R people do not go to these venues unless there is a very big buzz about the band already.

If you're in dance, the remix route is the way forward. Or for singers, doing sessions. Lisa Millett is a talented singer and she does sessions for different artists. Or you could try co-writing with people. Release material yourselves on white labels and send them to A&R staff at publishing companies—it's a sign of commitment. All publishers can and should help creatively. A&R in record companies is reactive—the best publishers have to be a bit more on the case and pro-active. The good A&R people in publishing know which new acts are worth considering. Effective publishers can be real facilitators—they find people who have a degree of talent—but remember, though, independent publishers have less capital and so it's harder for them to sign the same things; they may be more committed. Nevertheless, our experiences working closely with Universal Music Publishing in the UK over the past three or four years have shown that despite their comparatively large size they can still be as effective and focused creatively as any independent and their strategy of working with firms such as ours shows they recognise the value of the smaller creative unit.

✦✦✦✦✦✦✦✦✦✦✦✦✦✦✦✦✦✦✦✦✦✦✦✦✦✦✦✦✦✦✦✦✦✦✦✦✦✦✦✦✦✦✦✦✦

# MARA SCHWARTZ

Mara Schwartz is based in the US and has been the director of film, television, and new media at Bug Music, a publishing administration company, since

2003. The midsized company administers publishing for over three thousand songwriters, including Iggy Pop, the Faint, Peaches and Ryan Adams. Prior to this, Schwartz worked in television, video production and journalism.

## Why should a band pursue a publishing deal?

There's a lot of work involved in the maintenance of your song copyrights that you just don't have the time to do when you're recording or on the road touring. There's making sure all your songs are copyrighted with the Copyright Office, making sure all the cue sheets are filed with ASCAP, BMI or SESAC, making sure your mechanical royalties are collected from your record label. There's negotiation of sync licenses for film and television. The publisher does all these things for you.

## What is registering songs with a Copyright Office?

That's registering the copyright on the song so that in case there's a lawsuit later you can prove when you created the song.

## What is a cue sheet and why is it important?

It's a log of every piece of music in a TV show or film, and how long it is and when it was played. It's supposed to be provided by the production company, or a company hired to create it. It's something that the publisher gets and makes sure it gets filed with whichever performing rights organisation our songwriter is with. Then that organisation knows who to pay whenever that programme or film is broadcast.

## What is a mechanical licence?

It comes from mechanical reproduction, meaning the mechanical reproduction of your song on a CD. It originally referred to the mechanical reproduction of music on piano rolls. A mechanical license is a compulsory license, meaning that it has to be granted as long as the record company is willing to pay the mechanical royalties. It's kind of an interesting quirk of copyright law that any artist and label can cover anybody's song and they don't have to ask permission but they do have to obtain the mechanical license and pay the royalty.

The record label is responsible for paying either the songwriter or the publisher as a representative of the songwriter. A lot of times, they don't pay when they're supposed to, which is when publishers have to come in to sort things out. It's a lot easier if a songwriter is with a publisher who has to collect a lot of royalties for a number of songwriters from a particular record label. The label will often pay all of it in one payment to the publisher and have them make individual payments to each songwriter.

### And what is a sync license?

Whenever your songs are used on a TV show, movie, commercial, trailer, video game or stuffed animal that dances and sings, there has to be a sync license. It's a negotiation of rights to synchronize the music to picture. Nowadays, there's a lot more interest in placing previously created songs in television than there was before. Ten years ago, there were a lot more specially written jingles in commercials and a lot less licensed songs. There are a lot of opportunities for artists to get their music placed. The publisher has a creative department that will pitch songs for film and TV shows. They'll do a concentrated campaign when a new album is out, getting it out to all the music supervisors in TV and film companies for consideration. We're constantly listening out for new projects that might be able to use our music. It's really easy for people to remember a new song by an artist that's in the charts, but a film might be set in the 1930s and production company needs actual songs from that era so we go through out catalogues and see what we have that fits and we submit it to them to make sure they have everything in front of them.

### What's the difference between a publishing administrator and a co-publisher?

A co-publishing deal is a deal where the publisher typically will give the songwriter an advance. In exchange for the advance, they'll take a percentage, usually somewhere around half of the publishing ownership. A publishing administration deal is something where there's not usually an advance given. The ownership stays with the songwriter 100% and the publishing administrator takes a fee as payment for taking care of the paperwork. When we negotiate a sync placement as an administrator, we take a fee from that and from any other the work that we do for them. The only time we do advances is when there's pipeline income that the songwriter will definitely receive. For example, if they've already sold a significant amount of records and haven't collected the royalties from their label. Or they've had songs placed in film and television, so there is money they know is going to come in within the next year or so.

## Why is one better than the other?

Well, I'm biased of course towards the publishing administration side. Sometimes bands get into bidding wars where they get offered these co-publishing advances that are just huge, an amount of money that's just stupid for them to turn down. If they feel like they're not going to make the advance back, then it makes sense to agree to a co-pub deal even if they only have only 50% of everything and the publisher gets the other 50%.

## Does one work harder than the other because they have a greater stake in it?

I feel we work so hard. I don't know how we could work any harder because we collect all the money that's due to our writers and, since we get a percentage, we collect as much as possible. I'm sure if you asked a co-publisher, they would also say how hard they work for their writers.

## Do you do things like hooking up the artist with another songwriter?

We do that. The one thing we don't do is shop for a record deal and that's something that most co-publishers do. As an administrator, we usually don't pick up clients speculatively. We usually only pick up clients once they have some kind of mechanical royalties collection need. By that time, they've already got a record deal. Often, we do things that are above and beyond, like setting up showcases and get a lot of music supervisors to come out to the show. Even though we're not really involved in live performances, it's more about getting supervisors excited about the band so they'll want to use them in their next project.

## How do you feel about smaller publishers versus larger ones?

We're a medium-sized company so I can see both sides. If you are after a big advance, which a lot of people are, obviously it's the large publishers who can pay that. But sadly there are musicians who have been starving for so long, and not that much money is a big advance to them. Twenty thousand dollars isn't that big in the grand scheme of Universal or Sony, but for some guy who has been crashing on people's couches it's a fortune. But I do think the smaller to midsized publishers are going to be just as efficient in collecting your money for you and you'll probably get more personalized attention from your creative team.

## Are publishing deals like record deals in that they run out after a while or the artist might get dropped?

Most co-publishing deals have terms that are either year-to-year or album-to-album. Our administration deals are on a year-to-year basis with all our artists with an automatic rollover to the next year, unless they tell us otherwise. It shows confidence that people are going to be happy the deal, so we're comfortable giving them options to leave if they want.

## If a deal runs out and the artist/publisher decide not to renew it, are the songs the artist wrote during their time with that publisher still going to be half-owned by that publisher?

Publishing companies and administration companies do have retentions. If a song is placed in a film or TV show or the company has gotten another artist to release a cover version, the publishing company retains the rights to those songs or that particular version of the song, or that usage of the song for a period of time and that's something that's written into the contract. Many co-publishing deals do allow the publisher to retain the rights to all the songs they co-published during the songwriter's tenure there, but Bug is unique in that we only retain administration on songs we've gotten covers on or placed. A lot of old-school contracts from the Fifties and Sixties would tie up the songs in perpetuity, but people have gotten more savvy so the terms are usually somewhere between ten and fifteen years. I've seen a lot of people not be very smart about the deal that they've signed. We have a lot of artists here who are refugees from old, bad major publishing deals that they signed in the Seventies. They come here and they have this great body of work and they'll have one big hit that's tied up in perpetuity at a major publisher because they got it into a film or something.

## When should an artist look for a publishing deal?

If they're looking to get a record deal, some publishers can help them. What I always advise, and this is a little off the topic, but people don't utilise their performing rights societies. Any songwriter should use them. They should visit their local society, there are offices all over the country. They have a wealth

---

of resources. They put on showcases for unsigned songwriter, unsigned bands. It's amazing that more people don't take the time to visit ASCAP or BMI or SESAC. Although they don't do everything a publisher does, they can give you advice on publishers. I've had a lot of good clients put my way by ASCAP or BMI. They can get you pointed in the right direction and help you figure out what you want to do with your publishing and what kind of deal you want. And also, they can put you in some of the right steps towards getting you a record deal, getting you people to write with.

### How would you advise people to go about getting a publishing deal?
We don't take unsolicited material, just because of the possibility of future copyright infringement cases and things like that. We take submissions from managers who we know, attorneys who we know. But I honestly think the best way to get a deal is to play live out so much that we can't avoid you because everyone's talking about how good you are. If I go into Spaceland [a popular Los Angeles live venue] and I say hi to the bartender and he says, 'Have you heard so-and-so?' that's the point when a band is ready for a deal. If you really are as good as you say, you'll eventually get to the point when the bartender is talking about you.

✦✦✦✦✦✦✦✦✦✦✦✦✦✦✦✦✦✦✦✦✦✦✦✦✦✦✦✦✦✦✦✦✦✦✦✦✦✦✦✦✦✦✦✦✦

# collection societies and rights organisations

While the songwriter–publisher relationship is important, the fact is that most of your money as a writer or publisher is probably going to be channelled through one or more of the various societies and companies that act on your behalf in collecting and distributing royalties from thousands of 'music users'. These users range from record companies and broadcasters to concert venues, airlines and jukebox owners.

Most of these collection societies were set up in the early part of the twentieth century, when the music business was rapidly expanding and it was clearly impossible for an individual writer or publisher to keep track of where and when their songs were being performed, recorded and played on the radio. To solve this practical problem, writers and publishers banded together in collection organizations that could represent numerous copyright owners in making deals with the music users. Most of these deals set national rates for such things as radio play or concert performances that are enforced through legally binding contracts between the users and the collection organisations.

Whole books could be written about this system (and some have been), but here we aim to stick to the most practical aspects of how you can try to make sure you get paid properly for other people's exploitation of your creativity. And for many important uses of your music, there is no alternative but to join a relevant national collection society or company.

For practical purposes, there are three types of collection bodies, two representing you in your role as a writer and/or publisher and a third looking after your interests if you are a record label and/or recording artist. If you are a band, solo act or DJ writing your own songs or running your own label or handling your own (or other writers') publishing, you need to get involved with all three types.

These three categories of collection organizations are:

✦ Performing rights societies for songwriters and publishers (for example, ASCAP, BMI and SESAC in the US; SOCAN in Canada; PRS in Britain; and IMRO in Ireland)
✦ Mechanical rights bodies for songwriters and publishers (for example, the Harry Fox Agency in the US; CMRRA in Canada; and MCPS in Britain and Ireland)
✦ Performing rights bodies for recording artists and record companies (for example, PPL in Britain; PPL(I) and RAAP in Ireland; NRCC in Canada; and Sound Exchange in the US)

We are going to look at each of these in turn, beginning with the performing rights societies for songwriters and publishers. 'Performing rights' is a legal term that covers any kind of public performance of your copyright music. This includes not just live gigs but any use of recordings of your songs by radio, TV, club DJs, background tapes in shops and on Web sites, jukeboxes in bars and pubs, telephone on-hold music and many others.

## PERFORMING RIGHTS SOCIETIES

Performing rights organisations act on behalf of songwriters and music publishers in collecting royalties when music is played on radio, television, Internet, ringtones or live concerts. Also, they undertake what is called general licensing of bars, restaurants, shops and any other place where music is performed which is covered by the copyright act.

The performing rights is the biggest moneyspinner for songwriters and publishers, and in 2004, it brought in about £200 million in Britain and $1 billion in the US. This makes the companies that collect these fees key players in the business. We next hear from executives in the main performing rights bodies in the UK and US, starting with John Sweeney of PRS, who also works for MCPS, the British mechanical rights organisation.

✦✦✦✦✦✦✦✦✦✦✦✦✦✦✦✦✦✦✦✦✦✦✦✦✦✦✦✦✦✦✦✦✦✦✦✦✦✦✦✦✦✦✦✦✦✦✦✦✦

### JOHN SWEENEY

John Sweeney joined the Performing Right Society in 1978 and has worked in many areas of the organisation, including copyright, dispute resolution and membership. On the formation of the MCPS-PRS Alliance in 1997, John was

appointed director of membership, PRS and is now member relations director for the Alliance as a whole. He is also chairman of the PRS Foundation Ltd.—the UK's largest independent funding body purely for new music. He is a writer member of PRS and remains an active songwriter and performer.

#### What is the Alliance and what is its role in the music industry?

It's a combination of two companies that administer rights on behalf of composers and publishers in different areas. Starting with PRS, if you are a writer and you create a work, you have certain rights, including the right to have the work performed in public, have it broadcast, diffused by cable and used online. What that means is you are entitled to get some money when any of those acts happen, and what PRS does is pick up that money for you and pay it to you. PRS is needed because there would be mayhem if every writer individually went to every broadcaster and every shop and demanded their piece of the cake. So PRS acts on behalf of our forty-four thousand writer members and because of that we can command a significant figure.

## What does a new songwriter need to do to join PRS?

It's very simple. They have to have written just one song that they can notify us has been performed at least once live or on radio. The application form can be downloaded from the Alliance Web site. And there's a one-off admission fee, currently £100 for a writer and £400 per publisher to cover the paperwork. We also need a list of songs. We maintain a database of our members' work, of which there are now approximately five million.

## How does the writer get paid by PRS?

The BBC and certain venues have an obligation under the terms of their licence to not only pay us but to give us details of all the music that is broadcast or played live. We calculate how much each play is worth to the copyright owners. At present, for example, for three minutes of airplay we pay out about £115 for BBC 1 television and £50 for BBC Radio 1. With other stations, it will be a much smaller amount, like about £2.10 on a BBC local station such as Radio Shropshire. But we can only pay out to a writer if they register their songs with us and tell us how the money should be divided up.

## How do you mean, divided up?

If the member is a co-writer, say, in a band, they will have agreed to split the money, perhaps between four co-writers. And if the writers have a publisher, the publisher will be contractually entitled to some of the money, usually half of it, but no more than half.

## You said the BBC gives details of all the music it uses. What about other broadcasters and smaller venues?

With the BBC, the amount of money it pays us makes it economic for us to conduct an analysis of 100% of the music used. But with a smaller radio station, a 100% analysis would cost more than the actual money we get from the station. For these smaller stations, we take the music used on a number of days per month or per half-year and use that for distribution. We've increased this sample coverage considerably in the past year and we're looking at using new technologies to improve it further.

### What if I'm a PRS member and I know my song was played on a certain small station on a particular day that wasn't one of the sampling days?

Well, this is a frustration for members and this is why we're constantly trying to increase the sampling coverage. But even if you told us about this, we wouldn't pay you. There is no claims system for broadcasting, and in any case the principle of a random sampling system is that every member stands an equal chance of being included in a sample. If certain members are more able to tell us their songs were on a particular station—maybe they work there or live locally—they would receive a disproportionate amount of what PRS collects from that station.

### How about when my music is played on radio or television abroad?

When a songwriter or composer joins PRS, they usually join for the world, although they don't have to. There is an equivalent of PRS in most countries, and more than one in the United States and a few other countries. We have agreements with each of these, so that when our respective members have success in another country, the society in that country picks up the money and sends it to the writer's home society. So wherever a PRS member's work is being played in the world, subject to the arrangements between us and that country, they will be paid for it.

### How does PRS sort out payments from live shows?

Concert venues and live classical venues pay us 3% of their box office receipts and provide a full set list or programme. As with broadcasters, we can't afford to do a full census of smaller venues, such as pubs and clubs. Instead we employ an outside company and use a statistician to give them a number of venues to monitor on a rolling basis per year. The company sends a person with a clipboard to spend six hours noting down the music of a live event or DJ set, and also, if it's a pub, what is being played on the jukebox or what radio station is playing in the bar. Like with smaller broadcasters, it's a sampling system but with gigs and clubs there is a claims scheme. So, for example, a PRS member who is a regular performer of their own songs can send in a set list used at certain venues. It's very cheap for us to process and pay out. And we know this is especially beneficial to what we call 'specialist' music areas.

## Composers can also apply for funding from the PRS Foundation. How does that work?

The Foundation was set up in 2000 after PRS abolished a scheme that provided extra payments for certain types of music, mostly classical. Instead, PRS decided to fund a Foundation that would encourage the creation and performance of new music. The donation from PRS in 2006 is £1.25 million. The PRS Foundation doesn't support already established music but grassroots stuff. There are various programmes, including the New Music Award, which began in 2005 as our attempt to raise public consciousness of new music, as the Turner Prize does for the visual arts.

## You are also responsible for member relations at MCPS. What does that organisation do?

MCPS, which is the Mechanical Copyright Protection Society, deals with the right for composers to have their work copied. It exercises that right on behalf of the composer and publisher and charges a rate for the reproduction and pressing of a CD and for copying and recording music for a TV programme or a DVD.

## Is it correct that most members of MCPS are publishers?

There is no restriction on anybody joining MCPS and there is a surprisingly large writer membership. But whether a writer needs to join may depend on their contractual relationship with a publisher. When a writer joins PRS, they get paid directly but usually a publishing contract grants the publisher the right to receive 100% of the money from MCPS. The publisher then pays the writer.

## And what about the situation where a new, small company has a record label and a publishing arm and the label only records songs from its own publisher? Must that publisher join MCPS?

There would be little point, as MCPS would collect money from your right hand and pay it to your left hand and charge a fee for doing that! It's worth pointing out that both PRS and MCPS only exist to do something that composers can't do for themselves. In this case, you don't need MCPS. The time when you will need MCPS to collect on your behalf is when other record companies start putting out product containing those songs from your publisher's catalogue.

✦✦✦✦✦✦✦✦✦✦✦✦✦✦✦✦✦✦✦✦✦✦✦✦✦✦✦✦✦✦✦✦✦✦✦✦✦✦✦✦✦✦✦✦✦✦✦✦✦

# US PERFORMING RIGHTS ORGANIZATIONS

In the UK and almost all other countries, there is only one organization dealing with performing rights. The situation is different in the US, where three organizations compete for members among publishers and songwriters. These are the American Society of Composers, Authors and Publishers (ASCAP), Broadcast Music, Inc. (BMI) and SESAC. Each of the three does a similar job: licensing broadcasters, venues, retailers, etc. to use its members' copyright works.

But as a new songwriter or independent music publisher based in the US, how can you decide which of the three is the best for you to join?

You should approach this choice carefully, the same way you would choose an instrument to buy or select a band member. In many cases, you will remain connected with your performing rights society for many years, perhaps decades—that means through various projects and bands, changes in music trends, hair styles, and so forth.

A good strategy for choosing your performing rights affiliation would be:

+ What are your goals? What path do you expect your career to take? What sort of publishing goals do you have?
+ List the values you are looking for in a performing rights group. These might involve the image and business profile of the society, added value and services offered, how closely aligned the group is to the music and broader entertainment industry, the tone of the organization, the importance of tradition, the commitment to the future and new music, flexibility, probity, thoroughness, promotional reach, and so on.
+ If you have a manager, lawyer or record label or band situation, find out what advice on performing rights affiliation these professionals or peers will offer. For now, just get their advice; don't act on it prematurely. Try to develop a clear picture as to what your friends and peers think.
+ Get copies of the membership recruitment kits for any of the groups that you are considering joining. These can be found on the various Web sites (ascap.com; bmi.com; sesac.com). Study them carefully and then do a corresponding outline, one that describes the nature of each group and the key values it offers you.
+ Talk to a few people you trust who already have a performing rights affiliation. Ask them about their relationship with the society and the pros and cons they've experienced. Ask them about publishing and distribu-

tion, how are they treated, and so on. For most people, the choice boils down to two issues: which pays more, and how they are treated.

Next, officials of the two main organisations, ASCAP and BMI explain what they offer. First, ASCAP.

✦✦✦✦✦✦✦✦✦✦✦✦✦✦✦✦✦✦✦✦✦✦✦✦✦✦✦✦✦✦✦✦✦✦✦✦✦✦✦✦✦✦✦✦✦✦✦✦✦

## JENNIFER KNOEPFLE

Jennifer Knoepfle has been working with developing artists at ASCAP since 1999. Among her responsibilities has been the production of the *ASCAP Presents . . .* sampler CDs featuring new and emerging songwriters, such as the Killers and Midnight
Movies. She has also been instrumental in forging
a relationship with the Musician's Institute in creating open-mic nights and educational panels. She
currently serves as associate director of membership in the pop/rock division.

### Who should join a collection society?
A songwriter would join a society such as ASCAP
when they needed to make sure royalties were collected on their behalf when their songs are played
in the areas that we survey and we license, which are radio stations, television networks, cable networks, bars, clubs, Internet sites, jukeboxes, satellite
radio, theme parks, concert venues, etc. They don't have other means of getting royalties on such a widespread basis. I want to make a note here that we
don't actually pay artists unless they are songwriters also. We pay the songwriter; so if the artist did not write their songs, we're not paying the artist,
we're paying whoever wrote the song.

### When would a writer join a collection society?
A writer typically joins ASCAP when they have a completed commercial recording, something that would be getting played in the areas that we survey.
There's no need to join prior to that, but some people do. There are three things
you can have to join ASCAP. You can either have a commercial recording (and
that can be one song or it can be a whole record) or you will have played live

in some ASCAP-licensable venue such as the Troubadour or the Viper Room in Los Angeles or something like that; or you could have your work in a television show or a cable television show.

## What is the process of joining?
It's completely free to join. Every person who joins is a songwriter. Additionally, they would want to go through a publishing company. We pay royalties to the songwriters and the publishers separately.

## How often do ASCAP members get paid?
Our songwriters and publishers get paid on a quarterly basis. We have four international writer and publisher payments that come in as well. We pay approximately six to seven months after the performance happens.

## How does the money get split between the artist and the publisher?
The money gets split between the writer and the publisher exactly evenly. If they own their own publishing and they're the writer, they're going to get 100% of everything, 50% on the writer's side and 50% on the publisher's side. If they have a co-publishing deal with another company, the publishing royalty will be split.

## How does the money you collect get distributed?
We essentially distribute all the money that we get, with the exception of our overhead costs, which are the lowest costs of any performing rights organisation in the US. We have a 'follow the dollar' system in place. This means that the money we collect from radio stations gets distributed according to the music played on radio; the money we collect from television goes on the basis of television play. The money's distributed based on a weighting formula. A performance gets weighted based on a lot of different factors and from there we determine a credit value. That credit value is currently $6.70 per credit. The performance based on the weighting system would determine a certain number of credits, meaning it's half a credit, ten credits, five credits. You can get the information on how it's determined from our Web site. We also have reciprocal agreements with foreign societies.

## When was the company started and why?
ASCAP is the oldest performing rights society in the US. It was started in 1914 by songwriters like Irving Berlin and many of the people who wrote the stan-

dards of the day. They realised that they weren't getting paid for their works when they were being performed in the clubs and things of that nature. They came together to form ASCAP in order to protect the writers of the day and make sure they were paid for their performances.

## What success has the company had for its writers?

We do have a lot of artist development programs, meaning showcases and workshops where we've been pretty instrumental in helping newer bands get to the next level. For instance, we have showcases at all industry conferences, plus we have local shows, and a lot of artists that we've showcased have gone on to become really successful, like John Mayer early on, Jack Johnson, the Killers, and Damien Rice. When a band's successful, we don't necessarily contribute to the later phases of their career because we're just basically paying them at that point.

The membership requirement for BMI is similar to that of ASCAP and PRS: you must have had one of your songs performed. However, BMI does not charge writers for membership.

✦✦✦✦✦✦✦✦✦✦✦✦✦✦✦✦✦✦✦✦✦✦✦✦✦✦✦✦✦✦✦✦✦✦✦✦✦✦✦✦✦✦✦✦✦✦

✦✦✦✦✦✦✦✦✦✦✦✦✦✦✦✦✦✦✦✦✦✦✦✦✦✦✦✦✦✦✦✦✦✦✦✦✦✦✦✦✦✦✦✦✦✦

## TRACIE VERLINDE

Tracie Verlinde has been with BMI (Broadcast Music, Inc.) since 1997. She is senior director, writer/publisher relations in BMI's Los Angeles offices. She also helps in the production of the organization's 'Snowball' showcase at the Sundance Film Festival. Verlinde has been responsible for signing many writers to BMI, including Linkin Park, the White Stripes, the Shins, Death Cab for Cutie, and Rilo Kiley.

## When would a writer join BMI?

Basically, you will need a company like BMI if you've written or published songs that have the potential to be played on radio, television or the Internet and in restaurants or the thousands of other businesses that use music: the Gap, Starbucks, etc. Basically, it's an open-door policy. As long as you are not a member of another performing rights society you are able to join BMI if you have the desire to. You can't belong to BMI as well as ASCAP or SESAC.

## Is joining easy?

You can do it online and it's free. It's like filling out a Blockbuster card. It's name, address, social security number, and signature on both copies of the contract and you're done.

## Once someone registers with you online that's it, they're with you?

Yeah, it's a two-year term. They are able to leave after two years.

## Every time you write a song, do you have to register it?

Yeah, and you can do it online too. It's really easy.

## Does BMI need a copy of the song?

No, we don't require that.

## How do you determine who is getting what?

There's a different formula for each source of royalties, based on licensing fees and usage. There's a royalty information booklet on our Web site. In radio, there are different formulae for college radio and for large stations. In day-time television, there's a different formula for payment for theme music to that for background music. All the information goes in the computer and it spits out how much you will get paid based on usage of your song, how often it was played. If you're the only songwriter, how much you'll get will be more than if it's split it with co-writers, when obviously that money will be divided in two or three or four or more ways.

## How much can a writer get paid for one play of their song on the radio?

It varies, anything from twenty cents to maybe two to three dollars per one spin.

## That's obviously different from a live performance?

Yes. For live performances, we pay on the Top 200 tours in the US and that in-cludes opening acts. So if there are bands that played on the Warped Tour and the Warped Tour was one of the Top 200, they would get paid from us once they have provided us with set lists.

## How often do artists get paid?

We pay quarterly: January, April, July, October. Each payment goes back six to nine months, in terms of when the music was used. What also happens is we get reports and payments from foreign societies which appear on the writer's statement. If you wrote songs that were being played over in the UK or Spain, once those societies told us about those songs and that activity you'd see that on the same statement, under the headings of domestic earnings and foreign earnings.

## How do you split the money between writers and publishers?

In our system, the payment for a song is reckoned as 200%, and 100% of that goes to writers and 100% goes to publishers. So for us, it's an equal split.

## If a writer is already a BMI member and then they get a publishing deal, how does that work?

The publishing company will just register those works with BMI. The writer's deal with the publishing company can either be an administration publishing deal where the publisher makes 10% and just does the paperwork, or it might be a co-pub deal where they're taking 50%. But a publishing deal never touches the writer's share of BMI royalties. The writer's portion always goes straight to the writers.

## Why don't artists use performing rights organisations more often?

Partly because they don't know what we do. The other part is that once you join, you have to tell us about the songs you wrote. You have to actually say, 'Hey, I'm a BMI member and here's a list of my titles'. Bands will sign up or they'll forget they signed up and they won't register the works and those works will be getting played on college radio or whatever and they'll miss out on money. It's an area of the business that's so not sexy and cool that people don't really understand or know about it. It's not like, 'Hey, I signed to a label', or 'Hey, I signed with a manager, I got a booking agent'. It's more business, paperwork, so a lot of people don't know about it or care about it.

## What per cent of income does BMI keep?

We're a nonprofit organisation and we distribute more than 85% of our revenue, so we have about a 15% operating cost. Because it's nonprofit, we literally take our operating costs and the rest all goes back to our writers and publishers.

### Is there any difference between the three American performing rights organisations?

The main difference is that ASCAP and BMI operate on a nonprofit basis and SESAC is for-profit. There are a lot of differences in terms of how the business is run as far as the structure is concerned.

### How do you decide which company to go for?

Whoever you relate to. We always say it's our people who sell us. Other bands will be like, 'My favourite band is Deathcab for Cutie, they're with BMI', or 'Nirvana is my favourite band, they're with BMI'. It's kind of like Coke and Pepsi, your preference. If you have people at BMI who really believe in you and will help you, you should go there.

### What success has BMI had for its artists?

Huge. I'll give you some of the legendary people: John Lennon, Chuck Berry, Carlos Santana, John Williams, Danny Elfman, Mark Mothersbaugh. On the rock side we have Linkin Park, the White Stripes, the Foo Fighters. We have Mariah Carey, Little Jon. We have members from all the different areas of music. We've brought in more revenue this year than ever. We do a lot of artist development. We do showcases. We do things at industry events like CMJ and South by Southwest and Sundance. We have our own podcasts. We do things online with a little media campaign. There's a lot of artist development that we can actually do for people that no one's every heard of, taking them and being their best friend throughout their own creative process. We can absolutely help bands that need that extra push. I've bought bands groceries, given them free Levi's because we work closely with Levi's. We bought them lunch when they were broke.

✦✦✦✦✦✦✦✦✦✦✦✦✦✦✦✦✦✦✦✦✦✦✦✦✦✦✦✦✦✦✦✦✦✦✦✦✦✦✦✦✦✦✦✦✦✦✦✦✦

## SESAC

As a private company, SESAC does not publicize its membership requirements. In fact, its Web site states that membership is by invitation only. If you are interested in joining, you should contact SESAC direct.

## IMPLICATIONS FOR BRITISH SONGWRITERS

British songwriters will need to join one of these performing rights organizations if their recordings are issued in the US, or if they plan to tour there. This affiliation is generally made through PRS, which will affiliate its members with ASCAP, unless it is instructed to do otherwise by the songwriter. All three US organizations have London offices whose staff can explain the advantages of affiliation to British songwriters, publishers and managers.

British music publishers will normally arrange to be represented in the US by making a 'subpublishing' agreement with an American publisher. Under such an agreement, the American publisher acts as the representative of the British publisher's catalogue and it receives any performance royalties due to the British publisher's songs through the US performing rights organization to which it belongs. These are then forwarded to the British publisher. Generally speaking, the British publisher also acts as the UK subpublisher for its US partner.

## MECHANICAL RIGHTS SOCIETIES

'Mechanical rights' is a rather old-fashioned term dating back a century or more to when the reproduction of music by mechanical means, such as barrel organs, piano rolls and of course sound recording, was a novelty. Nowadays, the term still applies mainly to the recording and sale of music on CD, vinyl and tape, but it also includes various uses of music in video and film and the incorporation of music into broadcast programmes.

For complex historical reasons, the mechanical rights system in both Britain and the US is controlled by organizations owned by music publishers, in contrast to the performing rights bodies such as PRS and ASCAP, which are owned by both songwriters and publishers. The setup is similar in Ireland, Canada and Australia, while elsewhere in Europe and the Americas, the mechanical societies are similar in structure to performing rights bodies.

The practical result of this difference is that the mechanical rights bodies can seem to be less user-friendly for independent and independently minded publishers, songwriters and small labels. Instead, they tend to frame their rules and mode of activity according to the needs of the major publishers and labels. Nevertheless, the mechanical rights organizations carry out a vital task in licensing record companies and others, collecting royalties from them and distributing the royalties to publishers and songwriters. The basic royalty rate in Britain is 8.5% of the official dealer price of a release. The US rate is based on a fixed amount per track, which changes every year or so.

Britain and America each have one mechanical rights organization with a virtual monopoly of the business. The UK company is the Mechanical Copyright Protection Society (MCPS) while the US company is the Harry Fox Agency (HFA).

As we have seen already, MCPS is nowadays linked closely to PRS in the Music Alliance. This has practical benefits, notably in the registration of copyright songs. When you send a form to PRS, it can also be used for registration of your song with MCPS.

MCPS has two types of contract with record companies, depending on the size of the label. Under what is called the AP1 contract, bigger companies pay twice a year on the basis of actual sales of records to wholesalers and retailers. Small labels, however, must pay for every record pressed when they are pressed. MCPS can enforce this AP2 contract because it has agreements with pressing and duplicating plants that oblige those plants to inform MCPS of all the jobs they undertake. As John Sweeney mentioned in his interview, MCPS does, however, make an exception for records that involve artist/songwriters who are both their own label and their own publisher. If you are in such a position, MCPS does not require you to use its system.

A useful service provided by MCPS is advice on sample clearance. If you intend to use a sample taken from a commercially released track, MCPS can help you to identify the copyright owner of the song. Remember that the law in both the US and the UK requires you to get the permission of the copyright holder of the original song (usually a publisher) and the original recording (usually a label) before you release a track containing a sample.

## THE HARRY FOX AGENCY

The Harry Fox Agency (HFA) is the US equivalent of MCPS, collecting mechanical royalties on behalf of publishers and composers. HFA also represents many smaller US publishers and their writers abroad, notably in Asia, where HFA has set up an office to collect mechanicals from local labels that sell US music under licence.

## COLLECTION SOCIETIES AND RIGHTS ORGANISATIONS FOR LABELS AND ARTISTS

### PPL

In the UK, there is a separate performing right in sound recordings. This is additional to the performing right in the song that is administered by PRS. The organization responsible for licensing users of sound recordings is

PPL (Phonographic Performance Limited). PPL is similar to PRS in that it collects money from those who use recordings, and pays out the money to the owners of the recordings. The payout goes to two categories: record companies and recording artists. PPL splits this money equally between the two categories.

❖❖❖❖❖❖❖❖❖❖❖❖❖❖❖❖❖❖❖❖❖❖❖❖❖❖❖❖❖❖❖❖❖❖❖❖❖❖❖❖❖❖❖❖❖❖

## CLIVE BISHOP

Clive Bishop is director of operations for Phonographic Performance Limited (PPL). He was previously in the business affairs department of Warner Music and spent five years in the advertising industry before joining PPL in 2001.

### What does PPL do within the industry?

We've been around for seventy years and we licence sound recordings for broadcasting and public performance. So essentially we're licensing BBC television and radio and all commercial radio and television stations. In public performance, we licence all the uses of recordings in clubs, shops, etc. So we licence the same people as PRS, but whereas they licence on behalf of composers and publishers we represent the rights owners in sound recordings— who tend to be the record companies—and the performers on those recordings. Our members are about thirty-five hundred record companies from the major companies to small one-person labels. We also collect money due to the performers and pay out to thirty thousand of them, mostly British.

### How does the licensing system work?

The broadcast area is totally different from the public performance area. The BBC is our biggest licensee. They pay one lump sum a year, which allows them to play as much of our sound recording repertoire on all their stations. They send us details of all the tracks they broadcast, and the date and time they were used. Based on this, we divide up the money they pay by station and then divide that amount by the number of tracks played on each station. So we come up with a figure of the amount money per second of airplay. To give you one example, we allocate about £30 for a three-minute play on BBC Radio 1. With commercial stations, only the very large ones are legally obliged to provide PPL with 24/7 reports of what they play.

### How is the money divided up between record companies and performers?

Half goes to the rights owner and the other half is divided between all the musicians who contributed to that track. If it's a track with orchestral backing, the number of performers could be as many as sixty or seventy. Generally, the featured performer gets 65% of this money. The featured performer is the artist or group that is named as the recording artist on the CD. The other 35% is divided among the session musicians on that track.

### What about the public performance sector?

There are tariffs to be paid by the various types of music user. For example, a background music license for a small shop or restaurant would cost about £100 a year depending on size. There's a full list of tariffs available on the PPL Web site. As for distribution of that money, wherever possible we like to have reports of actual usage. Obviously, we won't get that from shops, restaurants and bars. So to decide on distribution methods, we have a committee made up of record company and performers representatives. It normally involves using analogies from other sources, for example, radio stations. If the money is from a club specialising in dance music, we'll use the music played on dance music radio stations or shows as the basis for distribution.

### And does PPL have a role in collecting money when UK records are played on radio or TV overseas?

We do offer a service relating to about twenty countries that have similar collection organisations to ourselves. The bigger record companies will usually have their own offices there or a local licensee to collect for them. So our service mainly appeals to the smaller independent labels and a broad spectrum of performers. We talk about it in terms of a pipeline. We have been laying the pipework in recent years, making agreements with the foreign organisations. When that's finished, we can turn on the tap and the income flows. It's quite an automatic process.

## How can labels and performers from the United States benefit from the PPL system?

Basically, PPL can only pay out to countries where the industry has the same public performance rights as the UK. Although we have a reciprocal arrangement with SoundExchange in the US for digital radio and Web-casting royalties, unfortunately, the US cannot reciprocate our terrestrial broadcasting and public performance rights. However, PPL still licenses repertoire recorded in the US if UK companies release it in the UK. And that UK rights owner receives 100% of the money when that repertoire is used. Whether any of that money finds it way to the US recording artist would be a matter for the UK or US label, not PPL. The only way a US artist could directly get paid from money collected by PPL would be if they had actually made their recording in a qualifying country such as Sweden, where there are the same rights as in the UK. The Swedish sister organisation of PPL would then pay them.

## If I have just started a label, when should I join PPL? After my label's first release is out?

No, that could be too late, because PPL can only licence the works of its members. So if your record is getting airplay before you join, we didn't licence that airplay and can't pay you anything for it. You should join as soon as you have a sound recording you have rights in. You can join before you release it. And it's free to join. The membership forms are on the Web site. We deduct our costs from what we pay you.

## How do I make sure I get paid if I'm a performer on a recording that's been released or about to be released?

PPL pays performers directly but the first point is that if your record label hasn't joined PPL, you won't get paid. So a conscientious artist or artist manager must make sure the company releasing your repertoire is a member. But you register for payment separately. You can come directly to PPL to join or you can join one of the performers' organisations, which will take care of this for you. We are working with those organisations in a Performers Alliance to streamline the process. The record company should provide full information on performers on each track to our CatCo database. You can go online to check the listing, and if your name is not there you can make a claim to PPL. You need to prove you were on that track, say, by showing your name was listed on the album sleeve or booklet.

**And what about payment when music videos are broadcast?**

We have a separate division called VPL (Video Performance Ltd.) for this. But the money we collect is only for the rights owner, i.e., the record company. Under UK law, the music video is defined as a film and performers don't have a legal entitlement to share in any public performance payments.

✦✦✦✦✦✦✦✦✦✦✦✦✦✦✦✦✦✦✦✦✦✦✦✦✦✦✦✦✦✦✦✦✦✦✦✦✦✦✦✦✦✦✦✦✦✦✦✦

As Clive Bishop says, recording artists must either register directly with PPL or become members of a society set up to collect money from PPL on behalf of musicians. At the time of writing, the two competing societies for recording musicians were PAMRA (Performing Artist's Media Rights Association) and AURA (Association of United Recording Artists). However, there are moves to co-ordinate the activities of these bodies, and by the time you read this, the system for musicians to register for payments from PPL may have changed. Check with the PPL Web site to find out the present position.

Again, as Clive points out, US copyright law does not include a general performing rights for sound recordings. Each time the US record industry and artists' unions tried to get Congress to bring in this right, the mighty US radio and TV industry called in its favours from representatives, who voted down the proposal.

## SOUNDEXCHANGE (US)

Despite this, the record industry in the US has started to get some money from so-called digital radio services. These offer twenty-four-hour multichannel music, usually as part of a cable television subscription package. The industry is also legally entitled to money from Internet companies, such as Webcasters. In 2000, an organization called SoundExchange was set up to collect money for these uses of music. SoundExchange is jointly owned by the RIAA (Recording Industry Association of America), A²IM (Association for Independent Music), the AFM (American Federation of Musicians) and AFTRA (American Federation of Television and Radio Artists). Next, John L. Simson, its executive director, explains more about SoundExchange.

## JOHN L. SIMSON

**What is SoundExchange, and how does it relate to other collection societies?**

SoundExchange is a performance rights organisation that licenses, collects and distributes royalties earned by the performers and copyright owners of sound recordings from digital, satellite and Internet radio services. We're similar to an ASCAP or BMI or SESAC, except they collect on behalf of the songwriter and the music publisher based on the song, and we collect for the artist and the label based on the actual recording. We work with the other collection societies on outreach efforts, such as copyright education. But we administer completely separate and distinct rights. Performers and owners of master recordings still need to sign up with us as well as the others.

In the UK, Phonographic Performance Ltd. (PPL) does what we do but their rights are greater than ours. They collect fees from the BBC and all other broadcasters, as well as any club or doctor's office that plays recorded music. In the US, we only have the right to collect on digital transmissions, so our royalty pool is much smaller but it's growing dramatically. With the rise of satellite (for example, Sirius and XM) and Internet radio, our revenues have gone in five years from $10 million a year to $40 million in 2005. We have a reciprocal arrangement in place with PPL, which means that a British label or artist member of that organisation would be able to get royalties collected by us. However, if anyone wants to, they can sign up directly with us to receive their royalties. It's free to join and all the forms needed are available at the Web site (Soundexchange.com).

**Tell us more about the organisation's history and how it's structured.**

We were originally built by the RIAA and then spun-off as a nonprofit in September 2003. These were the only people able to underwrite an entity like ours, as they would collect enough royalties to justify the expenditure. Knowing that this revenue stream was going to grow, we were very fortunate that the labels invested so that we could build a system. We did our first distribution in November 2001. We've processed over six hundred million distinct performances down to the individual track level. We have one of five systems recognised by the IFPI capable of doing track-level distribution, so that younger, smaller collecting societies that want to help can reach out to us and we will help them.

As a trade association and nonprofit organisation, we have no real owner. We represent the owners of copyrights and the performers of those copyrights. The board of directors is made up of nine artists or artist representatives, and nine labels or their reps. It's a very diverse board, with one rep from each of the major label groups, and the head of the new trade organisation representing independent labels, called the American Association of Independent Music ($A^2IM$), and two other independent label reps. There are six reps from the major labels and RIAA sector and three from the independent sector, which mirrors the collection breakdown—about two-thirds to the majors and one-third to the independents.

### How do you gather data on digital transmissions?

On a monthly basis, we get complete playlists from the satellite channels and many of the major services. So XM and Sirius send us complete lists, as do DMX and Muzak, which are cable or digital TV channels that play music. Web-casters have a different obligation based on the rules of the US Copyright Office. We wanted full playlists from them too, but they are only required to send us two weeks of every quarter, and it hasn't been specified what format it needs to be sent in. It could be on an envelope written in crayon. So we're working with the Copyright Office and licensees to establish the electronic format that we need to have.

Any of the larger services that are computer-savvy understand the easy ways to make this kind of playlist information available to us, but there are some political issues involved. The Web-casters say that if they're going to give us full census data then they want something in exchange; while we're saying that they're obligated to tell us what they're playing. They say that they only tell ASCAP and BMI three days out of every quarter; we say that was based on radio and that's basically the same thirty songs over and over again, while the Internet has tons of stations and they're playing a much wider variety of songs. So sampling will especially disenfranchise the smaller artists who are getting bits of play but not much. We've been fighting to get this, and it's the battle that I think matters in the data world, because we should be paying out accurately and the only way to do that is with complete information.

On the Web-casting side, there's still a lot of work in progress, in terms of how it affects distribution. Our members are keen on full census data because when they get a statement it tells them everything. Major label statements can be over three thousand pages. We have to aggregate the data, because when the rules were being negotiated the Web-casters said their playlists should be proprietary so that other people couldn't copy them. We thought this was bogus, but the Copyright Office accepted the Web-casters' argument.

## How will you cope with new technologies as they arise, for example, podcasts?

We've built a system that can essentially handle any kind of license or any kind of service. However, in the US, Web-casting and satellite radio are under a compulsory license, which means that they can play anything they want as long as they're paying and abiding by the rules of the statute. The only problem is that this is a streamed technology. If reproductions are being left on someone's computer as a download, then it falls outside of our mandate. Podcasts leave a reproduction, so they're really a download service and not a real radio service, so it's not us. We get revenues from iTunes radio streams, but not from the sales of downloads from iTunes. To do that, you need permission from the copyright owner and a negotiated deal. With us, they just take a statutory license and start playing.

## What advice do you have for young bands regarding collecting royalties?

Well, I dropped out of college to sign a record deal, went to London in 1971 to record my first album, and opened for Jethro Tull on the *Aqualung* tour in Albany, New York. Four thousand people yelling, 'You suck, we want Tull!' After that I went to law school and started managing bands. So I know how hard it is to break through. From my perspective, young bands need to know that there are all these new ways to generate revenue, and they need to exploit all of them. Our revenue stream is one that's a no-brainer, because any Web-caster can play your stuff once it comes out so you may as well be collecting the royalties that are due you. You have a choice with the use of your music on television or in films because those are negotiated deals, but for us there's no choice.

There's an organisation in the US called Alliance of Artists and Record Companies (AARC), and they collect a small stream of money in compensation for the private copying of recordings, maybe $4 million a year. Only $200 of it might be yours, but you know what, it's your money, so get it. If it pays for the van for the tour that week, then you should get it. I remember from when I did it, that it's not just the money from the gig, or from how many CDs I sold, or this much from T-shirts, or a small royalty cheque from someone else. All that money goes into a pool, and that's what keeps you from having to wait tables. So I'm very much a believer that you should be on top of these new sources of revenue and making sure you're collecting from them. Also, be careful when someone offers to get them for you. Think about what it's going to cost them to get the royalties for you, and what you have to give up in exchange. We've heard about people taking a fee for signing a band up with SoundExchange, and it's free and involves filling out two pieces of paper! Understand that everyone has to pay their costs, whether it's ASCAP or PPL in the UK. We have to collect the money, and from that we take our administrative costs off the top, about 15%, and distribute the rest. You have to expect that, because it's expensive to do what we do, but it's cheaper to do it for the entire industry than if individuals did it themselves.

◆◆◆◆◆◆◆◆◆◆◆◆◆◆◆◆◆◆◆◆◆◆◆◆◆◆◆◆◆◆◆◆◆◆◆◆◆◆◆◆◆◆◆◆◆◆◆

# INDUSTRY ASSOCIATIONS

We round off this part of the book with a brief review of a number of music industry bodies that you need to be aware of—and in some cases may decide to join.

These bodies exist to represent the common interests of companies or individuals in various parts of the industry. The most relevant ones are those that operate on behalf of professional musicians, songwriters, record labels and music publishers. Contact details can be found in the Toolkit section of this book.

## MUSICIANS' UNIONS

There are long-standing trade unions in both the US and UK catering to the needs of musicians. In both cases, however, the approach of the union has been felt by younger musicians to be somewhat old-fashioned, with priority given to such groups as classical orchestras and hotshot session players in the film and TV industries.

In Britain, the Musicians' Union (MU) has tried to counter this view by appointing a Music Business Officer geared to the contemporary scene and able to offer free advice to members on such issues as management and record contracts. The MU has also clarified its role in relation to DJs and (rather belatedly) stated that dance music DJs are eligible to join. Apart from free advice, the benefits of membership include good deals on insurance for instruments and other equipment, and legal backup when, for example, you are faced with a promoter who won't pay you for a gig you played.

The US union is the American Federation of Musicians (AFM). Both it and the MU have numerous local branches whose secretaries work part-time or full-time sorting out problems for union members. The AFM offers similar benefits to those provided by the MU. Next, we hear from officials of both unions, starting with the UK organisation.

✦✦✦✦✦✦✦✦✦✦✦✦✦✦✦✦✦✦✦✦✦✦✦✦✦✦✦✦✦✦✦✦✦✦✦✦✦✦✦✦✦✦✦✦✦✦✦

## NIGEL MCCUNE

Nigel McCune has been the music business officer of the UK Musicians' Union (MU) since 1998. Before that, he had been a promoter for London venues and local councils and an assessor for the Arts Council of applications for music subsidies.

### What role does the MU play in the industry?
We are first and foremost a trade union, not a service organisation or a trade association. Others spend a lot of effort on increasing the amount of music in the UK, whether in clubs, pubs or schools. This is all good news but somebody needs to be there to make sure the musicians actually doing that work are properly paid for it. That's where the MU comes in. Our members decide our priorities through our democratic structure. Then with the strength of our thirty thousand members behind us, we can negotiate pay rates for sessions or freelance orchestra players and we have a voice that's heard by the government, local authorities and other industry bodies.

### What type of musicians do you represent?
All kinds. A lot of what we do is bespoke to the contemporary music industry. We also have specialist sections for session musicians, freelance orchestral players, folk, jazz, writers of music and teachers. A lot of our members find teaching is a necessary part of the portfolio of work they have to create to survive and thrive. All the sections advise the union about their special problems.

### Why would a young musician, just starting out on a professional career, join the MU?

There's a whole host of reasons. The most tangible are benefits from insurance and legal advice. Immediately upon joining, everyone gets £10 million worth of public liability insurance. So if their speaker stack collapses at a gig and crushes, say, a small dog, the band is covered. There's also £1,000 worth of equipment insurance to be used against specific items that might get stolen or damaged. In addition, any contract a member is offered can be sent to the union and we will have it checked out by our lawyers free of charge. Then we have a partnership advice service. Whenever musicians are working together, as a band, DJ remix team or classical ensemble, it's important to make sure that none of them is responsible for another's debts or tax bills, etc. Our latest scheme is a registration of works service whereby members send examples of their own work on CD to us for safe storage so that it can be produced in any future dispute over ownership of copyright.

### So any member can come to you for help with a problem?

Yes. Probably the biggest benefit of joining the union is that we can help when a member gets ripped off—that's when, not if! When they're not paid for a gig or there's a royalty statement that doesn't add up or a contract they've signed in error, the union will take it up on their behalf. We pursue hundreds if not thousands of claims every year and recover hundreds of thousands of pounds in unpaid fees or royalties.

### What qualifications does a musician need to join?

None! We don't do auditions or anything like that. We aren't a talent agency. People join the MU because they want to, because they see it as essential to their career as a musician.

### Can DJs or vocalists join, as well as instrumentalists?

Yes, DJs are warmly welcomed now, although at one point the union made a distinction between ordinary club DJs and remixers—people who were manipulating sounds. But that became problematic and now we don't exclude any DJs and we have services in place for them, such as samples of remix contracts and standard DJ engagement contracts. As for vocalists, opera singers and singers in stage musicals generally find the actors union Equity to be their natural home. But vocalists in pop and rock groups, particularly those who write their own material, would find themselves better served by joining the MU or even joining both unions.

---

**How does the union communicate with the members as a whole?**
We have a very comprehensive Web site containing vast amounts of information, a magazine for members and every member gets a searchable directory on CD-ROM and as a printed book. It lists all members by instrument in every region of Britain. If a member is in the north of England and their drummer is stranded somewhere down south, they can use the directory to locate a local musician to deputise.

**What do you see the main challenges for musicians in the next five or ten years?**
There are various issues connected with the growing mobility of members these days. Already, I spend a lot of time on problems musicians are facing in transporting musicians by air. Then there is the high cost of visas to work in the United States and the difficulties of trying to qualify for a visa. Other international issues include those around international copyright directives and European law concerning health and safety regarding noise limits and other areas.

The other area that is growing in importance is rights, especially with regard to recordings and broadcasts and films. Because it is relatively easy and cheap to self-produce CDs, rights are at the forefront of people's thinking. But in many cases, upfront payments are relatively small. Musicians are persuaded to accept contracts with small payments on the promise of future payments from PRS, PPL and the other collection societies. The union has a role in making sure these work to the advantage of musicians and now, for example, our general secretary is a board member of PPL.

+++++++++++++++++++++++++++++++++++++++++++++++++

+++++++++++++++++++++++++++++++++++++++++++++++++

## TOM LEE

Tom Lee is president of the American Federation of Musicians (AFM), the major trades union representing musicians in North America. Tom Lee's career as a professional musician was mainly spent with the United States Marine Band in Washington, DC, where he reached the rank of Master Gunnery Sergeant. When he retired after twenty-four years, he had played piano for every president from Lyndon Johnson to George Bush senior. During this time, he was elected to the local AFM executive board in Washington, DC, and became the international organisation's president in 2001.

## What does the AFM do?

We represent approximately one hundred thousand musicians in the US and Canada, and have about two hundred and forty different locals throughout. These locals negotiate symphony orchestra contracts, theatre contracts, and small contracts for ballet shows or opera and, in addition, if there's any electronic media that's recording the music, say, television, they administer contracts in those areas. If it's just local television, they negotiate contracts. On the federation level, we negotiate national agreements, such as a recording contract that would cover all of the US and Canada, motion picture and television contracts, National Public Radio for the US, jingle agreements. All that and more.

## What are the benefits of being an AFM member?

Consider background musicians in the recording business in Nashville as an example. You play one or two sessions a day with an artist who sells a lot of recordings, and at the end of the year a certain amount of money from each one of the those recordings goes into a fund, and that money is divided up among all of those musicians who recorded that year on the basis of how many sessions they did. So if fifteen million dollars are collected, you take all the musicians and the number of sessions they did and, according to a weighted formula, those musicians will receive compensation for the next five years. Those who did the most sessions will receive a significantly higher payout than others. If you're in the motion picture industry and a film that you played on the score for goes into a new medium, such as DVD, 1% of the gross that is collected goes into a fund for motion picture musicians. So if you put 'Somewhere over the Rainbow' on a DVD, those musicians who recorded it originally make money from each DVD sold, whoever they were, and if they're not still alive their estates can collect money. In Los Angeles, we have a certain number of people who do a lot of movie scoring, so after twenty-five years of doing that, you can sometimes have significant amounts of money coming in from this fund.

## What about rock bands and independents in the industry? Are they members?

We have members from every genre, whether it's jazz, rock or blues, Top 40, or cover bands. The individuals in practically every major rock group would be members of our organisation.

**What is your relationship to other music organisations, like the Recording Industry Association of America or the Grammys?**

We're a big supporter and sponsor of the Grammys and the Future of Music Coalition. Regarding the RIAA, we're involved with it on a number of different legislative issues. We also have what we called a CEO retreat, which is when the leadership of the RIAA, NARAS, publishing companies, the performing rights organisations, Gospel Music Association, Country Music Association, and National Association of Record Merchandisers (NARM) meet up to discuss issues facing the whole industry. We are working closely with every other music organisation in order to effect legislative matters that will best help our industry.

**You mentioned funds for session musicians and motion pictures. Are there any other funds of that nature?**

We have a new use fund which covers such things as the TV broadcast of a movie.

We collect money for that and distribute it to the session musicians. If a pop group's music is put on a CD, not only do we collect a session fee for the musicians on the CD but there's also a new-use fee for that. If a TV show is rebroadcast, we collect money for that. There is now an intellectual property right for musicians and artists on recordings, not just for the recording companies, and we are now beginning to collect money that has been legislatively addressed. I serve on two boards in relation to this. One is the AFM Afterfund, which collects money on behalf of background musicians, and the other is SoundExchange, which collects money on behalf of artists from digital streams. We do other things as well. We have a national referral program on our Web site, so that if you're the father of a bride in San Francisco but need to find a band in another city where your daughter is getting married, you can go on the site and look for bands there.

**Why is now a good time to be a member of a musicians' union?**

It's more important now than ever for professional musicians to be members of a collective group that can lobby on their behalf. Musicians have a terrible time getting healthcare, so we are the largest entertainment union for musicians that lobby on Capitol Hill on behalf of healthcare for musicians. We want to expand this to intellectual property rights, so that if you're a young band and you create an album, we're going to collect money for you as long as you're a member and you follow our advice on how to protect your rights. We're also working to have a performer's rights that goes across the board, like you have in the UK, such that any time a record is played on the radio you collect money for the musicians that played on that track. There are so many issues that affect musicians, that if you're not part of a group that's working on your behalf you're going to get left behind. If we fail, it's going to be tougher for musicians to make it in this industry.

+++++++++++++++++++++++++++++++++++++++++++++++++++

## SONGWRITERS' ORGANISATIONS

The professional organizations for composers and songwriters are the Songwriters Guild of America (SGA) and the British Association of Composers and Songwriters (BACS). The relevance of such bodies is that, unlike the performing rights organizations, they exist solely to represent the views and interests of songwriters (not publishers).

The SGA is more practically oriented, helping its members to collect royalties, administer the publishing of their songs and operating an 'estate administration' service. The latter is useful after your death, when your heirs will continue to enjoy royalties from your songs for another seventy years!

In Britain, BACS offers business affairs workshops for budding writers and songwriting and promotional workshops where publishers and veteran writers give you instant feedback on your compositions. BACS publicity says it's 'not for the fainthearted'!

BACS is also the organiser of the Ivor Novello Awards for the best British songs of each year.

## RECORD LABEL GROUPS

There are bodies representing the interests of independent labels and distributors on both sides of the Atlantic. The US organization used to be known as NAIRD but a few years ago it changed its name to the American Federation of Independent Music ($A^2IM$). Indie labels can join for $300, and on its Web site there's a detailed account of what $A^2IM$ offers.

In Britain, the Association of Independent Music (AIM) was set up in 1998 and soon became an important player in the industry, taking some bold initiatives in the area of online marketing and Web-casting, while the majors were still floundering about and trying to decide whether Napster and mp3s were devils or angels. At the time of writing, it had over six hundred labels as members and if you have your own label, or are thinking of setting one up, we recommend that you make contact with AIM. The one-off joining fee for AIM is £100.

Some of the larger indies in both the US and Britain are also members of two other record industry organizations, the Recording Industry Association of America (RIAA) and the British Phonographic Industry (BPI). However, it is generally recognised that these bodies and their international equivalent, IFPI (International Federation of the Recording Industry), are basically the mouthpieces of the major companies. Their chairmen and presidents are usually current or past senior executives of such companies as Universal, Warners, EMI or Sony BMG, and their priorities are not always those of indie companies. Indeed, that's why A²IM. and AIM exist: to give a clear and separate voice for indies. That said, there is general co-operation between the various record industry organizations, especially when it comes to issues like piracy or the need for clear laws on Internet music.

Next we hear from the president of the US body.

✦✦✦✦✦✦✦✦✦✦✦✦✦✦✦✦✦✦✦✦✦✦✦✦✦✦✦✦✦✦✦✦✦✦✦✦✦✦✦✦✦✦✦✦✦✦✦✦

## DON ROSE

Don Rose, the inaugural president of the American Association of Independent Music (A²IM), has been in the music industry since the early 1970s. He ran record stores and a management company before he co-founded the Rykodisc record company. After a stint with Chris Blackwell's Palm Pictures in London in the early 2000s, during which time he was on the international committee of the Association of Independent Music (AIM), Don was recruited by the founders of A²IM to head up the new US trade association.

### Who makes up the membership of A²IM?
We went public in June of 2005, and within a few months we had over a hundred labels signed up as members. To be a regular member, you have to be in the business of producing and marketing recorded music. We also have an associate non-voting member program for other kinds of companies in the sector, such as distributors, digital distributors, retailers, law firms, manufacturers, etc. Not all of these associate members are completely independent per se. They're not voting members but they're doing business with the community and wish to support it. Even labels distributed by majors are very welcome to join. For example, we have Fontana as a member, and

they're wholly owned by Universal. Individuals aren't able to be full members, but we'll find a category for you if you wish to support the organization and the community.

## Was A²IM inspired by the UK's AIM?

It was, and there's a lot of need out there. But it's a difficult community to organise. They're not joiners; they're independent by nature. So it really takes a sort of cataclysmic event, which in this industry these days is all the digital issues and the transition to a digital economy, to bring them together. And independents see a lot of upside in these times, and a lot of headroom—a level playing field with a lot more access. On the other hand, precedents are being set, and we need indies to speak with a common voice in order to avert some bad precedents. For example, it's generally true that the digital download services pay the major record companies more per track than they pay to independent labels, even though the consumer price is the same. That's the kind of precedent that's particularly offensive to our community because it says that because you're small, your music is worth less. Our goal is to let the market set the value, but on the basis of the value of the music, not on the size of the gatekeeper.

## Is this the same with legislative and lobbying efforts? What's your relationship to the Recording Industry Association of America, which represents the interests of the major international companies?

It depends on the issue. There are some issues where we agree with the RIAA, and others where we'll stand aside without a position. For example, in the Grokster case in front of the Supreme Court in the summer of 2005, we neither supported nor opposed either side because there was such divergent opinion within our membership on that question. We don't have to have a position on everything. We exist to promote a common voice where such a thing exists. In the future, we may end up in opposition to the RIAA, but we are not specifically constituted as the anti-RIAA. We just have a different constituency.

## What are the major areas you focus on?

There's three basic avenues. Our fair-play agenda includes the digital market precedents I mentioned earlier, our legislative agenda involves lobbying the lawmakers as a trade group and then there's our service agenda, in which we can negotiate with other bodies on behalf of all our members. Right now this third part is young and underfunded, but it will include things like group health insurance, perhaps negotiated rates with FedEx, and certainly the Web site is intended to be a robust data and research source.

### How is A²IM funded?

By annual dues from our membership, based on a sliding scale related to market share. The founders (among them TVT and Roadrunner) have contributed two years of dues in advance. We also have Beggars Banquet, which was instrumental in setting up AIM in the UK. I was on the international committee of AIM when I lived in London. We don't have a formalized relationship with the UK AIM, but there's an ongoing dialogue. We're friendly cousins.

### Why is now an especially important time for indies to work together?

It's urgent now because of the changing rules related to the digital world. The sector desperately needs a seat at the table, as those rules are written by a complex organism that includes digital distributors, media companies such as Yahoo! and MSN, the labels big and small, music publishers, and the courts. It's a very interesting time. There is no specific group that has been empowered to write these rules; it's a matter of give and take and tugging and posturing. We need to have our interests represented in the discussions.

### Any last words of advice for people wanting to start an indie label themselves?

A lot of the benefits of what we're doing are going to trickle across the sector anyway, but it's very important to share ideas. You're not really competing with each other, you're competing with big record companies, with video games and movies and television and everything else. There can be a lot of camaraderie among the indies, especially at the startup level, and that's good to know.

+++++++++++++++++++++++++++++++++++++++++++++++++++++

# MUSIC PUBLISHER GROUPS

Finally, we should briefly mention the organisations devoted to the interests of music publishers. The principal bodies are the National Music Publishers Association (NMPA) in the US and the Music Publishers Association (MPA) in Britain. If you have a fully fledged publishing company, you might want to check them out. But rather like the RIAA and BPI, these organizations tend to be dominated by the publishing arms of the majors and other mega-publishers like Famous Music and Peermusic. There are also other bodies with some independent publishers as members in both Britain and the US, but they seem to be less active and less relevant to startup companies than their record label counterparts.

## GOVERNMENT AND CHARITABLE ORGANISATIONS

Youth Music (sometimes known as the National Foundation for Youth Music) provides and funds music-making opportunities for young people up to the age of eighteen who live in areas of social and economic need in the UK. It gives opportunities for children and young people to work with skilled musicians in their communities so that they can develop their skills, confidence and feel for music, from singing to performing to recording.

✦✦✦✦✦✦✦✦✦✦✦✦✦✦✦✦✦✦✦✦✦✦✦✦✦✦✦✦✦✦✦✦✦✦✦✦✦✦✦✦✦✦✦✦✦✦✦

## TREVOR MASON

Trevor Mason, the London regional co-ordinator for Youth Music, explains how young people can apply for funding for musical projects and what sort of projects it accepts. Trevor joined Youth Music in 2003 after working for Arts Council England as a Music Officer. His job entails advising applicants to Youth Music's funding programmes and guidance on Youth Music's objectives, criteria and priorities. Youth Music's twelve regional co-ordinators promote the work of Youth Music at a grassroots level, gathering information and contacts and acting as the link between the community and head office.

### What is Youth Music?
Youth Music is about all sorts of music for all sorts of children and young people—country to concertos, folk to funk, garage to gamelan, jazz to jungle, rap to ragga, songs to symphonies.

Youth Music is an innovative and independent charity which was set up in 1999 with £30 million of Lottery funding by the government Department for Culture, Media & Sport. It provides music-making opportunities for children and young people up to the age of eighteen who live in areas of social and economic need. It distributes £10 million per year of Lottery funding on behalf of Arts Council England to support music-making activities for young people across the UK. It does this by providing information and encouragement, as well as providing money. It aims to have reached three million by 2010. It has set up thirty Youth Music Action Zones across England, Scotland and Wales and funded thousands of projects to create music in each local area.

Youth Music wants to make a difference where there are few chances for young people to make music in their community, mostly outside school hours. To this end, it has established contact with many young people's organisations which concentrate on music, as well as those which include music as part of their work or are developing a musical tradition or culture. Youth Music's advice and support services are provided free to all organisations and individuals wishing to access its funds.

Through its Youth Music Action Zones (YMAZ), open programmes, Partnership Programmes and special initiatives, Youth Music has developed and implemented a UK-wide strategy in support of youth music-making that will:

+ Establish a legacy of music-making opportunities
+ Improve overall standards of music-making
+ Champion the value of music-making—proving that music has a positive effect on children and young people
+ Establish music-making opportunities as a force for regeneration in communities

## Who gets help from Youth Music?

Under the terms and conditions by which Youth Music is supported, it cannot send funds directly to individuals. This means that individual musicians who have identified a local need must collaborate with an organisation or group of organisations that want to support the initiative and that will become the fundholder for the life of the project if an award is made. The artistic leadership would remain with the music maker. Therefore, all applicants applying for funds from Youth Music need to be formally constituted in some way. This is to make sure that grants awarded are properly managed and that the fund is properly safeguarded. Youth Music invests mostly in music-making activities and not in equipment or instruments.

There are a number of different structures for organisations, from formal, legal ones to less formal. It is recommended that if you decide to go along the less formal route you have a set of written rules to show how you will operate and who takes responsibility for what. You may find that there are benefits in having something more formal than this, particularly if you are going to go on to do more projects in the future. Under the terms of the Lottery Directions, Youth Music is only able to make awards to organisations which are not intended for private gain. Youth Music also only funds organisations that can supply its last set of accounts.

Youth Music recognises, however, the need to offer support to people who want practical, hands-on experience to become leaders of music-making activities. There are already a substantial number of senior people working in music who provide an outstanding service by creating a setting for children and young people in which they can develop music skills. In all of Youth Music's programmes, high-quality musical leadership is a fundamental ingredient in developing musical confidence and expertise.

To ensure continuity and sustainability of programmes and schemes throughout the country (not only ones supported by Youth Music), it is essential that established and confident music leaders (sometimes known as animateurs) are asked and enabled to hand on their skills to younger people. To this end, where appropriate, Youth Music's funding programmes include opportunities for music leaders to help develop the skills of trainees simultaneously with the activities that are designed to enable children and young people to get to grips with music-making. The idea of working with trainees should not dominate the project in any way. The principal focus must be on music and children or young people. The handing on of skills as well as the benefit of having an 'extra pair of hands' should be an asset to a proposed project, not a burden.

It is widely acknowledged that involvement in music making improves learning and individual development, particularly where the involvement is from an early age. Youth Music funds programmes and schemes which support music making in a wide range of settings, including community centres, youth clubs, venues, village halls, schools, etc. where music making can be introduced and developed amongst young people who otherwise may not have the opportunity. Youth Music's funding complements music in the National Curriculum and it is quite common for Youth Music funded projects to be free to participants.

### How do young people apply for help?
Youth Music will consider applications from single organisations (except individual schools) or those (including groups of schools) who prefer to club together to make a consortium. A consortium can be made up of groups that are either similar or different to each other. For example, a group of schools clubbing together with an arts centre and a local band can make a consortium, as can a choir and a circuit of youth clubs. By creating a consortium, there is sure to be a more widespread effect on a locality.

Finding partners who will support your initiative will depend on local circumstances. You may already have contacts in the organisation which you feel will benefit and so the first step would be to talk to a person who works there. You might also find leads, especially if you are building a network. Those who should be able to offer advice about connections and contacts include your local council's Arts or Youth officers, workers at your regional office of Arts Council England and Local Education Authority.

In order to gain funding, an application form (downloadable from the YM Web site) needs to be completed and submitted to Youth Music. The form helps you to provide all the information Youth Music needs to complete an assessment of your bid for funding and to ensure it is consistent in its decision-making. Many people struggle with forms; they are put off by the apparent bureaucracy, but it's important to see them as giving a structure to your application—that will help Youth Music to assess your project fairly.

Along with the application form there are accompanying guidelines, or Hot Tips (also downloadable from the Web site). The Hot Tips explain a complicated question in terms that are easier to understand and give you a better 'feel' for what sort of activity and projects Youth Music wishes to fund. Youth Music operates three open programmes—First Steps, Vocalise and Make It Sound. To get the most up-to-date information about these programmes visit the Youth Music Web site (www.youthmusic.org.uk). For financial support, Youth Music will measure applications against the relevant Hot Tips.

### What sorts of projects are funded by Youth Music?

Youth Music funds opportunities for children and young people to work with skilled musicians in their communities so that they can develop their skills, confidence and feel for music. Running workshops, including collective music making, experimentation, playing, singing, recording, performing, listening and valuing the work of others, is all part of a Youth Music project. Youth Music supports imaginative and long-lasting proposals using a wide range of musical styles, cultures or genres. Such activity can take place as breakfast clubs, lunchtime workshops, and after-school clubs, at weekends or during school holidays.

The list is almost endless, but by way of illustration Youth Music can fund activity in the following music genres: African/Caribbean, Asian Classical, Asian Fusion, Blues, Choral, Country, Folk, Funk, Garage, Gospel, Hip-hop, Indie/Alternative, Japanese/Chinese, Modern Jazz, Opera/Music Theatre, Pop, R&B, Reggae, Rock, Samba/South American, Traditional Jazz, and Western Classical.

Projects should aim to provide children with access to as wide a range of music making opportunities as possible so that they are able to make an informed choice about their musical direction in the future. Experiencing and joining in a wide range of creative music making helps to develop an *ear* for music. Youth Music wishes to see children and young people very much involved in determining the direction of their music making developments, drawing on the diverse musical styles, cultural traditions, and different approaches to learning.

Music making takes place in various ways. These can be summarised as:

**Formal**—organised through statutory provision—schools, colleges, music services

**Nonformal**—activities that take place outside of the formal settings, for example, youth and community settings. These are usually supervised by adult professionals or volunteers

**Informal**—activities that young people organise and lead themselves without supervision

Each project provides an opportunity for people to get together and share skills, knowledge and ideas. Projects also train individual teachers, music students and youth group leaders working with children and young people (as trainees). Each project can be led by up to four music leaders who can come from a range of musical backgrounds but must inspire creative ideas and encourage anyone who teaches, or is involved in getting children and young people to make music, to approach music making with enthusiasm and confidence.

All projects funded by Youth Music will be expected to demonstrate what has been achieved. You will therefore need to collect information and data (monitoring) about your project which can be used as the basis of your final evaluation report. It is important to collect evidence throughout the project, at the beginning, during and when a project has finished to show the outcomes, what has been learnt and how things can improve in the future. Youth Music will also want to see that funding has been well used and to inform them of the effectiveness and value of particular funding programmes.

### What's a YMAZ?

Youth Music Action Zones work in areas of social and economic need and areas of rural isolation, creating musical opportunities for young people who are hard to reach. Each YMAZ is made up of a consortium of established, experienced music deliverers, linking together organisations from the public, voluntary and private sectors. Each YMAZ has a unique locally designed 'feel', and all music, artistic and social decisions are decided by local people.

They provide the bedrock for a strong and influential structure of support for youth music. Each YMAZ comprises a consortium of organisations which are able to

+ Deliver a wide range of music activities and encourage cross-over between music styles and genres
+ Provide workshops, rehearsals, performances and one-to-one teaching and mentoring
+ Develop partnerships between music and arts organisations, schools and commit projects to reach more children and young people
+ Co-ordinate and manage the development of music making activities within their zone

There are thirty YMAZs in the Highlands & Islands, Aberdeen & Grampian, Perthshire & Surrounds, Edinburgh & Lothians, Glasgow & Clyde Valley, South of Scotland, North East England, Humber, North Yorkshire, Greater Manchester, Lancashire, Liverpool & Merseyside, Cumbria, Merthyr Tydfil, Ynys Mon, Birmingham, Shropshire & Herefordshire, Staffordshire & Stoke-on-Trent, Corby & Kettering, Lincolnshire, Bristol & Gloucester, Cornwall, Plymouth, Norfolk, Thurrock, Portsmouth & South East Hampshire, South East England, Thanet, Slough, and London.

## What is MusicLeader?
Youth Music commissioned research in 2002 looking into the work, education and training opportunities on offer to professional musicians. The report, 'Creating a Land with Music', found both a need to expand training opportunities and for stronger links to be made between the music industry and training bodies. Young musicians of today, from all backgrounds, need to be trained for the kind of portfolio careers which are increasingly a reality. Youth Music's response to this research is MusicLeader, which aims to support and train the music leaders of the present and future. The initiative operates through regional MusicLeader Networks supported by an online resource, MusicLeader.net.

MusicLeader (www.musicleader.net) offers information on courses, training providers and networking events to support your professional development. You can use this resource to find out more about funding your training, along with information on accredited and nonaccredited learning. Its extensive search facility enables members to browse for information on training courses, training providers, networking events and music makers on a national or regional level. Its online forum can be used to air your views on the message boards, search the jobs section, take part in discussion groups and create your own blog. The forum is a great way to get in touch with people in your field of work and an easy way of networking with people from other sectors. It can also help you to keep up-to-date with the latest news in the youth music sector. Search our case study database for examples of music activities, training programmes and career profiles; download research, reports, tips and guidelines; or get to grips with the jargon buster.

By 2010, MusicLeader aims to have eleven thousand music leaders networked, enabling eleven hundred new practitioners to enter the sector, and provide twenty-five hundred others with skills development opportunities.

### How can I find out more about how Youth Music can help me?
Youth Music helps support hundreds of music projects around the country so there is likely to be one near you. If you visit the Youth Music Web site and click on 'Youth Music in your area' you can search for details of music projects in your local YMAZ. Failing that, you could always contact your local music service and they should be able to help point you in the right direction.

Youth Music's Web site, www.youthmusic.org.uk, offers online services as well as all the latest Youth Music news and events. There are also comprehensive links to other relevant music and funding organisations. Key features include an Events Section, Application Area, Funded Programmes Area, What We Fund, and Media and News sections. It is also home to Sound Station, Youth Music's Web resource for young musicmakers.

Also don't forget to contact your regional co-ordinator, whose details can be found on the Youth Music Web site.

### What other funding is available?
There are also other sources of funding available from organisations such as Arts Council England, Awards for All, Heritage Lottery Fund's Young Roots Programme, Big Lottery Fund's Young People's Fund, Performing Rights Society Foundation, local council grants' programmes and trusts and foundations such as Esmee Fairburn and Paul Hamlyn.

### Why was Youth Music set up?
The Department for Education and Skills (DfES) survey of Local Education Authority Music Services in 2002 found that, on average, 8% of young people in

---

England aged five to sixteen receive regular instrumental or vocal tuition. Of course, the pattern varies across the country, from 1% of pupils to 18%. This is a rather low take-up of subsidised instrumental tuition and confirmed the view that youngsters wish to pursue musical ambitions in a setting that related to music which interested them, rather than forms imposed upon them by the educational hierarchy.

Music Services are run by local education authorities or local authorities, or authority-supported independent organisations. They provide four main services for schools in their area: instrumental or vocal tuition outside of the main school curriculum, usually to individual pupils; out-of-school hours ensembles such as orchestras and choirs; support for classroom music teachers such as training days, advice, resources, instruments; and more recently, project-based activities such as community-based incentives.

Since 1988, the date of the Education Reform Act, cuts in Local Education Authority (LEA) spending, imposed by the Government, combined with the drive towards delegation of funding to schools resulted in a decade of reduction in the funds which helped maintain Music Services. Consequently, Music Service charges to customers rose steeply and an increasing proportion of these costs were paid by parents as LEA subsidy declined. The rise in tuition fees inevitably led to a dramatic drop in the number of school children undertaking instrument tuition through the schools music services. Despite efforts to reverse this trend, take-up levels have not altered dramatically.

The Government's Department for Culture, Media and Sport has recognised that the informal music sector could take a much bigger role in motivating teenagers who have fallen out of mainstream education—and who are, as a result, more likely to be demoralized and turn to drugs and crime. Formal music education, it was felt, often didn't appeal to young people, particularly the less motivated ones, especially when considering how large a part music plays in most teenagers' lives. Similarly, various writers have argued that many young people seek independence from mainstream organisations to give them a sense of authorship and ownership; making it on their own, in the market, is perhaps a critical test of their ability, whether in pop, computer games, design or fashion. Music can connect young people with the adult community to discover genuine artistic talent and address emotional development as a prerequisite for teaching basic skills.

Sound Sense, the UK development agency for community music, defines the informal or 'community' music sector as one that supports 'music that can happen anywhere and with anyone, because a "community" doesn't have to be a geographical one, but can be a group of people who share common interests, experiences or backgrounds'.

Given these developments, the ground was fertile for the launch of Youth Music.

✦✦✦✦✦✦✦✦✦✦✦✦✦✦✦✦✦✦✦✦✦✦✦✦✦✦✦✦✦✦✦✦✦✦✦✦✦✦✦✦✦✦✦✦✦✦✦✦✦✦

# SECTION 5

# TOOLKIT

# glossary

**a cappella**—vocals with no instrumental backing

**acetate**—one-off copy of a vinyl record, often used to test a track in clubs before mass-production

**ADAT**—a digital tape recorder (S-VHS) made by Alesis. Its connection standards have become widely used to link digital equipment.

**advance**—a sum of money that a record company or music publisher will pay to you on signing a record or publishing deal to help you to live while you are working on getting music out to the public. It is paid back out of your royalties.

**AFM (Associated Federation of Musicians)**—union representing musicians in North America

**AIM (Association of Independent Music Ltd.)**—the UK independent record label organization

**ASCAP (American Society of Composers, Authors and Publishers)**—collects money for performance of recorded works on behalf of the owner of the recording copyright and of musicians who play on recordings, for example, on radio, television, etc.

**A&R (artist and repertoire)**—the talent department of a record company

**back-line**—the amps and cabinets, and possibly also the drum kit, needed to play a live gig

**biog**—artist biography giving your musical, gigging, recording and press coverage history

**BMI (Broadcast Music, Inc.)**—acts on behalf of songwriters and music publishers in collecting royalties when music is played on radio, television, etc.

**buy-out**—when a company, for example, a games company, buys a track outright for use on its product rather than pay a royalty rate

**catalogue number**—a reference (usually numbers or letters and numbers) for a single or album used by manufacturers, distributors, retailers and press

**'choc block' terminal strip**—used for the safe connection/extension of bare-ended cables at low current

**click-track**—metronome beat used to keep players in time with sequenced music comping—compiling a recording from various takes on multi-track

**compressor**—processor which controls the maximum amplitude of the incoming signal to level out uneven volumes or to add density to the sound

**cover (version)**—a work played (or recorded) by someone other than the composer or original performer

**co-write**—a song composed by more than one person

**cross-fading**—on DJ mixing consoles, a fade between any two signal sources, usually two turntables

**demo**—a tape or CD of your music that demonstrates your style and ability, but which is not intended to be a releasable finished master recording

**DI box (direct injection box)**—converts between high-impedance (line) and low-impedance (mic) signals. Often gives signal-splitting and ground (earth) lift facilities.

**digi-pak**—paper-based alternative to the plastic CD box

**distributor**—the link between the record label and/or artist and the shops. For a charge, a distributor will sell in records to shops around the country, then physically deliver them to the shops.

**drop-in**—when a recording of a performance is kept until just before a mistake, then a new performance is recorded over it until the whole performance is approved

**dub plate**—see acetate

**EQ (equalization)**—tone controls, from simple bass and treble boost/cut to sections which control frequency, amplitude, bandwidth and shape of the effect very specifically

**filtered plug or plugboard**—three-pin, thirteen-amp connections which reduce or cancel the effects of sudden power surges, clicks and spurious electrical signals

**foldback monitor**—speaker system which allows musicians onstage to hear themselves and each other

**graphic**—an equalizer which affects preset frequency bands using a row of faders. These give a visual representation of the emphasis curve being applied.

**instrument jack**—quarter-inch mono connector used for line-level connections

**ISP (Internet service provider)**—for example, AOL, Freeserve

**jingle**—short piece of music for a commercial or TV channel identification (ident)

**lacquer**—metal plate cut by a mastering suite for vinyl production. There is one for each side of the record. The pressing plant will make its master plates from these.

**MCPS (Mechanical Copyright Protection Society)**—collects money in the UK for the use of composers' rights. Composers can register free. Those making a record have a legal requirement to register in advance their wish to mass-produce copyright material with MCPS and will pay a statutory rate for each unit made, which is collected on behalf of the composer(s).

**Midem**—the music business conference, held in Cannes, France, every January, which attracts thousands of delegates and showcases a variety of musicians and DJs

**mini-jack**—3.5-mm jack, usually stereo, as used for Walkman headphones

**MOBO**—Music of Black Origin awards ceremony (UK)

**monitor**—reference speaker; see also foldback

**mp3**—a compression standard for digital sound; standard format for Internet music delivery but likely to be superseded by more powerful standards

**'multicore' or 'snake'**—used live, a multiway cable which connects the mixer to the stage-box

**multimeter**—diagnostic tool for electrical equipment; gives readings of currents, etc.

**multiway DC adaptor**—converts AC mains to various DC voltages, with various connectors available for effects, small keyboards, etc.

**Musicians' Union (MU)**—an organization which protects the rights of UK musicians of all kinds and offers various services. Each member pays an annual subscription.

**noise gate**—processor which prevents signals passing through until a minimum level is reached. Noise is not heard until a 'good' signal opens the gate.

**PA**—(a) public address system for amplification of sound at gigs and in clubs; (b) personal appearance when an artist sings or mimes to backing tracks

**phono**—standard connector for domestic sound equipment, also known as an RCA plug

**playlist**—the list of records a radio station will play repeatedly during the day and early evening

**PPD (published price to dealer, or 'dealer price')**—the price charged by the distributor to retailers, before discounts. Used as a base figure for royalty calculations.

**PPL (Phonographic Performance Limited)**—in the UK, collects money for performance of recorded works on behalf of the owner of the recording copyright and of musicians who play on recordings. Typically, radio stations pay record companies through PPL for use of the recordings on air.

**production master**—a master tape or disc containing edited, treated and compiled recordings which are ready for mass-production

**promo**—promotional copy of a record. If appropriately labelled, it does not attract MCPS fees (in the UK).

**promoter**—the individual or organization which takes the full risk of live music events or club nights. The promoter hires the venue, pays for publicity and for performers, technicians and venue staff. In the US, a radio plugger is also called a promoter.

**PRS (Performing Right Society)**—collects performance revenue, on behalf of composers, for use of works on radio and in other public performances

**radio edit**—a track which has been shortened to fit the three-minute radio format, or rearranged to appeal to radio programmers

**radio format**—format radio began in the US, and the idea is for all records played on the radio station to be in a similar vein—AC (adult contemporary), pop, MOR (middle of the road), gold (oldies), rock, and so on. Most of the records are chosen and programmed into shows by computer. In contrast, on specialist radio stations or shows, most records are chosen by a panel or by the DJ presenting each show.

**radio: national**—radio programming that reaches the whole country, such as BBC Radio 1, 2, 3, 4 and 5 and Virgin Radio in the UK

**radio plugging**—a radio plugger, or promotions person, takes new, as yet unreleased records to radio stations and 'plugs' or promotes them to the head of music and to DJs in an effort to get them played

**radio: regional**—UK local radio reaching a defined area, such as Kiss FM in London

**reaction sheet**—a form sent out with promotional records, which DJs fill in and return to show what they and their audiences thought of the record and where they have been playing it

**recoup**—to recover from sales all expenditures made on a project, for example, advances and recording, video and tour support costs

**remix**—a marketing technique, taking the 'parts' of a record—vocals, instrumentation, etc.—and adding new musical parts to come up with a different version of the original

**roadie**—someone who goes on tour with a band to help load and unload equipment, drive, sell merchandise and so on

**royalty**—the fee paid by the user of a copyright work to the owner of the work. The use could be making copies (mechanical reproductions) of it for sale, broadcasting it, using it for a film, etc. Also, a fee per copy sold paid by a record company to a featured recording artist.

**scratching**—manually controlling the playing of a record on a turntable by spinning it with one hand, or the noise made by cueing the record in this way

**session musician**—freelance musician who moves from project to project doing live or recorded work or both, rather than belonging to a specific group

**show reel**—a tape or CD with a selection of your music to send advertising agencies or TV companies to promote your jingle or TV theme music capability

**SMPTE**—a time code used to synchronize audio (and video) machines; uses hours, minutes, seconds and frames (twenty-five frames per second)

**sound check**—procedure to check that each sound source onstage is reaching the sound engineer is adjusted for volume, EQ, etc. and can be heard satisfactorily by performers and audience

**sound engineer**—technician responsible for controlling the different sound sources and mixing them

**SoundExchange**—collects performance royalties on behalf of recording artists and labels

**stage-box**—box of XLR sockets onstage, linked to channels on a mixing desk

**streamable**—audio or video material accessed by a computer, which can be played in real time, within a few seconds of requesting it, rather than having to be stored on the computer first (downloaded) before it can be played

**test pressings (TPs)**—the first few copies of a vinyl record, which are used to check that there are no production faults before authorizing a full manufacturing quantity

**tribute bands**—bands that try to sound, and perhaps look, exactly like a successful band. Abba, the Beatles and the Spice Girls are some of the most commonly covered bands.

**URL (unique resource locator)**—Web address, for example, www.microsoft.com

**white label**—a record with no label artwork and packed in a white inner bag; used for promotional purposes, sent out to the press and to club and radio DJs before the finished records with full artwork

**XLR**—a three-pin connector (usually), found on microphones and high-quality connections

# contracts and agreements

The following pages contain a selection of the forms, contracts and other key documents you are likely to have to contend with in your music business career.

The first three contracts are those you sign as a writer in order to join the performing right organizations ASCAP, BMI or PRS. They are standard forms whose terms apply to all songwriters and you must complete one or other of them to qualify to receive royalties! The fourth contract is between a songwriter and MCPS, the UK mechanical rights organization.

As well as signing you up, the organization needs to know what songs you have written, so it can match up its information on airplay, record sales etc. Form 5 is an example of the UK registration form from MCPS-PRS. The second page is for 'unpublished' works—you use it if you don't (yet) have a publisher.

The remaining contracts and forms are examples of the kind of thing a small label needs to deal with. The contract on pp. 476–81 deals with the licensing of a track for a compilation. It is followed by a typical contract with a distributor.

Finally, on pp. 484–7 there is an application form for membership of the UK organization, AIM.

# 1. ASCAP Writer's Agreement

## ASCAP Membership Agreement

**Agreement** made between the undersigned (for brevity called *"Owner"*) and the AMERICAN SOCIETY OF COMPOSERS, AUTHORS, AND PUBLISHERS (For brevity called *"Society"*), in consideration of the premises and of the mutual covenants hereinafter contained, as follows:

1. The *Owner* grants to the *Society* for the term hereof, the right to license non-dramatic public performances (as hereinafter defined), of each musical work:

Of which the *Owner* is a copyright proprietor; or

Which the *Owner*, alone, or jointly, or in collaboration with others, wrote, composed, published, acquired or owned; or

In which the *Owner* now has any right, title, interest or control whatsoever, in whole or in part; or

Which hereafter, during the term hereof, may be written, composed, acquired, owned, published or copyrighted by the *Owner*, alone, jointly or in collaboration with others; or

In which the *Owner* may hereafter, during the term hereof, have any right, title, interest or control, whatsoever, in whole or in part.

The right to license the public performance of any such musical work shall be deemed granted to the *Society* by this instrument for the term hereof, immediately upon the work being written, composed, acquired, owned, published or copyrighted.

The rights hereby granted shall include (a) All the rights and remedies for enforcing the copyright or copyrights of such musical works, whether such copyrights are in the name of the *Owner* and/or others, as well as the right to sue under such copyrights in the name of the *Society* and/or in the name of the *Owner* and/or others, to the end that the *Society* may effectively protect and be assured of all the rights hereby granted.

(b) The non-exclusive right of public performance of the separate numbers, songs, fragments or arrangements, melodies or selections forming part or parts of musical plays and dramatico-musical compositions, the *Owner* reserving and excepting from this grant the right of performance of musical plays and dramatico-musical compositions in their entirety, or any part of such plays or dramatico-musical compositions on the legitimate stage.

(c) The non-exclusive right of public performance by means of radio broadcasting, telephony, "wired wireless," all forms of synchronism with motion pictures, and/or any method of transmitting sound other than television broadcasting.

(d) The non-exclusive right of public performance by television broadcasting; provided, however, that:

(i)This grant does not extend to or include the right to license the public performance by television broadcasting or otherwise of any rendition or performance of (a) any opera, operetta, musical comedy, play or like production (whether or not such opera, operetta, musical comedy, play or like production was presented on the stage or in motion picture form) in a manner which recreates the performance of such composition with substantially such distinctive scenery or costume as was used in the presentation of such opera, operetta, musical comedy, play or like production (whether or not such opera, operetta, musical comedy, play or like production was presented on the stage or in motion picture form); provided, however, that the rights hereby granted shall be deemed to include a grant of the right to license non-dramatic performances of compositions by television broadcasting of a motion picture containing such composition if the rights in such motion picture other than those granted hereby have been obtained from the parties in interest.

(ii) Nothing herein contained shall be deemed to grant the right to license the public performance by television broadcasting of dramatic performances. Any performance of a separate musical composition which is not a dramatic performance, as defined herein, shall be deemed a non-dramatic performance. For the purposes of this agreement, a dramatic performance shall mean a performance of a musical composition on a television programme in which there is a definite plot depicted by action and where the performance of the musical composition is woven into and carries the plot and its accompanying action. The use of dialogue to establish a mere program format or the use of any non-dramatic device merely to introduce a performance of a composition shall not be deemed to make such performances dramatic.

(iii)The definition of the terms "dramatic" and "non-dramatic" performances contained herein are purely for the purposes of this agreement and for the term thereof and shall not be binding upon or prejudicial to any position taken by either of us subsequent to the term hereof or for any purpose other than this agreement.

(e) The *Owner* may at any time and from time to time, in good faith, restrict the radio or television broadcasting of compositions from musical comedies, operas, operettas and motion pictures, or any other composition being excessively broadcast, only for the purpose of preventing harmful effect upon such musical comedies, operas, operettas and motion pictures or compositions, in respect of other interest under the copyrights thereof; provided, however, that the right to grant limited licenses will be given, upon application, as to restricted compositions, if and when the *Owner* is unable to show reasonable hazards to his or its major interests likely to result from such radio or television broadcasting; and provided further that such right to restrict any such composition shall not be exercised for the purpose of permitting the fixing or regulating of fees for the recording or transcribing of such composition, and provided further that in no case shall any charges, "free plugs," or other consideration be required in respect of any permission granted to perform a restricted composition; and provided further that in no event shall any composition, after the initial radio or television broadcast thereof, be restricted for the purpose of confining further radio or television broadcasts thereof to a particular artist, station, network or program. The *Owner* may also at any time and from time to time, in good faith, restrict the radio or television broadcasting of any composition, as to which any suit has been brought or threatened on a claim that such composition infringes a composition not contained in the repertory of *Society* or on a claim by a non-member of *Society* that *Society* does not have the right to license the public performance of any such composition by radio or television broadcasting.

2. The term of this *Agreement* shall be for a period commencing on the date hereof and continuing indefinitely thereafter unless terminated by either party in accordance with the Articles of Association.

3. The *Society* agrees, during the term hereof, in good faith to use its best endeavors to promote and carry out the objects for which it was organized, and to hold and apply all royalties, profits, benefits and advantages arising from the exploitation of the rights assigned to it by its several members, including the *Owner*, to the uses and purposes as provided in its Articles of Association (which are hereby incorporated by reference), as now in force or as hereafter amended.

4. The *Owner* hereby irrevocably, during the term hereof, authorizes, empowers and vests in the *Society* the right to enforce and protect such rights of public performance under any and all copyrights, whether standing in the name of the *Owner*, and/or by others; to prevent the infringement thereof, to litigate, collect and receipt for damages arising from infringement, and in its sole judgement to join the *Owner* and/or others in whose names the copyright might stand, as parties plaintiff or defendants in suits or proceedings; to bring to suit in the name of the *Owner* and/or in the name of the *Society*, or others in whose name the copyright may stand, or otherwise, and to release, compromise, or refer to arbitration any actions, in the same manner and to the same extent and to all intents and purposes as the *Owner* might or could do, had this instrument not been made.

5. The *Owner* hereby makes, constitutes and appoints the *Society*, or its successor, the *Owner*'s true and lawful attorney, irrevocably during the term hereof, and in the name of the *Society* or its successor, or in the name of the *Owner*, or otherwise, to do all acts, take all proceedings, execute, acknowledge and deliver any and all instruments, papers, documents, process and pleadings that may be necessary, proper or expedient to restrain infringements and recover damages in respect to or for the infringement or other violation of the rights of public performance in such works, and to discontinue, compromise or refer to arbitration any such proceedings or actions, or to make any disposition of the differences in relation to the premises.

6. The *Owner* agrees from time to time, to execute, acknowledge and deliver to the *Society*, such assurances, powers of attorney or other authorizations or instruments as the *Society* may deem necessary or expedient to enable it to exercise, enjoy and enforce, in its own name or otherwise, all rights and remedies aforesaid.

7. It is mutually agreed that during the term hereof the Board of Directors of the *Society* shall be composed of an equal number of writers and publishers respectively, and that the royalties distributed by the Board of Directors shall be divided into two (2) equal sums, and one (1) each of such sums credited respectively to and for division amongst (a) the writer members, and (b) the

publisher members, in accordance with the system of apportionment and distribution of royalties as determined by the Board of Directors in accordance with the Articles of Association as they may be amended from time to time.

8. The *Owner* agrees that the apportionment and distribution of royalties by the *Society* as determined from time to time by the Board of Directors of the *Society*, in case of appeal by him, shall be final, conclusive and binding upon him.

The *Society* shall have the right to transfer the right of review of any apportionment and distribution from the Board of Directors to any other agency or instrumentality that in its discretion and good judgement it deems best adapted to assuring to the *Society*'s membership a just, fair, equitable and accurate apportionment and distribution of royalties.

The *Society* shall have the right to adopt from time to time such systems, means, methods and formulae for the establishment of a member's apportionment and distribution of royalties as will ensure a fair, just and equitable distribution of royalties among the membership.

9. "Public Performance" Defined. The term "*public performance*" shall be construed to mean vocal, instrumental and/or mechanical renditions and representations in any manner or by any method whatsoever, including transmissions by radio and television broadcasting stations, transmissions by telephony and/or "wired wireless"; and/or reproductions of performances and renditions by means of devices for reproducing sound recorded in synchronism or timed relation with the taking of motion pictures.

10. "Musical Works" Defined. The Phrase "*musical works*" shall be construed to mean musical compositions and dramatico-musical compositions, the words and music thereof, and the respective arrangements thereof, and the selections therefrom.

11. The powers, rights, authorities and privileges by this instrument vested in the *Society* are deemed to include the World, provided, however, that such high grants of rights for foreign countries shall be subject to any agreements now in effect, a list of which are noted on the reverse side hereof.

12. The grant made herein by the owner is modified by and subject to the provisions of (a) the Amended Final Judgement (Civil Action No. 13-95) dated March 14, 1950 in *U.S.A. v. ASCAP* as further amended by Order dated January 7, 1960. (b) the Final Judgement (Civil Action No. 42-245) in *U.S.A. v. ASCAP*, dated March 14, 1950, and (c) the provisions of the Articles of Association and resolutions of the Board of Directors adopted pursuant to such judgements and order.

SIGNED, SEALED AND DELIVERED, on this _____ of _____, _____.
                                                day              month           year

Owner {       Sign your name here       _____

              _____

Society {     AMERICAN SOCIETY OF COMPOSERS, AUTHORS AND PUBLISHERS

              By _____
                        President and Chairman of the Board

# ASCAP Writer Application

**1. PLEASE TYPE YOUR FULL LEGAL NAME IN THE FIELD BELOW**

Check one: ☐ Mr. ☐ Ms. ☐ Miss ☐ Mrs. ☐ Dr. ☐ Other: [          ]

Full Name: [                    ]

IMPORTANT: If you only enter one name, you must provide proof of such name.

**1a. PLEASE LIST ANY PSEUDONYMS, STAGE NAMES OR PROFESSIONAL NAMES YOU ARE USING, IF DIFFERENT FROM YOUR LEGAL NAME.**

Pseudonyms: 1) [                ]   2) [                ]

**1b. PLEASE LIST THE NAME OF THE BAND OR MUSICAL GROUP OF WHICH YOU ARE A MEMBER (IF ANY).**

Band Name: [                    ]

**2. DATE OF BIRTH: (mm / dd / yyyy)** [     ] [     ] [        ]

**3. ADDRESS:**
E-mail*

[                    ]

Street Address                                   Apt #

[                    ]

City                          State                Zip

[                    ]

Phone Number                        Fax Number
( [   ] ) [                ]        ( [   ] ) [                ]

\* ASCAP will use your email address for ASCAP correspondence only. We will not share or sell your email address. You may opt out of receiving ASCAP email correspondence at any time.

**3a. ROYALTY ADDRESS:**
(only if you would like your royalties and performance statements sent to a different address than above)

Name: [                    ]

Street Address                                   Apt #

[                    ]

City                          State                Zip

[                    ]

Phone Number                        Fax Number
( [   ] ) [                ]        ( [   ] ) [                ]

**4. ARE YOU A U.S. CITIZEN OR A RESIDENT ALIEN OF THE UNITED STATES?**

☐ YES   ☐ NO

If no, what is your country of permanent residence? [                    ]

**5. SOCIAL SECURITY NUMBER:** [                    ]

(required for U.S. citizens and residents)

**6. I AM CURRENTLY (or) I HAVE BEEN A MEMBER OR AFFILIATE OF:**

☐ ASCAP   ☐ BMI*   ☐ SESAC*   ☐ Other*

As:   ☐ a writer   ☐ and/or a publisher

*PLEASE ATTACH A COPY OF YOUR RELEASE FROM THIS ORGANIZATION. APPLICATIONS WITHOUT NECESSARY RELEASES CANNOT BE PROCESSED.

If affiliated as a publisher, please list company's name below:

[                    ]

**7. I AM APPLYING AS A:**   ☐ Composer (music)   ☐ Author (lyrics)   ☐ Both

To qualify for membership in ASCAP, you must be the writer or co-writer of at least one musical work or song that has been commercially recorded, performed publicly in any venue or medium licensable by ASCAP, performed in any audio visual or electronic medium, or published and available for sale or rental as sheet music, a score or folio.

Title of ONE musical work or song: [                    ]

Please check ONE of the following requirements you meet to qualify for membership in ASCAP and provide the information requested based on the musical work or song listed above:

☐ **A commercial recording**

Recording Artist: [                    ]

Date Of Release: [                    ]

Record Label: [                    ]

**OR**

☐ **Public performance in any venue licensable by ASCAP**
(Club, live concert, symphonic concert or recital venue, college or university, etc.)

Performer: [                    ]

Name of venue: [                    ]

Date of Performance: [                    ]

Where? [                    ]

**OR**

☐ **Performance in any audio visual or electronic medium**
   (film, television, radio, Internet, cable, pay-per-view, etc.)

Medium (film, television, radio, Internet, etc.): [                    ]

Title or name of film, television program, web site or radio station:

[                    ]

Date of performance: [                    ]

**OR**

☐ **Published sheet music, score or folio available for sale or rental**

Title of published sheet music, score or folio: [                    ]

Publisher: [                    ]

**8.** PLEASE CHECK HERE IF YOU PRIMARILY COMPOSE CONCERT MUSIC (WORKS FOR ORCHESTRA, CHAMBER ENSEMBLE, CHORUS, WIND ENSEMBLE/CONCERT BAND, ELECTRO-ACOUSTIC FORCES, ETC.): ☐

**9. CONFIDENTIALITY OF MEMBER ADDRESS:**

Under certain circumstances, ASCAP members are entitled to examine a list of all members names and addresses, unless a member wishes his or her address to be kept confidential. Please indicate whether you wish ASCAP to keep your address confidential (for reasons of privacy or otherwise) in these circumstances.

☐ Please keep my address confidential.

**10. WARRANTIES & REPRESENTATIONS:**

A. I represent that there are no existing assignments or licenses, direct or indirect, of non-dramatic performing rights in or to the musical work listed in #7 above, except to or with the publisher(s) of this work. If there are assignments or licenses other than with publishers, I have attached copies of such assignments or licenses.

B. I have read ASCAP's Articles of Association, Compendium of Rules and Regulations, and the Second Amended Final Judgment entered in *U.S. v. ASCAP* ("AFJ2") and agree to be bound by them, as now in effect, and as they may be amended, and I agree to execute agreements in such form and for such periods as the Board of Directors shall have required and shall hereafter require for all members.

C. I represent that I meet the eligibility requirements for membership as set forth herein. I understand that ASCAP reserves the right to request substantiation of eligibility at any time.

D. I warrant and represent that all of the information furnished in this application is true. I acknowledge that any agreement entered into between ASCAP and me will be in reliance upon the representations contained in this application, and that my membership will be subject to termination if the information contained in this application is not complete and accurate.

### Optional: Writer Digital Home Recording ("DART") Royalties Election

Under the Audio Home Recording Act of 1992, royalties are paid by manufacturers and importers of digital audio recording equipment and recording media (e.g., blank tapes or discs). The royalties are shared by writers, publishers, recording artists and record companies. ASCAP can act on behalf of those members who specifically designate ASCAP to represent them in digital audio royalty matters under the Act. SEE <u>DART FACT SHEET</u> FOR MORE INFORMATION BEFORE MAKING YOUR DECISION. IF YOU ARE UNDECIDED, YOU MAY LEAVE THIS SECTION BLANK.

☐ YES, Applicant grants the American Society of Composers, Authors and Publishers ("ASCAP") the exclusive right to collect and distribute digital audio royalty payments as provided in Public Law No. 102-563 (the Audio Home Recording Act of 1992, as such law may be amended and payments for home recording of Applicant's copyrighted musical works outside of the United States, with respect to all of the musical works described in the ASCAP Membership Agreement.

☐ NO, Applicant does not wish ASCAP to represent me regarding home recording rights.

PLEASE SIGN YOUR LEGAL NAME HERE:

_____          _____

Sign Here                                                                                      Date

_____          _____

Signature of parent or guardian if applicant is under 18                   Date

NOTE: APPLICATIONS THAT ARE NOT SIGNED WILL BE RETURNED TO THE APPLICANT.

06/2002

# 2. BMI Writer's Agreement

**BMI** · 320 West 57th Street, New York, NY 10019-3790 · 212-586-2000 · FAX 212-245-8986

Date

Dear

The following shall constitute the agreement between us:

1. As used in this agreement:

(a) The word 'Period' shall mean the term from        to
and continuing thereafter for additional terms for two years unless terminated unless terminated by either party at the end of said initial term or any additional term, upon notice by registered or certified mail not more than six (6) months or les than three (3) months prior to the end of any such term.

(b) The words 'Work' or 'Works' shall mean:

(i) All musical compositions (including the musical segments and individual compositions written for dramatic or dramatico-musical work) composed by you alone or with one or more co-writers during the Period; and

(ii) All musical compositions (including the musical segments and individual compositions written for dramatic or dramatico-musical work) composed by you alone or with one or more co-writers prior to the Period, except those in which there is an outstanding grant of the right of public performance to a person other than a publisher affiliated with BMI.

2. You agree that:

(a) Within ten (10) days after this execution of this agreement you will furnish to us a completed clearance form available in blank from us with respect to each Work heretofore composed by you which has been published in printed copies or recorded commercially or in synchronization commercially with film or tape which is being currently performed or which you consider as likely to be performed.

(b) In each instance that a Work for which a clearance form has not been submitted to us pursuant to sub-paragraph 2(a) is published in printed copies or recorded commercially or in synchronization with film or tape or is considered by you as likely to be performed, whether such Work is composed prior to the execution of this agreement or hereafter during the Period, you will promptly furnish to us a completed clearance form with respect to each such Work.

(c) If requested by us in writing, you will promptly furnish us a legible lead sheet or other written or printed copy of a work.

3. The submission of each clearance form pursuant to paragraph 2 shall constitute a warranty and representation by you that all of the information contained thereon is true and correct and that no performing rights in such Work have been granted to or reserved by others except as specifically set forth therein in connection with Works heretofore written or co-written by you.

4. Except as otherwise provided herein, you hereby grant to us for the Period:

(a) All the rights that you own or acquire publicly to perform, and to license others to perform, anywhere in the work, any part or all of the works.

(b) The non-exclusive right to record, and to license others to record, any part or all of any of the works on electrical transcriptions, wire, tape, film or otherwise, but only for the purpose of performing such work publicly by means of radio and television or for archive or audition purposes. This right does not include recording for the purpose of sale to the public or the purpose of synchronization (i) with motion pictures intended primarily for theatrical exhibition or (ii) with programs distributed by means of syndication to broadcasting stations, cable systems or other similar distribution outlets.

(c) The non-exclusive right to adapt or arrange any part or all of any of the Works for performance purpose, and to license others to do so.

5. Notwithstanding the provisions of sub-paragraph 4(a):

(a) The rights granted to us by sub-paragraph 4(a) shall not include the right to perform or license the performance of more than one song or aria from a dramatic or dramatico-musical work which is an opera, operetta or musical show or more than five (5) minutes from a dramatic or dramatico-musical work which is a ballet, if such a performance is accompanied by the dramatic action, costumes or scenery of that dramatic or dramatico-musical work.

(b) You, together with all the publishers and your co-writers, if any, shall have the right jointly, by written notice to us, to exclude from the grant made by sub-paragraph 4(a) performances of Works comprising more than thirty (30) minutes of a dramatic or dramatico-musical work, but this right shall not apply to such performances from (i) a score originally written for or performed as part of a theatrical or television film, (ii) a score originally written for or performed as part of a radio or television program, or (iii) the original cast, sound track or similar album of a dramatic or dramatico-musical work.

(c) You, the publishers and/or your co-writers, if any, retain the right to issue non-exclusive licenses for performances of a Work or Works in the United States, its territories and possessions (other than to another performing rights licensing organization), provided that within ten (10) days of the issuance of such license we are given written notice thereof and a copy of the license is supplied to us.

6. (a) As full consideration for all rights granted to us hereunder and as security therefor, we agree to pay to you, with respect to each of the Works in which we obtain and retain performing rights during the period:

(i) For radio and television performances of a Work in the United States, its territories and possessions, amounts calculated pursuant to our then current standard practices upon the basis of the then current performance rates generally paid by us to our affiliated writers for similar performances of similar compositions. The number of performances for which you shall be entitled to payment shall be estimated by us in accordance with our then current system of computing the number of such performances.

You acknowledge that we license performances of the Works of our affiliates by means other than on radio and television, but unless and until such time as such methods are adopted for tabulation of such performances, payment will be based solely on performances in those media and locations then currently surveyed. In the event that during the Period we shall establish a system of separate payment for performances by means other than radio and television, we shall pay you upon the basis of the then current performance rates generally paid by us to our other affiliated writers for similar performances of similar compositions.

(ii) In the case of a Work composed by you with one or more co-writers, the sum payable to you hereunder shall be a pro rata share, determined on the basis of the number of co-writers, unless you have transmitted to us a copy of an agreement between you and your co-writers providing a different division of payment.

(iii) Monies received by us from any performing rights licensing organization outside of the United States, its territories and possessions, which are designated by such performing rights licensing organization as the author's share of foreign performance royalties earned by your Works after the deduction of our then current handling charge applicable to our affiliated writers in accordance with our then current standard practices of payment for such performances.

(b) Notwithstanding the provisions of sub-paragraph 6(a), we shall have no obligation to make payment hereunder with respect to (i) any performance of a Work which occurs prior to the date on which we have received from you all the information and material with respect to such Work which is referred to in paragraphs 2 and 3, or (ii) any performance of a Work as to which a direct license as described in sub-paragraph 5(c) has been granted by you, your co-writers, if any, or the publishers, or (iii) any performance for which no license fee shall be collected by us, or (iv) any performance of a Work which you claim was either omitted from or miscalculated on a royalty statement and for which we shall not have received written notice from you of such claimed omission or miscalculation within nine (9) months of the date of such statement.

7. In accordance with our then current standard practices, we will furnish periodic statements to you during each year of the Period showing the monies due pursuant to sub-paragraph 6(a). Each such statement shall be

accompanied by payment of the sum thereby shown due to you, subject to all proper deductions, if any, for taxes, advances or amounts due BMI from you.

8. (a) nothing in this agreement requires us to continue to licence the works subsequent to the termination of this agreement. In the event that we continue to license your interest in any Work, however, we shall continue to make payments to you for such work for so long as you do not make or purport to make directly or indirectly any grant of performing rights in such a Work to any other licensing organization. The amounts of such payments shall be calculated pursuant to our then current standard practices upon the basis of the then current performance rates generally paid by us to our affiliated writers for similar performances of similar compositions. You agree to notify us by registered or certified mail of any grant or purported grant by you directly or indirectly of performing rights to any other performing rights organization within ten (10) days from the making of such a grant or purported grant and if you fail so to inform us thereof and we make payments to you for any period after the making of any such grant or purported grant, you agree to repay to us all amounts so paid by us promptly with or without demand by us. In addition, if we inquire of you by registered or certified mail, addressed to your last known address, whether you have made any such grant or purported grant and you fail to confirm to us by registered or certified mail within thirty (30) days of the mailing of such inquiry that you have not made any such grant or purported grant, we may, from and after such date, discontinue making any payments to you.

(b) Our obligation to continue payment to you after the termination of this agreement for performances outside of the United States, its territories and possessions, of Works which BMI continues to license after such termination shall be dependent upon our receipt in the United States of payments designated by foreign performing rights organizations as the author's share of foreign performance royalties earned by your Works. Payment of such foreign royalties shall be subject to deduction of our then current handling charge applicable to our affiliated writers and shall be in accordance with our then current standard practices of payment for such performances.

(c) In the event that we have reason to believe that you will receive, are entitled to receive, or are receiving payment for a performing rights organization other than BMI for or based on United States performances of one or more of your Works during a period when such Works were licensed by us pursuant to this agreement, we shall have the right to withhold payment for such performances from you until receipt of evidence satisfactory to us that you were not or will not be paid by such other organization. In the event that you were or will not be paid or do not supply such evidence within eighteen (18) months from the date of our request therefor, we shall be under no obligation to make any payment to you for performances of such Works during such period.

9. In the event that this agreement shall terminate at a time when, after crediting all earnings reflected by statements rendered to you prior to the effective date of such termination, there remains an unearned balance of advances paid to you by us, such termination shall not be effective until the close of the calendar quarterly period during which (a) you shall repay such unearned balance of advances, or (b) you shall notify us by registered or certified mail that you have received a statement rendered by us at our normal accounting time showing that such unearned balance of advances has been fully recouped by us.

10. You warrant and represent that you have the right to enter into this agreement; that you are not bound by any prior commitments which conflict with your commitments hereunder; that each of the Works, composed by you alone or with one or more co-writers, is original; and that exercise of the rights granted by you herein will not constitute an infringement of copyright or violation of any other right of, or unfair competition with, any person, firm or corporation. You agree to indemnify and hold harmless us, our licensees, the advertisers of our licensees and their respective agents, servants and employees from and against any and all loss or damage resulting from any claim of whatever nature arising from or in connection with the exercise of any of the rights granted by you in this agreement. Upon notification to us or any of the other parties herein indemnified of a claim with respect to any of the Works, we shall have the right to exclude such Work form this agreement and/or to withhold payment of all sums which become due pursuant to this agreement or any modification thereof until the receipt of satisfactory written evidence that such claim has been withdrawn, settled or adjudicated.

11. (a) We shall have the right, upon written notice to you, to exclude from this agreement, at any time, any Work which in our opinion is similar to a previously existing composition and might constitute a copyright infringement, or has a title or music or lyric similar to that of a previously existing composition and might lead to a claim of unfair competition.

(b) In the case of Works which in our opinion are based on compositions in the public domain, we shall have the right, upon written notice to you, either (i) to exclude any such work from this agreement, or (ii) to classify any such work as entitled to receive only a fraction of the full credit that would otherwise be given for performances thereof.

(c) In the event that any work is excluded from this agreement pursuant to paragraph 10 or sub-paragraph 11(a) or (b), all rights in such a Work shall automatically revert to you in ten (10) days after the date of our notice to you of such an exclusion. In the event that a Work is classified for less than full credit under sub-paragraph 11(b)(ii), you shall have the right, by giving notice to us, within ten (10) days after the date of our notice advising you of the credit allocated to the Work, to terminate our rights therein, and all rights in such Work shall thereupon revert to you.

12. In each instance that you write, or are employed or commissioned by a motion picture producer to write, during the Period, all or part of the score of a motion picture intended primarily for exhibition in theaters, or by the producer of a musical show or revue for the legitimate stage to write, during the Period, all or part of the musical compositions contained therein, we agree, on request, to advise the producer of the film that such part of the score as is written by you may be performed as part of the exhibition of said film in theaters in the United States, its territories and possessions, without compensation to us, or to the producer of a musical show or revue that your compositions embodied therein may be performed on the stage with living artists as part of such musical show or revue, without compensation to us. In the event that we notify you that we have established a system for the collection of royalties for performance of the scores of motion picture films in theaters in the United States, its territories and possessions, we shall no longer be obligated to take any such action with respect to motion picture scores.

13. You make, constitute and appoint us, or our nominee, your true and lawful attorney, irrevocably during the Period, in our name or that of our nominee, or in your name, or otherwise, in our sole judgement, to do all acts, take all proceedings, execute, acknowledge and deliver any instruments, papers, documents, process or pleadings that, in our sole judgement, may be necessary, proper, or expedient to restrain infringement of and/or to enforce and protect the rights granted by you hereunder, and to recover damages in respect to or for the infringement or other violation of said rights, and in our sole judgement to join you and/or others in whose names the copyrights to any of the Works may stand; to discontinue, compromise or refer to arbitration, any such actions or proceedings or to make any other disposition of the disputes in relation to the Works, provided that any action or proceeding commenced by us pursuant to the provisions of this paragraph shall be at our sole expense and for our sole benefit. Notwithstanding the foregoing, nothing in this paragraph 13 requires us to take any proceedings or other action against any person, firm, partnership or other entity or any writer or publisher, whether or not affiliated with us, who you claim may be infringing your Works or otherwise violating the rights granted by you hereunder. In addition, you understand and agree that the licensing by us of any musical compositions which you claim may be infringing your Works or otherwise violating the rights granted by you hereunder, shall not constitute an infringement of your Works on our part.

14. BMI shall have the right, in its sole discretion, to terminate this agreement on at least thirty (30) days' notice by registered or certified mail if you, your agents, employees or representatives, directly or indirectly, solicit or accept payment from writers for composing music for lyrics or writing lyrics to music for reviewing, publishing, promoting, recording or rendering other services connected with the exploitation of any composition, or permit use of your name or your affiliation with us in connection with any of the foregoing. In the event of such termination no payments shall be due to you pursuant to paragraph 8.

15. No monies due or to become due to you shall be assignable, whether by way of assignment, sale or power granted to an attorney-in-fact, without out prior written consent. If any assignment of such monies is made by you without such prior written consent, no rights of any kind against us will be acquired by the assignee, purchaser or attorney-in-fact.

16. In the event that during the Period (a) mail addressed to you at the last address furnished by you pursuant to paragraph 20 shall be returned to the post office, or (b) monies shall not have been earned by you pursuant to paragraph 6 for a period of two consecutive years or more, or (c) you shall die, BMI shall have the right to terminate this agreement on at least thirty (30) days' notice by registered or certified mail addressed to the last address furnished by you pursuant to paragraph 20 and, in the case of your death, to the representative of your estate, if known to BMI. In the event of such termination no payments shall be due to you pursuant to paragraph 8.

17. You acknowledge that the rights obtained by you pursuant to this agreement constitute rights to payment of money and that during the Period we shall hold title to the performing rights granted to us hereunder. In the event that during the period you shall file a petition in bankruptcy, such a petition shall be filed against you, you shall make an assignment for the benefit of creditors, you shall consent to the appointment of a receiver or trustee for all or part of your property, or you shall institute or shall have instituted against you any other insolvency proceeding under the United States bankruptcy laws or any other applicable law, we shall retain title to the

performing rights in all Works the rights to which are granted to us hereunder and shall subrogate your trustee in bankruptcy or receiver and any subsequent purchasers from them to your right to payment of money for said Works in accordance with the terms and conditions of this agreement.

18. (a) You hereby authorize us to negotiate for and collect any royalties or monies to which you may become entitled as a writer pursuant to the Audio Home Recording Act of 1992 and/or any amendments thereto or substitutions therefor and, to the extent possible, collect for and distribute to you royalties arising from or as compensation for home recording in countries outside the United States, its territories and possessions. This authorization with respect to royalties and monies under the Audio Home Recording Act of 1992 may be revoked by you at the end of any calendar year on prior written notice by you to us by registered or certified mail. Such revocation shall be effective beginning with the calendar year subsequent to the time of notice and shall in no way effect the Period of this agreement with respect to any of the other rights granted to BMI by you hereunder.

(b) We agree to distribute to you royalties and monies collected by us pursuant to the authorization granted in sub-paragraph 18(a), pursuant to our then prevailing practices, including deduction of our expenses therefor.

19. All disputes of any kind, nature or description arising in connection with the terms and conditions of this agreement shall be submitted to the American Arbitration Association in New York, New York, for arbitration under its then prevailing rules, the arbitrator(s) to be selected as follows: Each of us shall, by written notice to the other, have the right to appoint one arbitrator. If, within ten (10) days following the giving of such notice by one of us, the other shall not, by written notice, appoint another arbitrator, the first arbitrator shall be the sole arbitrator. If two arbitrators are appointed, they shall appoint a third arbitrator. If ten (10) days elapse after the appointment of the second arbitrator and the two arbitrators are unable to agree upon the third arbitrator, then either of us may, in writing, request the American Arbitration Association to appoint the third arbitrator. The award made in the arbitration shall be binding and conclusive on both of us and shall include the fixing of the costs, expenses and reasonable attorneys' fees of arbitration, which shall be borne by the unsuccessful party. Judgement may be entered in New York State Supreme Court or any other court having jurisdiction.

20. You agree to notify our Department of Writer/Publisher administration promptly in writing of any change in your address. Any notice sent to you pursuant to the terms of this agreement shall be valid if addressed to you at the last address so furnished by you.

21. This agreement constitutes the entire agreement between you and us, cannot be changed except in a writing signed by you and us and shall be governed and construed pursuant to the laws of the State of New York.

22. In the event that any part or parts of this agreement are found to be void by a court of competent jurisdiction, the remaining part or parts shall nevertheless be binding with the same force and effect as if the void part or parts were deleted from this agreement.

Very truly yours,

BROADCAST MUSIC, INC.

ACCEPTED AND AGREED TO:

By ............................................

By ............................................
Vice President

Virtually Indispensable

══════════════════════════════════════════════════════════════ Join

Please complete the following information to apply to join BMI. Should you need any assistance please contact the BMI Writer Administration Department at (212) 586-2000.

\* Denotes Required Field

| FULL LEGAL NAME | |
|---|---|
| Prefix (check one) \* | ○ Mr. ○ Mrs. ○ Ms. ○ Miss |
| First \* | |
| Middle (leave blank if none) | |
| Last \* | |
| Suffix (Jr., III) | |

| | |
|---|---|
| Mother's Maiden Name \*<br>(Last Name Only) | |

| | |
|---|---|
| Social Security Number \* | - - |

| | |
|---|---|
| Date of Birth \* | Month   Day   Year |

| COMPLETE MAILING ADDRESS | | | |
|---|---|---|---|
| Address Line 1 \* | | | Apt # |
| Address Line 2 (if needed) | | | |
| City \* | | | |
| State (\*Required for US and Canada) | Please Select | | |
| Zip Code \* | | | |
| Country \*<br>(of Residence for Tax Purposes) | Please Select | | |
| Citizenship \* | Please Select | | |
| Phone \* | Country Code<br>1 | Area Code<br>( ) | Number<br>- |
| Fax (leave blank if none) | Country Code<br>1 | Area Code<br>( ) | Number<br>- |
| | (U.S. Country Code is 1) | | |

**E-Mail** *

Pseudonyms, AKAs (Also Known As)

**List any other names or forms of your legal name that you may use as a writer. Do not list co-writer, band, or group names. Maximum fifty (50) characters. (Leave blank if none)**

**First**
**Middle**
**Last**
**Suffix (Jr., III)**

**First**
**Middle**
**Last**
**Suffix (Jr., III)**

**First**
**Middle**
**Last**
**Suffix (Jr., III)**

Please check any of the following boxes that best describe your genre of music: *

| | | |
|---|---|---|
| ☐ Pop/Rock | ☐ Urban | ☐ Classical/Concert |
| ☐ Gospel | ☐ Jazz | ☐ Commercial Jingle |
| ☐ TV/Film | ☐ Theatre | ☐ Promos |
| ☐ Latin | ☐ Country | ☐ New Age |

Please check one of the following boxes: *

○ I have never been a member of BMI, ASCAP, SESAC, or any foreign performing rights organization.

○ I am currently or have been previously affiliated with ASCAP, SESAC, or a foreign performing rights organization.

# 3. PRS Writers Agreement

## Writer membership agreement

*Please note that this is an important document. By signing it you will hand over certain rights to us. It also sets out precisely what you can expect from us and what we can expect from you whilst you are a member.*

**1. Definitions**

**In this Agreement:-**

(a) words and phrases which are not defined shall have the same meaning as in our constitution,

(b) "Constitution" means our Memorandum of Association, Articles of Association, Rules and Regulations (which are all available from us upon request);

(c) "we" means the Performing Rights Society Limited of 29/33 Berners Street, London W1P 4AA and "you" means...

Forename(s)                          Surname

Address

                                     Town or City

County

Full post code

"us", "our", "your" and "yourself" shall be construed accordingly;

(d) "transfer" means (depending on the context) assign or assignment; and

(e) "the rights" means, in respect of any musical work:-

(i) the performing right; and
(ii) the film synchronisation right (subject to our obligation to assign or licence this right to you in accordance with our Articles of Association).

**2. The Transfer**

(a) you transfer to us absolutely for all parts of the world the rights which belong to you on the date of this Agreement or which you may acquire or own while you remain our member.

(b) the transfer mentioned in clause 2(a) shall last for so long as you remain a member and for any additional period which is specified in our constitution.

**3. Our Obligations**

**We will:-**

(a) use our best endeavours to administer the rights in accordance with our published service standards;

(b) use our best endeavours to pay you any royalties due to you under our Constitution. If we do not do so, we will pay you compensation up to the limit which is set out in our service standards;

(c) use our best endeavours to license on the best achievable terms as many users of the rights as practicable (taking into account business constraints, our resources and the interests of our membership as a whole);

(d) maintain a complaints procedure which you can use if you are not happy with the way in which we apply our Constitution or policies. If that complaints procedure has been exhausted and you are still not satisfied, you will have access to an independent appeals procedure;

(e) treat information about your royalty earnings as confidential, subject to any practical or legal obligation to disclose such information to any authority or person with the legal power to compel such a disclosure;

(f) return to you all or part of the rights in so far as this is permitted by our Constitution;

(g) maintain a suspension of royalties procedure which we will apply to you if there is a dispute involving the rights; and

(h) give you upon request details of the service standards, complaints procedure, appeals procedure and suspension of royalties procedure which are mentioned above as soon as practicable after you have requested such details.

## 4. Your Obligations

**You:-**

(a) warrant and represent that you own or have full power to transform the rights and that the musical works (the rights in which you have transferred to us under this Agreement) do not and will not infringe the copyright in any other musical work;

(b) accept that you are bound by our Constitution; and

(c) promise to:-

(i) indemnify us and keep at all times fully indemnified from and against all proceedings, claims, demands, costs, expenses, awards and damages arising directly or indirectly in respect of the rights which you have transferred (or have purported to transfer) to us under this Agreement;

(ii) give to us such documents as we may reasonably require to enforce the rights;

(iii) do all such acts as are necessary to vest the rights in us and enable us to enforce all or part of the rights;

(iv) insert in each relevant contract you make with a third party a clause expressly reserving to us the rights and to make such contract subject to this Agreement;

(v) refrain from licensing any of the rights and from otherwise dealing with the rights;

(vi) avoid doing anything which is likely to prejudice our ability to meet our obligations to you and to our other members; and

(vii) pay any annual membership fee or charges for special services rendered by us.

Your signature                          Our signature

This agreement made on the following date:

**Compositions;** in order to join you need to fulfil our criteria for membership. Usually this means being a writer of three songs. If unsure, refer to booklet What is PRS? or call us on 0171-306-4341.

**These are the three compositions in which I have an interest, and are my reason for applying for PRS membership.**

Title of composition 1

Title of Composition 2

Title of Composition 3

**I enclose all of the following in support of my application.** We cannot admit you without all of these items!

☐ A) copy of my commercial recordings. (*Alternatively, evidence of broadcasts or live performances for three of my compositions within the past two years.*)

☐ B) photocopy of my birth certificate or passport.

☐ C) signed Membership Agreement.

☐ D) Admission fee of £50, inclusive of VAT. (cheque payable to PRS Ltd).

**PLEASE NOTE – IF WE DO NOT RECEIVE FROM YOU ALL OF THE ABOVE ITEMS WE WILL NEED TO CONTACT YOU. THIS WILL RESULT IN A DELAY IN YOUR APPLICATION WHICH MAY LEAD TO A LOSS OF ROYALTIES.**

**Please read this:** The attached Membership Agreement, which only takes effect if your application for membership is successful, vests in the Society the ownership of your performing and film synchronisation rights. Please note this is a legal document concerning the transfer by you of certain rights to the Society and if you are in any doubt as to its effects you are advised to take legal advice before signing it.

The assignment of the rights will normally be for the territory of the world but you may be entitled to exclude certain countries from the scope of the Society's administration of your rights.

Please do not sign the Agreement if you are applying to exclude any country from the territorial extent of your assignment.

Please also note that the society reserves the right to disclose certain information concerning any of your registered compositions to authorised members using the Society's Repertoire On-Line Membership Enquiries System and any associated e-mail or telephone enquiry system(s) (collectively referred to as "ROME"). Please contact the Society's Membership Representatives Department (0171-306-4354), if you require further information about this service. Finally, it should be noted that a member may not receive royalties relating to compositions featured in samples, record sales charts and other information which is used by PRS to identify the performance of music in situations where accurate compositions details cannot be collected at a reasonable cost. In addition the society is not under any obligation to make distributions of royalties to you in respect of any public performance, broadcasts or cable transmission of your compositions which take place prior to the date from which your admission to membership is deemed to be effective. This is normally the 1st January or 1st July immediately preceding the date when admission is formally granted at a meeting of the Society's Directors.

Signature                    Date

Help us: how did you hear about PRS? e.g. friend/publisher/another writer/PRS leaflet?

What best describes the type of music you compose?

**Thank you for your application – we will get back to you very soon and we look forward to looking after you as one of our valued writer members. Please return this completed form to: Writer Admissions, PRS, 29/33 Berners Street, London W1P 4AA.**

# PRS writer member application form

**NAME AND ADDRESS DETAILS**

Surname

Forename(s)

Full postal address

Date of birth

Nationality

Telephone number (inc. STD code)

Daytime/mobile telephone number

E-mail address

**PAYMENT DETAILS**

Name of bank or building society

Sort code

Address of bank

Account number

Name in which account is held

Pay reference details

**PSEUDONYM DETAILS**

Surname

Forename(s)

Surname

Forename(s)

**ADDITIONAL DETAILS**

Which category best describes the type of music you compose?

Title of one composition in which you have a writer/composer interest

Broadcast/live performance details regarding your composition(s)

Reason for applying for PRS membership

I enclose all of the following in support of my application:-

☐   documentation confirming performances(s) of my composition(s)

☐   photocopy of my birth certificate, marriage certificate or passport

☐   fully completed and signed Membership Agreement

☐   admission fee of £100.00, inclusive of VAT (Cheque payable to PRS Ltd.)

PLEASE NOTE - IF WE DO NOT RECEIVE ALL OF THE ABOVE ITEMS OR THE APPLICATION FORM HAS NOT BEEN FULLY COMPLETED WE WILL NEED TO CONTACT YOU. THIS WILL RESULT IN A DELAY IN YOUR APPLICATION WHICH MAY LEAD TO A LOSS OF ROYALTIES.

Your Signature            Date

Thank you for your application - we will get back to you very soon.

Should you have any questions concerning this form please call us on 020 7306 4805 or email us at admissions@prs-alliance.co.uk

Please return this form to Writer Admissions, PRS, 29-33 Berners Street, London, W1T 3AB, UK.

writer member

*application*

The Mechanical-Copyright Protection Society Limited

**E-Mail** *

---

Pseudonyms, AKAs (Also Known As)

**List any other names or forms of your legal name that you may use as a writer. Do not list co-writer, band, or group names. Maximum fifty (50) characters. (Leave blank if none)**

**First**

**Middle**

**Last**

**Suffix (Jr., III)**

---

**First**

**Middle**

**Last**

**Suffix (Jr., III)**

---

**First**

**Middle**

**Last**

**Suffix (Jr., III)**

---

Please check any of the following boxes that <u>best</u> describe your genre of music: *

| | | |
|---|---|---|
| ☐ Pop/Rock | ☐ Urban | ☐ Classical/Concert |
| ☐ Gospel | ☐ Jazz | ☐ Commercial Jingle |
| ☐ TV/Film | ☐ Theatre | ☐ Promos |
| ☐ Latin | ☐ Country | ☐ New Age |

---

Please check one of the following boxes: *

○ I have never been a member of BMI, ASCAP, SESAC, or any foreign performing rights organization.

○ I am currently or have been previously affiliated with ASCAP, SESAC, or a foreign performing rights organization.

# MCPS Writer Membership Application Form

*Complete all relevant sections. Where a particular section is not relevant, please state **not applicable** or **n/a**.*

**NAME AND ADDRESS DETAILS**
Enter <u>true name</u> as stated on official documentation i.e. birth certificate, passport, deed poll or marriage certificate.

Surname | Forename(s)

List any other names you write under. Group/band names or company names will <u>not</u> be accepted.

Surname | Forename(s)

Surname | Forename(s)

Address (including full postcode)

Date of birth

Nationality

Telephone number | Daytime/mobile telephone number | E-mail address

**ROYALTY PAYMENT DETAILS**

Name of bank or building society

Sort Code

Branch address

Account Number

Name in which account is held

Building society roll number/pay reference (if relevant)

Should you require your royalties to be paid to an account outside of the UK, options are available using TAPS. Please refer to our website (www.mcps.co.uk) for further info.

**DISTRIBUTION DETAILS**

Please confirm if you require your royalty statement in disk format
and we will contact you with regard to technical specification.

Yes ☐    No ☐

**EXPLOITATION DETAILS**

Detail one composition (in which you have a writer/composer interest) which has been subject to mechanical usage.

| Title | Area of Usage i.e. CD, Video, Film | Catalogue No./ Transmission No. | Band Name (if relevant) |
|---|---|---|---|
| | | | |

**TERRITORY REPRESENTATION DETAILS**

If you are a direct member of any other mechanical rights organisation, please detail below.

| Name of overseas society | Territory of representation |
|---|---|
| | |

NB. While MCPS licenses directly in the UK (and in Europe subject to central licensing arrangements), in all other territories licences are via affiliated societies. Collection and distribution of overseas royalties is subject to rules laid down by the MCPS board from time to time. In most cases, this involves members making a claim using an International Royalty Claim Form, to be submitted every time their compositions are released in foreign territories. These forms are available on request.

**I enclose all of the following in support of my application:-**

☐ Documentation/evidence confirming mechanical usage of my composition(s)

☐ photocopy of my birth certificate, passport, deed poll or marriage certificate

☐ fully completed and signed Licensing and Collection Mandate

☐ admission fee of £50.00, inclusive of VAT (cheque payable to MCPS Ltd)

☐ signed letter from a solicitor, accountant or bank manager **if applying for an AP2/2A exclusion**

## FAILURE TO PROVIDE ALL OF THE ABOVE ITEMS WILL DELAY YOUR APPLICATION

I acknowledge receipt of the MCPS Membership Agreement (Document Reference MA2) and the three accompanying annexes (Rental and Lending, Multimedia, Online Exploitation), which I have read and considered.

I hereby apply for membership of MCPS and I understand that the submission of this completed Membership Application form constitutes an offer by me to enter into a legally binding agreement with you on the terms and conditions referred to in the Membership Agreement in accordance with my wishes expressed on the Licensing and Collection Mandate. I also understand that acceptance of this offer takes place when MCPS notifies me that membership has been granted.

| Signature | Date |
|---|---|
| | |

Please return this form to:

**MCPS – PRS Alliance Ltd, Writer/Publisher Admissions, 29 – 33 Berners Street, London, W1T 3AB, UK.**

# MCPS Writer Licensing And Collection Mandate

*This is an important document. Please read it carefully. By completing and signing it you give MCPS the authority (mandate) to license, collect and distribute royalties for a particular use of a work or catalogue.*

## 1. PRODUCT BLANKET LICENSING

**Audio/Video Product (AP/VP/ECL)** - This mandate is automatically included, subject to any exclusions specified below. MCPS operates the following types of licensing agreement under the Audio/Video Product Schemes:

- **Sales Agreement Companies** - MCPS will license all parties which fall under this agreement on the basis of net shipments and charge commission on the royalties distributed. These companies account quarterly and MCPS will distribute within seven working days of receipt of the royalties for audio products and within one month of the receipt of the royalties received from both sales agreement and non sales agreement video product companies.

- **Non-Sales Agreement Companies** - MCPS will license all parties seeking a licence on the basis of manufacturing quantities and charge commission on the royalties distributed.

- **European Central Licensing (ECL)** - ECL deals occur where the royalties for sales throughout Europe are collected by one society and distributed to the society in the territory where the sales took place for onward distribution to the copyright owner. ECL royalties are distributed quarterly.

## *EXCLUSIONS:*

This section applies to applicants who own a record company and/or video company.

**Sales Agreement Companies:** If a Member wishes to exclude any audio product sales agreement company from MCPS collection, **all** AP.1/AP.6 companies will be excluded (in accordance with clause 3 of the Membership Agreement). Collection then becomes the responsibility of the Member but licensing remains the responsibility of MCPS and a higher commission rate will apply.

**Non-Sales Agreement Companies:** A Member may exclude a record company on a manufacturing agreement (AP.2/AP.2A), provided the record company and the Member are "Related Parties" (see clause 16.20 of the Membership Agreement). Where a record company is excluded, MCPS will continue to license that record company, but the Member will collect royalties direct in relation to their own repertoire.

A 5% commission fee will be applied to members who earn royalties from MCPS' administration of Related Party Exclusions and do not collect their royalties via MCPS. The fee will be calculated quarterly in arrears at 5% of the excluded royalty rate, subject to a minimum charge of £25 per quarter, and will be invoiced within 14 days of the end of the quarter. Invoices will be subject to payment terms of 28 days from the date of issue. If no excluded royalties have been earned for a quarter, then no charge will be levied for that period.

The standard AP.2/AP.2A commission rate will apply for any record company not excluded.

**To apply for an AP.2/AP.2A Exclusion, you must provide a letter from a solicitor, accountant or bank manager on their official headed paper, giving the name and full postal address of the record company and confirming that you and the record company are related parties.**

**VP.1/VP.2:** A Member may exclude any Video Company from MCPS licensing and collection, however a higher commission rate will be charged on those companies MCPS does license.

Record Company/ies and/or Video Company/ies you wish to exclude:

**2. BROADCAST BLANKET LICENSING**

This mandate is automatically included in the Membership Agreement. Exclusions not available.

**3. OTHER LICENSING**

Although your works may not have yet been subject to the following usages, it is mandatory to complete this section.

For the use of non-production music in **Audio and Audio-Visual Productions**, you have the option to exclude these licences from MCPS control. The options are as follows:

**MCPS ONLY:**       MCPS has exclusive right to issue the licence for the relevant use after having gained prior approval for the use from the Member.

**MEMBER ONLY:**     MCPS has no right to license or negotiate on the Member's behalf for the relevant mandate.

**MCPS ON 1ST CALL:** Either the Member **or** MCPS has the right to issue the licence, depending upon whom the user of the music contacted first. If MCPS is contacted first, MCPS must still get prior approval for the use from the Member.

Please indicate who you authorise to issue licence by ticking one box only for each mandate.

| Audio and Audio-Visual Product Mandates | MCPS ONLY | MEMBER ONLY | MCPS ON 1st CALL |
|---|---|---|---|
| Theatrical motion pictures | | | |
| TV advertisements | | | |
| Radio advertisements | | | |
| TV programmes | | | |
| All other non-retail sound bearing copies | | | |

**4. ADDITIONAL ANNEXES TO MEMBERSHIP AGREEMENT MA2**

Please indicate if you wish to take advantage of the terms and conditions as specified in the relevant annexes.

| | YES | NO |
|---|---|---|
| Rental and lending annex | | |
| Multimedia annex | | |
| Online annex (*as modified in our letter dated 4 December 2001*) | | |

Please note it is not necessary for MCPS to gain prior approval from the Member in respect of the additional annexes.

<u>**FAILURE TO COMPLETE SECTIONS 3 AND 4 WILL INVALIDATE YOUR APPLICATION**</u>

**Signature:**

**Name (Block Capitals):**

**Date:**

Return to: **MCPS–PRS Alliance Ltd, Writer/Publisher Admissions, 29 – 33 Berners Street, London, W1T 3AB, UK.**

# 5. MCPS-PRS Registration of Works Form

**WRITERS JOINT NOTIFICATION (WORKS) FORM**
**FOR UNPUBLISHED WORKS**

Title ...................................................
Secondary Title ...................................................
Duration ........................

Title for Advertising 'Jingle' ...................................................
Product ...................................................    Agency ...................................................
Script Title ...................................................    VT / Radio No. ...................................................

Description ...................................................

| Writers Names. (if appropriate indicate registered pseudonym only) | Writer Designation (See *) | Share of Royalties | | Enter your CAE number, if known, alternatively part of your address | For Office Use |
| | | Performing | Mechanical | | |
| 1 | | ✓ | % | | |
| 2 | | ✓ | % | | |
| 3 | | ✓ | % | | |
| 4 | | ✓ | % | | |
| 5 | | ✓ | % | | |
| 6 | | ✓ | % | | |

Tick box for:
☐ ☐ Amended Registration
☐ Dramatico-Musical Work
for PRS:
☐ SESAC   ☐ BMI
Licence     Licence
for MCPS:
☐ Authority **not** given
☐ for First Recording

* Writer Designation: Indicate appropriate combinations : 'C' for Composer 'A' for Author; Arr for Arranger etc.

Instrumentation ...................................................

Performance Details / Other Relevant Comments ...................................................

Commercial Recording Details and Numbers ...................................................
Information supplied will be used for registered purposes under the Data Protection Act 1984

**THIS FORM IS ONLY TO BE USED BY WRITER MEMBERS TO NOTIFY WORKS AS FOLLOWS:**

1. UNPUBLISHED works for which specific performance activity is known (past or future) - indicate venue, performance date, concert, artiste, etc.

2. UNPUBLISHED works issued on commercial recordings - indicate recording label, number, artiste etc.

3. UNPUBLISHED commissioned music or lyrics for cinema, television and video productions. Contracts with production companies or television contractors are also required for commissioned music or lyrics. USE FORM JNF / A4 FOR PUBLISHED COMMISSIONED MUSIC AND LYRICS

4. UNPUBLISHED arrangements of non-copyright music should be notified if specific performance activity (past or future) is known or if they have been issued on commercial recordings. A copy of every such arrangement notified must be sent to PRS with this form for grading purposes and will be returned on request. Alternatively, the reverse side of the PRS copy may be used, but please write out in full at least part of the arrangement.

5. PUBLISHED works assigned to a foreign or non member British publisher must be notified on FORM JNF / A4 (enclosing a copy of your contract)

NOTE PLEASE DO NOT NOTIFY WORKS ASSIGNED TO A PRS/MCPS PUBLISHER MEMBER THIS IS THE RESPONSIBILITY OF THAT PUBLISHER

The undersigned assigns to The Performing Right Society Limited (PRS) the performing right as defined by the Articles of the Society and agrees to the division of the royalties indicated

Signature of Writers: 1 ........................  2 ........................  3 ........................  4 ........................  5 ........................  6 ........................

Date ........................

Stock No. JNF MS-190

# 6. Licensing Agreement for Compilation Album (UK)

AGRRREEMENT

THIS AGREEMENT is made on the           day of          199

BETWEEN:

(1)

    of

    ("Licensor")

(2)   Zip Dog Records (a firm) of _____
     ("Licensee")

1.   <u>Definitions</u>

In this agreement these terms are defined as follows:

| | |
|---|---|
| "the Act" | Copyright, Designs and Patents Act 1988 (and any statutory modification or re-enactment) |
| "Album" | Masters with a playing time equivalent to one CD length album and provisionally entitled "Club Meets Dub v2.0" |
| "Artist" | whose recording[s] are the subject of this agreement |
| "Masters" | finished master stereo tape or digital equivalent of Recordings technically and commercially suitable for use in the manufacture of Records |
| "Record" | any contrivance now known or subsequently invented by which Recordings may be reproduced for exploitation in all media including but not limited to all types of phonograph records compact discs tape recordings whether embodying sound alone or by which both picture and sound can be played back simultaneously |
| "Recording(s)" | the original sound recording(s) set out in part 1 of the Schedule |
| "Rights" | the rights granted and assigned as set out at clause 3 |
| "Schedule" | the schedule which forms an integral part of and is annexed to this agreement |
| "Term" | the period set out at clause 2 |
| "Territory" | the World |

2.   <u>Term</u>

The Term of this agreement shall be for 3 years commencing on the earlier of the date of first release of the Album in the UK or 30th September 1996.

- 1 -

3.    Grant of Rights

Licensor grants to Licensee by way of licence free of all encumbrances the following rights (the "Rights") which may only be exercised in Territory:

(a)    the exclusive right to manufacture distribute and sell Records reproducing the Album

(b)    subject to the interest of the appropriate performing rights society the exclusive right to authorise public performances of Records

(c)    the exclusive right in all media to advertise publicise and exploit Records

(d)    the right to use Artist's name(s) likeness and biographical material for all purposes of this agreement

(e)    the right to use artwork and promotional material as may be supplied by Licensor

(f)    the right to engage third parties to manufacture, distribute and/or publicise Records

(g)    the right to sub-licence the exploitation of the Recording(s)

4.    Licensor's warranties and undertakings

Licensor warrants to Licensee that:

(a)  `  Licensor owns or controls sufficient rights in Recording(s) to grant the Rights

(b)    underlying musical material comprising Recording(s) will be available to Licensee for use in the manufacture of Records on standard terms and conditions for licensing copyright material

(c)    there are no subsisting licences granted by Licensor to third parties for exclusive exploitation of Recording(s) in Territory nor will such an exclusive licence be granted by Licensor during Term

(d)    there are no outstanding claims known to Licensor which could affect the Rights

(e)    Licensor has full power and authority to enter into this agreement

(f)    Licensor has obtained such consents as may be necessary to enable Licensee to exploit Rights including the consents of all those who contributed to the production and making of the Records to exploit their performances in all ways provided for by this agreement

(g)    Recording(s) are copyright for all purposes defined in the Act

(h)    exploitation of the Recording(s) will not be obscene nor defamatory of any person nor infringe moral rights of any person; for this purpose the term "moral rights" shall include those rights subject of Chapter IV of Part I of the Act and any other or similar "droit moral" arising in Territory

(i)    none of the material included in the Recording(s) is or will be sampled but to the extent that any such material is sampled then Licensor will obtain at its cost and expense all and any necessary releases and consents to enable Licensee to fully exploit any such sampled material

- 2 -

5. Licensee's warranties and undertakings

5.1 Licensee shall be responsible for making payments for mechanical licences necessary to exploit Recording(s)

5.2 Licensee shall endeavour to exploit Recording(s) to maximise the income for both Licensor and Licensee

5.3 During the last six months of Term or last three months of Option Period (as may be appropriate) Licensee shall not manufacture quantities of Records in excess of numbers manufactured during the previous three month period

5.4. Licensee shall not incur nor hold himself out as authorised to incur any liability on behalf of Licensor

5.5. Licensee shall immediately notify Licensor of any infringement by any third party of the Rights in Territory of which Licensee becomes aware and Licensee shall take such action including legal proceedings at its own cost to which Licensor will, wherever necessary, be a party and Licensee shall account to Licensor for one half of net monies recovered (if any) as a consequence of such action or proceedings after deducting all of its legal fees incurred in relation thereto

6. Delivery of Materials

Licensor shall deliver to Licensee:

(a) Masters of all Recording(s) together with replacement Masters from time to time as Licensee may reasonably request

(b) label copy and a list of appropriate credits

(c) such further or other materials as Licensee may reasonably require.

7. Consideration

In consideration of Licensor granting the Rights Licensee shall make payments of royalties to Licensor being the amounts set out at paragraph 1 of part 2 of the Schedule ("Royalties")

8. Accounting obligations

8.1 Licensee will deliver to Licensor a financial statement setting out details of Licensor's account with Licensee within 90 days of 30th June and 31st December in each year accompanied by payment of any sums due to Licensor

8.2 The procedures set out at paragraph 2 of part 2 of the Schedule shall apply to the computation of payments due to Licensee

9. Further Assurance

Licensor undertakes that it will at the Licensor's expense give such further assurance and execute such further or other deeds or documents as may be necessary to give effect to the provisions of this agreement

-3-

10. Termination

10.1 No breach of this agreement shall be considered as material unless notified in writing, the party in breach being thereby given 30 days to remedy such breach in default of which the party serving the notice may terminate this agreement immediately.

10.2 Upon termination of this agreement Licensee shall deliver to Licensor all Masters and derivatives and parts produced from Masters together with all artwork and other originals and transparencies of packaging and promotional material.

11. Sell off Period

11.1 Upon the expiration of Term or, if applicable, Option Period, Licensee shall immediately cease manufacturing Records but may continue to sell off existing stocks of Records for a period of three months ("Sell-off Period") provided that prices shall not be reduced without Licensor's prior consent

11.2 Upon expiration of the Sell-off Period at Licensor's option Licensee will either sell any remaining stock to Licensor at cost or alternatively destroy such stock and furnish an affidavit to Licensor verifying this

12. Indemnity

The parties shall each indemnify the other against breaches of this agreement

13. Notices

13.1 Any notice required to be given under this agreement shall be in writing and shall be delivered to the other party's last address either by hand, by telex or by telefax but shall in any event be confirmed by its being sent by prepaid registered or recorded delivery post

13.2 Any notice to be given or served pursuant to this agreement shall be treated as having been received no later than two working days after the date upon which such notice has been posted within the United Kingdom and 12 working days if posted outside the United Kingdom

13.3 The addresses stated at the beginning of this agreement shall be the appropriate addresses for service unless and/or until a new address is notified, it being the obligation of each party to keep the other informed of any changes of address

14. Miscellaneous

14.1 Failure, delay or partial exercise of any right of either party shall not operate so as to preclude any further exercise thereof or the exercise of any other right. Each party's rights and remedies are cumulative and not exclusive of any rights and remedies provided by law

14.2 This agreement shall constitute the entire understanding between the parties, any agreed amendments to be in writing and signed by both parties

14.3 Neither party has the right to rely on any representation made by one to the other unless expressly set out in this agreement

14.4 If either party's performance of this agreement is delayed or becomes impossible or impracticable because of any act of God, fire, earthquake, strike, civil commotion, act of government or any other event of force majeure, that party may upon notice to the other suspend its performance of this agreement for the duration of such interruption and upon its conclusion the number of days equal to the number of days of such suspension ,shall be added to Contract Period in which delay occurred

14.5    In this agreement headings shall be for ease of reference only and shall not affect construction

14.6    Voidability or unenforceability of any one or more provision or part provision shall not constitute voidability or enforceability of any of the other provisions or part provisions which shall remain in full force and effect

14.7    In this agreement where the context admits the singular shall mean the plural and vice versa and the masculine the feminine and vice versa.

14.8    This agreement shall be governed in all respects by the law of England and Wales and all disputes shall be submitted to [the High Court in London]


## SCHEDULE

### PART 1

**(Recording(s))**


### PART 2

#### (Payments)

1.    Royalties

1.1    Licensor's Royalties shall be computed by dividing 50% of the total of Net Profits as defined below by the total number of recordings including Recording(s) comprising the Album.

1.2    For the purposes of computing the amounts to be paid to Licensor "Net Profits" shall mean the total of all monies, fees, royalties and advances ("Gross Income") actually received by Company derived from exploitation of Recording(s) after deduction of:

   (a)    the total cost to Licensee of originating, mastering, manufacturing, packaging, marketing, promoting, advertising and distributing Records

   (b)    all legal and accounting fees of and occasioned by the negotiation and conduct of all and any licensing and distribution arrangements made with third parties for exploitation of Recording(s) to include (but not limited to) audit costs and all costs incurred in litigating any matter arising from such exploitation by third parties but only a proportion of such legal and accounting costs incurred by Licensee shall be deducted from Gross Income where such licensing/distribution arrangements are made by Licensee for the benefit of enabling it to exploit Recording(s) with Recording(s) of others of its artists

   (c)    all mechanical licensing fees and other fees payable to owners of copyright in any composition used in Recording(s)

1.3    All payments made hereunder are inclusive of equitable remuneration in respect of rental, lending, satellite and cable re-transmission rights

1.4    No Royalties shall be paid on Records given away in reasonable numbers and consistent with industry practice for promotional purposes or on records sold as deletions or cut outs

1.5    Licensee may make reasonable reserves against returned Records

2.    <u>Accounting procedures</u>

2.1    For the purposes of computing amounts payable to Licensor:

    a)    where payments are derived from overseas exploitation of Recording(s):

        (i)    foreign currency shall be converted at the date of receipt of payments by Licensee from its overseas licensees and distributors

        (ii)    payments to Licensor shall be subject to the deduction of any withholding tax that may be retained by such overseas licensees and distributors

        (iii)    Licensee shall be under no obligation to make payments to Licensor until Licensee has received payment from its overseas licensee and/or distributor

    (b)    VAT or any other sales or similar tax shall be deducted and/or payable on all sums referred to in this agreement subject to the provisions of the appropriate VAT or other invoice

    (c)    payments to Licensor shall be subject to the deduction of any withholding tax that may be retained by such overseas licensees and distributors

    (d)    Licensee shall be under no obligation to make payments to Licensor until Licensee has received payment from its overseas Licensee and/or Distributor

2.2    Licensee shall keep full and complete books of account of its exploitation of the Recording(s) which Licensor may at its own expense inspect (either alone or by way of its appointed representative) once in each year on giving at least 14 days prior Notice in writing and if any inspection reveals an underpayment to Licensor of ten per cent (10%) or more then Licensee shall pay the reasonable costs of the inspection.

Signed for and on behalf of Licensor:        in the presence of:

_____        _____

Signed for and on behalf of Licensee:        in the presence of:

_____        _____

# 7. Distribution Contract (UK)

## TERMS AND CONDITIONS OF TRADING

### 1. Stock

a) You shall supply stocks of records in their sleeves or other packaging together with all inserts (ready inserted) and any promotional or other material intended for distribution with records sufficient to meet our orders and you shall be responsible for design and manufacture of all materials.

b) You shall be responsible for planning and execution of all marketing, advertising and promotion of your records.

c) We shall have the right to decline to distribute promotional or other similar material but if we accept such material for distribution with records or in connection with records we shall be under no obligation to ensure that such material is distributed and while we will take reasonable care of such material while it is in our possession, we shall have no liability in respect of any loss or damage thereto, howsoever occurring and we shall have no obligation to account to you for such material.

d) In the event that records are returned to us by any of our dealers in accordance with our standard returns policy or because they are faulty, wrongly ordered or wrongly despatched we shall be entitled to replace such returned records from stocks of your records or to give the dealer a credit in respect thereof, at our discretion and we will debit your account in respect thereof. In the event that a record is returned because it is faulty we will not credit the amount of stocks of your records by such returned record but will make such record available for collection by you.

e) We shall not be liable for loss of stocks of records, howsoever arising, of up to 2% of the annual actual sales of records. In excess of the above, howsoever arising, our liability shall be limited to the proven cost of manufacture of such lost records SAVE THAT in the case of loss by any insured peril including without limitation fire and theft our liability shall be limited to the amount received from our insurers in respect of such lost records.

f) We may from time to time, at your request, supply strike forces with numbers of your records. We shall not be responsible to account to you in respect of any of such records lost or given away by such strike forces. We shall not be liable to account to you for records sold by strike forces to customers unless at the time that we are notified by the strike force of such sale we maintain a credit account with such customer which is not on hold or unless we actually receive payment in respect of such sales.

### 2. Disposal of Stock

a) If we have an excess of stock we will notify you. You shall have the right to come and collect the excess stock within 30 days. If you have not done so within that 30 day period we will be entitled to dispose of the ecess as we see fit.

b) We shall be entitled to dispose in any manner we think fit, of any record (with it's sleeve ) or sleeve which is returned to us as defective unless you shall have given to us written notice not to dispose of the excess as we see fit.

c) At our request you shall collect all stock held by us and unsold and any promotional publicity or other like material held by us, and in the event of failure by you to collect such stock or other material within 30 days we shall be entitled to dispose of such stock or material in any way we shall decide (including destruction).

### 3. Warranties

a) You hereby warrant and represent to us:-

i) That the distribution of your records hereunder will not infringe the patent, trade mark, service mark or copyright of any third party.

ii) That all recording costs and expenses, artist and copyright fees and royalties in respect of records distributed hereunder have been or will be borne otherwise than by us.

iii) That none of the material comprised in any of the records is defamatory or of an obscene nature or is such that the distribution thereof will render us liable to criminal and/or civil proceedings and that you have obtained the consent of all parties whose performances are included in the records to be distributed for their performances to be so included.

iv) That the distribution of your records  will not involve us in any form of liability to any third party.

v) You hereby indemnify us against all liabilities, costs, damages and expenses which we may suffer or incur as a result of any breach or non-performance of any of your warranties or undertakings.

1

## 4. Sales and Discounts

a) All standard file discounts given to customers within the United Kingdom shall be borne by us. All other discounts shall be borne by you.

b) In the event that we make your records available to customers on a consignment basis which we shall not do without your prior approval, we will not account to you in respect of such records until such time as such customers have accounted to us that they have sold those records.

## 5. Taxes Arising on Sale

We shall be responsible for the payment of VAT on records and cassettes sold by us and for the accounting to HM Customs in respect thereof and we shall keep you fully and effectually indemnified in respect thereof.

## 6. Statements

a) Statements shall be rendered to you at your nominated address or such subsequent nominated address within twenty-one days of the end of each calendar month showing the nett sales of records invoiced by us during the preceding calendar month and the amount due to you.

b) We shall pay to you the sums shown to be due to you in respect of sales to customers within the United Kingdom within 15 days of the end of the calendar month in which the statement is rendered or the receipt by us of your invoice therefor (whichever is the later). We shall pay to you the sums shown to be due to you in respect of sales to customers based outside of the United Kingdom within 45 days of the end of the calendar month in which the statement is rendered or the receipt by us of your invoice therefor (whichever is the later). We shall pay you by Company cheque drawn in Pounds Sterling. You shall supply us with an invoice in respect of the monies shown to be due to you or (in the event that the amount deducted from your account in respect of returns exceeds the amount credited to your account or your account is for any reason shows a negative amount due to you) a credit note within seven days of the receipt by you of our statement.

c) We may maintain reasonable reserves against anticipated returns and credits, which reserves shall not exceed twenty five percent (25%) with respect to those sums shown due in any applicable accounting period save that we shall only maintain reserves where we consider that returns may exceed sales (for example because a notice of termination of this agreement has been served or because you do not have an adequate number of releases scheduled) and in respect of television advertised albums we shall be entitled to maintain reserves of forty per cent (40%) in any event. Each reserve established shall be liquidated within SIX (6) accounting periods from the accounting period in which such reserve was established.

d) You may at your own expense, appoint an independent duly qualified accountant to inspect, examine and audit our books and records insofar as such books and records relate to distribution hereunder or any monies payable to you hereunder and such inspection may be made within seven (7) days written notice during normal business hours but not more than once in any period of six (6) months. In the event that such inspection reveals an underpayment we will forthwith pay to you the amount of such underpayment.

## 7. Charges for Additional Service

If we shall undertake at your request any additional service, whether in connection with your records or otherwise, you shall pay to us our reasonable and proper charges in relation to such services and we shall be entitled to deduct such charges from payments due to you.

## 8. Legal Actions and Claims

If we shall receive notice (actual or otherwise) of any legal claim or dispute of whatever nature concerning any recording or record thereof or packaging held by us or distributed by us , then we shall be entitled to retain any and all sums owed which may become owing from us to you under until such time as such claim or dispute shall have been disposed of (whether by legal action or otherwise).

## 9. Insurance of Stock

We insure stock against fire damage and other third party perils to the manufactured cost of the stock. Claims will be settled at the discretion of the insurance company and we will not be liable in any way in the event of a dispute. We will however use our good offices to promote and safeguard the interests of one of our labels in a dispute.

2

# 8. AIM Membership Agreement

## AIM MEMBERSHIP FORM - PART 1
## APPLICATION FORM (RECORD LABELS & DISTRIBUTORS)

Please read AIM's Membership terms (see Part 5) and send in your completed and signed application form (together with a cheque for: £117.50 for labels or £998.75 for distributors and completed Parts 1, 2 and 3).

| COMPANY NAME | | | |
|---|---|---|---|
| BPI MEMBER: | YES/NO (delete as necessary) | Date you became a BPI member: / / | |
| PPL MEMBER: | YES/NO (delete as necessary) | PPL membership number: | |
| ADDRESS | | | |
| | | | |
| CITY | | POSTCODE | |
| TELEPHONE | | FAX | |
| MOBILE or DIRECT LINE | | | |
| E-MAIL | | WEBSITE | |

| What are the names and job titles of your company directors? | |
|---|---|
| NAME | JOB TITLE |
| | |
| | |
| | |
| ...and the name of one main contact for AIM. | With their e-mail address. |
| | |

BUSINESS: ☐LABEL, ☐DISTRIBUTOR, ☐ON-LINE LICENSEE/DISTRIBUTOR, OTHER (please specify):_____

- *I want to become a member of AIM, and ask that you process this application.*
- *I have provided the other information requested in the form entitled "Further Information" (Part 2).*
- *I have declared my interests in other relevant companies on the form entitled "Declaration of Interests in Companies (including label imprints)" (Part 3).*
- *I confirm that I satisfy and agree to the terms and conditions of AIM Membership as set out "AIM's Terms of Membership" (Part 5).*
- *I enclose a cheque for £117.50 (£100 plus VAT) made payable to The Association of Independent Music Ltd.*
- *I agree to pay an annual subscription to AIM. If I am a record company, this is a flat fee of £120 plus vat (payable in advance from the January following registration) PLUS a percentage of my PPL income. I confirm that I am a member of PPL and register my repertoire with PPL and that my signature below is confirmation of my authority to PPL to deduct and pay direct to AIM an annual subscription which is a percentage of my PPL income (agreed on an annual basis by the AIM board - currently 12%). I authorise PPL to make these deductions from each of PPL's distributions to me during any annual year in which I am or have been a member of AIM. I understand that if I am (and remain) a member of the BPI, the PPL deduction is currently set at 7%. AIM will raise an invoice to reflect any deductions made. If I am a distributor I agree to pay an annual subscription of £750 plus vat (in advance, at the beginning of every calendar year).*
- *I agree that PPL / CatCo can supply my repertoire information to AIM on my behalf.*
- *I agree to the mandate on negotiating internet deals as per attached (resolution passed at AIM AGM 2001).*

Signed_____ Name _____ Date _____

**Association of Independent Music Ltd**                    AIMMembershippack05.doc Page 3 of 9
Lamb House, Church Street, Chiswick, London, W4 2PD
T 020 8994 5599   F 020 8994 5222   E info@musicindie.com   W www.musicindie.com
Registered in England and Wales  Company number: 368 5877
Registered office: Second Floor, Quadrant House (Air Street Entrance), 80-82 Regent Street, London W1B 5RP

## AIM MEMBERSHIP FORM– PART 2a
### MORE INFORMATION

**About the company**

NO OF EMPLOYEES ☐

YEAR ESTABLISHED ☐

**Territories (Please tick all that you supply)**

☐ UK
☐ EUROPE
☐ JAPAN
☐ USA
☐ OTHER (please specify) _____

**Music type (Please tick all which apply)**

☐ AMBIENT/N. AGE
☐ ASIAN
☐ BLUES
☐ BRASS BAND
☐ BUDGET
☐ CHILDRENS
☐ CHORAL
☐ CLASSICAL
☐ COMPILATIONS
☐ COUNTRY
☐ DANCE

☐ EARLY MUSIC
☐ FOLK
☐ CHRISTIAN
☐ HIP HOP/RAP
☐ INDIE ROCK
☐ JAZZ
☐ MOR
☐ NOSTALGIA
☐ S.T./CAST/TV
☐ POP
☐ PUNK

☐ R&B/SOUL/FUNK
☐ REGGAE
☐ REISSUES
☐ ROCK
☐ ROCK N ROLL
☐ SPOKEN WORD
☐ WORLD
☐ OTHER (see below)

Please give us more details about the above, or any other relevant information:

**Association of Independent Music Ltd**
Lamb House, Church Street, Chiswick, London, W4 2PD
**T** 020 8994 5599   **F** 020 8994 5222   **E** info@musicindie.com   **W** www.musicindie.com
Registered in England and Wales  Company number: 368 5877
Registered office: Second Floor, Quadrant House (Air Street Entrance), 80-82 Regent Street, London W1B 5RP

AIMMembershippack05.doc Page 4 of 9

## AIM MEMBERSHIP FORM - PART 2b
## ADDITIONAL STAFF CONTACTS

Please take the time to fill out this form in order that AIM can keep their database up to date.

Boxes have been left blank at the bottom for you to let us know the details of any other key members of staff.

| Position | Name | Email | Telephone |
|---|---|---|---|
| Managing Director | | | |
| PA to MD | | | |
| Marketing Director | | | |
| Head of Promotions | | | |
| Finance Director | | | |
| Head of International | | | |
| Head of Business Affairs | | | |
| Head of Production | | | |
| | | | |
| | | | |
| | | | |
| | | | |

**Association of Independent Music Ltd**
Lamb House, Church Street, Chiswick, London, W4 2PD
**T** 020 8994 5599   **F** 020 8994 5222   **E** info@musicindie.com   **W** www.musicindie.com
Registered in England and Wales   Company number: 368 5877
Registered office: Second Floor, Quadrant House (Air Street Entrance), 80-82 Regent Street, London W1B 5RP

## AIM MEMBERSHIP FORM - PART 3
### DECLARATION OF MEMBERS' INTERESTS IN COMPANIES (including label imprints)

Member's Name: _____

Is more than 50% of the Member owned by another company or group of companies:
**YES / NO ?**

If yes, please provide name of that company/group: _____

**Companies which the Member (or its holding company) owns or controls (e.g. 51% shareholding):**
N.B. The companies which are in the record label or distribution business and form your corporate group,
have joined AIM with you.  AIM terms, conditions, and annual subscriptions apply to them.

| NAME OF COMPANY AND CONTACT DETAILS   (e.g. Name of Label head, Address, Telephone number, email) | TYPE OF BUSINESS (label/label imprint, distributor, on-line licensee/distributor or other – e.g. publisher) | PPL INFORMATION If the company is a label or label imprint, who is registered with PPL to collect income? |
|---|---|---|
|  |  |  |
|  |  |  |
|  |  |  |
|  |  |  |

**Companies in which the Member (or its holding company) owns or controls 50% or less :**

| NAME OF COMPANY AND CONTACT DETAILS (e.g. Name of Label head, Address, Telephone number, email) | TYPE OF BUSINESS (label/label imprint, distributor, on-line licensee/distributor or other – e.g. publisher) |
|---|---|
|  |  |
|  |  |

**Association of Independent Music Ltd**
Lamb House, Church Street, Chiswick, London, W4 2PD
**T** 020 8994 5599    **F** 020 8994 5222    **E** info@musicindie.com    **W** www.musicindie.com
Registered in England and Wales   Company number: 368 5877
Registered office: Second Floor, Quadrant House (Air Street Entrance), 80-82 Regent Street, London W1B 5RP

AIMMembershippack05.doc Page 6 of 9

# web addresses/contacts

**A2IM (American Association of Independent Music)**
Web site: www.a2im.org

**AFM (American Federation of Musicians of the United States and Canada)**
Web site: www.afm.org

**The Agents' Association (Great Britain)**
Web site: www.agents-uk.com

**AIM (Association of Independent Music)**
Web site: www.musicindie.com

**AMIA (Association of Music Industry Accountants)**
Email: amia_uk@hotmail.com

**APRS (Association of Professional Recording Services)**
Web site: www.aprs.co.uk

**ASCAP (American Society of Composers, Authors and Publishers)**
Web site: www.ascap.com

**AURA (The featured performer society)**
Web site: www.aurauk.com

**BACS (British Academy of Composers and Songwriters)**
Web site: www.britishacademy.com

**BMI (Broadcast Music Incorporated)**
Web site: www.bmi.com
www.benedict.com (the copyright Web site)

**BPI (British Phonographic Industry)**
Web site: www.bpi.co.uk

**British Promotional Merchandise Association**
Web site: www.martex.co.uk

**British Underground**
Web site: www.britishunderground.net

**CMJ (College Media, Inc.)**
Web site: www.cmj.com

**Copyright Advice and Anti-Piracy Hotline**
Web site: www.copyright-info.org

**Department for Culture, Media and Sport**
Web site: www.culture.gov.uk

**DTI (Department of Trade and Industry)**
Web site: www.dti.gov.uk

**E Centre UK (for bar-coding and e-commerce standards)**
Web site: www.e-centre.org.uk

**HFA (Harry Fox Agency Inc.)**
Web site: www.nmpa.org

**IFPI (International Federation of the Phonographic Industry)**
Web site: www.ifpi.org

**IMRA (Independent Music Retailers Association)**
Web site: www.worldprofit/imramusic

**IMRO (Irish Music Rights Organization)**
Web site: www.imro.ie

**International Association of Entertainment Lawyers**
Web site: www.iael.org

**IPA (Independent Publishers Association)**
PO Box 3163, London NW1 5HJ
Tel: 020 7704 8541 Fax: 020 7704 8540

**Law Society**
Web site: www.lawsociety.org.uk

**MCPS (Mechanical Copyright Protection Society)**
Web site: www.mcps.co.uk

**MMF (Music Managers Forum)**
Web site: www.ukmmf.net

**MOBO (Music of Black Origin)**
Web site: www.mobo.com

**Music Education Directory**
Web site: www.bpi.co.uk

**MPG (Music Producers Guild)**
www.mpg.org.uk

**MPA (Music Publishers Association)**
Web site: www.mpaonline.org.uk

**Musicians' Union**
Web site: www.musiciansunion.org.uk

**NAS (National Academy of Songwriters)**
Web site: www.nassong.org

**National Association for Campus Activities**
13 Harbison Way, Columbia, SC 29212-3401, USA
Tel: 001 803 732 6222 Fax: 001 803 749 1047

**National Foundation for Youth Music (Youth Music)**
Web site: www.youthmusic.org.uk

**National Union of Students Entertainments**
Web site: www.nus-ents.co.uk

**NMPA (National Music Publishers' Association)**
Web site: www.nmpa.org

**NMPA**
Email: pr@nmpa.org
Web site: www.nmpa.org

**PAMRA (Performing Artists's Media Rights Association)**
Web site: www.pamra.org.uk

**PLASA (Professional Lighting and Sound Association)**
Web site: www.plasa.org

**PPL (Phonographic Performance Ltd)**
Web site: www.ppluk.com

**Prince's Trust**
Web site: www.princes-trust.org.uk

**PRS (Performing Right Society)**
Web site: www.prs.co.uk

**RIAA (Recording Industry Association of America)**
Web site: www.riaa.com

**SESAC**
Web site: www.sesac.com

**SGA (Songwriters Guild of America)**
Web site: www.songwriters.org

**SoundExchange**
Web site: www.soundexchange.com

**SPARS (Society of Professional Audio Recording Services)**
Web site: www.spars.com

**Student Radio Association**
Web site: www.studentradio.org.uk

**The Band Register**
Web site: www.bandreg.com

**The Radio Academy**
Web site: www.radioacademy.org

**VLA (Volunteer Lawyers for the Arts)**
Web site: www.vlaa.org

**Women in Music**
Web site: www. womeninmusic.org.uk

# other useful web addresses

**www.benedict.com** (the copyright Web site)
**www.collegemusic.com** (US college music)
**www.edirol.co.uk** (Roland)

---

**www.gearsearch.com** (equipment site)
**www.indie-music.com** (US indie music)
**www.inthecity.co.uk** (trade fair)
**www.midem.com** (trade fair)
**www.mudhut.co.uk** (unsigned music site)
**www.musesmuse.com** (songwriters' newsletter)
**www.musicianswalk.com** (musicians' resources)
**www.musiciansweb.net** (host site for audio/video)
**www.music-media.co.uk** (UK industry directory)
**www.nemis.co.uk** (New music in Scotland)
**www.nus.org.uk** (National Union of Students)
**www.panasonic.com/consumer_electronics/technics-audio**
   (Technics turntables)
**www.recordingconnection.com** (US site for studio jobs)
**www.songlink.com** (newsletter for music publishers and songwriters)
**www.sky.co.uk/RFTS** (Reach for the Sky)
**www.demon.co.uk/studiobase** (UK studios information)
**www.taxi.com** (US independent A&R site)
**www.vestax.co.uk** (Vestax mixers and other products)
**www.wightweb.demon.co.uk/bandit** (Bandit A&R newsletter)
**www.wipo.org** (World Intellectual Property Organization)
**www.yamaha.com** (Yamaha official site)

# INDEX